American Patriots and the Rituals of Revolution

American Patriots and the Rituals of Revolution

Peter Shaw

HARVARD UNIVERSITY PRESS
Cambridge, Massachusetts
1981

To my daughter, Jennifer

Library of Congress Cataloging in Publication Data

Shaw, Peter, 1936–
  American patriots and the rituals of revolution.

  Includes bibliographical references and index.
  1. United States—History—Revolution, 1775–1783—
Causes. 2. Collective behavior. I. Title.
E210.S49   973.3'11   80-18657
ISBN 0-674-02644-6

Contents

Introduction   1

I   Crowds and Crisis
1   *The Rehearsal of Revolution*   5
2   *Their Kinsman, Thomas Hutchinson*   26
3   *John Wilkes and the Earl of Bute*   48

II   Conscience Patriots
4   *James Otis*   77
5   *John Adams*   109
6   *Joseph Hawley*   131
7   *Josiah Quincy*   153

III   The Revolutionary Impulse
8   *The Child, Revolution*   177
9   *Festival, Ritual, and Revolution*   204
10   *The Rituals of the American Revolution*   227

Notes   233

Acknowledgments   273

Index   275

Illustrations

Description of the Pope   17
Broadside, 1769. Courtesy of the New-York Historical Society

Thomas Hutchinson   29
Edward Truman, 1741. Courtesy of the Massachusetts Historical
Society

The Wicked Statesman   42
Massachusetts Calendar, 1774. Courtesy of the American Antiquarian
Society

America in Distress   51
Paul Revere, 1775, *Royal American Magazine*. Courtesy of the
American Antiquarian Society

Claudius Pouring Poison into the King's Ear   54
Oxford Magazine, 1769. Courtesy of the Trustees of the British
Museum

The Colossus   56
Political Register, 1767. Courtesy of the New York Public Library

John Wilkes   59
William Hogarth, 1763. Courtesy of the Trustees of the British
Museum

James Otis   79
Joseph Blackburn, 1755. Courtesy of the Frick Art Reference Library,
collection of Mrs. Carlos Hepp

John Adams   111
Benjamin Blyth, 1766. Courtesy of the Massachusetts Historical
Society

Josiah Quincy   156
Gilbert Stuart, 1825. Courtesy of the Museum of Fine Arts, Boston,
collection of Edmund Quincy

A View of the Year 1765   181
Paul Revere, 1766. Courtesy of the American Antiquarian Society

The Deplorable State of America, 1765   183
John Singleton Copley, 1766. Courtesy of the Library Company of
Philadelphia

Poor Old England Endeavoring to Reclaim His Wicked
American Children   187
Anonymous, 1777. Courtesy of the Trustees of the British Museum

Guy Fawkes   192
George Cruikshank, 1825–1826. From William Hone, *The Every-Day
Book.*

The Life and Humble Confession of Richardson, the Informer   193
Broadside, 1770. Courtesy of the Historical Society of Pennsylvania

French Revolutionary Procession   218
Anonymous French print, late eighteenth century

Lords Bute and Grenville Hung in Effigy   219
Boston-Gazette, 1766. Courtesy of the New York Public Library

A Representation of the Figures Exhibited and Paraded
through the Streets of Philadelphia   221
Charles Willson Peale, 1780. Courtesy of the American Antiquarian
Society

Introduction

THE AMERICAN REVOLUTION began in a series of protests against English revenue measures: the Sugar Act in 1764, the Stamp Act in 1765, and the Townshend Acts in 1767 and 1768. Yet interpretations of the Revolution have always stressed deeper causes for the discontent of Americans. John Adams's famous remark that the Revolution took place "in the Minds and Hearts of the People" assumed an underlying change in what he termed the "Religious Sentiments" of Americans. He related these sentiments to the Puritan tradition of religious revivals, calling the 1760s and 1770s, with which the present study is chiefly concerned, "AN AWAKENING and a REVIVAL of American Principals and Feelings."[1] Modern explanations of the Revolution have come to stress other underlying causes—economic, social, ideological, and even moral; but these have held in common with Adams an assumption that the American colonists were not entirely aware of the forces that moved them.

The sense of something that does not quite meet the eye has been especially remarked in the Revolution's political rhetoric and, more recently, in the collective discontent expressed by its public demonstrations. It has been clear for some time, for example, that the legal and political arguments advanced in patriot writings were flawed in logic, and that furthermore they were couched in an "inflated," even "paranoiac" rhetoric. As for the revenue measures that they excoriated, these "in retrospect appear to have been no more than a series of justifiable and not very sinister actions by the parent state."[2] There is no need to adopt recent suggestions that patriot writers expressed a mass delusion arising from a kind of universal psychological disturbance. But historians now agree that the Revolution cannot be

1

accounted for without assuming that there were powerful, unconscious forces at play.[3]

The overheated prose of American patriot writers found an echo in the public's fierce resistance to the same English revenue measures. Crowds of demonstrators, sometimes breaking into riot, displayed visual symbols of various kinds to depict the horrors of British rule described by patriot writers. Yet although both the anomalies of the rhetoric and the collective emotionalism of Americans have been studied, the relationship between them has not. In this connection the history of the 1960s offers certain perspectives on the 1760s. In the 1960s the interactions of crowds, crises, and personal conscience touched virtually everyone in America. At the time one came to appreciate the significance of symbolism in political writings and demonstrations, and to feel the political impact of youth as an idea, especially when it was conveyed by the presence of young people at demonstrations. The effect of similar elements in the pre-Revolutionary atmosphere of the 1760s and 1770s in America amounted to what I term a "ritual of revolution." Just as in the 1960s, the ritualization of politics took place at once in the minds and hearts of the patriots, and in the actions of revolutionary crowds.

The historical questions posed by the symbolism of American Revolutionary protest—in rhetoric as well as among crowds—call for an eclectic approach that can include the insights of psychoanalysis, anthropology, and literary criticism. The present study, accordingly, amounts not to a historical interpretation of the Revolution in the strict sense, but to a reading of its ritual language. This reading takes into account patriot writings, cartoons, and plays, the symbolism of crowds, and the behavior of patriots who participated in the collective ritual of revolution. A chapter is devoted to the scapegoat of these rituals, Thomas Hutchinson of Massachusetts, and another to their sources in the expressive politics of England during its troubled domestic passasge through the 1760s and 1770s. The last chapters deal with the intimate connections among festival, youth, and revolution by tracing the rituals in question back to their origins.

I

Crowds and Crisis

CHAPTER ONE

The Rehearsal of Revolution

T HE STAMP ACT RIOTS of August 1765 shocked the English-speaking world. Despite a history of far more violent crowd disturbances in the American colonies, these gatherings elicited special concern. Opponents of the Stamp Act expressed as much surprise and dismay as its supporters, and both sides took steps to prevent a repetition of the violence. Two hundred years later, in the 1960s, street disturbances in which a few people were injured could similarly elicit sharper reactions than acts of violence in which scores were killed. At both times the expressive behavior of crowds proved more important than their actual deeds. Repeatedly the rioters emphasized, and the authorities reacted to, this behavior rather than the situation objectively considered. To participants and observers alike, the ritual proved more important than the reality.[1]

The 1765 riots came two years after England's victory over France in its protracted Great War for the empire. During the war the English had used their American customs service in an unsuccessful effort to eliminate illegal trade with the enemy. Then, starting in 1760 when the fighting ended in North America, English ministries had attempted to offset their crushing war expenses by again using the customs service—this time hoping to improve its efficiency in order to collect more revenue. Just as during the war, however, smuggling by merchants in Boston and other American cities frustrated the ministry's plans. The Stamp Act of 1765 represented but one in a series of attempts to raise money and was not the first to be resented. It affected far more people than the previous acts, however; whereas before ship-borne commerce alone had been taxed, the Stamp Act called for revenue stamps on virtually all paper transactions and published materials. As a result, newspaper publishers and lawyers joined the opposition. They would be the chief users of stamped paper, and they stood to be taxed for the first time.

In general, Americans were agreed in theory that they ought to help pay for a war that had removed the French from their borders, and they thought it fair that they be partly liable for the continued, expensive presence of the British military that patrolled their continent.[2] When it came to the proposed Stamp Act, however, there was widespread opposition based on a number of fears. It was said that the new act would worsen the postwar depression (which many falsely attributed to the Sugar Act of the previous year); it was feared that the collections would drain away cash essential to the economy; and, far more broadly, it was charged that the act represented the opening wedge in a plot to deny English freedoms in America for the purpose of enslaving its people. Stamp acts were not unheard of in British history, and some thirty years later the new American government itself would have recourse to one. But this particular Stamp Act raised special passions.

In Boston two riots in August 1765 set a pattern for the rest of the colonies. The first riot began as a demonstration against the appointed stamp distributor, Andrew Oliver, whose wine cellar was invaded and whose house was partly damaged. The second riot started as a series of break-ins at the homes of customs and province officials. Whatever official documents could be found were destroyed, and at the same time wine cellars were opened, so that the crowd got drunk—as it had at Oliver's. This time, however, the drunkenness had far more vicious results. At the last house broken into, not only were papers scattered and torn, but the building, which belonged to the lieutenant governor, was stripped down to its shell. The first riot, which was reported in newspapers throughout the colonies, set off a chain reaction of similar demonstrations and destructiveness. Each began with an elaborate parade of effigies representing officials believed to be responsible for the Stamp Act. And everywhere, as in Boston, a mocking, festival-like behavior prevailed among the protesters.

Despite the demonstrations, the Stamp Act remained scheduled to go into effect on November 1, 1765. Protests were set for this day, too, with Boston arranging safeguards to prevent a repetition of its August violence. Sporadic but orderly demonstrations continued during the next few months after November, until the Stamp Act was finally repealed. The news of repeal was greeted with a final series of celebratory crowd pageants in May 1766. Thus, the Stamp Act episode began and ended with public, symbolic demonstrations by crowds, marking it as an event of emotional as well as political significance.

If the ritual symbolism employed by the crowds accounts in a general way for the demonstrations' stunning effect on public opinion, it does not explain why large crowds mobilized to oppose this particular revenue act. That shipping merchants, lawyers, and newspaper owners should join the demonstrations made sense. But most of those in the crowds lacked a direct interest in the matter. The mechanics, apprentices, dock workers, seamen, servants, slaves, and boys whom the professional men and businessmen joined would not be required to use the stamps when the act went into effect. They might expect to come in contact with a revenue stamp at the witnessing of signatures for an apprenticeship or a term of indenture, but on these occasions their masters presumably would be the ones to pay. It is true that playing cards would require stamps, and it was rumored that marriage licenses would, too. But these were hardly grounds for riot. Furthermore, special exclusions were provided for seamen, one of the most prominent groups at the demonstrations.[3]

Many loyalists explained the Stamp Act riots as a delayed reaction to the crackdown on smuggling brought about by the Sugar Act of 1764. Much later, a nineteenth-century historian, Andrew Preston Peabody, explained the Stamp Act mobs in a similar way: he viewed them as a delayed reaction to the Sugar Act—by drunkards in particular. He pointed out that the Sugar Act affected at least twenty distilleries in Boston, each of which was dependent on cheap, smuggled molasses. "This state of things," wrote Peabody in 1888, "alone can account for the turbulent and obstreperous patriotism of the class of men who would have been the chief clientage of the distilleries, but who had very little concern in the impending Stamp Act, which was an atrocious grievance to the merchants and the men of business, but which, had it preceded the molasses act [that is, the Sugar Act], would hardly have been understood or cared for, still less opposed and resented, by the populace."[4] It was true that the Stamp Act crowds made straight for the liquor when they broke into a house. Futhermore, thirty years earlier a rise in the price of alcohol had led to the somewhat similar Gin Act riots in London. But in the English case the crowd's symbolization, which involved a figure known as "Mother Gin," and ritual burnings of the act, made clear the subject of its anger.[5] In the case of the Stamp Act, the symbolic and real figures made no such clear sense.

In Boston, for example, the crowd reserved its greatest violence, both actual and symbolic, for the lieutenant governor of the province, Thomas Hutchinson, and for the earl of Bute, the predecessor of the current prime minister. Remarkably, neither of these men was a supporter of the act. In a similar fashion, two Englishmen, John Wilkes and William Pitt, were incorrectly celebrated as the champions of America in this crisis. In fact, Wilkes was not at the time interested in American affairs, while ironically Pitt was the prime minister who had begun the customs assault on American smuggling during the recent war.

Why rumors should have persisted that Bute, though out of office, had instigated the Stamp Act, and that Hutchinson, who was working to oppose it, was its leading American supporter, is a question in itself. In the case of Bute, it might be said that the pervasive suspicion and hatred of him in England was transferred to an unthinking crowd. But Hutchinson was hated not only by the crowd, but also by the patriot leaders, who had more leisure for reflection. Their rhetoric—in its treatment of Bute and Hutchinson, and in its tendency toward exaggeration and violence—amounted to a written equivalent of the illogicalities and excesses of American crowds. Patriot writers treated the customs acts as part of a conspiracy to undermine traditional American probity in order to enslave the colonists.[6] They made Hutchinson and Bute the archfiends in this conspiracy, and England itself a cruel, unnatural parent dashing out the brains of its loving children. Not surprisingly, the loyalists were at a loss to account for such language, and tended to regard it either as a cynically calculated means of inflaming the crowd, or as simple hysteria.

It was apparent from the first that resistance to the Stamp Act expressed far more than disapproval of the act in particular. In the disturbed atmosphere of protest, there reappeared personal quarrels, old resentments, business rivalries, and unhealed political wounds. Furthermore, it was not difficult to see that geography and population destined Americans at some point to change their relationship to England. And finally, as the intensity of the Revolution eventually suggested, the sentiment of personal autonomy that was growing everywhere in the Western world during the eighteenth century was especially strong in America.

All these forces were made manifest by the colonists in public forms. These tended to be symbolic and ambiguous, and to be accompanied by various degrees of violence, both verbal and physical. Through these forms, Americans of the 1760s and 1770s conducted what may be termed a "ritual of revolution." Strictly speaking, "ritual" implies the formal enactment of a prescribed ceremony or routine, whereas American crowds added routines of their own to the traditional practices that they adopted. On the other hand, both the traditional and the innovative elements remained strongly religious, as with all politics during this period in America. The religious emphasis has led one analyst to describe the entire revolutionary process as the collective ritual of a new American "civil religion."[7]

In the discussion that follows, "ritual" is used to indicate not only the influence of religion, but also symbolization and behavior similar to that which anthropologists have found in formal ritual. In the case of political demonstrations by patriot crowds, the imitation of quasi-religious festivals, along with behavior that was not fully rational and controlled, produced events that may be termed ritualistic in nature. In the case of patriot rhetoric, the word "ritualized" may be applied in the sense accepted in literary criticism, where it signifies any incantatory, partly unconscious use of language.

Both the rituals of individual patriots and those of the crowds served to convey those cultural imperatives of the colonists that could not gain explicit expression until a nation had been declared. The process was evident in the first, most important, and most fully described American crowd of the Revolution: the August 1765 demonstration and riot in Boston against the Stamp Act.

This protest was staged shortly after word reached America that the Stamp Act had been passed in May 1765. At 5 A.M. on August 14, market day, a large elm tree opposite the Boylston market was hung with two effigies and surrounded by Stamp Act protesters. One effigy, made of straw and dressed in a gentleman's breeches, represented Andrew Oliver, secretary of the province and the man designated as Boston's stamp tax collector. Next to it hung a boot, representing Lord Bute. In the approving words of the *Boston-Gazette*, the boot "concealed a young imp of the D——l [Devil] represented as peeping out of the Top—On the Breast of the Effigy was a Label, in

Praise of Liberty, and denouncing Vengeance on the Subvestors of it." The "Label" pinned to the effigy of Oliver read:

> Fair freedom's glorious cause I've meanly quitted
> For the sake of self;
> But ah! the Devil has me outwitted,
> And instead of *stamping* others, I've *hang'd* myself.

On the left arm were Oliver's initials, "A.O." Attached to his right arm was the warning: "PS Whoever takes this down is an enemy to his Country." The devil's imp, who held a pitchfork ("an Horrid Fork") aimed at Oliver, had pinned to it a paper representing the Stamp Act. In the punning spirit of the boot symbol, which was borrowed from England, the *Boston News-Letter* reported that the figure peeping out of it was "said by some of the Printers to be the Devil or his Imp"—a play on the term "printer's devil."[8]

Every farmer on the way to market was forced to stop and, in a physical play on words, have "his Articles stamped by the Effigy." The onlookers were reported as "Joyous" and universally participating in a spirit of "Ridicule." One Bostonian wrote to a friend, "You would have laughed to have seen two or three hundred little Boys with a Flagg marching in Procession on which was King, Pitt & Liberty."

Afterward, the figures were left hanging until "about dusk" when they were taken down and placed in a coffin. The whole affair had been planned as a mock hanging, funeral, and burial. The "labels" on the effigies, with their cautionary messages, played on the "dying speeches" of the condemned that were sold at hangings in Puritan New England. Like the supposed words of Oliver, these speeches typically confessed a crime and warned others to avoid the evil ways that led to it. Many in the crowd accompanied the procession wearing signs of mourning, thus making it into a mock funeral. In the same spirit of mockery and word play, the effigies were "not covered with a Sheet," explained the *Boston Post-Boy*, "except the Sheet of Paper which bore the Inscription." Supported by six men, the coffin was carried in a mock-solemn funeral procession led by "forty or fifty tradesmen, decently dressed." The accompanying chants were "Liberty and Property" and "No Stamps." The procession stopped at Governor Bernard's residence, "went up his Yard gave 3 Huzzas, on which all the People ran out [of the house] in great surprise." From here the crowd proceeded to the Town House, or city hall, where the governor and council were meeting on the upper story. They had been in touch with events since morning, at which time they had sent the sheriff to take down the effigies. He had been frightened off, and since then they had been unable to find any other civil officer willing to act. The crowd carried its "pageantry" through the ground floor of the building, gave three cheers, and departed.[9]

Thus far the protest had gone according to plan, and was proceeding to its culmination in a bonfire on Fort Hill, where effigies traditionally were burned. But along the route, part of the crowd broke away to tear down a building under construction by Oliver. This contingent acted under the false assumption that the building was intended as a Stamp office. Oliver's house was also on the way to Fort Hill; there the crowd threw stones through the windows, conducted a mock hanging of Oliver's effigy, sawed off its head, and burned it. Then all proceeded to the hill, where the second effigy was "stamped" on and then burned with wood taken from the supposed stamp building previously torn down. This was the intended ending of the demonstration, and at this point the "Directors of the People" went home, leaving behind a group drinking around the bonfire. After a time the drinkers returned to Oliver's. They tore down and burned the fences, broke into the ground floor and cellar, drank the wine, and scattered the silver, "none of which however was missing the next Day," according to the *Gazette*.[10]

When Governor Bernard wrote that "there never was such a Mob known in the Province," he had in mind not the violence done, but the apparent involvement of all classes. Never before, he continued, had there been "so many Abettors of Consequence; it is said there were 50 Gentlemen Actors disguised in Trawsers & Jackets." Heretofore mobs had been strictly lower-class phenomena, it would seem. This time not only had "gentlemen" participated, but they had come dressed as workers. (Another report had it that the gentlemen had dressed as "decent tradesmen"; if this was so, then they had moved themselves down the ladder of class by only one rung rather than two.) The trousers and jackets, though, hardly provided a very effective disguise: they had far more significance as a gesture of solidarity with the working class.[11]

Gentlemen stood for authority, and had always been so identified at times of festive turmoil such as New England's Pope Day holiday, during which their homes and dignity were traditionally violated. On that day the paraded effigy was dressed, like Andrew Oliver's, in breeches. By joining the parade in trousers of their own the gentlemen of Boston in August 1765 replaced their usual reluctant tolerance of the lower-class ethos with deference toward it. Later, during the French Revolution, the wearing of trousers grew so important that the term *sans-culottes*—"without gentlemen's breeches"—came to signify working-class and hence radical affiliation. From the eighteenth century onward, dress bespoke politics. In the early twentieth century, intellectuals wore work shirts as a gesture of solidarity with the working class. More recently, youths in the 1960s returned to the gesture of 1765 when they dressed in the dungarees that had been the nineteenth-century version of workmen's trousers.[12]

The symbolism of the Stamp Act protests has been traced to the religious imagination of New Englanders. The devil, who regularly appeared in effigy, verses, and accompanying broadsides during the Revolution, may be regarded as an embodiment of the familiar villain of Puritan sermons. In traditional Manichean-symbolic fashion, the giant elm hung with effigies came to be known as the Liberty Tree, which taken together with the devil symbolized "good against evil."[13] The ritual in which these symbols were embodied, however, was not religious alone. The processional with its straw effigies, the sacralized tree, the symbolism of death by hanging, the bonfire—all these elements suggested rites older than those of American Calvinism.

The crowd's playful mood evoked the holiday atmosphere of New England. Significantly, the day's activities had been planned on a holiday—the Prince of Wales's birthday (August 12)—and they took place on another—Boston's Market Day (Thursday). The humor associated with such days, a humor dependent on reversals and word play, called to mind pagan sources, notably the mock reversals of the Roman Saturnalia. The patriots' running joke had it that the protesters themselves were "stamp" men. They stamped farmers' goods, stamped on Oliver's effigy, and even stamped on the wood taken from his supposed stamp office. Here, one observer reported, "If any piece happened to be cast on the fire before it was stamp'd it was pull'd off and the ceremony had upon it and put on again." In a pun, the meaning of a word is reversed yet retained, just as here, and just as with social positions in the Saturnalia, where servants and masters temporarily changed places. The newspapers tried to capture the mock tone of the proceedings by improving upon the puns. Thus the green sole that was meant to suggest Lord Grenville became a "Green-vile" sole in print, making two puns where there had been one.[14]

All this playfulness did not allay the crowd's anger. And yet one cannot fail to be struck by the newspaper report that nothing had been stolen from Oliver. This circumstance has been variously attributed to the deferential habits of colonial society, and to a "self-discipline" among crowd members inspired by "convictions and a sense of the importance of the cause they were engaged in." But such restraint was not at all unusual among crowds. As Gustave Le Bon pointed out seventy-five years ago, "A crowd may be guilty of murder, incendiarism, and every kind of crime, but it is also capable of very lofty acts of devotion, sacrifice, and disinterestedness, of acts much loftier indeed than those of which the isolated individual is capable."[15] As examples, Le Bon cited extraordinary cases of riots during the French revolutions of 1789 and 1848 in which, just as at Oliver's house, no looting took place. Such restraint was possible, he argued, as a direct consequence of the crowd's irrational state of mind.

According to this theory, which was later taken up by Sigmund Freud, the crowd is mesmerized by a psychically powerful leader, whose instructions are carried out to the letter. But the virtue of Le Bon's approach lies not in its insistence on irrationality and the charismatic crowd leader, neither of which applies particularly well to the American crowd, but in its recognition of two extremes in crowd behavior—one restrained and the other hysterical. These extremes were evident on August 14, 1765, when there took place both a particularly orderly procession and an outbreak of destructiveness. Rather than Le Bon's having hit upon an irrational phenomenon, however, it may be suggested that he described a ritualized one. Groups participating in a ritual may act in ways that can neither be termed irrational, nor described as being entirely in accordance with their customary good sense, either. Sanctioned by the ritual proceeding, they may engage both in violence and in the kind of restraint remarked by Le Bon and by those who observed the August 14 demonstration.

The concept of ritual accounts for other anomalies of crowd behavior as well. For example, it has puzzled historians to note that so-called bread riots in France in the eighteenth century did not, as it was long assumed, coincide with periods when prices rose to their heights. Peasants and the urban poor responded to more than hunger alone. Despite being cruelly put down by the king's soldiers, moreover, these protesters maintained a seemingly inexplicable reverence for the king. It has been suggested that such contradictions are characteristic of "primitive rebels"—preindustrial and preorganized workers who were anticipating the proletarian revolutions of later times.[16] The American case, though, offers an exception to this theory. For not only did its preindustrial workers exhibit a dogged reverence for the king, but its sophisticated political theorists did so as well.

Despite overwhelming evidence of George III's complicity in the policies that were driving them toward revolution, Americans of all classes on the patriot side sustained their loyalty to the king throughout the period from 1760 to 1776. Thus, in 1769 and 1770 when the king personally refused to so much as receive grievance petitions from his subjects in England, he rendered insupportable the claim that not he but his ministers were responsible for the government's actions. Yet the most that can be found in patriot writings at this point are "tell-tale qualifications" in the continuing "assertions of the King's goodness."[17]

The phenomenon of loyalty was not restricted to any particular time or place in the years prior to 1776. George III was widely and quite incorrectly regarded as "one of the earliest and most dedicated opponents of the Stamp Act, and as the most important single force in the movement for its repeal." The king's name was loudly upheld and his health drunk enthusiastically at the earliest Stamp Act demonstrations, the dedication of Liberty Tree, Stamp Act Repeal Ceremonies, and subsequently at virtually every anti-British demonstration up to 1776. During this period his birthday continued to be celebrated with similar enthusiasm throughout the colonies.[18]

In 1768 the king was looked to as the best hope of repealing the Townshend Acts, which he approved, and after the Intolerable Acts of 1775 he continued to be trusted by many. Indeed, "on the very eve of the Revolution, in late 1774 and early 1775, a remarkable upsurge of American faith in and dependence on George III appeared." Among certain members of the Continental Congress this faith lasted until the vote for independence. In continuing to support their king up to the moment of revolution itself, protesting Americans resembled both sixteenth-century French tax rebels and nineteenth-century Italian peasant revolutionaries.[19]

When they decided to declare independence, Americans turned on George III with a fury as remarkable as the loyalty that preceded it. By all accounts the precipitant was a single pamphlet, Thomas Paine's *Common Sense,* which by laying the blame for the troubles of the colonies on monarchy in general and the king in particular ignited the revolutionary spark. Suddenly, Paine made the much-praised king "a butcher," and the "cruelest . . . *tyrant."* On reading *Common Sense* in 1776 the patriot Joseph Hawley declared in the Puritan terminology of religious preparationism that "every sentiment has sunk into my well prepared heart." Whereas until now the singularity of American political writings had lain in their mildness toward the king when compared with those of British contemporaries, they began to surpass these in temerity. In some ways the most shocking example was the Declaration of Independence. Like *Common Sense,* the Declaration treated the king in a new way. For, after a decade of arguments directed at Parliament, it suddenly offered a long and detailed list of misdeeds which it attributed exclusively to him. Following public readings of the Declaration, George III was burned in effigy and interred in mock burial; his statues were pulled down, and his coat of arms burned in a frenzy of destruction not experienced in America since the Stamp Act.[20]

The great outburst of 1776 has been aptly termed a "killing of the king"—an orgy of symbolic destruction necessary to the establishment of popular sovereignty. So it was. And it can be added that this killing completed the ritual process begun in 1765 with the symbolic killings of effigial substitutes for the king. Once again, as in the case of the underlying causes of the Stamp Act opposition, an unconscious process took a ritual form, expressing the enmity toward the king which earlier symbolizations had succeeded in containing. For years this enmity had been systematically denied by professions of loyalty to the king in patriot writings and by toasts and shouts of loyalty to him at crowd gatherings.[21] When the enmity surfaced, it manifested itself not only in the explicit language of *Common Sense* and the Declaration of Independence, but also as a collective ritual expression.

If this expression on the part of the crowds had parallels in the written word, it nevertheless had a ritual language of its own. The crowd's richly evocative insurrectionary symbols derived, as everyone knew, chiefly from New England's Pope Day. This November 5 holiday was an adaptation of the English Guy Fawkes Day, the annual commemoration of the 1605 Gunpowder Plot against the king. In England "guys"—effigies of the leader of the plot—were carried in processions and then burned. In New England the Catholic Guy Fawkes was replaced by the pope, and accompanied by the devil. These substitutions reflected an American religious bias: a plot against the king almost automatically suggested a popish conspiracy, and hence the devil. A third figure was sometimes added in America: the pretender to the throne, James III, who had invaded Scotland in 1715, and whose son, James IV, still alive in the 1760s, had led a similar invasion in 1745. The Pretender figure represented a suggestive updating of the earlier powder plot against the king.

The traditional parades of the two Boston pope carts were arranged by workmen and apprentices from the north and south ends of the town. Each cart had a stage built upon it.

> At the front of the stage was a large lantern of oiled paper, four or five feet wide and eight or nine feet high. On the front was painted in large letters, "The devil take the pope"; and just below this "North end forever" or "South end forever." Behind the lantern sat the pope in an arm chair, and behind the pope was the devil standing erect with extended arms, one hand holding a smaller lantern, the other grasping a pitchfork. The heads of pope and devil were on poles which went through their bodies and the stage beneath. Boxed up out of sight sat a boy whose mission was to sway the heads from side to side as fancy suggested.[22]

The devil effigy was accompanied on the stage and alongside the cart by other boys with blackened faces and in jester's caps. These devil's "imps" harassed and mocked the pope effigy. In the evening, the effigies were usually burned on Fort Hill. Afterward, men and boys entered many of the town's finer houses, where they performed mummeries and were given alms and drink. A contemporary called the participants "Anticks" and described them as being dressed "in filthy clothes and oftimes with masked and blackened faces" as they went about collecting money. In each house they "would demean themselves with great insolence."[23]

In Boston a rivalry troublesome to peace officers sprang up between the north and south ends of the town. Each attempted to seize and destroy the other's cart and pope. The fist-fighting and stone-throwing grew bloodier year by year and the organization of the two groups more elaborate. Each had a leader who arranged the display and directed the battle. In 1764, the year before the Oliver and Hutchinson riots, a boy was run over and killed by one of the carts. The sheriff was ordered to put an end to the processions, and was able to seize and destroy the north end pope. Its followers, however, soon retrieved and rebuilt it, only to lose it again late in the day to the south-

Defcription of the POPE, 1769.

Toafts on the Front of the large Lanthorn.
Love and Unity.---The American Whig.---Confufion to the
Torries,and a total Barifhment to Bribery andCorruption.
On the Right Side of the fame.---An Acroftick.

J nfulting Wretch, we'll him expofe,
O 'er the whole World his Deeds difclofe,
H ell now gaups wide to take him in,
N ow he is ripe, Oh Lump of Sin.
M ean is the Man, M--n is his Name,
E nough he's fpread his hellifh Fame,
I nfernal Furies hurl his Soul,
N ine Million Times from Pole to Pole.
Labels on the Left Side.

Now fhake, ye Torries ! fee the Rogue behind,
Hung up a Scarecrow, to correct Mankind.
Oh had the Villain but receiv'd his Due,
Himfelf in Perfon would here fwing in View :
But let the Traitor mend within the Year,
Or by the next he fhall be hanging here.
Ye Slaves ! ye Torries who infeft the Land,
And fcatter num'rous Plagues on ev'ry Hand,
Now we'll be free, or bathe in honeft Blood ;
We'll nobly perifh for our Country's Good,
We'll purge the Land of the infernal Crew,
And at one Stroke we'll give the Devil his Due.
Labels on each Side the fmall Lanthorn.
WILKES and LIBERTY, No· 45.

See the Informer how he ftands, If any one now takes his Part,
An Enemy to all the Land, He'll go to Hell without a Cart
May Difcord ceafe, in Hell be jam'd,
And factious fellows all be dam'd.
From B-----, the verieft monfter on earth,
The fell production of fome baneful birth,
Thefe ills proceed,—from him they took their birth,
The Source fupreme, and Center of all Hate.
If I forgive him, then forget me Heaven,
Or like a WILKES may I from Right be driven.
Here ftands the Devil for a Show, }
With the I--p---rs in a row,   }
All bound to Hell, and that we know. }
Go M--n lade deep with Curfes on thy head,
To fome dark Corner of the World repair,
Where the bright Sun no pleafant Beams can fhed,
And fpend thy Life in Horror and Defpair.
Effigies,—M--n, his Servant, &c.--A Bunch of TOM-CODs.

Description of the Pope, Boston 1769

A politicized Pope Day procession directed against John Mein, the loyalist
newspaper publisher. The engraving shows the traditional pageantry, with
the devil standing behind the pope and in front of the pope an illuminated
lanthorn. The verses contain such motifs of patriot rhetoric as hanging,
blood, Bute as evil versus Wilkes as savior, and punning (on Mein's name).

enders, who were usually defeated by the north. The south-enders then "burnt Both of [the Popes] . . . at the Gallows on the Neck."[24]

The insurrectionary potential in this rowdy holiday was evident. Its threats to peace officers, together with a certain wantonness of symbolism, breathed defiance of authority in general. In substituting the pope for Guy Fawkes, moreover, Americans had put their own anti-Catholic concerns ahead of the holiday's concern with treason against the king. Later, when they substituted the effigies of political figures for the pope, they continued to defy logic by including Bute and Grenville. Whatever the immediate issues, the larger issue thus expressed was the colonies' relationship to England. It was commonly said that this relationship was one of dependence resembling that of a child to its parents, with now either the child or parents, depending on one's political point of view, beginning to behave unnaturally.

The patriot conception of the Revolution as a familial drama has been perpetuated both by historians of the Revolution and by writers of fiction up until the present—with all concurring in a picture of the break from England as a kind of national coming of age. In fact, public demonstrations were often dominated by children and youths, and many of the patriots were young men in their twenties. Although they might be married and have families of their own, the idea of many personal rites of passage has always seemed an apt description of their Revolutionary experience. Writers of fiction, accordingly, have commonly symbolized the whole Revolutionary process, both personal and collective, by a teen-aged youth.[25] His coming of age typically adumbrates the coming of age of the nation. Among tales of the Revolution that include such a youth there is one so dense in suggestion and so steeped in actual history that its symbolizations offer profound insights into the meanings of the Revolution.

Nathaniel Hawthorne's "My Kinsman, Major Molineux" concerns a teen-aged boy's coming to colonial Boston, where his involvement in a crowd enacts his own coming of age while predicting that of the country. In part, the story is a commentary on the process of sublimation and ritual substitution that was typical of the American Revolution. Hawthorne had in mind victims like Andrew Oliver and Thomas Hutchinson, whom he mentions at the outset. The manner in which they were made scapegoats for the king sets the pattern for the central scene of scapegoating in the story.

The time is the 1730s, a period that saw frequent crowd disturbances, as Hawthorne emphasizes. But the story's details of behavior by the crowd and its leader are meant also to suggest the 1760s and 1770s. Major Molineux, a member of "the court party," the colonial ruling elite, is to be tarred and feathered and ridden out of Boston on a cart. Earlier the same night his nephew, Robin, unaware of the preparations, arrives in Boston. Robin's well-placed relative has promised to help him make his way in the world. Not until the end of the night does Robin comprehend why the townspeople, who know about the tarring and feathering, turn away his requests for directions to his kinsman's home. As they don disguises for the night's work, the conspirators create an atmosphere of phantasmagoria and dream that engulfs the reader, who shares Robin's ignorance. Finally the shrieking crowd arrives, and its leader halts the procession to let Robin see his tarred and feathered kinsman. The two mutely recognize one another, and then, in a stunning development, Robin lets out a shout of laughter "louder than all the rest." Interpretation of the tale rests on the social, political, and psychological sources of this apparently inappropriate reaction.

Above all, "My Kinsman, Major Molineux" concerns a young man's initiation, the setting for which is an act of revolt that anticipates the American Revolution. Typically, Robin's coming of age involves two warring emotions: the wish to defy and break free of authority, and the fear of having to stand alone without its protection. Robin exhibits his dependence on his relative by repeatedly invoking his name, and by thinking of his own future strictly in terms of the name's influence. (Major Molineux, whom Robin repeatedly refers to as "my kinsman" who will set things right, may be regarded as a surrogate father.) Even as Robin is placing his dependence on Molineux, though, he unconsciously expresses his revolt. For although he is anxious to locate his kinsman, he repeatedly acquiesces in evasions by the townspeople that prevent his doing so. His gullibility thus betrays a wish *not* to succeed in his search. Of course he eventually does succeed—only to release in laughter the unconscious resentment he has harbored throughout his search.

Hawthorne brings together the crowd and the young man at a crucial point for each. The boy's psychology is underlined by the fact that the crowd is carrying out a political overthrow of authority that parallels his personal drama. At the same time the boy's experience tells something about the crowd. As one critic has put it, the story could have been subtitled, "America's Coming of Age."[26] The crowd, having fixed on Major Molineux as representative of the authority it has grown ready to overthrow, enacts a scapegoat ritual that predicts but is not yet an actual act of revolution. This ritual proves to have a profound effect on Robin. Its derisive, ritualized laughter ignites his laugh and brings about his coming of age.

Robin's development parallels the growth of revolutionary senti-ment in America from 1765 to 1776. Like Robin with his kinsman, American crowds and American patriots directed at substitutes like Thomas Hutchinson what they actually felt toward the king. Whereas Robin begins in elaborate dependence on authority, as represented by his kinsman, Americans elaborately expressed their loyalty and sub-mission to the king in writings and crowd events. When Robin is con-fronted with a ritual that expresses defiance of authority, and that sud-denly makes explicit his real feelings toward his kinsman, he explodes with a seemingly irrational emotionality. Just so with American crowds when suddenly confronted with the Declaration's total reversal of atti-tude toward the king.[27]

This is not to suggest that Hawthorne attempts to reduce the Rev-olution to a childlike event. He imputes no childishness to the adults who conduct the proto-Revolutionary ritual witnessed by Robin, but on the contrary makes clear that it is an affair of the town elders. On the other hand, Robin's presence seems both to be essential to the proceedings and to throw light on them. Hawthorne, it would appear, is suggesting that the process of Revolution was conducted *in terms of* coming of age. It is in this sense that Robin, like the other young men of Revolutionary fiction, can serve as a symbol. Neither is Hawthorne implying that the Revolution itself was only a kind of ritual, for he emphasizes that his tale takes place well before the 1760s, let alone 1776. Just so, the rituals of revolution employed by Americans be-tween 1765 and 1776 were not revolutions in themselves but rather anticipations of one to come. In their dramatic processionals and dis-plays they enacted what may be termed a rehearsal of revolution.

Interpreters of "My Kinsman, Major Molineux" have pointed out that the break from authority in coming of age includes a release of accumulated hostility. The same was true of the American Revolution. There, so long as it was ritualized, violence remained at a remarkably low level, especially when compared to the French Revolution or mod-ern revolutions. But the great impact of the Stamp Act riots depended on the widespread impression that they had released unprecedented violence. Observers reacted not so much to the destruction of property and the physical intimidation of a few individuals, frightening as these were to those directly involved, as to the symbolic executions and immolations that accompanied these actions. They reacted, that is, to the *ritual* violence of the protests.

Stated another way, the shocking element in Revolutionary crowds came from expressions of hostility and licensed regression characteristic of the coming-of-age ritual. It was no wonder that, although these processes proved fascinating to the patriots, for whom in many cases they dramatized hidden feelings, they also caused embarrassment and dismay. The revivalism of the Puritans, most recently resurrected in the Great Awakening, was evidence of an American capacity for mass enthusiasm, and it was with some justice that loyalists disparaged the Stamp Act riots by reference to American history.[28]

Politically speaking, the patriot movement attached itself to the progressive ideas of the age—the elimination of corruption, greater individual freedom, freedom of the press, more pure representation. When the movement took to the streets, however, it could be embarrassingly regressive, and not just politically. Patriots in various places were associated with folk punishments against adulterers and prostitutes, and these punishments were strongly reminiscent of the Puritan era. The patriot Continental Association issued prohibitions against various kinds of games and entertainments, and forbade stage plays. In 1766 the New York Sons of Liberty "pulled down the play house the beginning of the 2nd act, put out all the lights, then began picking of pockets, stealing watches, throwing Brick Bats, sticks and Bottles and Glasses, crying out Liberty, Liberty then proceeded to the Fields or Common and burnt the materials."[29]

In two significant instances patriots were associated with superstitious hysteria over smallpox inoculation. In Norfolk, Virginia, in 1768 and 1769 the agitation against inoculation appears to have been aroused partly because the physician in charge was a loyalist, partly as a means for debtors to attack their creditors, and partly as an expression of anti-Scots prejudice against one of the merchants who had had his family inoculated. The organizer of the Norfolk anti-inoculation mobs had received his training in the Stamp Act agitation, when he had been involved in a tarring and feathering. This time, a "drum and flag" were used for recruitment, there were effigy burnings, and a

group of patients including women and children, some of them fe-
verish from their inoculations, were driven out of doors and marched
to the town pest house.[30]

In Marblehead, Massachusetts, in 1773 and 1774 a debate over
methods of inoculation—English or American—arose among patriot
leaders. The question arranged itself along chauvinist lines, and reflected the town's division between Old and New Lights in the religious controversies of the Great Awakening. In the seventeenth century Marblehead had undergone a similar episode—one that has been
compared to the witchcraft obsession in nearby Salem. Now the town
once again employed measures dating back to the seventeenth century, among them the killing of the inhabitants' dogs. Other old superstitions and antiscientific fears were revived when a group of citizens erected a building on a nearby island for the purpose of giving
smallpox inoculations. Tarring and feathering mobs intimidated users
of this hospital, which was finally set afire. Patriot leaders, who were
among those supporting the inoculations, now found themselves opposed by mobs consisting of the same people who had supported them
in opposing the Stamp Act and later English measures. In protest
against the behavior of the crowd, some of these leaders resigned from
the local committee of correspondence.[31] In both Norfolk and Marblehead the patriot crowd had identified itself with superstition, intolerance, prejudice, and brutality.

One can only imagine the embarrassment occasioned by anti-inoculation riots in a patriot like John Adams. His pride in marrying into
the distinguished Boylston family often brought to his mind the illus-
trious ancestor of his wife who had braved superstition to introduce
smallpox inoculation in Boston in 1721. Adams himself underwent inoculation at about the time that the Marblehead hospital was being attacked, and his wife and family were inoculated at about the time of
the Norfolk attacks. Yet Adams and his fellow patriots underwent
their own rituals of separation from England, displaying versions of
the ritualized regression found in crowd behavior. It is possible to
trace the sources of such behavior not only in Adams but also in three
of his fellow patriots from Massachusetts: James Otis, Josiah Quincy,
and Joseph Hawley. The differences in age and temperament among
the four were wide, not to speak of their political differences. And
whereas Adams, Otis, and Hawley came from the same rural, up-
wardly mobile yeoman class, Quincy was their social superior. Never-

theless, each underwent a revolutionary experience that had analogies with the crowd's anticipatory rituals. And each shared in crucial ways the others' experience of revolution.

There were certain proximate relationships among the four. Quincy and Adams grew up in the same own. Adams looked up to Otis, was presented by him for admittance to the Massachusetts bar, and replaced him as a patriot representative to the provincial legislature after Otis's breakdown. Hawley, like Adams, was influenced by Otis's politics; Adams worked with and consulted Hawley in the Massachusetts legislature and later at the beginning of the first Continental Congress. But these connections were less important than the shared experiences of the four. Each underwent the doubts and anxieties of a phenomenon that may be termed "conscience patriotism."

For patriots and loyalists alike, as it has been pointed out, the typical experience of the Revolution was a *crise de conscience* consisting of an anguished ordeal of choice between patriotism and loyalty.[32] The anxieties attendant on this process gave it a resemblance to the personal rituals by which the American Puritans had prepared themselves for salvation. These had been episodes of ritualized introspection, self-doubt, and generally misdirected anxieties. When completed, they had tended to produce a sense of absolute conviction—one that rendered the Puritans terrifying figures, both as moralists and as revolutionaries. In a similar fashion the patriot sons of the Puritans underwent a period of preparation during the 1760s and 1770s. Their rituals, too, permitted the expression of strong emotions, while disguising revolutionary implications. And they, too, strengthened personal resolve by directing anxiety toward an external enemy. In the end, the rituals of revolution produced a species of conviction that gave independence, when it came, a moral strength reminiscent of Puritanism.

The crises of conscience undergone by the four patriots in question took place at different times and in varying political terms. But for each the result was a real or apparent wavering in allegiance to the patriot party, or else a similar wavering in conviction about the desirability of separation from England. That these questions were matters of conscience rather than expediency was clear from the rest of their political behavior. In common with many other patriots, all four men prided themselves on not being office-seekers.[33] Throughout the period Otis, Adams, and Hawley talked constantly of resigning, and actually did resign offices that they held by virtue of their patriot connection. They stood ready to risk both unpopularity and loss of income in support of their principles. Otis made himself unpopular with the patriot party by changing his position on crucial issues more than once; Hawley publicly opposed the party's new constitution for Massachusetts; and Adams and Quincy together risked ostracism by representing the British soldiers indicted for the Boston Massacre.

The psychic costs of this conscience politics were indicated by the frequent complaints of ill health in the political writings of these patriots. All four suffered imagined or real illnesses, both mental and physical, as did many of their loyalist opposites. Their symptoms—depression, hypochondria, nervous excitement—reflected the anxieties inflicted on them by the times. In the course of the Revolutionary period, all underwent episodes of psychic stress. Although these were of varying seriousness, the dates in each case indicate a connection with political crisis.

It has been said that the first precondition for revolution is a state of unfocused anxiety, experienced as ambiguity toward established order. This is followed by the choice of a "responsible agent," who becomes the focus of emotions. Among the American patriots it became an article of faith that "a malevolent design" against the freedom and purity of America lay behind the actions of the government in Britain and its officials in America. The patriots assumed various causes for this supposed conspiracy and believed that they had identified a number of responsible agents, among them Lord Bute in England. But "to John Adams, Josiah Quincy, and others the key figure in Massachusetts from the beginning to the end was Thomas Hutchinson."[34]

Adams, Quincy, Hawley, and Otis were not the only ones in Massachusetts to single out Hutchinson. They were joined by James Otis, Sr., Samuel Adams, Edmund Trowbridge, Benjamin Thacher, and others in their circle of lawyers and judges. Nevertheless, these men, intimately thrown together with Hutchinson daily in court and often traveling with him in a group through Massachusetts and Maine on legal circuit, made a very small and select assemblage. Thus, they hardly represent a scientific sample of patriot thought and emotions. On the other hand they may be said to represent a suggestive microcosm—almost a little family in which there was played out the larger drama of a fledgling America separating from its parent country.

Hutchinson, who became lieutenant governor, then governor of

Massachusetts, remained at the center of agitation from 1760 until his removal from the governorship and departure for England in 1774 after the Boston Tea Party. During this period he was the focus of demonstrations and crowd violence as often as he was attacked in print by patriot writers. His ordeal at the hands of both reveals much about the nature of the American Revolutionary impulse.

CHAPTER TWO

Their Kinsman, Thomas Hutchinson

T HOMAS HUTCHINSON served as lieutenant governor of Massachusetts from 1758 to 1770, was twice acting governor during that period, and was royal governor of Massachusetts from 1771 to 1774. By 1760, when he was appointed chief justice of the Superior Court at the age of fifty, he had seemingly earned a secure place in the history of his province. He had carried forward with distinction a tradition of service going back over one hundred twenty-five years. In this tradition first clerics and then businessmen like Hutchinson's father and himself devoted a portion of their time to government. Hutchinson began serving in the legislature in 1737. Here a few men were able to combine ability with family eminence so as to achieve political advancement. "Honorable to a fault, sincere, industrious," Hutchinson progressed in the approved manner. He started with committee chairmanships, was elected speaker of the house, moved to the council, or upper house, and finally, in 1758, received royal appointment as lieutenant governor. He continued to hold this last office simultaneously with his chief justiceship and other judgeships, but as of 1760 he retired from business.[1]

In manner Hutchinson appears to have presented a typical eighteenth-century American combination of gravity and kindliness: he was formal in public, but genial and sometimes witty among friends and family. He had a tender streak that showed in his concern for the poor. Accordingly, on being appointed chief justice he retained his probate court judgeship (although resigning as a judge of common pleas) in order to continue his charitable work. It was ironic that soon afterward the patriot party included the probate post in their attacks on his "plural office holding." Also ironic was the fact that Benjamin Franklin's sister should have blessed Hutchinson for his service to her as probate judge whereas Franklin later held up the same man to his son William as an example of broken public trust.[2]

Hutchinson's loyalty to friends was intense, and he often adhered to it at his own political expense. Somewhat similar was his loyalty to the memory of his wife, who died in 1754. In a marked "exception to eighteenth-century matrimonial custom," he did not remarry. He remained close to his children but presented a lonely figure as the patriots increasingly ostracized him from the community.[3]

Hutchinson was strikingly tall for the times—about six feet—and slimly graceful. Here, too, he differed, for his opponents tended to be short, portly men like the Adamses and the Otises. In contrast to them he was sometimes called vain of his appearance. No doubt Hutchinson's somewhat lordly air helped make it possible to imagine him an ally of British royal tyranny. But neither his appearance, nor his putative vanity, nor anything else in his character or actions sufficiently explains the passions that he inspired in the patriots.[4] Among his contemporaries there was agreement that the source of Hutchinson's problems could be traced to the 1740s and the colony's oldest, fiercest, and most persistent internal issue, the redemption of paper money. And yet, even at that early date, the agitated tone "of the town meeting's reports against a currency based on silver is difficult to understand in view of the voters' election of Hutchinson and leaders of the hard-money party to at least two places in the town's delegation to the General Court in the 1740s."[5]

The monetary struggle of the 1740s itself went back at least to the beginning of the eighteenth century. At that time two parties emerged over the issue of how to fund the province currency. They reflected the opposition between hard-money creditors and easy-money or inflationist debtors. The creditors in this case advocated a basis in silver, the debtors a paper currency secured in various ways, the most original of which was by the prospective value of land. The scheme of a "land bank" was undertaken privately in the 1740s after repeated attempts to have it endorsed by the legislature. Its failure was attributed by some to Hutchinson, who had been one of its leading opponents. The land bankers were at least one generation older than the patriots who made the Revolution, but they bequeathed two legacies connected with the experiment: resentment over its defeat, and legal problems connected with debts that had been paid with land notes.

For the Hutchinson family, opposition to paper money and inflation went back to a hard-money bill proposed by Thomas Hutchinson's father in 1734. Although the elder Hutchinson had profited by speculating in paper money, he "had great merit," as John Adams later put it, in advocating a less volatile currency. Thomas Hutchinson took up his father's position in print in 1736, and was subsequently a witness to the passions connected with the issue during Massachusetts' political crises in the 1740s. In 1749 when a chimney flue set fire to the roof of his house, a crowd of onlookers, many of them made hostile by the money issue, stood by shouting, "Let it burn!" A few years earlier a shortage of cash in the province had been partly responsible for the ouster of Governor Belcher after he refused to extend the life of the paper money in circulation.[6] Among those responsible for driving him out was Deacon Samuel Adams, the father of the revolutionary. In 1741 the deacon put much of his fortune into the land bank scheme. Then, when Parliament ruled the land bank illegal, the deacon suffered extensive losses. There were plans for a demonstration march that provoked rumors of a possible uprising in the countryside, and a legend arose of an abortive "rebellion" of 1741. At this time Deacon Adams became a figure in the popular party, and in 1747 he was negatived from the council by the governor, as his son and other patriots would be in the 1760s and 1770s. After the deacon's death the following year his son Samuel began his political career by joining with friends to form a club and start a newspaper, the *Independent Advertiser,* to espouse the popular side in politics. His articles amounted to attacks on the incumbent governor, William Shirley.[7]

In the late 1740s Hutchinson began to push his own hard-money scheme through the legislature, and by 1750 it appeared to many that he had given the "Massachusetts inflationist party its death blow by outlawing paper money through Parliamentary legislation." Samuel Adams, who had married in 1749, lost his wife in 1757. In 1758 he nearly had his property seized to satisfy claims left over from his father's losses in the land bank. Adams prevented the seizure by threatening in a newspaper advertisement to prosecute anyone attempting to carry out a sheriff's auction of his property on the designated day. It is usually said that Adams emerged as a political figure in response to the Stamp Act, but Hutchinson wrote of the 1758 incident that "the son first made himself conspicuous on this occasion." On his part, Samuel Adams regarded the Hutchinson party's "Design" against the colony's freedom as having its origins in the 1750s.[8]

Disputes over monetary questions appear to concern economics

Thomas Hutchinson

alone, yet in America they have frequently inspired religious fervor. The Puritans, as Herbert L. Osgood observed, applied their conceptions of the orthodox and the heretical "to a question of economic belief and practice, and the heretics, as usual, were charged with moral obliquity."[9] (Similar attitudes reappeared much later in American history, notably in the rhetoric of "Coin Harvey," the nineteenth-century monetary hysteric described by Richard Hofstadter in *The Paranoid Style in American Politics.*)

The old Puritan attitudes, as Osgood showed, continued on through the 1740s and 1750s. Since the land bank memories lasted into the 1760s as well, monetarism may be said to have forged a link between Puritanism and the Revolution itself. While Hutchinson's party held sway, the easy-money party was made to represent heresy, and its members were hounded legally and extralegally by the hard-money establishment. (Since easy money hurt ministers, widows, and orphans, along with others on fixed incomes, Hutchinson and his party could view its advocates with righteousness and resentment.)[10] On the other hand, the resentments of the easy-money party amounted to a combination of just complaints and the accumulated passions engendered by the question over a period of at least sixty-five years.

Thomas Hutchinson thus shared with his patriot foes a measure of Puritan certainty. Like his fellow loyalists, he regarded the patriot opposition as the work of "designing, artful men"—just as the patriots regarded him as a self-seeking schemer. On the patriot side more than on his, there was never any softening of views. After Hutchinson's death in 1780 John Adams still believed that he was perhaps "the only man in the world who could have brought on the controversy between Great Britain and America."[11]

The demonizing that led to such an inflated charge appears to have resulted from a combination of local circumstances and the wider implications of Hutchinson's role in Massachusetts politics. On the one hand matters like his hard-money policies accumulated political enemies. The most notorious instance was his acceptance of the appointment as chief justice of Massachusetts, thereby denying James Otis, Sr., a post on the Superior Court. This earned for Hutchinson, as all were aware, the lasting enmity of the Otis family. At the same time, the chief justiceship carried a weight of symbolic importance, as the fulsome eulogies for Hutchinson's predecessor indicated. Given Hutchinson's long prominence in Massachusetts, his native birth, and his offices of lieutenant governor and chief justice, he seems to have be-

come the most visible embodiment of kingly authority in Massachusetts—even more so than the newly appointed governor, Francis Bernard. Edmund Trowbridge came to regard the entire American Revolution as the result of Hutchinson's appointment, which he had
supported. "I freely believe," he wrote in 1779, "this war would have
been put off many years if Governor H had not been made Chief Justice."[12]

The 1760s in Boston, like the 1740s, developed into a period of
heightened emotions. In 1760 a fire in the city caused widespread destruction, and led to higher taxes. It "embittered the people and made
them extraordinarily sensitive to any real or imagined abuses in the
years that followed." As a result of the fire, "every act after 1760
echoed the issues and bitterness of former conflicts in Boston's history"—which is to say that, as often as not, Thomas Hutchinson was
at issue. At about the same time there arose fears that England would
impose an American episcopate, an issue exploited by James Otis and
by the itinerant revivalist minister, George Whitefield, who had been
the voice of the Great Awakening in the 1740s. (Whitefield now returned to preach in Boston.) Finally, smallpox, last broken out in the
1720s, also returned.[13] The situation had the overtones of Sophocles'
Oedipus Tyrannos, in which the disturbed citizens of a plague-infested
city feel that they must find a scapegoat to release them from their
cursed situation.

Between 1760 and 1765 James Otis, Jr., was chiefly responsible
for the campaign against Hutchinson. In 1764, together with Samuel
Adams, he was instrumental in keeping Hutchinson from being sent to
England to remonstrate against the Sugar Act. Both men apparently
preferred weakening Hutchinson to working against the act. Also in
1764, with the prospective Stamp Act under discussion, Samuel
Adams wrote the Boston Instructions, which accusingly "referred in
everything but name to Hutchinson." In the course of Adams's subsequent anti–Stamp agitation, his prime aim remained the ouster of
Hutchinson. Eventually, according to John C. Miller, who as Adams's
biographer understandably emphasized his subject's role, Adams
ended with "success in making [Hutchinson] the scapegoat of the
Stamp Act." Starting in this period Hutchinson came to be referred to
as a cloven-footed devil figure. Years later, Samuel Adams attacked
him under the fitting pseudonym, "Cotton Mather," and referred to
him as "that Fiend, Hutchinson."[14]

The Stamp Act agitation crystallized both the patriot movement as a whole and, in Massachusetts, its anti-Hutchinson bias. Samuel Adams, John Adams, and Joseph Hawley all emerged as patriots over this issue. The American Revolution was born, one could say, with the eruption of resentment against the Stamp Act in general, and Thomas Hutchinson in particular.

Not only did Hutchinson oppose the Stamp Act but, unknown to the patriots, he was instrumental in procuring its repeal. Furthermore, in one of the great ironies of the period, he proves to have helped formulate both the terms of patriot opposition to England and its rhetoric. Hutchinson himself was probably unaware of the role played by the anti–Stamp Act argument that he wrote and sent to England in 1764. But it has recently been shown that his paper strengthened British opposition to the act, and very probably influenced the most famous Parliamentary speech of the debate. This was Colonel Isaac Barré's reply to Charles Townshend, who had accused the American colonists—"Children planted by our Care, nourished up by our Indulgence untill they are grown to a Degree of Strength & Opulence"—of ingratitude for their reluctance to pay a fair share of the expenses for their military protection. Barré declared to Townshend: "They planted by your Care? No! your Oppressions planted em in America . . . they grew up by your neglect of Em." In words that carried across the Atlantic and echoed throughout the Revolutionary period, Barré went on to accuse England of having sent over corrupt officials, "to Spy out their Lyberty, to misrepresent their Actions & to prey upon Em; men whose behaviour on many Occasions has caused the Blood of those Sons of Liberty to recoil within them."[15] In response, patriot groups across America adopted the name "Sons of Liberty," along with the concept of England as a nonnurturant parent.

Although it is true that "there is no similarity of phraseology to suggest that Barré was speaking from Hutchinson's manuscript," Barré's close reading of Hutchinson is suggested by another kind of similarity—one of imagery. Hutchinson told the story of a neighbor of his, a poor farmer with "ten or twelve Sons" who was "so unnatural to his own flesh and Blood" as to hire them out to work or to fight in the navy. "I could not help thinking of the Nation and her Colonies," Hutchinson commented. And further on, more pointedly, he asked whether it was "from a parental Affection to the Colonists" that Britain had protected them, or from a wish to preserve her lucrative trade with them.[16] It seems likely that it was in Hutchinson's manuscript that Barré found his powerful answer to the administration's familiar parent-child analogy: the parent, not the child, was unnatural.

Hutchinson appears to have taken the arguments that he transmitted to England from none other than James Otis, Jr. It has been pointed out that Hutchinson adopted a position similar to that held by Otis in the *Rights of the British Colonies,* a work written the same year and sent along by Hutchinson with his own paper.[17] But in addition, Hutchinson's arguments had been anticipated by Otis in his 1761 speech on Writs of Assistance. There, speaking in court before Hutchinson himself, Otis had offered an exhaustive history of the colonies similar to the one in Hutchinson's paper. At every point in that history, Otis argued, England had profited from its colonies while exerting itself on their behalf minimally or not at all.

Hutchinson's reaction to Otis's speech was not recorded, though John Adams claimed that because of its powerful argument against the statute in question, Hutchinson "dared not utter a word in its favor."[18] Clearly, Hutchinson listened with care to the young Otis, and three years later transmitted his arguments to England. Toned down and sent under the aegis of authority, they made their way into Parliament, and from thence back to America. There, instead of bringing glory to Hutchinson, they were directed against him as the representative of British authority. In this way he was rendered the author of his own downfall.

The ironic drama of Hutchinson's fate centered on the mob action that destroyed his house. Hawthorne used the event as the background of "My Kinsman, Major Molineux," though he had to turn to other crowd events for most of his details. This was because the Hutchinson riot, as it came to be known, was an example not of ritual but of planned, probably hired hooliganism. Nevertheless, it took its place in the popular imagination as a link in the series of ritualized protests against the Stamp Act. Furthermore, in the end it left a kind of symbolic residue in the mystery of why Hutchinson had been attacked at all.

On the night of the first Stamp Act riot, Hutchinson, who was Stampmaster Oliver's brother-in-law, had come twice to the besieged house, the second time with the sheriff of Boston. When Hutchinson tried to address the crowd, "a Ringleader cried out, the Governor and the Sheriff! to your Arms, my boys!" and a shower of stones sent the two men into retreat. Whether the ringleader's use of "governor" represented a condensation of "lieutenant governor" or a popular apprehension of Lieutenant Governor Hutchinson as the leading man in the province is not clear. But in any case Hutchinson had fatally associated himself with Oliver and the Stamp Act by appearing on the scene. (Earlier in the day Hutchinson had been the one to send the sheriff on his unsuccessful attempt to take down the effigy of Oliver hung in the Liberty Tree.) It was no wonder that a rumor should soon circulate making Hutchinson responsible for the Stamp Act. Convinced of his innocence, though, when accosted by a window-breaking crowd at his own house the following night, he refused to appear and contradict the rumor.[19]

Disturbances continued during the next several days in Boston, with the focus of crowd resentment shifting to officers of the customs. Then on the night of August 26 there were break-ins at the houses of the comptroller of customs and two officials in the Court of Admiralty (which tried customs cases). Just as on August 14, there appears to have been both a plan and a popular overwhelming of that plan. This time, however, the plan itself included housebreaking and the destruction of private property. To begin the evening a group of boys started a bonfire in front of the Town House, which was "an usual signal for a mob." Once a crowd had gathered, it was split into two groups of "disguised ruffians," and led off "in Regular March," shouting "Liberty and Property." Fired up by stolen liquor, the crowd ended the night with its attack on Hutchinson's house. According to Governor Bernard, Hutchinson, "being conscious that he had not in the least deserved to be made a party in regard to the Stamp Act or the Custom House . . . rested [at home] in full security that the mob would not attack him."[20]

At dinner with his family, he received warning just in time to escape, leaving behind everything he cared for: books, papers, the manuscript of his history of Massachusetts, clothing, plate, hangings, paintings, money. The crowd arrived not only in liquor and in anger, but apparently with a purpose, for after destroying papers and possessions, as at its previous stops that night, it undertook the systematic destruction of Hutchinson's house. By dawn the rioters had torn out virtually every window and partition, the wainscoting and roof tiles, part of a cupola at the top of the house, and part of the shingling. They destroyed everything, including the fruit trees in the garden, "the furniture of a kitchen only excepted." The next day Josiah

Quincy, Jr., wrote that "the destruction was really amazing." Another observer wrote, "I could not think that so much work could be done by 20 skillfull men in 50 hours—all in the Dark!" Hutchinson called it "the most violent outrage . . . that ever was known in America."[21]

Hutchinson's unpopularity in connection with the Stamp Act undoubtedly had a bearing on the destruction, even if only as a pretext. But numerous other causes suggested themselves to Hutchinson, and his contemporaries as well as historians up to the present have speculated along the same lines. Governor Bernard believed that Hutchinson was being punished for presiding over the Writs of Assistance case. Others felt that enemies still bitter over the hard-currency bill of 1749 had hired the mob. There were other possibilities as well, having to do with smuggling and Hutchinson's judicial role in suppressing it.[22] But it now appears that one particular rumor of the time was probably true: namely, that a group of speculators dealing in Maine lands wanted to destroy papers in Hutchinson's possession that were unfavorable to them. These same men may well have spread the rumor that Hutchinson favored the Stamp Act.[23] However, the actual cause of the riot matters less than the existence of these and other possible motives for attacking Hutchinson. Each possibility represented a political past in which Hutchinson had made enemies although acting with propriety. Thus, whether any or all of the reasons given for the attack proved true or untrue, the fact would remain that no wrongdoing on his part was at issue, or even any substantive political difference between him and the patriots. It seems evident that Hutchinson was being punished in the role of a scapegoat. Furthermore, whether the mob was hired or not, its fury when it reached Hutchinson's house was out of all bounds with its behavior at the break-ins earlier in the evening. Unlike the Oliver crowd, this one got out of hand not so much from ritual stimulation as from entering the house of Thomas Hutchinson.

Governor Bernard obviously was a more logical choice for such an attack, and in fact his official residence, the Province House, did suffer broken windows on August 15 and was surrounded though untouched just before the crowd marched to Hutchinson's on the twenty-sixth. Bernard had removed himself to the Castle in Boston harbor on both occasions, so that the mob may have turned to Hutchinson in compensation. It has also been suggested that they left the Province House intact because their own taxes would have had to pay for its repair.

Nevertheless, Bernard showed surprise when writing from the Castle on the day following the Hutchinson riot: "My House was not attacked at all; which I wondered at: for the other Persons having offended them only by being in Office under the King, I should have thought, that I should have been reckoned the most offencive."[24] The "governor" in Massachusetts, somehow, was not Francis Bernard, the English lord, but Thomas Hutchinson, the native of the province.

The destruction of Hutchinson's house gained him little sympathy. When, after repeal of the Stamp Act early in 1766, Bernard used his veto power to disallow James Otis's appointment as Speaker in the legislature, Hutchinson was blamed as "the real policy maker of the Administration." The unrelenting campaign against him seems to have had its effect. At the end of 1766 he underwent attacks of dizziness after moving back into his rebuilt house. Then came a paralytic stroke in 1767, followed by a severe depression which he termed a "nervous disorder."[25] Cast in the same mold of conscience as his patriot opponents, Hutchinson suffered illnesses of mind and body similar to theirs when he could no longer support the anxieties of his position. Like them he recovered, henceforth suffered fears for his health, and repeatedly set these aside at the call of duty.

That call next came in 1769 when Francis Bernard was forced by his unpopularity to retire to England, and Hutchinson was appointed acting governor. Soon afterward, at the beginning of 1770, there came another wave of crowds and crisis arising from a combination of English and American issues. In England the case of the government versus John Wilkes resumed, and reports that Wilkes was being denied his seat in Parliament renewed American concern over constitutional liberties. At the same time the king's refusal to receive petitions from his English subjects darkened the horizon. In America the nonimportation movement came to a head, partly spurred by inflammatory newspaper reports from England, with resultant crowds and riots not only in Boston, but in New York as well.[26]

Hutchinson's accession as acting governor in 1769 marked a turning point in the patriot-loyalist struggle. He now stood unequivocally as the chief representative of the king's policies in Massachusetts (all the more since, unlike Bernard, he at first had no lieutenant governor serving under him who might have deflected opposition). Some of the seventeenth-century governors of Massachusetts had been virtually deified figures, and a measure of their awe remained connected to the office when Hutchinson assumed it. In January 1770 the nonimportation issue focused on Hutchinson, partly through his sons, who were importers. Confronted at his house by a crowd among whose leaders marched James Otis and the notorious agitator, William Molineux, Hutchinson reminded everyone that he was now his Majesty's highest representative in Massachusetts. The crowd withdrew this time, but passions in Boston remained high. Thousands were soon assembled for the funeral of Christopher Seider, a boy shot by the stray bullet of a besieged loyalist.

A month later came the Boston Massacre. Immediately after the shootings, Hutchinson rushed to the scene in a characteristic attempt to calm the enraged crowd. He was chased, but returned to give a much-heckled speech urging everyone to go home; he then took evidence at a late-night judicial hearing, and ordered the soldiers arrested. Nevertheless, after the Massacre the patriots concerted to hold him responsible. He refuted every false charge, but of course was not believed. In Mercy Warren's propaganda play, *The Adulateur,* he is first associated with the killing of Seider, then made responsible for bringing soldiers into the town, and finally shown instructing their captain to have them shoot if accosted by the citizens. (In the case of Seider, Hutchinson had in fact ordered the sheriff to the scene before the shooting, but neither this official nor any other had the temerity to interfere.) The Massacre itself is depicted in *The Adulateur* as a resultant slaughter of innocent children by the soldiers. In the same spirit John Adams privately sketched a dramatic "letter from the grave" addressed to Hutchinson from Crispus Attucks, who had been killed in the Massacre. Attucks holds Hutchinson "chargeable before God and Man, with our Blood."[27]

Nathaniel Hawthorne's treatment of this period in the story "Edward Randolph's Portrait," which draws on the same tradition of Hutchinson's guilt for the Massacre, throws an imaginative light on 1769–1770 as a turning point. In January 1770 the fictional Hutchinson has just "assumed the administration of the province, on the departure of Sir Francis Bernard," and now must make a crucial decision. He has been instructed from England to restore order. These, of course, are the soldiers who in a few weeks will fire on the crowd. Hawthorne has rearranged chronology here, and omitted Hutchinson's efforts to have the troops removed in order to avoid just such bloodshed as occurred.[28] But Hawthorne's purpose is neither exoneration nor blame. He is exploring the process by which Hutchinson became the scapegoat of the Massacre.

Before he signs the fatal order, Hawthorne's Hutchinson is reminded of Edward Randolph, an earlier royal official. Randolph will forever be remembered "as the destroyer of our liberties." Hutchinson the historian, observing that his research has shown the popular tradition about Randolph to be based on "old women's tales," dismisses the parallel with himself. He fails to realize that his reputation is as subject to the popular spirit as Randolph's. Hutchinson's niece warns him of "the awful weight of a people's curse," and he is struck by her words. But he sees his choice as one between "the rebuke of a king" and "the clamor of a wild, misguided multitude." The king, he decides, is "more to be dreaded." Furthermore, the mob may run wild. "Would you have me wait," Hutchinson asks, "till the mob shall sack the Province House [the governor's official residence], as they did my private mansion?"

Clearly, Hawthorne perceived Thomas Hutchinson as a tragic figure in history. Once placed between the mob and the king, he is the prisoner of forces beyond his control. And his antiquarian historian's instinct only makes more ironic his unremitting fate as the scapegoat of revolution in Boston. Like the real Hutchinson, Hawthorne's character falls as a result of his opposition to the popular will. "I set my foot upon the rabble," he declares, "and defy them." This is something that no "ruler" in America can hope to do, for the popular will has roots deep in the life of a people. Hawthorne exposes the superstitiousness on which this will is based, though not entirely to degrade it. Rather, he seems to be suggesting that its origins lie in layers of human history deeper than Hutchinson is equipped to penetrate.

Following the public agitation that surrounded the Boston Massacre in early 1770, there came a settling of emotions that has come to be known as the "quiet period" of the Revolution. In Boston, however, all was not entirely quiet following Hutchinson's appointment as full royal governor early in 1771. "The news, long rumored in the newspapers, set off a train of protest and recrimination that lasted for months." One newspaper writer branded Hutchinson "a traiterous usurper, a most ungrateful, subtle, cruel, and ambitious tyrant." Later in the year another writer, in what a government newspaper called probably the "most daring production ever published in America," called him "a monster in government," who should be deposed. Specifically, the patriots challenged the new governor's right to change the venue of the legislature. The issue was typical of the period in being more symbolic than real, for it concerned a governor's "prerogative." This was the question that began the English liberty movement against the king early in the 1760s; it had perhaps contributed to Bernard's fall, though his moving of the legislature shortly before his departure aroused nothing like the protests that erupted when Hutchinson took the same step. Hutchinson was himself opposed to moving the legislature, but complied with an order from London.[29]

In 1773 this and all other minor issues were swept away. First, Hutchinson delivered a defense of Parliamentary sovereignty that was answered by a committee of leading patriots. The document, which has been called "one of the most important of all the revolutionary papers," was written and amended by Joseph Warren, Samuel Adams, Joseph Hawley, and John Adams. Taking up Hutchinson's premise that there could be no compromise between Parliamentary authority and independence, the patriots as much as concluded that by this reasoning theirs was indeed a condition of independence. John Adams later referred to the committee's conclusion as the first Declaration of Independence. He might have added that as a matter of course such a declaration had emerged in Massachusetts as a response to Thomas Hutchinson. As for the king, who was more significantly concerned in this implied revolt of his subjects than Hutchinson, the patriot document asserted that the people "humbly look up to his present Majesty . . . as children to a father."[30]

Soon afterward, Hutchinson's private letters to England came into the hands of the patriots. They had been written in 1768 and 1769, when the atmosphere of disorder in Boston had been at its height, and they discussed the problems of maintaining order. Hutchinson wrote that stricter measures would have to be taken, and that these would result in "an abridgment of what are called English liberties." Here and elsewhere in the letters, as Bernard Bailyn has written, Hutchinson uttered "no sentiment that he had not elsewhere, and publicly expressed." But when the letters were published in a pamphlet they were advertised as containing proof that Hutchinson had engaged in a conspiracy which, as the title put it, "Threatned Total Destruction to the Liberties of All America."[31]

This publication raised a furor of denunciation. In verse, essay, print, and play Hutchinson was vilified as a traitorous, Machiavellian devil. The incident, as Lawrence H. Gipson judiciously observed, had "only an indirect bearing upon the larger issue." But it elicited as much feeling as any other crisis of the period in Massachusetts—far more than that which accompanied the similar publication of Bernard's letters in 1769 before he left the governorship. When word reached America a few months later that Alexander Wedderburne had attacked Benjamin Franklin in Parliament for procuring Hutchinson's private letters, Wedderburne joined the proscribed list. Thousands watched as he and Hutchinson were together burned in effigy in New York and Philadelphia.[32]

These effigy burnings culminated a newspaper campaign against Hutchinson "unequaled in the previous decade, during which he had been the main butt of popular party propaganda." Again Mercy Warren's verse plays caught the popular emotion, and especially the logic of reversal whereby he could be termed a parricide. In *The Adulateur* (1772) Hutchinson had been depicted as "Rapatio," the duplicitous, grasping tyrant of Upper Servia, who will "smile at length to see my country bleed." There, in addition to greed and power lust, he is motivated to line his pockets by recollection of the time when his house was broken into and he was "flung . . . helpless, / Naked and destitute, to *beg* protection." In *The Defeat* (1773) Rapatio is seen squeezing widows and orphans to rebuild his house. As the play ends he is standing with a scaffold behind him and his brother-in-law predicts: "A lifeless Effigy wont long suffice, / But you and I as Forfeiture must pay, / Our hoary heads to this much injur'd State."

During the same period Hutchinson Street in Boston was changed to Pearl Street, while the town of Hutchinson, Massachusetts, resolved no longer to bear the name "of one who had acted the part of a traitor and parricide." The name was changed to Barre, after Colonel Barré.[33] This was the crowning irony. Not only had Barré gained fame by using Hutchinson's 1764 protest against the Stamp Act as the basis for his Sons of Liberty speech, but now he was rewarded through the usurpation of Hutchinson's very name.

Hutchinson was stunned both by the breach of privacy that permitted his letters to be published, and by the unfair way in which their meaning was twisted to suggest that he had plotted against American liberties. He had been falsely blamed and had had his role exaggerated from the 1740s, when he was said to have influenced Parliament against the land bank, through the Stamp Act, the Townshend duties, and the Boston Massacre. Now "hovering at the edge of collapse" as in 1767, Hutchinson, believing himself the victim of a "plot," wrote: "I fall in the cause of government." William Franklin, a loyalist, reported to his father after the letters appeared that "the Govr. is gloomy and low spirited, and seems by no means pleased with his situation." Benjamin Franklin, who shared responsibility for his condition, responded with merciless accuracy: "I don't wonder that Hutchinson should be dejected. It must be an uncomfortable thing to live among people who he is conscious universally detest him."[34]

The patriots now began to call for Hutchinson's removal as governor, and they soon had their way. The tea crisis that precipitated the Revolution devolved almost as a matter of course into patriot defiance of Hutchinson. Yet again, he had privately opposed the government policy that brought about the crisis, was forced to uphold that policy, and ended by being held personally responsible for the outcome—in this case the Boston Tea Party. When announcement was made of the Boston Port Bill, the royal response to the Tea Party, Hutchinson was hanged in effigy in Princeton, Charleston, Newport, and of course Boston.[35] All that remained of preparation for revolution was a transfer of anger from Hutchinson to the king. This took place about a year after Hutchinson's replacement as governor by General Gage in 1774.

The rising tide of public hatred for Hutchinson, marked by the actions of mobs and the burning of effigies, closely followed the pattern of expected but never-realized anger at George III from 1765 to 1776. Each time the crowd rose in opposition to the king it declared itself undyingly loyal to him but implacably committed to the destruction of Hutchinson. It was no wonder that Benjamin Franklin, in defending himself for procuring Hutchinson's letters, should have regarded their author and his correspondents as "like the scape-goats of old": sacrificial figures whose role it was to carry "away into the wilderness all the offenses which have arisen between the two countries."[36]

Just as popular antipathy to Hutchinson had moved parallel with patriot writings about him since 1765, the effigy burnings that greeted the Declaration of Independence had parallel references to Hutchinson in the text of that document itself. The Declaration's accusation that the king had ignored American petitions logically included one of 1773 calling for Hutchinson's removal from the governorship. And the Declaration's assertion that the king had "called together Legisla-

The Wicked Statesman

Thomas Hutchinson, his copy of Machiavelli at his feet, is caught in the act
of misusing public money. The devil and the viper of patriot rhetoric and
earlier cartoons have, as it were, here turned on their accomplice.

tive Bodies at Places unusual, uncomfortable, and distant from the Depository of their public Records, for the sole Purpose of fatiguing them into Compliance with his Measures" was clearly a reference to Hutchinson's relocation of the Massachusetts legislature from Boston to Cambridge. Yet from 1770 to 1772 whenever Hutchinson protested that he was acting on the express order of the king, he was not believed.[37]

In English exile after 1774, Hutchinson lobbied to relieve Boston of its burdens under the Port Bill and to bring about some kind of reconciliation. But he had become a figure in history more symbolic than real. The patriots continued to regard him as the enemy, and believed that he was behind the very measures of Parliament that he sought to ameliorate. When his mansion outside Boston was broken into in 1775 another batch of his letters was found. These were no different in substance from the ones previously released by the patriots. But they were again presented selectively, slightly reworded, and accompanied by tendentious analyses that made Hutchinson appear to have conspired against Massachusetts freedoms since 1760.[38] In the months before the Declaration of Independence, as the letters continued to appear, they coincided with and contributed to the final stage of the patriot movement.

Thomas Hutchinson spent the rest of his life in England, where he completed his three-volume *History of the Colony and Province of Massachusetts Bay.* It was by reference to an irony concerning this work that Hawthorne indicated a connection between the Major Molineux of his story and Hutchinson. For not only was the *History* one of the story's sources for descriptions of crowds, but the manuscript of the very volume that contained these descriptions had been trampled in the mud when Hutchinson's house was destroyed in 1765. The *History* also described the often unhappy careers of Hutchinson's predecessors in the offices of governor and lieutenant governor. Its last volume, written in England, brought the story up to date, and hence chronicled his own demise. Thus, Hutchinson first studied the early New England precedents for his ouster from office, then suffered a mob attack similar to though more extensive than any he had described, and finally recorded the events that had led to his own downfall. Through it all he never could account for the false accusations of patriots and the fury of mobs against him.

When John Adams came to London a few years after Hutchinson's death, he wrote that, "hardened as my heart had been against him . . . I was melted at the accounts I heard of his condition . . . Fled, in his old age, from the detestation of a country, where he had been beloved, esteemed, and admired, and applauded with exaggeration—in short, where he had been every thing, from his infancy—to a country where he was nothing; pinched by a pension, which, though ample in Boston, would barely keep a house in London." Adams was told by Lord Townshend that Hutchinson "put an end to his own life," a story he did not believe.[39]

Hawthorne ended "Edward Randolph's Portrait" with Hutchinson's death in London. He did not mean to suggest the historical circumstances, but rather the kind of superstition that surrounded a man popularly regarded as the last traducer of Massachusetts liberties. Thus, Hawthorne's Hutchinson,

> when, far over the ocean, his dying hour drew on . . . gasped for breath, and complained that he was choking with the blood of the Boston Massacre; and Francis Lincoln, the former Captain of Castle William [where the troops were garrisoned], who was standing at his bedside, perceived a likeness in his frenzied look to that of Edward Randolph. Did his broken spirit feel, at that dread hour, the tremendous burthen of a People's curse?

The actual Hutchinson most certainly did feel the people's curse. And among his other testimonials of popular hatred was one that might have come from a story by Hawthorne. For in 1778 Hutchinson learned that when his country house was broken into, the Continental soldiers had stabbed holes in his portrait with their bayonets.[40]

Hutchinson's actual death came when he was sixty-nine years old, ailing, and living in Brompton Park, London, a short distance from the Houses of Parliament. On June 2, 1780, a mob approached Parliament from the opposite direction. It was the first day of the Gordon riots, the bloodiest and most extensive of a turbulent century. By night the London sky was aflame, and no one knew how far the rioting might go. Since February Hutchinson had been sick. He had no sooner recovered from an illness following his son's death than his daughter had died, and he had again fallen ill. Eleven days before his death he stopped keeping his diary, though on the first of June he made an entry in his account book. On June 3 "he conversed well and freely upon the riot in London the day before." He also expressed "his expectations of dying very soon." When it came time for his daily carriage ride he walked out the door, collapsed on the stairs of his house, then died a few moments after being carried inside.[41]

In Paris when he heard the news of the riots, John Adams was aghast at the "Bigotry and Fanaticism" and the "Violences of the most dreadful Nature." "G[overnor] Hutchinson died in the Beginning of the Affray," he commented, and "Lord Mansfields House underwent a worse Fate, than his." Adams's secretary, apparently echoing Adams, presumed that the spectacle of the mob had "killed him." Also in Paris, Benjamin Franklin wrote on that same day: "Governor Hutchinson, it is said, died outright of the fright."[42] Both Franklin and Adams could imagine what a riot would mean to Hutchinson. His son, it is worth noting, expressed fear of the crowds when, three days later, he observed its members wearing blue ribbons about their heads—the sign of support for the popular hero, John Wilkes. "For my own part," he wrote ironically, "I left my mouth open to bawl out, no *Popery*, and ready to inquire for *blue Ribbons.*" A few years earlier Hutchinson had moved into a house formerly belonging to Wilkes. On that occasion he had joked about the possible influence of "popular notions" over him.[43] Now, with these notions apparently triumphing in the streets, he could not have failed to think of the American mob. Whether or not the resultant memories of his past sufferings hastened his death, its occurrence during a riot made a sadly fitting end to his ordeal.

The meaning of this ordeal lay in the nature of the popular will that Hawthorne summoned up in his stories. As long as the Massachusetts colonists could not admit the sentiment of revolution, especially to themselves, they needed to express it indirectly and symbolically through a scapegoat. Hutchinson, like his fictional counterpart in "Edward Randolph's Portrait," did not understand the extra-logical forces that led to his being assigned this role. And yet it would be hard to find a contemporary any more sensitive than he to the workings of the popular will. His failing—one shared with later historians who held a similar common-sense view of crowds as purely political phenomena—was an inability to imagine that a crowd might be organized by the Whig leadership and at the same time express the popular will.

On one occasion Hutchinson did speak of a "frenzy" in the behavior of his opponents, and he related it to the outbreaks of Puritan hysteria that he had chronicled in his history. Significantly, the comparison occurred to him in connection with a symbolic issue: a patriot demand in 1770 that the portraits of two Catholic kings, Charles I and James II, be removed from the Massachusetts Council chamber. Hutchinson compared the fanaticism behind the demand to the atmosphere in which his great-grandmother, Anne Hutchinson, had been banished from New England. Emotions in the seventeenth century, he wrote to a friend on the anniversary of the day his house had been destroyed by the mob, had not been higher "when they hanged the Quakers, when they afterwards hanged the poor innocent Witches, when they were carried away with a Land Bank, nor when they all turned new Lights [in the Great Awakening] than the political frenzy has been for a Twelve month past."[44] So charged with menace was the atmosphere that he referred to, and, presumably, so fresh the recollection of Bernard's departure being hastened by the theft and publication of his letters, that Hutchinson crossed out this sentence before sending his letter.

As late as 1773 during the frenzy caused by the release of his own letters, Hutchinson wrote that the "deception can't last longer than it did in the time of the witchcraft." He viewed his patriot opponents, then, not as mad but as temporarily possessed. On the other hand, he recognized that he was caught up in a process analogous to an emotional overthrow of paternal authority. In planning a "History of the Revolt of the Colonies" he appropriately chose as an epigraph lines from the beginning of Isaiah suitable for utterance by the king: "I have nourished children and brought them up, and even they have revolted from me." Attacks on Hutchinson were automatically part of this revolt, and by virtue of the traditional language of kingly absolutism they were as much acts of symbolic regicide or parricide as verbal attacks on the king himself. The patriots themselves were disturbed by these implications and vehemently denied the applicability of the regicidal terminology to themselves. Instead they applied it, in a strained manner, to the loyalists. These supporters of "Caesar," the patriots charged, were the real "Paracides of their country," and also "the murderers of their own children and families."[45]

Like Lord Bute in England, Hutchinson loomed in the patriot imagination as America's nation-destroying Caesar. But for all their insistence on calling this Caesar a parricide, patriots like John Adams and Mercy Warren imagined *him* as the one to be overthrown. Though the loyalists are called "parricides" in Mercy Warren's plays, it is "Brutus" (a figure meant to represent her brother, James Otis) who is urged to "bravely plunge" his sword into Rapatio-Hutchinson (who is explicitly compared to Caesar).[46] By making Hutchinson their scapegoat and identifying *him* as a parricide, the patriots transferred to him the most frightening implication of their political resistance. As a result, they were able to regard themselves as continuingly loyal to the king even as their readiness for separation matured.

In this light the relationships to Hutchinson of the leading Boston patriots on the one hand, and the crowds on the other, emerge as crucial to the process of revolution in America. The patriots defined their politics by reference to Hutchinson, suffered crises of confidence over the way he was treated by the crowd, and ended their careers in uncertainty regarding him. The crowds virtually began their agitations with attacks on Hutchinson in 1765, and conducted their final symbolic demonstrations before 1776 upon his departure for England. One may say that the beginning of revolution in America had much to do with Thomas Hutchinson—with his image in the streets, and with the struggle in the minds of the Massachusetts patriots over their relationships to him.

CHAPTER THREE

John Wilkes and the Earl of Bute

T HE CAMPAIGN AGAINST Thomas Hutchinson, the Stamp Act disturbances, and the subsequent disorders in America up to 1776 all had intimate connections with events in England during the 1760s. Just as it is tempting to speculate how this decade in America would now be viewed if no revolution had followed, it is tempting to speculate on how the same years in England would be viewed if a revolution *had* taken place there. For English riots were far more extensive than those in America, and had deeper roots in social and economic discontents. Furthermore, the atmosphere of both Parliamentary politics and newspaper debate was more heated than in America. In an England beset by successive depressions, droughts, and famines, the portents of civil dissolution mounted with an accumulating intensity.

English political passions were at least as important an export as Whig ideas. These passions tended to come across the sea in visual and symbolic form, with the principals on either side of the constitutional struggle taking on the stature of folk heroes representing good and evil. At the first American Stamp Act demonstration on August 14, 1765, the effigy hanging next to that of Andrew Oliver, the prospective distributor of stamps, consisted of a boot with a devil's imp peeping out of it. The boot, as everyone knew, stood for Lord Bute. Everyone knew, too, that when the marching youths cried, "King, Pitt, and Liberty," their slogan included Bute's most prominent opponent in Parliamentary politics.

Though no one remarked the incongruity, the Bute effigy and the cry for Pitt lacked any firm basis in reality. Although Americans followed the British opposition in holding Bute responsible for the Stamp

Act, he had actually been "overt" in his opposition to it. In contrast, "no one, friend or enemy, knew where Pitt stood." His famous speech against the Stamp Act was delivered six months after its passage, in *response* to American opposition. On the other hand, as prime minister, in 1760 Pitt had inaugurated an active British policy toward illegal American trade by calling for "the most exemplary and condign Punishment" of those trading with the French enemy.[1] American sentiment for Pitt and against Bute, then, had to do not with immediate realities but with something that had come to be symbolized in their opposing personal figures.

John Stuart, third earl of Bute, was a slightly impoverished Scottish nobleman of retiring, scholarly ways. A "botanist of distinction," he produced a nine-volume work on the subject. At his isolated estate on the Isle of Bute he sponsored private theatrical productions and "masquerades," in which he also performed. Together with his acting, his somewhat foppish good looks helped to make him appear "cold and severe"—just like the similarly studious Hutchinson. He was taken up by the royal family and in the 1750s became tutor to George, the future king. Then at the death of George II in 1760, at about the time that Hutchinson was elevated to the chief justiceship, Bute became the most powerful man in England. As "the favourite," he was the young king's chief adviser, and in 1761 formally entered the government as secretary of state, the equivalent of prime minister.

At this time he became the object of a campaign of vilification unprecedented and apparently unaccountable in its savagery. He was "libeled in songs, pamphlets, newspaper essays, poems, squibs, and handbills."[2] In over four hundred cartoons he was shown deceiving the king and undermining precious English liberties. If anything, his role was magnified by American caricaturists such as Paul Revere, who regularly adapted the English cartoons. The accompanying verses on American versions of these were heavy with Biblical allusions: Bute became "the great serpent" or else the Beast of Revelation. Frequently he was shown alongside a ravished, dying figure of Liberty who represented America.

In 1763 the London Chimney sweeps selected Bute as their target at the beginning of agitation for reform in their working conditions. On May Day the child sweeps, wearing enormous periwigs, came begging at Bute's door following their traditional holiday procession. Here, it was reported, they were refused money. Whether or not this was true, Bute was made to appear unfriendly to an English tradition, and was thereafter opposed by the sweeps and other groups of workers. By the end of 1763 he was forced to resign political office. Yet this step did not end his "misfortunes." With an irrationality that recalled Hutchinson's ordeal before and after his expulsion from Massachusetts, Bute continued to be regarded as "the author of all our present ills."[3]

This charge was made in 1766, by which time Bute had been forbidden so much as to enter the king's presence, lest he influence him. Apparently, after 1763 "for a year or so George III still turned to him as a sort of father-figure who would bolster up his morale." And it appears that the king did consider returning his friend to government in 1765. However, the constitutionally retiring Bute refused a renewal of power, and the king never spoke to him again. Nevertheless, on into the 1770s and even the 1780s both the people and highly placed members of Parliament regarded Bute as the secret influence behind nearly every sinister political event—even though there is "certainly no evidence to prove his illicit involvement in politics after 1766."[4]

By 1769 Bute, like Hutchinson, was broken in health by unremitting personal attacks. On April Fool's Day, 1771, at the height of a crisis over freedom of the press and involving John Wilkes, Bute was presented in effigy even though he had nothing to do with the issue. "A hearse, followed by two carts, was drawn through the city, and accompanied by a very great mob." Bute's effigy appeared in the first cart, accompanied by "a Chimney Sweeper, who acted the part of a Clergyman" to him. When the procession reached Tower Hill, Bute was "pretendedly beheaded, then put into the hearse and carried off." By this time, partisan politics of a certain kind could hardly find their expression without using him as a scapegoat. In a somewhat similar fashion Bute was reviled in America as late as 1778 in a broadside song distributed to Revolutionary troops. At this late date he was unnecessarily designated "B——," as though mention of his name could still bring retaliation.[5]

Bute's character undoubtedly contributed to his false reputation. Apparently unfit for public business, which he viewed in a generalized, romantic light, he anticipated his failure as a politician from the beginning and spent his ineffectual time in office looking forward to bittersweet defeat and resignation. He was decidedly not a sinister mover of events. Above all, he wished to retain the conviction that, as he put it

America in Distress

Paul Revere based this illustration on an English print, "Britannia in Distress." The ever-swooning female figure of Britannia (as Liberty) in the original is here designated "America"; her identifying shield has been replaced by the fallen bow, quiver of arrows, and headdress of an Indian maiden. A recognizable likeness of Hutchinson at the left has replaced one of the figures in the original, and Bute, third from the left, has replaced another—a horned, bewigged, man-devil figure.

in a letter to George III, he had gained friendship and influence with the king by "honest noble means," and not by "the wretched arts thro' which minions have too often fascinated their prince; and rendered the very name of favorite odious to every worthy man."[6] But by acting to preserve his own self-esteem above all else, Bute helped to fix on himself the very reputation that he wished to avoid.

Today it is easy to see that a theory of conspiracy, especially the idea that sinister forces were at work to undermine the Constitution, frequently amounted to the only satisfactory explanation of politics for both Englishmen and Americans in the mid-eighteenth century. Hutchinson has been called the "scapegoat" of such theories in America, and Bute their "scapegoat" in England. Oddly enough, both men were blamed in the same way: Hutchinson for complicity in a British attempt to undermine American liberties, and Bute for originating it. The American patriots considered the two to be allied in this conspiracy.[7]

It is uncertain for whom or what, exactly, Bute stood as a scapegoat. In some accounts his imposition of a cider tax in 1762 is regarded as the greatest source of his unpopularity. It resulted in his being hanged in effigy in Exeter, and in his being burlesqued by "a figure in a Scottish plaid with a blue garter ribbon [which] paraded through the towns leading by the nose an ass royally crowned."[8] Bute's misfortunes can be further traced to his period as tutor to the young heir apparent. By inculcating the future monarch with the doctrines of Bolingbroke's *Patriot King,* he laid the groundwork for George III's attempt to restore the royal prerogative. This attempt, of course, sparked the liberty movement of the 1760s and 1770s. And when George III chose to assert his prerogative over ministerial appointments by elevating Bute, he made him the obvious focus of the opposition. Hutchinson was placed in a similar position. His elevation to the chief justiceship by Bernard, which also was viewed as a corrupt extension of the prerogative, helped make him the focus of the American liberty movement.

The doctrine of ministerial responsibility has also been suggested as a source of Bute's plight. According to this doctrine, the king never does wrong and therefore cannot be criticized. Any problems that arise under the king's authority are traceable to his advisers, especially the chief minister. Bute in England and Hutchinson in America both suffered under this convention. Yet Bute came in for more abuse than the traditional scapegoating of a chief minister. And afterward not his successors to the office but he himself, now the supposed "minister behind the curtain," continued to be held responsible for the errors of government. By all indications, Bute had become involved in a new kind of symbolic politics.

One source of this politics was William Pitt, the Great Commoner. At the end of the 1750s he came to represent the national ideal of conscience, above all as it concerned itself with the good of the nation. His supposedly selfless idealism amounted to the contemporary definition of "patriotism," one that had a particular appeal to the righteous American temperament.[9] In the early 1760s, as Pitt's name was growing into a byword for patriotism, Bute's came to stand for its opposites: corruption, self-seeking, tyranny. Moreover, unfortunately for Bute, two important objects of Pitt's attacks in Parliament were the Scots and the Jacobites. The Pretender's Rebellion in 1745 had taken place in Scotland, and memory of this fact, together with the ever-present English prejudice against the Scots, produced a kind of hysteria against the Scotsman, Bute. (Hence, the Scotch plaid along with the garter of office to identify him in caricatures.) To make matters still worse, Bute's name was by coincidence John Stuart, which falsely suggested a connection with the family of the Pretender. As early as 1761 Bute's carriage was pelted as he entered and left Parliament, and the shouts of the crowd included "D——n all Scotch rogues!" "No Bute!" and "Pitt for ever!"[10]

The final source of popular hysteria over Bute was the persistent rumor that he was having an affair with the king's mother, the Princess Dowager. Just as in cartoons Bute peeped out from behind a curtain to influence politics, so was he popularly imagined as sneaking about backstairs at the palace for purposes of sexual intrigue. Accordingly, when he was paraded in effigy, as on April Fool's Day, he was typically accompanied by the Princess Dowager—or a petticoat representing her. Bute's political enemies made capital of the situation by enforcing a distantly historical parallel with Roger Mortimer, the evil regent to Edward III, who was his queen's secret lover. The play, *The Fall of Mortimer*, was reissued with a new preface by John Wilkes. The preface pushed home the implications of the parallels with Bute by wittily insisting that none of them applied to the present reign. Then, referring to Bute's reputation as an amateur actor, Wilkes ironically praised him for his excellence—especially in "the famous

Claudius pouring Poison into the King's Ear, as he is Sleeping in the Garden. — Scene in Hamlet Act I. Scene III

Claudius Pouring Poison into the King's Ear

Lord Bute and the Princess Dowager as Gertrude, murdering George III. This is an illustration of John Wilkes's ironic praise of Bute for his supposed performance in *Hamlet*, where *"you pour fatal poison into the ear* of a good, unsuspecting King."

scene of *Hamlet,* where you *pour fatal poison into the ear* of a good, un-suspecting King." Bute had been so depicted in more than one car-toon. The parallel suggested, of course, both an affair with the queen and a hand in the death of the former king.[11]

In disparaging the Bute-Dowager rumors, L. H. Gipson wrote that all of them "may be passed over by the historian." But according to a recent biographer of Wilkes, the Mortimer parallel amounted to "the boldest and most brutal attack yet made on this or, indeed any Prime Minister." Wilkes's insinuations in the preface to *Mortimer* and elsewhere, in fact, brought about "the end of Bute."[12]

The image of Bute as a kind of evil and traducing father of the king was made possible first of all by the youth of George III. The king had succeeded not his father, who died in 1751, but his grandfa-ther, with whose age his youth contrasted sharply. Finally, under George III there was for a time no heir apparent. Traditionally the opposition formed around this figure. Such a situation, Richard Pares has written, existed only "between 1769 and 1782, when the heir ap-parent was a minor." It is possible, he speculates, that otherwise the opposition might not have developed "their anti-monarchist constitu-tional doctrines." Whatever the political results, from a symbolic point of view Bute and the Princess Dowager were left to represent the par-ents in the royal family. Repeatedly, the king was represented in car-toons as a child being duped by the princess with the aid of Bute.[13]

When Wilkes and others who aided in creating the public image of Bute drew on this configuration, they were aided by a popular ap-prehension of the tutor's paternal role in the family. For as novels of the period show, "tutors and court ministers are as emphatically 'true parents' as natural parents." In the iconography of attacks on Bute there is no mistaking his identity as a father. In a cartoon of 1767, for example, he is depicted as a giant towering over petitioners for office. They cringingly look up as one of them, crippled, passes under him. Beneath the cartoon appear lines spoken by Cassius in Shakespeare's *Julius Caesar,* with some pointed alterations:

> Why man he doth bestride this narrow World
> Like a COLOSSUS; and we petty ministers
> Walk under his huge Legs, and peep about
> To find ourselves Posts, Peerages, and Pensions.[14]

The colossus here is, of course, Julius Caesar. Cassius actually refers to "petty men" and "dishonourable graves" rather than "Petty minis-

The Colossus

A resplendent, tartaned Lord Bute, standing astride the pillars of Fraud and
Lust (a reference to his putative affair with the Princess Dowager), is
associated with Caesar by the amended quotation from Cassius' speech.

ters" and "Posts, Peerages, and Pensions," but the political point about tyranny and corruption is similar.

In the lines quoted from the play, Cassius is being presented by Shakespeare as a resentful son who rebels against one whom, consciously or unconsciously, he thinks of as a father. His image of himself and the others in the band of brothers who unite against Caesar perfectly catches a boy's vision of his father as both admirably commanding and oppressively overbearing. For, the son-like figures whom he imagines as walking under the giant's legs are, psychologically speaking, looking up at their father's genitals. Thus, the figure used by Cassius and borrowed by the cartoonist may be interpreted as one of Oedipal envy and fear.

John Adams ended one of his essays with a phrase from *Julius Caesar:* "Cassius from Bondage shall deliver Cassius." The New York Sons of Liberty signed one of their papers "Brutus," while a writer in the Boston *Gazette* attacking Hutchinson at the height of anger against him in 1773 signed himself "Casca." In Virginia, Patrick Henry provoked shouts of "Treason!" by declaring that "tarquin and Julius had their Brutus, Charles had his Cromwell." Several years later Henry's speech containing his most famous utterance—"Give me liberty, or give me death"—may have been based on Cassius's indictment of Caesar just before he likens him to a colossus.[15] Both Thomas Hutchinson and Lord Bute, then, were conceived of as father-like Caesars opposed by patriots who likened themselves to the group of symbolic sons who united to overthrow a tyrant.

This scenario was manipulated by an opposing political faction for avowedly propagandistic reasons. Yet the imagery elicited its own, powerful response—one that helps account for the triumph of opposition theories of politics over those of Bute. Just as in the contention between Hutchinson and the American patriots, the Butean principles were remarkably popular in conception. Bute aimed to restore probity to government just as Pitt did. His Bolingbrokian doctrine of the patriot king implied a figure standing above politics, who would purify the corruptions of the state. As everyone knew, corruption was rife when George III came to power. The Americans made this corruption their leading argument against customs taxes, for example, pointing out that the collectors were placemen come to make quick fortunes through their percentages of duties. Not surprisingly, then, when John Adams read George III's high-toned accession speech he devoutly approved its principles. He called the new king "a friend of Liberty" (an epithet that later became opposition currency) and found his sentiments "worthy of a king—a [Bolingbrokian] Patriot King."[16]

In this context the widespead conviction of Bute's corruption after 1763 becomes doubly extraordinary. For not only did Bute resign, but at the same time Pitt, his opposite and symbol of the liberty party's virtues, fell in the public esteem. His acceptance of a baronetcy and pension from the king raised a cry of betrayal, and may have influenced the public's choice of a new champion, the "God of Liberty," John Wilkes. As Edmund Burke remarked in 1768, "since the fall of Chatham [that is, Pitt], there has been no hero of the mob but Wilkes."[17] The result of Wilkes's accession was a state of national agitation, with demonstrations, effigy burnings, and riots that lasted into the 1770s and had a profound influence on American politics.

The paradoxical career of John Wilkes has attracted increasing interest. A notorious rake, he stirred the moral conscience of the nation. A scurrilous newspaper libeler, he sparked the battle against censorship. A place-seeker, he advanced the principle of free elections. A snob, he attracted the love of the common people and elevated their self-respect. His first great cause arose when he was arrested for libel. As a member of Parliament (he had bought his seat in the normally corrupt manner of the day), he attempted to claim a member's privilege against prosecution. But in the meantime his arrest electrified the nation and became the occasion for agitation against open or "general warrants," the English equivalent of Writs of Assistance. As a result, Wilkes quickly became a hero in America for espousing a cause similar to James Otis's.

In 1768 and 1769 Wilkes stood as a popular candidate for Parliament and was elected four times—only to be refused his seat each time. Wilkes eventually won the right to take his seat, and went on to become lord mayor of London. He consistently represented himself as a friend to American freedom, and thus remained a popular figure in America throughout the 1770s. In contrast, the long departed Lord Bute continued to personify the assault on liberty in general and American freedoms in particular.

The symbolism of the crowds who supported Wilkes has elicited particular interest in the past few years. George Rudé, in studying grievances ranging from the cider tax to the constitutional questions raised by the king's favoritism toward Bute, has found a tendency on

John Wilkes

Drawn from the life for an engraving during Wilkes's interrogation concerning Number 45 of the *North Briton*. Wilkes is immediately identifiable by the liberty staff and peleus, and by his squint, which is more pronounced in the engraving. Also added to the engraving are the designations "North Briton Number 45" and "North Briton Number 17" on the newspapers to the left of Wilkes, and the word "Liberty" on the peleus.

the part of protesters to associate the causes of these grievances with Wilkes. Rudé believes it "no coincidence" that the price riots and industrial disputes of the 1760s dovetailed with Wilkite demonstrations.[18] Others believe that this *was* a coincidence, and that the Wilkite demonstrations attracted people entirely different from those concerned with wages or food prices.

In a study of the Wilkes phenomenon, John Brewer has treated the liberty movement in anthropological terms. Wilkes functioned as a kind of jester-harlequin figure or a lord of misrule, Brewer suggests. His physical ugliness and squint-eye resembled the deformities often associated with jesters, and he was known to attend masques dressed in motley. In a similar manner, other historians have tried to deal with the absence of a modern class-consciousness in the crowds of this period by noticing the ritual and festival element in their behavior. Though these studies reach different conclusions about the nature of the Wilkes phenomenon and about crowds in general, they have begun to take into account extra-political and extra-economic motives of the sort that were crucial in America.

Such motives, with their festival-like overtones of revolt, were evident throughout Wilkes's campaign against Bute. When Bute set up a newspaper, *The Briton,* to support government, Wilkes organized his opposition paper, the *North Briton.* Its very title, referring to the part of England that includes Scotland, pointed to Bute, and it consisted mostly of diatribe against "the favourite." Here Wilkes trembled on the verge of capital libel, since any attack on the favorite implied an attack on the king himself.[19] The doctrine of royal infallibility, however, protected Wilkes by assimilating his attacks to a tradition in which the sovereign's errors and wrongdoings could be safely assigned to his leading minister. In light of this convention, it can be said that Bute progressed with the help of Wilkes from a position as quasi-legal, political scapegoat for the king to one as a scapegoat more immediately and emotionally perceived.

In the forty-fifth number of the *North Briton* Wilkes overstepped the bounds of propriety, causing the government to order seizure of the paper and his arrest. Yet it has never been satisfactorily explained why this issue was any more offensive than others. "Its references to the King," it has been pointed out, "were couched in terms of the profoundest respect." Wilkes himself made this point a year after the Number 45 incident, arguing that if one examined his text, "the sovereign is mentioned, not only in terms of decency, but with that regard and reverence which are due from a good subject to a good king."[20] Wilkes had managed to evoke more apprehension by praising the king than he would have by ignoring him.

Well before Number 45 appeared, the *North Briton* was known for its heavy irony. As in the preface to *Mortimer,* Bute was invariably praised in extravagant terms—for bringing other Scots into office, for arranging a supposedly disastrous peace with France, for setting the country on the road to Jacobitism. Number 38, for example, consisted of a supposed letter from Charles Stuart, the Pretender, to his "kinsman," Bute. Here Wilkes raised the specter of regicide, employing an ironic tone that automatically undercut his professions of good faith toward the sovereign. When he began Number 45, therefore, by apparently exculpating the king, he achieved a similar effect of insolence. *"The King's Speech,"* he wrote, referring to George III's formal opening of Parliament, "has always been considered by the legislature, and by the public at large, as the *Speech of the* [Chief] *Minister."* In 1761, at the king's first opening of a Parliamentary session, Wilkes had quipped with reference to Bute that this was the speech of the minister, "though of what minister I cannot tell."[21] This time, however, Wilkes was writing after Bute's resignation from the government. Why, then, did he continue to attack Bute, and why did the government respond even though Bute had left office?

The role of scapegoat became so much Bute's alone, it would seem, that no minister who replaced him had the necessary symbolic weight to assume it. At first his special role was not entirely clear. Thus, when he was attacked as he entered and left Parliament in 1762, one account reported: "It is said, but it is denied also, that the King was insulted." Only a year later, however, Bute could write of the campaign against him, "I am the mark for the party, but the whole is in reality aim'd at the King himself." (Prophetically, George III himself had warned, "Whoever speaks against Lord Bute, I shall think speaks against me.") Wilkes appears from the beginning to have been chipping away at the divinity that hedges a king. Early in George's reign Wilkes was reported to have refused an invitation to play cards by protesting, "I cannot tell the difference between a king and a knave." Later, there could be no mistaking Wilkes's crocodile tears over the honor of the crown when he wrote in Number 45, "I lament to see it sunk even to prostitution."[22]

But even more remarkable than Wilkes's indirect attack on the king was the government's response. It was ordered that a copy of the *North Briton* Number 45 be publicly burned by the hangman. The ceremony would amount to a symbolic assertion of legitimacy—one evoking the ultimate power of the state to take a life. The resultant riot marked a turning point in English and American consciousness, and provided the vocabulary of dissent for the rest of the period leading to American independence.

Wilkes's arrest a week after the appearance of Number 45 caused a great stir. He contrived to make it into a public affair in which his being taken into custody for questioning, his trial, and his release all could be viewed from the streets. After he received his first judicial hearing the cry went up, "Liberty! Liberty! Wilkes for ever!" On his release a crowd awaited him at home; here the cries were "Whigs for ever and no Jacobites!" and "Wilkes and Liberty!"[23] The latter was to echo in both England and America for a decade. With it, Wilkes had come to embody the patriot-liberty movement with an intimacy of association never conceived of under Pitt.

Eight months later, on the day set for burning Number 45, the crowd was ready with a counter-ceremony. On December 3, 1763, a London sheriff set out to bring a copy of the paper to the hangman. His carriage was impeded by a great crowd so that he had to walk to "the place where the paper was to be burnt"—that is, the Cornhill, a square used for public hangings. Here he read the official order for the burning and had Number 45 set to the torch. The onlookers surged forward and may have saved some of the scraps. Then the "mob," when it spied an accompanying city marshall, "hissed, and pelted him with mud, and struck him, and spit in his face, crying out, 'Wilkes and Liberty.'" The crowd then offered its counter to the official ceremony: the burning of "a jackboot and petticoat."[24]

The paradox of Wilkes's impact on history could not have been better expressed than in the simultaneous uses of the cry "Wilkes and Liberty!" and the continued use of the jackboot and petticoat. The cry expressed the oppositionist political implications of the incident, the effigies its retrograde, psychological ones. The latter had to do in one way or another with the decline of kingship. Michael Walzer, who in *Regicide and Revolution* describes the dread ceremonies of kingship, argues that the mystery of royalty died in England with the judicial murder of Charles I in 1649. In the eighteenth century the tradition of awe surrounding the kingship continued to decay. Nevertheless, the frantic reaction to Wilkes's symbolic challenge demonstrates a continuing loyalty to the old idea of kingship. Although it is true that earlier in English history the perpetrator of Number 45 and not the manuscript would have been dealt with by the hangman at Cornhill, the ceremony nevertheless retained much of its awesomeness.

In the meantime, constitutional government had taken upon itself not only regal powers but some of their old mystique as well. Thus, in 1764 when a work called *Droit Le Roy* asserted the ancient prerogatives of kingship, there was outrage on all sides in Parliament, comparable to that evoked by Number 45. *Droit Le Roy* was denounced as being "Jacobitical, and violating the Bill of Rights and the [Glorious] Revolution." Without a dissenting vote it was ordered to be burned by the public hangman at two separate places in London. In this case the sentence was carried out without public opposition.[25]

Wilkes himself, significantly, was not present at the attempted burning of Number 45. His influence, all observers agree, was as a symbol of opposition, not its leader. At the end of 1763 he was expelled from Parliament as "the libeller of his king," fought a duel in which he was wounded, and fled to France. In exile, and with his case suspended, Wilkes continued to be identified during the next four years with the numeral 45.

A disquisition could be written on the uses of 45 in connection with Wilkes and his followers. It appeared on commemorative cups and other crockery, in cartoons, and in popular jests; it was chalked on the doors and displayed in the windows of private houses; it determined the number of toasts at banquets, and the amounts of almost any item appearing in a patriotic context. Whether the actual Wilkite celebrations or the journalistic accounts of them were more extravagant in their uses of the number would be hard to say. In November 1769, for example, the following item appeared in the London *Public Advertiser:*

Saturday last, being Mr. Wilkes's Birth Day, 45 independent Gentlemen belonging to Deal, met at the Hoop and Griffin Tavern in that Town, had 45 Pounds of Beef roasted, 45 Turnips, 45 Potatoes, and 45 Carrots boiled; and after having drunk Mr. Wilkes's Health . . . to the Amount of 45 Glasses, each Man fired 45 Pieces of Cannon, and concluded the Evening with Bonfires, the Room where they sat illu-

minated with 45 Candles, Dancing &c. and departed with greatest
Friendship and Satisfaction exactly 45 Minutes after Eleven.[26]

The same mode was adopted in America, where followers throughout
the land were "infatuated" with Wilkes and 45. A celebration for him
in Charleston, South Carolina, met at "45 Minutes after Seven
o'Clock" and lasted until "45 Minutes past 12." When the effigy tree
at the first Stamp Act protest in Boston was sacralized as the Liberty
Tree, its branches were thinned out so as to number forty-five. Later
the Bostonians "strung 45 lanterns on Liberty Tree when celebrating
the repeal of the Stamp Act; two years later, in 1768, a group at Norwich, Conn., eating from plates marked 'No. 45,' downed 45 patriotic
toasts, while a nearby Liberty Tree flew a flag inscribed, 'No. 45,
WILKES & LIBERTY'; and a gathering of 45 New Yorkers on the 45th
day of the year 1770 consumed 45 pounds of beefsteak cut from a
bullock 45 months old."[27]

The uses of 45 have been called "symbolic," "talismanic," and
"cabalistic," and it has been suggested that they reflect the tradition of
Biblical numerology.[28] But above all, their spirit of excess and mockery again recalls the Saturnalia. Every joke about the number 45 perpetuated this spirit, thereby contributing to an international counter-
ritual of challenge to authority.

Wilkes returned to England in 1768 as an outlaw. He had repub-
lished Number 45 in pamphlet form in 1763, and had given further
offense with an obscene parody of Alexander Pope called *An Essay on
Woman.* Though he had not planned to publish the parody, after a
handful of copies had been bound by his private press the government
seized one of these as an excuse for prosecution. Wilkes's strategy on
his return was to make a public issue of himself again. If he could secure election to Parliament as a result of his notoriety, he would once
more be rendered safe from prosecution. At the beginning of his campaign he lost an election in the city of London. But it was possible to
stand at one election after another, and he soon won his way into Parliament through the nearby borough of Middlesex. His victory there
began a species of Wilkite celebratory demonstration that monopo-
lized English and American attention for the next three years. On
election day passersby in Middlesex were forced to shout for "Wilkes
and Liberty" while passing coaches were marked with the number 45.
When Wilkes's victory was announced on the following day, the

celebrations intensified. "Until three o'clock in the morning the metropolis was a blaze of light, a candle at least in each window being demanded by the mob. Upon every door in the town 'No. 45' was scrawled in large figures. No vehicle was allowed to pass through the streets unless the driver wore the popular colours [blue and white]. The first nobility were compelled to decorate their coachmen and grooms with blue favours, and to cheer for 'Wilkes and Liberty.' " Those windows that were not illuminated were broken. Some time during the day the crowd seized the Count de Seilern, the Austrian ambassador, described as "the most stately and ceremonious of men." They pulled him out of his coach and "chalked 45 on the sole of his shoe."[29] The celebration obviously had to do not only with the cause of liberty, but with a widespread impulse to flout authority. The government responded repressively, as is frequently the case, thereby stimulating the crowd to more explicit expression of its impulse.

Despite popular support for him, Wilkes was arrested on the standing libel charge directed at Number 45 and the *Essay on Woman*. He was incarcerated in the King's Bench Prison, which soon became the empire-wide focus of sympathy for him. The King's Bench was no Newgate. It contained a garden, a concourse with shops, a coffeehouse, and a tavern where gentlemen being held in the desirable tower apartments could entertain. Wilkes, the notorious roué, was able to entertain ladies privately.[30] Nevertheless, the popular hero had been imprisoned, and crowds gathered outside the King's Bench in April and May 1768 while his case remained in doubt.

As fate would have it, they came at a high point of agitation in the decade. On May 8 sailors protesting economic conditions assembled in St. George's Fields adjacent to the prison. On the following day the Thames watermen conducted a related demonstration, just as the hatters went on a strike of their own. None of these actions started out to do with Wilkes, but the coincident demonstrations by his supporters contributed to the disturbed atmosphere of the city. Thus, whether the workingmen were clashing with or displaying sympathy toward the Wilkites—and both occurred—they lent themselves to the Wilkites' purposes.[31]

On the night of the hatters' strike "a large mob" of Wilkites "assembled before the Mansion-House, carrying a gallows with a boot [for Bute] hanging to it, and a red cap." These objects were then carried "along Cornhill." Unlike the workers in their concern for wages,

these demonstrators focused on symbols of authority (albeit from out
of the past): they were interested in government leaders and the Mansion House, the seat of city government.[32] For the next week both
kinds of demonstrations continued, especially those of workingmen.

In the midst of these disturbances there took place the Massacre of
St. George's Fields on May 10. Significantly, it was set off by a symbolic gesture. When a soldier tore down a pro-Wilkes handbill he
came to blows with one of the onlookers. Soon the soldiers were attacked by the crowd, the riot act was read, and the soldiers fired, killing and wounding about a dozen people, including innocent bystanders. They then chased and killed William Allen, an innocent farmer,
thinking him a ringleader. Throughout the day, the fact that the soldiers were Scots Guards had served to exacerbate the situation. In the
aftermath, Wilkites pointed to this circumstance as evidence of yet
another Butean conspiracy. The Massacre became a motif for subsequent Wilkite demonstrations over other issues. It was depicted on
handbills and in cartoons and was publicized in America, where it influenced responses to the Boston Massacre two years later.[33]

The government, ever inept, soon provided new opportunities for
demonstrations. A few weeks after the Massacre, Wilkes received a
sentence of twenty-two months' imprisonment in the King's Bench for
his publication of Number 45 and *An Essay on Woman.* There was
some street agitation in anticipation of the sentence, but no large outbreak. Then, early in 1769, Parliament used the pretext of his conviction for libel to deny him the seat that he had won in the Middlesex
election. Wilkes now went from the embodiment of the movement for
liberty on the issues of general warrants and freedom of the press, to
its embodiment on the issue of the sanctity of free elections. Middlesex
elected him three more times during the next several months, and as
many times Parliament denied him a seat. The elections were occasions for further demonstrations, and during these it became apparent
just what kind of a symbol Wilkes had become for the people.

In the first place, Wilkite crowds tended to be celebratory rather
than protesting. The people turned out not when Parliament rejected
Wilkes but on election days and the days following, on his birthday,
and—after his release from prison—on days when he was scheduled to
appear in Parliament. The very day of his incarceration was turned
into a kind of celebration; for the first of his three reelections in 1769
Wilkes himself gave a dinner and had the King's Bench illuminated;

and there was, of course, a celebration upon his release in 1770. On this occasion windows were illuminated throughout England and America. One English town hung an effigy of Wilkes's opponent in the Middlesex election; in another, the familiar "BOOT, filled with combustibles, after being for some time suspended upon a gibbet, was blown up amidst the universal acclamations of the populace."[34]

Though Lord Bute remained an object of Wilkite hatred well into the 1770s, beginning with Wilkes's return to England in 1768 the liberty question stood out as a contest between Wilkes and George III. Nevertheless, just as in America, "almost every Wilkite ballad maintained, in a way that we perhaps would regard as incongruous, the compatibility of ardent support for the Crown with allegiance to 'Wilkes and liberty.' " Typically, at the birthday celebration for Wilkes held at the Forty-five Tavern in 1769, the first toast went to the "King & his Royal Consort," and only the second to "Mr. Alderman Wilkes and his Family." (Remarkably, it has been said that Wilkes himself in all his career only once wrote anything "personally directed against George III," and this was a phrase in a private letter.[35]

On the other hand, the popular, stylized obeisance to Wilkes insolently imitated the rituals of royalty, especially the king's birthday. In celebration of royal birthdays and anniversaries, as of military victories, the common practice was to place candles in the windows of both public buildings and private houses. The enforced illuminations in celebration of Wilkes had an obvious, mocking reference to the patriotism of this gesture. Thus, after the first Middlesex election, "the mob paraded . . . obliging every body to illuminate and breaking the windows of such as did not do it immediately. The windows of the Mansion House, in particular, were demolished all to pieces . . . they demolished all the windows of Ld. Bute."[36] The easy transitions on this occasion were ominous for authority: from mockery through the medium of illuminations, to destruction of state property, to a menacing gesture toward the king through the by-now-traditional surrogateship of Bute.

After 1768 these implications grew more explicit. "Royal and loyal toasts were drunk" to Wilkes, he was called "the Father of his Country," and taverns changed their names to "Wilkes Head" in imitation of "Kings Head" taverns. At demonstrations the cry, or song, arose of "Great Wilkes Our King." Soon the crowds went still further. The cry "No King!" was heard, and then "Wilkes and No

King!" By 1769 a member of government could write angrily that "it is no longer a struggle whether He (Wilkes) is the first Man in the Kingdom, but no Body else shall be address'd, no, not even Majesty Himself." On one occasion "No Wilkes No King" was followed by "This is the most glorious opportunity for a Revolution that ever offered."[37]

After 1770 the Wilkes issue gradually died down. There were sporadic effigy burnings of Bute and the Princess Dowager, along with more demonstrations when Wilkes was invested as alderman in 1770 and as lord mayor of London in 1772.[38] These last demonstrations coincided with a peaking of public emotions in both England and America in 1770 and 1771. Afterward there came a transatlantic calm that has yet to be fully explained. The "quiet period" in America lasted until the end of 1773; the next widespread rioting in England took place in 1780. In emotional terms, at least, it would appear that in both countries the public demonstrations between 1768 and 1771 had satisfied the populace.

The problem of identifying the discontents that led to the demonstrations continues to engage historians. In America the question is identical with that of the causes of the Revolution; in England it has to do with the nature of the Wilkite movement. In both cases the neglected element has been the extra-political motivation of the crowds. During the period of quiescence there were sufficient political and economic issues to stir up the populace on both sides of the Atlantic. But the crowds did not again rise and resort to a symbolic language until they were aroused by *religious* issues. In America the Quebec Act of 1774, and in England the Catholic Relief Act of 1778, both of which extended privileges to Catholics, led to far greater actions in the streets than any political event for the rest of the decade, with the possible exception of the Declaration of Independence.[39]

These religious issues were very different from either those of the English liberty movement or those of the American resistance to taxation, yet many of the cries and symbols of the crowds remained the same as they had been in the 1760s. In America effigial processions, buryings, and burnings were revived in 1774, while in England in 1780 the protesters chose St. George's Fields as their meeting place, wore the Wilkite blue cockade, and raised the unifying cry of nearly every English-speaking crowd of the previous two centuries: "No Popery!"

The English "Protestant Mob" had risen or threatened to rise at crises since the Glorious Revolution of the seventeenth century. This mob feared and hated the Irish, the French, English Catholics, and any tendency that could be identified with the pope. In the eighteenth century "anti-Catholicism remained part of the political tradition of the people, continually nourished by Republican, Whig or nationalist agitation." Protestant emotions surfaced in the religio-political Sacheverell riots of 1709, the Pretender's Rebellion in 1715, the Gin Act riots of 1736, the agitation against the Jewish Naturalization Act of 1753, many of the agitations of the 1760s and 1770s, the Gordon riots of 1780, and finally the Priestley riots of 1791.[40] Most striking about the cry of "No Popery!" on most of these occasions was its independence of any political tendency. It came from both left and right, from both workingmen and the middle class, and it surfaced in political, social, and nationalist-chauvinist contexts alike.

The religious element tended to predominate when Catholics and other minorities were at issue, whereas nationalism came to the fore after wars. (The latest peace treaty seemed always to have surrendered the fruits of English conquests at arms, as in the case of the unfair attacks on Bute for the treaty of Paris in 1763.)[41] In the campaign against Bute during the 1760s, religious and nationalistic emotions were united with Whig conspiracy theory. The Wilkite movement took this potent mixture to the streets, where it was embodied in a traditional manner—that is, in outbreaks of political emotionalism on royal days such as the king's birthday. In America such disturbances, whatever their timing, tended to adopt the symbolism of Pope Day.

The English origin of Pope Day, Guy Fawkes Day, amounted to a celebration of the king apparently very like those conducted on his own special days. For in marking the anniversary of the popish plot against a former king's life, the populace affirmed its loyalty to the reigning monarch. On the other hand, just as the pope's effigy in America came to stand as the champion of the north and south end factions in Boston, the Guy Fawkes effigy grew into a kind of beloved mascot. And, disguised by playfulness though it was, the Guy's popularity revealed a degree of sympathy with the regicidal intention of the real Guy Fawkes. This buried sympathy provided the impulse for the eighteenth-century political outbreaks that coincided with the holiday.

The Sacheverell riots, for example, resulted from a fierce anti-Tory sermon preached on Guy Fawkes Day, 1709. In it Dr. Henry

Sacheverell spiced his political anti-Toryism with xenophobic fears over the safety of the Protestant church. These fears were automatically heightened by their implied reference to the day's observance of the Popish Plot. At the time that Sacheverell preached, Guy Fawkes Day additionally commemorated the November 5 landing of William of Orange at Torbay in 1688, an event popularly interpreted as a freeing of England from popery. Just as with Number 45, the government ordered Sacheverell's sermon burned, and riots broke out.[42] At the end of the century the Priestley riots of 1791 were sparked by another sermon preached on Guy Fawkes day.

Between 1709 and 1715, first the succession crisis, as the crown passed from Queen Anne to George I in 1713, and then the uprising in favor of the Pretender were punctuated by demonstrations and riots on royal days. In 1715 Jacobites attacked the new king and the Hanoverian succession on Queen Anne's accession day and her coronation day, on the king's birthday, on the anniversary of Charles II's restoration, on the Pretender's birthday, and on Queen Elizabeth's Day. They burned effigies of Oliver Cromwell and William III, two figures responsible for interruptions of the former succession; in response, the Whig government employed the stocks, pillory, hanging tree, and drawing and quartering. Anti-papal pageants were organized on the king's coronation day, on anniversaries of victories over the Pretender, on Guy Fawkes day, and on the same Queen Elizabeth's Day employed by the opposition. The government's days included the usual celebratory bonfires and illuminations, but its pageants emphasized punishment: effigies were haltered, ridden skimmington, hanged, and burned. Each side conducted processions in which the other was shown in mock triumph.[43]

The papal sympathies of the Jacobites left a residue of anti-Jacobitism for the rest of the century. When Lord Bute was obliged to leave the country in 1768 his supposed connection with the Pretender came into play. A communication in the *Political Register* describing his ignominious departure suggested that the day, August 1, was an anniversary "marked out by heaven to be ominous to the house of Stuart." This day, the writer explained, "has been remarkably auspicious to liberty; first in giving us the accession of the mild house of Brunswick, and then in securing the succession by giving birth to a Prince of Wales, thereby blasting, it is hoped, for ever, the most distant gleam of hope in the tyrant house of Stuart, of succeeding to the throne of these kingdoms."[44] The strained symbolism of royal births and anniversaries in this attack was typical of the way in which hatred of Bute assimilated itself to the most deeply held prejudices of Englishmen.

Quite as remarkable as the duration of such prejudices was their tendency to break out in political form on days of festivity. The Wilkite high points tended to come on festival days, one of which, Wilkes's birthday, temporarily joined the traditional calendar. When thus related to the calendar, the lord-of-misrule aspect of Wilkes pointed out by John Brewer calls to mind the Roman Saturnalia. In that festival of overthrow the lord of misrule presided over festivities at the end of the Roman calendar year. During a week of sexual and other behavioral excesses, masters changed places with their servants, who mocked the principle of authority by lording it over their temporarily subservient masters. On the last day the mock ruler was turned into a scapegoat. He was himself mocked and overthrown, after which order was reinstated.[45]

The Saturnalia, through its successive overthrows of legitimate and illegitimate rulers, made possible the expression of ambivalence toward authority. (In "My Kinsman, Major Molineux" the saturnalian crowd ousts and humiliates Major Molineux, while at the same time paying him homage by its ritual worship of him.) The Roman masters were mocked and humiliated, but the strongest mockery was reserved for the scapegoat ruler. His overthrow, which coincided with the reinstatement of the true masters, symbolized obedience to authority. At the same time it symbolized resentment of authority, inasmuch as the scapegoat was himself nominally a ruler.

Starting with the Stamp Act, Americans conceptualized their local crises in terms of the unfolding Wilkes drama. The general warrant used to arrest Wilkes appeared to have its parallels in the Writs of Assistance and unfair customs taxes; the "irregular" proceedings against Wilkes paralleled British enforcement of the new American customs regulations; the killings by soldiers in St. George's Fields during a Wilkes demonstration coincided with the introduction of troops into Boston, and later appeared to have presaged both the shooting of Seider and the Boston Massacre in 1770. When the patriot James Otis was injured in a coffeehouse brawl with a customs commissioner, he was mistakenly presumed to be an innocent victim—one who had suffered at the end of a series of assaults on champions of liberty that had begun with attacks on Wilkes.[46]

In London it was possible to view Bute and Wilkes on their ways

to and from Parliament, or to learn about them from gossip, and
though in this manner their reputations were much inflated they nevertheless remained men as well as symbols. But in America the political importance of the two was distorted far more, perhaps because
they were known only from highly emotional newspaper reports of
disturbances or from cartoons.[47]

The public drama of opposition between Bute and Wilkes answered a need that commonly arises when the authority of king and
state has come to be doubted. "Authority cannot be apprehended as
both good and bad at the same time." Thus, in periods like the 1760s
one may expect to find the formula of a "king deceived by his ministers" coming into prominence, along with a dramatization in which
one political figure receives undue "reverence" while his opposite receives the full weight of anger aroused by the times. In such a situation
there may also appear "primitive methods of expression and representation to take the place of contemporary ones." In America domestic
events were guided by the methods of expression accompanying the
major English crises of the eighteenth century. Thus in the 1730s and
1740s Boston disturbances like the market riot, impressment riots, and
disorders in connection with the land bank issue were sparked by "a
series of newspaper reports on contemporary British actions of opposition violence."[48]

The American crises of the 1760s closely followed the English
riots and effigial displays of the decade, especially the struggle between
Bute, "a favourite of the Crown," and Wilkes, "a favourite of the
people," as Josiah Quincy, Jr., phrased it. According to Thomas Hutchinson, in 1763 "the sound of 'Wilkes and liberty' was heard in Boston, in proportion to the number of inhabitants, as much as in London."[49] The same year a Boston newspaper carried the report of a
Devonshire protest against the cider tax in which Bute was displayed
in effigy next to a verse that ended with the phrase "Liberty, Property, and No Excise." Along with other news of British disturbances,
this provided the basis for the symbolism of the first Stamp Act displays. In 1765 reports first of weaver "mobs" in London and then of
riots among striking glovemakers preceded the August Stamp Act
riots. After the Oliver riot the *Boston Gazette* observed, "All America
is in commotion, and the people very exactly copy the example of their
brethren at home." Later, "throughout 1768–1769, the colonists
were subjected to a barrage of news from England concerning that fa-

mous political character, John Wilkes." To one observer, these reports appeared to have been responsible for the riot over the customs seizure of John Hancock's ship, the Liberty, at which the cry of the crowd was "Hancock and Liberty!"[50]

Throughout this period Wilkes's portrait appeared in American almanacs, and his birthday was publicly celebrated with enthusiasm, especially in 1770 when he returned to prominence. The result was a patterning of American events according to the English liberty party's scenario: a conspiracy against liberty conducted by Bute and opposed first by Pitt and then by Wilkes and his followers. In American cartoons and oratory Hutchinson and other royal governors tended to be assimilated to the Bute image, while in several colonies one or more champions of the opposition came to be called "the American Wilkes."[51]

The term suited the leaders of crowds to a certain extent, and applied to the speeches and rhetoric of many patriots, but for the most part it did not describe the sober, moralistic men who initiated the Revolution. Although they tended to assimilate local politics to the Bute-Wilkes model, theirs was hardly a saturnalian passage to resistance. Rather, they may be thought of as caught up, like Hawthorne's Robin, in a popular movement whose expressive style colored their private experience. The patriots who are discussed in the chapters that follow were at pains to dissociate themselves from the opportunism and self-aggrandizement associated with Wilkes: theirs was a politics of principle. And yet, in essential ways, their strength derived from the popular rehearsal of revolution going on around them in Massachusetts.

II

Conscience Patriots

CHAPTER FOUR

James Otis

A FTER THE DESTRUCTION of Lieutenant Governor Hutchinson's house in 1765 it was widely assumed that James Otis, Jr., had been responsible. Though Otis in fact opposed mob violence, the rumor arose from the well-known fact that he and his family had a personal feud with Hutchinson. This feud was used to explain not only the Hutchinson mob but also the major controversies of Massachusetts politics during the 1760s. Governor Bernard attributed to it the eventual downfall of Hutchinson himself. "Without the Union of Popular Politicks with private Revenge," Bernard wrote, "it is impossible to Account for the Ruin of the Lieutenant Governor."[1] Bernard spoke from experience. For upon arriving in Massachusetts in 1760 as the new governor he had almost immediately found himself embroiled in the Otis-Hutchinson rivalry.

One of Bernard's first official tasks was to name a chief justice of the Superior Court to replace the recently deceased Stephen Sewall. The Otises regarded a position on this court as politically due to Colonel James Otis, Sr., a politician and local judge in Barnstable, Massachusetts. James Otis, Jr., lobbied unsuccessfully on his father's behalf, at one point discussing the matter with Hutchinson himself. When Hutchinson told him that he did not intend to seek the chief justiceship, Otis took his words as an engagement not to *accept* it. Soon afterward Bernard, who did not have to honor political debts owed by others to Colonel Otis, offered the chief justiceship to Hutchinson, who did accept it. Bernard later wrote that he went ahead with the appointment despite being warned by Otis that "if his Father was not appointed Judge, he would set the whole Province in a flame, tho' he perished in the attempt." Soon after Hutchinson accepted the appointment, Otis "swore revenge."[2]

77

The story of Otis's threat to Bernard circulated widely in Massachusetts and was taken as a key to Otis's conduct during the rest of the 1760s. However, it did not quite reveal the secret of his contradictory behavior. Otis, as Hutchinson remarked at the end of his career, carried out his threat, consuming himself in the process.[3] He began his agitation directly after Hutchinson became chief justice, emerging as the leading patriot figure in Massachusetts and remaining so until 1770. After the Revolution his fellow patriots agreed that he had done as much as any single person, and far earlier than any but Samuel Adams, to foster the revolutionary spirit in Massachusetts. On the other hand, his career, which ended in mental breakdown, was marked by a series of bewildering tergiversations and apparent betrayals that perplexed friends and enemies alike. This behavior has never been explained.

Historians have been right to dismiss the assumptions of contemporaries that Otis was motivated simply by disappointment on behalf of his father. The self-destructiveness of his political reversals confirms the impression that he struggled selflessly over the key issues of the day. Nevertheless, "the explosive quality" of Otis's opposition to Hutchinson, writes Hugh F. Bell, "and its consequent disruption of Massachusetts politics for a decade, is an intriguing puzzle, the solution of which would contribute greatly toward an understanding of the eventual breakdown of imperial relationships in New England." Moreover, as Merrill Jensen has written, Otis's fight with Bernard and Hutchinson was "so entwined with rising opposition to British policies that it is impossible to separate one from the other."[4]

Within ten years of his threat to set the province in flames, Otis, after several years of increasingly erratic behavior, began to act so bizarrely in public that his family saw fit to remove him to the country, where he could be looked after by a farmer and his wife. Tradition had it that he suffered a mental collapse after a political enemy beat him on the head with a cane. But it now appears that the once famous fight, which Otis himself started, though it resulted in a cut on the forehead, did not bring about Otis's mental illness. If this was the case, then there are important implications for the beginnings of the American Revolution in Massachusetts. For if Otis's final breakdown was not brought about by a beating in 1769, then it is likely that, as many contemporaries charged, he was mentally disturbed earlier in the 1760s. This was the period during which he laid the "Foundations," as

James Otis

John Adams put it, of the American Revolution, though not without undergoing the unaccountable reversals that exasperated his own party as much as the government. "The chief consistency in his career," it has been suggested, "was his hatred of Thomas Hutchinson." And, indeed, he both began and ended his patriot activities with reference to Hutchinson.[5]

Before the chief justiceship came up, both Otis and his father were "friends to government," with no reason to dislike Hutchinson. According to an anecdote about Otis as a young lawyer—one meant, like Washington's cherry tree story, to illustrate his honesty—he is supposed to have been congratulated by Hutchinson for a selfless gesture. Halfway through a case, Otis, realizing that his client was pressing a trumped up complaint, refused to go on. The judge, Hutchinson himself, "without knowing at the time, the particular reasons for Otis's proceeding [to drop the case], paid him some natural compliments on his frank and manly conduct, and took the occasion to remark, how much time might be saved, if it were generally imitated.[6]

Although Hutchinson was the constant in Otis's politics, Colonel Otis, his father, was the precipitant. The reiterated charges of contemporaries that the colonel's disappointment explained his son's actions give the impression of a close father-son relationship. Yet despite Otis's fierce concern that his father be appointed to the court, their relationship was anything but warm. Their letters to one another during the 1740s and the 1750s have a uniformly businesslike tone. Beginning when Otis was at college from 1739 to 1743, he painstakingly detailed for his father all his expenses, and sent along the receipts. To be sure, New England youths commonly were brought up to appreciate thrift. But this did not necessarily exclude intimacy of feeling or the expression of hopes, fears, and convictions, as in this case. After Otis became a lawyer, money remained the chief subject between him and his father. As they exchanged business letters about the family interests, neither correspondent expressed any more intimacy than they would have, had the two been unrelated partners.[7]

As a beginning lawyer in Plymouth, Otis sometimes found himself in competition for clients with his father in nearby Barnstable, and sometimes had to oppose him in court. Though at the outset he won two cases in which they were opposing attorneys, he was not able to accumulate enough clients to support himself. Eventually he was forced to move to Boston, where he was reduced to serving as his father's "factotum."

Colonel James Otis appears to have mistreated all of his sons. "The image of the old man projected by the sons is that of an awesome, overbearing, and jealous *pater familias* intent upon retaining control." The colonel was a provincial in every sense of the word—in family relations, business, and politics. He painstakingly built a fortune through hard work and sharp dealing in a seemingly infinite number of transactions. Beginning as a clerk and general overseer for his already well-established mercantile and farming family, for twenty years he turned small profits in wools, foodstuffs, fish, pork, lumber, rum, manufactured goods, silks, satins, linen, and ribbons. Part of the time he appears to have been the local shoemaker.[8] When he turned to legal work, he succeeded by accumulating a large number of small fees. Again it was a matter of adding penny to penny, and again the colonel (his title came from a militia appointment during this period) made a good deal of money.

Through family connections the colonel began to accumulate appointive offices in Barnstable, and uncontestedly gained election to the legislature in 1745. He quickly became an ally of Governor Shirley, and soon came to be known as his henchman. In tandem with Hutchinson in the council, or upper house of the legislature, he engineered the appointment of William Bollan, the governor's son-in-law, as province agent to London. During the Seven Years War, like Hutchinson and Peter Oliver, with whom he also was friendly, he made money by supplying the army. More obviously grasping than they, he did not scruple to take a leading role in recruiting soldiers in his native Barnstable while at the same time securing the contract to outfit them.

The colonel's problems began in 1757 when he resigned his lower-house seat in order to make himself available for election to the council. When his attempt failed, he found himself both out of province office and without influence in the new administration of Governor Pownall. When he tried for council election in 1759 his opponents, who were of Hutchinson's circle, again defeated him. Presumably referring to his numerous patronage appointments in Barnstable, they argued that he already had "too much Power." To make matters worse, at about the same time his business practices appear to have come under adverse scrutiny under Governor Pownall. In 1757, just after his first defeat for the council and in anticipation of the new Pownall administration, Colonel Otis wrote a memo recording a conversation about himself. Someone reported to him that in the council it had been predicted that "my Business Would then Be Effectually Done upon the new Governours comeing for Mr T Hutchinson and Mr Olliver would Be his advisers and that they had a Bad opinion of my Conduct and that Mr Hutchinson had said that I never Did Carry things while in the [General] Court By any merit But only By Doing Little Low Dirty things for Governor Shirley such as Persons of ~~merit~~ worth Refused to medle with and that Shirley made use of me only as a Tool for [their?] Purposes."[9] Much is revealed by this long sentence. Hutchinson and Oliver have come to disapprove of Colonel Otis partly out of aristocratic hauteur, no doubt, but partly out of a sense of political ethics as well. Colonel Otis does not deny their charges. Instead, he deals with what for another man might appear as a slur on his character strictly as a matter of prospective loss of "my Business."

Despite his cool response, the colonel had cause to feel the slur, and to resent it all the more for its evident accuracy. It was said that "for many Years" the colonel "almost idolized" Hutchinson. Whether or not this was so his frustration is easy to imagine when, bent on rising to Hutchinson's level of "~~merit~~ worth," he first failed to join him on the council, and then lost a place on the court to him. But what of the colonel's son? James Otis, Jr., took his father's side, of course, but only at some cost in consistency. For his own character and values made him appear more a son of Hutchinson than of the colonel. Like Hutchinson, the antiquarian and author of a history of Massachusetts, Otis was bookish. After college he spent a year and a half studying literature and philosophy before turning to the law under the tutelage of Jeremiah Gridley, the most demanding and decidedly the most philosophically minded lawyer in Massachusetts. Soon after Otis began in practice, his brother explained to their ever-demanding and complaining father that James was "Excusable" for not writing home. He was making up for "misspent time" by studying so intensely that "he Scarcsly allows himself time to Eat Drink or Sleep." (The brother's need to apologize for James when he was twenty-five years old and in practice for himself testifies to the colonel's ability to intimidate his sons.) During the years of rivalry with his father and thereafter, Otis sacrificed time that might have been spent on his business to write a book on Latin prosody, which he published, and another on Greek prosody, which remained in manuscript. Later, when difficult points of law arose, Otis's colleagues were able to consult the rare books in his library.[10]

By 1760 Otis was known as a learned, selfless, distinguished member of the bar, though perhaps something of an eccentric and trouble-maker as well. He appears to have cultivated a character directly at odds with his father's. For the colonel's ambition he substituted indifference to professional success, at times "almost completely" neglecting his law practice in favor of politics. For his father's slow accumulation of profit through many small transactions he substituted a broad, theoretical approach to the law (he was known particularly for brushing aside technicalities in favor of fundamental issues), and an unconcern over fees (as when he donated his services to defend some young people in trouble for public misbehavior). Whereas the colonel was a creature of patronage, his son made a name for himself as an orator and political writer. The Writs of Assistance case in 1761 first brought Otis prominence and election to the legislature. After this, though, rather than seeking additional offices as did the colonel, he twice made ostentatious displays of resigning his seat.[11]

When Otis launched his attacks on Hutchinson, he depicted the new chief justice as a man sunk in a mean ambitiousness just the opposite of his own high-mindedness. The striking fact about his characterization was that it was wrong. But if it did not fit Hutchinson, it applied very well to the colonel.[12] The younger Otis's leading charge against Hutchinson was that of self-enrichment through plural office holding—exactly what was being implied in saying that the colonel held too much power. The colonel's unabated accumulation of public offices throughout the 1760s occasioned acute and continuing embarrassment to his son. Under the circumstances it was natural for contemporaries in both political parties to conclude that Otis's fierce opposition to Hutchinson had to do with the colonel. Yet they did not realize, as it appears in retrospect, that Otis's campaign on his father's behalf concealed disapproval of the colonel.

Significantly, the years of Otis's lawyerly rivalry with his father coincided with a political alliance between the colonel and Hutchinson. In fact, it was on the basis of the colonel's support of a money bill authored by Hutchinson in 1749 that the Otises expected Hutchinson to stand aside if offered the chief justiceship in 1760. Years later Otis wrote of the connection between the two that "Col Otis for years made himself more enemies by espousing his Honor's interest, than by all the rest of his conduct in life." But Otis's first attacks on Hutchinson, though they referred to the money bill, never acknowledged the colonel's connection with it.[13]

Hutchinson by now had grown into a figure of political and social authority who was the equivalent, much in the manner of a king, of the father in a family. By 1760 he was lieutenant governor of the province, and had just served as acting governor while awaiting Bernard's arrival to replace Governor Shirley. At the same time he was a member of the governor's council, and was the newly appointed chief justice. When Otis stood up to argue the Writs of Assistance case before Chief Justice Hutchinson, he had to deal with the subject of kingly authority before a man who had come to represent for him both the legitimacy of authority in general and, by association, a father's betrayal of the paternal responsibility to be perfectly upright.

The Writs of Assistance were open warrants that authorized customs officials to search for smuggled goods. They had been in use for some time, but now Otis was challenging them on behalf of the merchants whose warehouses were being searched for smuggled goods. His case, a weak one, was directed against their constitutional legality, but his summation amounted to more than a legal argument. Delivered with impressive drama, it proved to be a political speech as well, and one with both personal and philosophical implications. Otis's ringing assertion that the writs violated fundamental law and were therefore void is a part of the drama of the American Revolution. "Then and there," wrote John Adams, "the child Independence was born." But another drama was played out in the writs courtroom at the same time—one concerning Otis's feelings toward Thomas Hutchinson.

Had Colonel Otis received the appointment that he coveted, his son would have been arguing before *him,* and very possibly on the side of the crown. This was because at the time of Hutchinson's appointment the younger Otis had held the position of deputy advocate general of this very court. In his argument he pointed this out. He recently had "renounced that office," he asserted, in order to switch from having to defend the writs to challenging them. But his motive for resigning cannot be established with certainty: it could as easily have been pique over Hutchinson's appointment as chief justice as a looking forward to the writs case.[14] Given Otis's passionate intertwining of the personal and the political, one would have to guess that both motives operated.

Before he turned to his constitutional argument Otis delivered a lengthy personal vindication. In it for the first time he claimed for himself a character distinctly unlike his father's. His remarks amounted to telling Hutchinson that James Otis, Jr., could not be despised on the grounds of venality and lack of principle. Out of "principle," Otis insisted, he had accepted and gone on to take "more pains" in this "popular cause" than he ever would take again. Furthermore, he now stood forth despite the fact that he had "raised much resentment." In other words, he had given up an office and gone over to the "popular" but weaker side despite certain loss of favor among Hutchinson's party and class. Furthermore, to his "dying day," Otis grandly asserted, he would argue his convictions "whether under a fee or not (for in such a cause I despise a fee)." That his resignation as an officer of this court resulted in his giving up far less income than was popularly thought only underlines his concern to depict himself as a figure of selfless, sacrificing principles.[15]

Remarkably, despite attacks on him for acting to elevate his father to office, Otis never was accused of self-seeking. His was a subjective, self-involved career, but one genuinely different in spirit from his father's. Thus, he had some right to the closing words of his writs oration: "Let the consequences be what they will, I am determined to proceed. The only principles of public conduct, that are worthy of a gentleman or a man, are to sacrifice estate, ease, health, and applause, and even life, to the sacred calls of his country. These manly sentiments, in private life, make the good citizen; in public life, the patriot and the hero."[16]

If the figure of Colonel Otis lay behind his son's opposition politics, and if Thomas Hutchinson was their object, then King George III became their operative symbol. For in the writs case Otis inaugurated his practice of bringing the monarchy into his arguments. By alluding to the new king's accession speech he cast the writs proceedings in the light of succession, legitimacy, and prerogative—the leading issues on which opposition to the royal party in England was based. The king had figured recently in Francis Bernard's accession speech on being sworn in as royal governor of Massachusetts. On that occasion Bernard had declared that the new "Sovereign is acknowledged to be the Maintainer of the Privileges of His Subjects, and the People are become the Supporters of the Prerogative of the Crown." It was this prerogative that Otis dedicated himself to attacking, sometimes in the person of the king, and sometimes in the more familiar persons of the governor and lieutenant governor.[17]

Following the Writs of Assistance argument Otis was elected in early 1761 to the lower house of the Massachusetts legislature for the first time. There he immediately joined with his father, long-time Speaker of the house, in opposition to Hutchinson and Governor Bernard. The first major issue to arise had to do with counterfeiting and coinage, and it soon developed into a private battle between the younger Otis and Hutchinson. The subject at hand, which included monetary theory concerning the relationship among gold, silver, and paper currency, retained a philosophical cast from the debates of the previous century—debates that had involved John Locke and, later, Newton. But as Miss Prism points out in Oscar Wilde's *The Importance of Being Earnest,* "even these metallic problems have their melodramatic side."

For Otis the unrevealed melodramatic side concerned the fact that his father and Hutchinson had joined together to pass the money bill of 1749. Now, when opposition arose to Governor Bernard's new proposals with regard to counterfeiting, Hutchinson published an article defending him. "I think," he wrote, referring to 1749, "I may be allowed to call myself the father of the present fixed medium." The currency question, it will be recalled, had been the basis of an entire party's resentment, and it was the reason frequently given by contemporaries for the destruction of Hutchinson's house. "It may even be," Clifford K. Shipton went so far as to speculate, that—as Hutchinson "came to believe"—the resentment of the easy-money or inflationist party "was the decisive factor in bringing on the Revolution in Massachusetts." When, just as his article was about to appear, Hutchinson jokingly remarked to Otis that its contents had cut out some work for him, he spoke better than he knew, for Otis answered him in two remarkable essays of his own.

In the first of these Otis began with a note depicting his argument with Hutchinson in heraldic terms. He had been afforded the rare opportunity of "entering the List with a Gentleman . . . much One's Superior." This was "certainly very tempting." Hutchinson, he declared, had done him the "Honour" of issuing a "personal challenge," and he proposed to take up the gage. Hutchinson's little joke before publication implied, of course, no such challenge, and the currency questions at hand certainly did not call for the personal tone of Otis's articles. It was in these articles that Otis repeatedly mentioned the currency bill of 1749, held Hutchinson responsible for it, and yet never mentioned Colonel Otis's involvement, much less the fact that the colonel had claimed the chief justiceship in reward for his support of the bill.[18] Otis was content to accept Hutchinson as the "father" of the bill, and to direct his attack solely at him.

The following year, 1762, Otis mounted a campaign against William Bollan, the colonial agent in Britain. This made some sense if Otis wished to embarrass the governor's party, which for years had maintained Bollan in his position. But Otis's intensity seemed excessive to contemporaries. Furthermore, Otis leveled the "curious charge" that Bollan had attempted to undermine Congregationalism in Massachusetts. This was the first hint of the religious issue that the patriots later exploited, and to which the crowds, especially, responded. When questioned about his peculiar opposition to Bollan, whose removal he eventually secured, Otis admitted his unconcern either with Bollan or the religious issue (personally, Otis appears to have been a "rationalist," or agnostic). "But," he said, "I hate the L[ieutenant] G[overnor] should prevail in any thing."[19] Once again, though, there was a more private motive involved. For Bollan was Governor Shirley's son-in-law, and had originally been appointed through the combined influence of Hutchinson and Colonel Otis. Bollan was part of the system of nepotism in which the colonel was entangled and against which, on a higher level, the younger Otis directed much of his energy during the 1760s.

There now commenced the tergiversations for which Otis became famous. Each authority who has written on his career tends to single out one of these as mysterious, while dismissing the rest. Otis is said inexplicably to have made peace with the administration in 1762, in 1763, in 1765, or 1767, but in whichever case for a short time only. The first truce, which lasted for a few months, came soon after Otis had established himself as leader of the opposition, and it elicited considerable surprise. As Hutchinson later explained, Governor Bernard "flattered himself that he should be able to reconcile to him, both father and son." He began by arranging government appointments for both the colonel and Otis's brother, Joseph. Otis apparently responded by voting in favor of a bill deeding public land to Governor Bernard; then, after the appointments went through, he returned to the opposition. It is unlikely that this was a simple case of nepotism. Otis typically would have had a higher reason for his vote, though he might not have recognized the process of rationalization that lay behind it. It is possible that at the same time he was attempting to get at Hutchinson by splitting him away from Bernard.[20] Whatever the reason, had Otis been a calculating politician he would hardly have timed his reconciliation with Bernard so obviously, nor have broken it as precipitously as he did.

The obscure, bizarre incident with which Otis recommenced his opposition indirectly involved his father once again. The office that the colonel had just won was none other than the seat in the council he had coveted in 1757. On finally gaining it in 1762 he resigned his seat in the lower house, which replaced him as Speaker with Timothy Ruggles, a member of the court party. Otis, in Judge Peter Oliver's description, "interested himself most infamously" to keep Ruggles from the post, though as far as anyone could tell he had no reason to oppose the man.

When John Adams admitted to Judge Oliver that Otis had delivered a "distracted Speech" on Ruggles, but asserted that he nevertheless continued to respect his talents, Oliver replied pointedly, "I have known him these 20 Years and I have no opinion [that is, no good opinion] of his Head or his Heart. If Bedlamism is a Talent he has it in Perfection." This implication that Otis was mad in 1762 came from a relative of Hutchinson and a future loyalist. It would not be long before charges of madness came to be leveled against one another by loyalists and patriots alike—a circumstance that was not surprising, given the times. Modern psychology affirms that divisions in the state portend both divisions in families and disturbances within individuals.[21]

Yet Oliver's slur was not the only hint of early mental instability in Otis. At a meeting of the Massachusetts Historical Society in 1858, a Mr. Savage presented a letter from Otis's brother Samuel to their father that "contained evidence of the existence of a tendency to insanity in the younger Otis, which manifested itself at an early period of his life." Unfortunately, this letter was never printed, and it appears to have disappeared. Other youthful portents of Otis's later behavior exist, though all are based on hearsay evidence. During a college vacation, for example, Otis is supposed to have played the violin for a group of friends to dance by. The party took place at "his father's house." After the dancers "were fairly engaged, he [Otis] suddenly stopped and holding up his fiddle and bow, exclaimed 'So Orpheus fiddled, and so danced the brutes!' and then tossing aside the instrument, rushed into the garden." Whether or not Oliver had this incident in mind, Otis seems to have shown signs of instability before and during 1762.[22]

The striking feature of Otis's politics from this point forward was his shifting back and forth from opposition to cooperation with the incumbent administration. As Oliver noted, Otis's chief obsession was with Hutchinson, whom he denounced and praised by turns: "He will one Time say of the Lieutenant Governor, that he had rather have him than any Man he knows, in any one office, and the next Hour will represent him as the greatest Tyrant, and most despicable Creature living." For a while in 1762 and 1763 Otis's changeableness appears to have phased in three- or four-month intervals, leaving contemporaries and later historians alike quite unable to make sense of his politics. But the point is that, with Otis, politics and his obsession with Hutchinson ran along together. And in both of these Colonel Otis was never far in the background, as Oliver also noted.[23] Eventually politics, Hutchinson, and the colonel came together late in 1762.

In October of that year Otis wrote a private letter containing his most complete version of Hutchinson's infamy. He began by distinguishing the conservative from the radical party in Massachusetts, designating the conservatives as the "court" party. This accords well enough with modern understanding of the "Tory" or "government" faction of the time. But Otis also called this faction the "church party" and, referring to the previous governor, "the Shirlean faction." Colonel Otis, of course, had been nothing if not a Shirlean. As usual, Otis did not mention his father. But his letter went on to give an account of local politics that made Hutchinson responsible for the moral decline of the Shirley party—the charge brought by Hutchinson against Colonel Otis—with the result, presumably, that upright men like the Otises were forced to leave the party:

> At the head of this party [Otis wrote] is the Lieutenant Governor who by the superficial arts of intrigue, rather than by any solid parts, by cringing to Governors and pushing arbitrary measures [the typical charge brought against Colonel Otis, never Hutchinson], has so far recommended himself to Mr. Shirley and to our present Governor that by their means, tho' he was bred a merchant, he is now President of the Council, Chief Justice of the Province, Lieut. General and Captain of castle William, the Capital fortress in the Province, [and] Judge of the Probate of Wills for the County of Suffolk, the first County in the Province.[24]

Here, attributed to Hutchinson, are the colonel's toadyism, plural office holding, and even his merchant's lack of preparation for the Superior Court. (Hutchinson, in fact, had had nearly ten years of experience as a judge, albeit in a lower court, even though, unlike the colonel, he had never practiced as a lawyer.)

In contrast to his treatment of Hutchinson, Otis made no such sweeping condemnations of Governor Bernard, the man directly responsible both for the colonel's disappointment and, presumably, the affairs of the colony. For the most part, Otis's opposition to Bernard took the form of attacks on Hutchinson. Then, in 1762, Otis shifted his attack to yet another substitute figure of authority: the king. The tract in which he did so, *A Vindication of the Conduct of the House of Representatives,* is generally regarded as his sanest and most influential work. It has been called "one of the earliest and broadest statements of the principles" of the American Revolution. Beginning as a protest against executive incursion on the right of the legislature to control tax money, it expanded into a statement of the fundamental rights and equality of all men. Yet this essay had in it an element of the bizarre as well. The local history of the *Vindication,* in particular, throws an odd light on the essay's constitutional arguments. These, it develops, concerned not so much the House of Representatives as Otis himself.

In 1762 the governor requested the House's approval of a small military expenditure authorized by him during its usual long recess. Otis protested that approval would be tantamount to surrendering the House's prerogative over money matters. Such jealousy of legislative prerogative was an old story both in England and the colonies, so it was not surprising that the House agreed with Otis and authorized him to write a remonstrance to the governor. In this paper, which he read to the House for its approval, Otis elevated the issue to one of tyranny. It would be "of little consequence to the people," he declared, "whether they were subject to George, or Lewis, the king of Great Britain, or the French king, if both were arbitrary, as both would be, if both could levy taxes without Parliament." When this passage was heard, its familiar use of the king's name shocked one member into exclaiming, "Treason! Treason!"[25]

The reaction was not inappropriate, given the political-symbolic climate of the day. George III had already made clear his intention to reassert kingly prerogative, and the liberty party in England had begun to oppose him. Wherever the king's political powers were questioned the issue linked itself intimately with his ceremonial function. Thus, in 1762 one's manner of addressing the king had not only its age-old symbolic importance, but political overtones as well. In England John Wilkes was conducting his campaign against prerogative by indiscretions similar to Otis's use of first names. Wilkes "introduced for the first time into political discussions the practice of printing the names of the chief persons in the State at full length instead of indicating them merely by initials."[26] Wilkes presently overstepped the unspoken bounds of permissible criticism of the king just as Otis overstepped them in America. In Otis's case the shock effect of his usage was increased by the fact that he was arguing in the especially sensitive area of prerogative. The governor, like the member of the House who cried "Treason!" promptly disapproved of the passage in question as insulting to the king.

In response, Otis wrote his *Vindication.* His purpose, he declared, was to "clear from ambiguity" his reputedly "seditious, rebellious and traitorous" remarks, which were in fact "very . . . harmless." Yet in defending himself Otis but increased the impression of insolence. With pointed wit he alternated propositions like "God made all men naturally equal" with pious declarations such as "The king of Great Britain is the best as well as the most glorious monarch upon the globe, and his subjects the happiest in the universe." One critic, in an analysis that calls to mind Wilkes's Number 45 of the *North Briton,* has called the essay "an avowal of loyalty to the king so hyperbolical as to suggest its dangerous nearness to irony." Calculatedly insolent, Otis repeated his bandying about of the first names of kings. Then, escalating his use of first names in the legislature, he remarked that it was immaterial what kings are called: the monarchs of Europe, including George III, might as well be referred to as *"Tom, Dick or Harry."*[27]

Otis's second truce with the Bernard administration came in 1763, a year after the first. It, too, coincided with appointments for Colonel Otis: two Barnstable judgeships which he received in October. The king again became "the best and greatest Prince in the world," and Otis proposed to reconcile the two parties in the present dispute over prerogative. "Liberty and prerogative," he could prove, were "the same." These were the two warring principles to which Otis alternately devoted himself. He planned three essays that would finally settle the matter and announced them in an advertisement. "The last" of these, he promised, "will be dedicated to the KING." His own interest in politics was selfless, Otis indicated, as for the second time he announced his retirement from the legislature.[28]

Not surprisingly, none of the promised essays ever appeared. A month later Otis resumed his opposition, recommencing as usual with Hutchinson. By this time the other party's references to Otis as mentally disturbed had become more frequent, along with his denials. Jonathan Sewall referred to his "mad rant," and reported Otis's own servant remarking, "There goes the crazy Man." Another administration writer, possibly referring to yet another reversal on Otis's part, asked "whether a certain Writer who advertised publishing a Book to be dedicated to the King, was *raving Mad,* either at the Time of Writing, or at the Burning of his Copy?" The same writer, apparently referring to one of Otis's unaccountable departures, this time from the legislature, asked "whether it was Madness when a certain Gentleman abruptly left a great Assembly for reasons known only to Self-sufficiency? Whether his early and humble Return was an Evidence of the Return of his Senses?"[29] Once again this was political rhetoric. And yet Otis seems to have been the political figure most consistently attacked in these terms, which become suggestive in light of his later behavior.

Otis began his new antigovernment campaign by publishing an article intended to dispel the popularly accepted view that his was a politics of resentment on behalf of his father. He admitted the resentment but denied that it ruled all his actions. As to the charge that he had threatened to "set the province in a flame," he had no recollection of it. He vehemently denied all charges against himself, then dilated on his resentment at Hutchinson's failure to answer a letter—the one Otis had carried to him from the colonel on the subject of the chief justiceship. As when he had imagined a formal, "personal challenge" in Hutchinson's banter, Otis now imagined an insult in Hutchinson's supposed neglect of a formality—toward the colonel, not himself. (In contrast to his own democratic-familiar use of royal first names, Otis was demanding the strictest observance of courtesy on Hutchinson's part.)

In his article Otis revealed more than he realized with his continued attitude of awe toward Hutchinson's public character. The lieutenant governor was in effect the American prime minister, he pointed out, and deserved to be called the *"Father of his Country."* As for his own father, Otis had to admit that the colonel had solicited for an appointment to the Superior Court—something Hutchinson had never done. This admission inadvertently contrasted with Otis's own proud claim elsewhere in his article that "I never asked a Court Favour."[30]

For the first time Hutchinson answered directly, giving his own account of his and Otis's meetings in 1760, and arguing convincingly that he had neither intended nor given insult in omitting a letter to the colonel after speaking with his son. Otis answered in turn, making this the most personal newspaper debate of the period. Once again he exposed his deeper feelings, both with his wit and his arguments. His first piece, he now protested, "was written in the spirit of love and meekness, and so shall this be." This ironic self-abasement was followed by a confession containing further irony. Hutchinson's reply had given him, Otis wrote, "imaginations" of being "again on a footing [of equality] with his Honor," whose grandeur contrasted with his own humble estate.[31] The irony of these elaborate terms of address, which were almost identical to Otis's first newspaper attack on Hutchinson in 1761, cannot disguise a genuine awe of Hutchinson.

A few days later, with regard to Otis's ostensibly conciliatory second essay, Hutchinson remarked with characteristic blandness and insight that Otis "professes to have buried the hatchet every three or four months," but that whenever he is given offense, "instead of returning the affront to the person from whom he received it, he wreaks all his malice and revenge upon me." Significantly, Colonel Otis harbored no such emotional resentment. In fact the colonel attempted to reach an understanding with Hutchinson. "I told him," Hutchinson wrote of the colonel's approach,

> he could not be insensible of the injurious treatment I had received from his son and that the Monday before he had published the most virulent piece which had ever appeared [the one just quoted, begun "in the spirit of love and meekness"], but if he would desist and only treat me with common justice and civility I would forgive and forget everything that was past. He replied it was generous; and yet his son has gone on in the same way ever since, and have no reason to think the father dislikes it.[32]

The modern debate over Otis's reversals passes over those of 1762 and 1763 to concentrate on the following two years, 1764 and 1765. Chiefly, this debate involves his contradictory responses to the Stamp Act, and the controversy that these aroused. The problem then and since has been one of determining just what Otis meant in his essays on the Stamp Act. His apparent change of opinion from opposition to acceptance of the act resulted in impassioned resentment against him. Historians have both defended him as consistent and found him guilty as charged. In question are three works: *The Rights of the British Colonies Asserted and Proved* (1764), *A Vindication of the British Colonies* (1765), and *Brief Remarks on the Defence of the Halifax Libel, on the British-American Colonies* (1765). The first two preceded the arrival of news that the Stamp Act had been voted into effect, but recognized the likelihood of passage. Stripped of the complexities of the argument, the charge against Otis was that in 1764 he denied Parliament's right to tax the colonies, and then recanted in his two essays of 1765. One modern scholar has concluded that the essays of 1765 show not merely the "wavering" and "retreat" with which Otis was charged at the time, "but a complete defection on constitutional issues."[33]

But the problems go further than this, for taken by itself the 1764 essay, *The Rights of the British Colonies,* has itself been called "confused and contradictory." Bernard Bailyn has responded that "properly understood, the [*Rights*] . . . is not self-contradictory, nor did Otis repudiate it [in the essays of 1765]." Yet Bailyn vividly describes the "jumbled," erratic composition of the *Rights* and its frequent digressions. And he summarizes Otis's argument as follows: "Thus Parliament can do anything, but there are some things it cannot do. It is hardly surprising that Otis's contemporaries were confused." It should be added that in the *Rights* Otis was characteristically ambivalent in expressing both awe and contempt for authority. Even as he challenged Parliament's right to tax he wrote with filial piety, "If I have one ambitious wish, 'tis to see Great-Britain at the head of the world, and to see my King, under God, the father of mankind."[34] Despite its problems of content and tone, the *Rights* clearly challenged Parliament. On the other hand, the essays that followed in 1765 undoubtedly continued his pattern of vacillation toward authority.

Otis's subject in both 1764 and 1765 continued to be that of prerogative, with Parliament replacing the lieutenant governor, governor, and king as the focus of the question. And, just as from 1761 to 1763, the patriot responses to Otis were admiring so long as he seemed to challenge authority, then outraged when he seemed to abandon his position. The administration sensed another truce; some later historians found reasons for the reversals; other historians deny that any reversals took place at all.[35]

The *Rights* was a sober response to news from England of impending taxes: "of all [Otis's] political writings, this is the most sedate." The essays of 1765, in contrast, were responses to a defender of

Parliament. Their tone is personal and often hysterical, making the political argument more difficult to abstract. These later two essays replied to newspaper attacks by Martin Howard, a loyalist of Newport, Rhode Island. Howard, writing as a "Gentleman at Halifax," very ably exposed the ambivalences of the 1764 *Rights* in regard to both content and tone. He charged Otis with making contradictory assertions about Parliamentary authority, and he identified Otis's characteristic tone of menace. For example, it was equivalent to "sedition," Howard pointed out, for Otis to compare the present situation with 1649—the year in which Charles I had been beheaded. Howard ridiculed Otis for his "stile," his "diction," and his organization—all under the ironic pretense of praising the *Rights.*[36]

As it grew clear during 1765 that the Stamp Act would certainly go into effect, opposition to it changed from argument against something proposed, to preparations for actual resistance. If Otis did recant in his replies to Martin Howard, he may, as it has been suggested, have been retreating in the face of the likelihood that his position could lead to violence. Howard subsequently explained Otis's apostasy as a reaction to the unfavorable reception given the *Rights* in England.[37] Howard's attack, and the fact that it made explicit Otis's veiled threats to the king, proved especially disturbing to Otis, though he protested most vehemently at what appeared to be a relatively mild sally.

Howard had scoffed at Otis's resort to the familiar argument that the colonists could not properly be taxed as long as they had no direct representation in Parliament. This oft-repeated maxim, he wrote, "like the song of *Lillibullero,* has made all the mischief in the colonies." It was in his anger at this passage that Otis, in the *Vindication of the British Colonies,* his first essay of 1765, appeared to retreat from his constitutional position. Quoting Howard's sentence, Otis replied that the colonies were bound by acts of Parliament, that this was "implied in the idea of a supreme sovereign power," and "if the parliament had not such authority, the colonies would be independent, which none but rebels, fools or madmen, will contend for. God forbid these colonies should ever prove undutifull to their mother country! . . . America would be a meer shambles of blood and confusion." That Howard's mention of "Lillibullero" conjured up for Otis a terrifying vision of revolution would not have surprised contemporaries. For this army marching song retained vivid associations with the revolution and overthrow of King James in 1688. By its reputation it had "sung a king out of three kingdoms."[38]

Earlier in the *Vindication* Otis expressed not his horror at the ingrate child, revolution, toward the mother country, but an equal and opposite fear of the unrestrained power of the father over the son. He did so by way of illustrating the doctrine of supreme, sovereign power through the paternal analogy. The king is as the father of a family, for whose children his "unbounded will" is "law." Here Otis quoted the political theorist, Filmer, on the absolute power of a father, twice repeating Filmer's illustration of a father's ancient right to "castrate" his children. The second time Otis quoted this he added italics and inserted a parenthesis so that the example read: "whereupon we find the power of *castrating,* and making eunuchs (for singing songs like Lillibullero, &c.) much in use in old times." In alternately conjuring up the overthrowing son and the castrating father, Otis expressed his own contradictory attitudes toward authority at the same time as he participated in, or perhaps helped to inaugurate, a style of literary protest that has been called "Whig Sentimentalism." In plays, essays, and cartoons beginning at the time of the Stamp Act this style shared both Otis's tone of hysteria and his fascination with parental neglect—the latter expressed in the lopping off of parts of the body. As early as 1763 Otis had imagined "the commonwealth" with "an army of Banditti . . . encamped round about and a strong party of Patricides cutting out her bowels."[39]

Martin Howard, in a *Defence* of his "Gentleman at Halifax" letter, objected to the spirit of disrespect toward authority manifested by Otis (and others), but also pointed out Otis's ambivalence. For despite a savage attack on Howard for supporting Parliament, Otis had reversed himself in the *Vindication* by proclaiming the authority of Parliament with "the zeal of a new convert." In a fury, Otis replied a second time, with his *Brief Remarks on the Defence of the Halifax Libel.* He now insisted that all his writings were consistent. However, when he failed to renounce explicitly the doctrine of Parliamentary supremacy, "the rage against him in the town of Boston seemed to be without bounds," and Otis was called "a reprobate, an apostate, and a traitor, in every street in Boston."[40]

Clifford K. Shipton has written that Otis's two replies to Martin Howard "in their confusion and violence show the failing of his mind."[41] Certainly the argument in the second of these, the *Brief Re-*

marks, can hardly be followed. It would require a separate study to explain all the allusions, latinisms, expletives, and verses that appear in this piece in connection with denunciation of Martin Howard. The references to "Lillibullero" are especially obscure, though it is clear that the intent is to label Howard as a rebel-like singer of this song. Despite such diversions and despite the obscurities of the piece, its contemporaries thought they understood Otis quite well. On the one hand the patriots took offense at Otis's support of Parliament, while on the other hand Governor Bernard took this support as a sign of his "sincere" repudiation of the oppositionist position he had taken in 1764.

In "Sackcloth & ashes" Otis, in Bernard's view, was begging forgiveness "in humblest Manner" for the "liberties" he had taken with Parliament in his *Rights of the Colonies.* With regard to the constitutional question Bernard no doubt had in mind Otis's declaration, "I have not a syllable to say against the jurisdiction or authority of parliament, never having entertained the least doubt of it, nor to my remembrance ever expressed any." The governor presumably was further pleased when Otis refused "to say a single" word against the Stamp Act: "I humbly, dutifully, and loyally presume . . . that the supreme legislative of Great-Britain do, and must know infinitely better what they are about and intend, than any without doors."[42]

In the understandably ignored bombastic part of his reply to Martin Howard, far from being humble Otis reached a height of rhetorical excess, expressing himself in his by now habitual terms of familial disorder and violence. To "the wisdom and goodness of our most gracious Sovereign" and his supporters he contrasted the attitude of the Halifax gentleman, Martin Howard: he, not Otis, was the true rebel. Whereas other loyalist defenders of the administration, one of whom had shown the "tenderness of a parent" in his manner, deserved to be honored, Martin Howard displayed "the rage malice and fury of an Orestes, tearing out the bowels of his mother, stabbing his sister, killing his own sons and daughters, and plucking out his own eyes." Not content with this evocation of filial revolt gone wild, Otis once again evoked the Pretender. Howard and his friends were a crew of "Jacobites [that is, followers of the Pretender] & Jew jobbers." They were a "little, dirty, drinking, drabbing, contaminated knot of thieves, beggars and transports, or the worthy descendants of such, collected from the four winds of the earth, and made up of Turks, Jews and other Infidels, with a few renegado Christians & Catholics."[43]

In this second reply to Howard, denunciation replaced argument. And soon denunciation itself broke off abruptly—at a significant point and in a suggestive way. Howard had brought up the old question of Otis's addressing the European monarchs by their first names, a usage he labeled treasonous in intent. Otis paused over this accusation to complain of being himself ill treated: "The humanity and philanthropy of this attack [by Howard] on a gentleman [Otis] who has been long in a very ill state of health, and now unable to answer for himself, is very remarkable."[44] Since Otis was writing anonymously, he was able formally to deny being the one who had misappropriated the king's name. But his identity was obvious. His complaint of ill health, therefore, rings true psychologically. One can hardly avoid the conclusion that Otis railed at Martin Howard principally for making explicit his own inner conflict between obedience to and defiance of authority.

Despite his two attacks on Howard, Otis proved unable to allay charges that he was a backslider, and as a result he stood to lose his seat in the legislature. By good fortune, though, it seems that he was saved politically by a Tory attack on him in the form of a scurrilous poem that appeared just before election day. This served to restore his radical credentials and led to his reelection and eventual appointment to the Stamp Act Congress in New York. Why this poem, only one attack among many, should have had the power to reverse Otis's fortunes has never been explained. The answer probably lies in its connection with the Martin Howard exchange, to which it alluded with its title, "Jemmibullero." The poem's author, Samuel Waterhouse, showed a devastating insight into Otis's ideas and a close familiarity with his character and history, along with an awareness of the degree to which Otis had been disturbed by Martin Howard's allusion to "Lillibullero." "Jemmy," as well as being a nickname for "James," was a "popular derisive epithet" of the time. It had appeared in *The Beggar's Opera,* where it designated a turncoat. The appellation had been applied to Otis before (as noted by Howard) and it stuck to Otis henceforward. In "Jemmibullero" Waterhouse's refrain, "tititumti, tumtititi, tititumti, tee," was a joke on Otis's having published a treatise on prosody. The subtitle, "A Fragment of an Ode of Orpheus," may have referred to the violin-playing incident in Otis's youth when, before abandoning his friends, he had mentioned Orpheus.[45]

With equally pointed insult, Waterhouse enforced the popular notion that Otis's political actions could be traced to his father: "So

Jemmy rail'd at *upper folks* while Jemmy's DAD was out,/But Jemmy's DAD has now *a place,* so Jemmy's turn'd about." Waterhouse called Otis a "madman" as well. He also inserted a line that may clarify Otis's reference to his ill health in the *Brief Remarks:* "And Jemmy *pleads* his bloody nose when quarrels he wou'd settle!" Otis had been twitted for "the aptness of thy nose to bleed" in an anonymous newspaper attack in 1763. And a few months after the appearance of "Jemmibullero" the colonel reported that James suffered "a Fitt of Bleeding of the Nose which was Troublesom Some days." Frequent nosebleeds, presumably the symptom of his ill health that Otis referred to, appear as a suitable accompaniment to his violent temper. His indirect reference to them when accused of treason suggests that in his mind the symptom was connected with revolt against authority.[46]

That the use of the tune "Lillibullero" should have coincided with a crisis in Otis's fortunes indicates the heightened awareness of political symbolism that he shared with his opponents. A look at the lyrics of this well-known old revolutionary tune reveals the source of its contemporary applicability. Rather than being directed against its actual object, King James, the song is supposed to be sung in a stage Irish accent by one of the king's supporters. Unwittingly this supporter mocks both himself and the king. He is anticipating the arrival in Ireland of James's deputy, Talbot, in 1687, the year before the English Revolution. With Talbot's aid, along with a "dispence ... from de Pope," the singer and his fellow Irishmen will "hang Magna Charta and dem [Protestants] in a rope." Talbot's supporters "shall have commissions gillore" while the Protestants will be forced to convert to Catholicism.

The situation in the Massachusetts Bay colony, like Ireland a "separated" part of the empire, was in 1765 similar in outline. The king had sent over Bernard as governor, and in the eyes of Otis and his party improper customs commissions had been given out in the manner of Talbot. In addition, the patriots suspected a plot to install "popish" Episcopalianism in the colony. (Otis, especially, took up this religious fear.) The Massachusetts opposition to the king was expressed in tracts like Otis's, which, like "Lillibullero," instead of attacking His Majesty, accused others of being his enemies. Such men as Martin Howard supposedly proved themselves "patricides" and enemies of the king by supporting one of his deceiving ministers: Talbot in Ireland, Bernard or Hutchinson in America. In both Ireland and America, it may be said, the king was sung out of his dominion by an opposition that attacked not him, but his royal deputies.

When Martin Howard mentioned "Lillibullero" he did so to accuse *Otis* of rebellion. By the time Waterhouse published "Jemmibullero," the tune could serve to mock Otis as a false, ambiguous rebel: "And Jemmy is of this mind, & Jemmy is of that,/And Jemmy'd fain make something out, but Jemmy can't tell what." Waterhouse was right about Otis's ambiguity, which he characterized more accurately than he may have realized. For "Lillibullero" itself expressed ambiguity about the king, his governor, and revolution—the three subjects that engrossed Otis's existence. All of these could be seen in Otis's Stamp Act waverings, especially as punctuated by incidents concerning Thomas Hutchinson. To follow Otis's career from 1765 to 1770 is to describe a man of this mind and of that—one who, indeed, would fain make something out but can't tell what.

Early in 1765, as he leaned toward acquiescence in the Stamp Act, Otis voted to restore the salary for Hutchinson that he had voted to take away from him in 1762. During this period, John Adams later recalled, "there was appearance of coalition between Otis and Hutchinson." When the homes of Hutchinson and Martin Howard were wrecked in August 1765 and Otis was blamed, his "thorough detestation" of such violence was countered by his statement in public that "he knew for a fact that the whole idea of a Stamp Act had been hatched by Hutchinson and Bernard," and that (as Bernard reported him saying) he "knew the room (meaning in my House) the time & the Company when the Plan was settled."

Soon afterward Otis was sent to the Stamp Act Congress that met in New York City in fall 1765. Here, to everyone's surprise, he took positions in support of royal prerogative that were more conservative "than the most rabid of the Massachusetts Tories." As if in expiation for his behavior, on the day following his return from the Congress Otis attacked Hutchinson in print, using terms that he himself soon characterized as "acrimonious" and "ludicrous." He then delivered "a most inflammatory Harangue" at the town meeting, in which he "inveighed against the Lieutenant Governor in terms most suitable to have raised another Mob against him."[47]

In late 1765, as the public waited for news of repeal of the Stamp Act, Otis went through yet another bewildering series of reversals.

These came within a matter of months and days, just as in 1762 and 1763. A few days after his attack on Hutchinson he returned to denouncing Stamp Act mobs. In January 1766 he again denied Paliamentary authority in print. During the same month he said in conversation "that Parliament had a Right to tax the Colonies and he was a d——d fool who deny'd it, and that this People never would be quiet till we had a Council from Home, till our Charter was taken away, and till we had regular Troops quartered upon Us." Two months later, in April 1766, Bernard reported, "Otis has today been quite mad, and has declared that he heartily wishes the Stamp Act may not be repealed." These reversals were accompanied by new shifts of attitude toward Hutchinson and the administration.[48]

In April, a month after Bernard heard Otis oppose repeal, it was reported that Parliament had voted the Stamp Act out of existence. At this point Otis was able to bring his ambivalence toward the act into phase with the split in his king-governor feelings. For the Massachusetts House he prepared two committee documents: a reply to the governor's opening speech, and an address to the king. Both were responses to repeal, which had been officially announced by Bernard in his speech. The answer to the governor was insulting. But, as an early biographer noticed, the thanks to the king for repeal "glowed with the most affectionate loyalty; thereby placing in a strong light the difference of their [that is, the committee's but actually Otis's] feelings towards the sovereign, or 'his representative.' "[49]

From repeal of the Stamp Act in 1766 until 1770, Otis's public activities, which gradually diminished, focused largely on Hutchinson and prerogative. In 1768 Otis was present in the House of Representatives at a discussion of an allegedly libelous newspaper letter attacking Governor Bernard. Apparently stimulated by the letter's insult to authority, "Otis upon this Occasion," Bernard wrote, "behaved in the House like a Madman; he abused every one in Authority and especially the Council in the grossest Terms." When Hutchinson was put up for election to the council the same year, "our great incendiary," wrote Hutchinson, "like an enraged Daemon ran about the House." "In a fury," Otis, carrying "votes for my Competitor," cried, "Pensioner or no Pensioner [that is, was or was not Hutchinson a time-server of the English government?], a term which among Americans conveys a very odious Idea & upon a third trial prevailed against me." At about the same time, in his typical compensatory manner, Otis

wrote to England asserting the colonists' "loyalty to their king, and
. . . affection for the mother Country."[50]

By this time, over a year before the affray that was to take place
with Commissioner John Robinson, Otis was regularly displaying
rapid shifts from one side to the other on political questions, and from
obsequiousness to insolence toward individuals, especially Hutchinson.
He was, as John Adams had put it as early as 1765, "sometimes in Despondency, some times in a Rage." Once again his opponents heaped
contempt on him in satiric verses with titles such as "The Jemmiwil-
liad, An Ode" and "Jemmicumjunto, An Ode For the New-Year
1768."[51]

In 1769, after a House speech by a colleague taking the governor's side, Otis rose and declared, "Mr. Speaker, the liberty of this
country is gone forever! and I'll go after it." Then he once again
walked out of the legislature. Just two days before his fight with Robinson in September 1769, Otis, his logorrhea completely out of control, interrupted all attempts at conversation among a group of fellow
patriots. Before and after the fight he appeared publicly "in black
gloom." He "had ruined his Country," he said, but "had acted with a
good intention, & stretching forth his hand, cursed the day on which
he was born."[52]

On the day of the fight Otis and Robinson "met, alike prepared
with canes purchased that day at the same shop." After a brief struggle, during which Otis was cut on the head, they were parted by onlookers at the coffee shop to which they had come. Otis's wound had
no discernible effect on his already deteriorating mental condition.
Thus he was taking up much where he had left off when he appeared
at a lawyers' discussion group early in 1770 and rambled disconnec-
tedly for an hour trying to tell a simple anecdote. At one point on that
occasion he said that "he hoped he should never see T[homas] H[ut-
chinson] in Heaven." John Adams, who reported the incident in his
diary, feared he was "not in his perfect Mind," adding, "I fear, I
tremble, I mourn for the Man, and for his Country. Many others
mourne over him with Tears in their Eyes."[53]

Then, on January 29, 1770, Otis marched with Molineux at the
head of the crowd that confronted Hutchinson. (As recently as 1767
Otis had published his disapproval "of all tumultuous and riotous Proceedings.") At first Otis had refused to join the crowd. Then he
"made a speech . . . but no body could understand from what he said

whether he condemned or approved of the measure." Finally he joined the committee. When Hutchinson appeared to face the crowd he singled out Otis, saying that he was "greatly surprised to see him there, who could not be ignorant of the illegality of such proceedings." When his house had been destroyed in 1765, Hutchinson went on, by some of the very people he now saw before him, he had been in effect a private citizen, though lieutenant governor; this time he was the recently appointed acting governor. "I am now the representative of the greatest monarch upon earth," he warned them, "whose Majesty you affront in thus treating my person." The crime involved presumably was treason, the correct term for an attack on the king's highest representative, as Josiah Quincy had pointed out in the town meeting.[54]

The event that appears to have directly affected Otis's mental equilibrium was the funeral of the boy martyr, Christopher Seider. This display amounted to a vast projection of the Whig Sentimental vision of murderous authority that permeated Otis's attacks on loyalists. On the day of the funeral, John Adams reported that Otis "has been this afternoon raving Mad—raving vs Father, Wife Brother, Sister, Friend &c." From this point on he sank rapidly. He seems to have been drunk much of the time, and the object of jibes in the street.[55]

On March 16, 1770, "Mr. Otis got into a mad Freak to night & broke a great many windows in the Town House." A month later, on April 22, in a similar incident on the sabbath, "Mr. Otis behaved very madly, firing Guns out of his Window that Caused a Large Number of people to assemble about him."[56] It was after this second incident that his family removed him to the country. Yet even at this juncture Otis's actions contained an underlying political logic, for his attack on the Town House windows implied a coherent symbolism.

The Town House, or town hall, resembled London's Mansion House, which was the focus of many Wilkes demonstrations. At the first Stamp Act demonstration the crowd had marched through the Town House while the governor was presiding over a meeting of the province's Council. For years the building's windows had carried symbolic import, as was demonstrated by an incident in which Otis was involved in 1763. Just before one of Otis's attacks on Hutchinson in the Boston *Gazette* that year, a group of youths broke several windows at the Town House. Otis mentioned the incident in the course of his article (the one in which he took up for the first time Hutchinson's appointment as chief justice). A group of playful youths had acted up a bit, Otis wrote, at which the governor's council overreacted by issuing a proclamation. But this was a case of high spirits on Accession Day, a celebration already unduly restricted by old laws.

> It seems some of our Fathers took a strong aversion to bonfires, squibs and crackers [two kinds of exploding fireworks], in consequence of which the populace were refrained from those marks of loyalty on the anniversary of the King's accession, I think it was. Some of the little Boys and negroes vented their rage at this disappointment upon the lower windows in the Town-House. This affair was dress'd up in the proclamation [which similarly restricted the celebrations] in such a manner, that I fear a stranger would mistake us all for a parcel of Jacobites, it being impossible to find by the proclamation that loyalty misguided was the occasion of this loss of glass to the public.[57]

Otis's own breaking of these windows may have represented a demented return to the naughty defiance of the child who desecrates the edifices of authority. But it was precisely such childlike defiance that appeared in the many patriot demonstrations that were accompanied by children. Furthermore, in seizing on the misbehavior of the youths in 1763, Otis had displayed his genius for probing into the symbolic underpinnings of the state. For the celebration of the monarch's accession was in fact the origin of Guy Fawkes Day and Pope Day.

When Otis wrote that he was not certain what the exact occasion for celebration had been, he presumably was thinking that it was either Accession Day or the king's birthday. On both a spirit of revelry prevailed, and on both the Town House windows were illuminated at night. In this context Otis's familiar mention of "Jacobites," followers of the Pretender, summoned up the very figure of menace to the king that had been adapted to Pope Day celebrations by New Englanders.

Otis's own window-breaking contained one other element of symbolism implicit in the date on which it took place. Up until the previous year contemporaries could not have helped commenting that Otis was breaking windows on the eve of St. Patrick's Day. For until that year it had been a New England practice to combine the St. Patrick's holiday with celebration of the Stamp Act's repeal. The result was an amalgam similar to the results of combining Pope Day symbolism with opposition to the Stamp Act. Starting in 1770 the Boston Massacre replaced the celebration of repeal as Boston's annual March patriotic observance. But Otis appears to have assumed that the older celebration day would serve to express public emotion on a current issue as well—just as it had in the past. His intention, however, which was to reenact the patriot passion play as it had evolved since 1765, evidently went unnoticed in the aftermath of the Boston Massacre.

Yet another incident from Otis's past serves to indicate the sympathy that he felt with regard to the symbolism implicit in these origins. As a young lawyer he defended a second group of youths, this time in Plymouth, Massachusetts, after a frolic on Pope Day. In the traditional manner the young men of the town had forced homeowners to illuminate their windows, and then had gone on a window-breaking spree (presumably of unlit windows). Otis's biographer reports the story from family tradition: "Thinking the prosecution [of the young men] to have been illnatured and vindictive, [Otis] kindly engaged in their defence, exerted all his powers of humour and argument, described it as a common, annual frolic, undertaken without malice, and conducted without substantial injury; obtained their acquittal and refused all fees."[58]

Otis's own last frolic was followed by an act of contrition toward Thomas Hutchinson. With it Otis summarized his personal symbolism of revolt against king, father, and governor. After being removed to the country following his window-breaking and gun-firing in March and April 1770, Otis was allowed to wander about freely. In August, drunk and disheveled, he made his way to Hutchinson's summer house in Milton, Massachusetts. Acting Governor Hutchinson, ever understanding of his foes, had him shown in. Otis announced that he had come to apply to Hutchinson for protection. Then, as Hutchinson recalled it, in a disconnected way Otis referred to his ten-year campaign of vilification against Hutchinson: "God knows, clapping his hand to his heart, that I had no hand in it." This was followed, however, by a declaration that amounted to an apology for that campaign. Otis said that he now rested "in the peace of God and the king," and added that he considered Hutchinson, as governor, the "Representative of the King, and the King, as the Representative of God."[59] Unlike his patriot contemporaries, Otis, once faced with Hutchinson's elevation to the kingly authority of acting governor, no longer could oppose him. He challenged him at the head of a crowd and then suffered a breakdown. In his subsequent remorse he acknowledged Hutchinson's power and his own dependence by requesting "protection," and ended by proclaiming Hutchinson's religious, political, and fatherly legitimacy.

From this time forward Otis faded in and out of sanity, continuing to alternate his opinions so as to outrage everyone, especially his fellow patriots. In May 1771 he appeared to have recovered, and he returned to the legislature. The following month he opposed Samuel Adams and supported Hutchinson's "undoubted Right," or prerogative, to relocate the legislature. Hutchinson, Otis argued in his speech supporting him, was a "a good Man." Some thought Otis again "distracted," while others regarded this as a "Conversion to Toryism." (John Adams never changed his opinion that the reversal was a result of Hutchinson's having "destroyed" him.) By August Otis began to fade, and in December he had to be "bound hand and foot," placed in a post chaise, and driven away. He was well in 1772, when he again took the government side in the legislature, using "banter and ridicule" to dismiss John Adams's contention that Americans were in danger from a British ministerial conspiracy "to make them absolute slaves." Later in the same year, however, he supported a newspaper article attacking the king—possibly the most direct and potentially treasonous essay of its kind before 1776.[60]

Thus it continued through independence, which Otis opposed, then embraced. In 1775, while visiting his brother-in-law, he "behaved well till dinner, was almost done and then in the old way got up went off where I know not." He showed up at the battle of Bunker Hill with a borrowed gun and there "went among the flying Bullets." In July 1776 he petitioned the Revolutionary Massachusetts legislature for an amount of money due him, and referred to himself as "James Oates." Titus Oates was the madman who had set all England aflame in the seventeenth century with false reports about a popish plot against the king's life. Like him, Otis had feared that with the aid of the pope, a Pretender would invade England and overthrow the king—who in Otis's version would be rescued by fleeing to America. Otis's pun on his own name in July 1776 recalled the tradition of English revolutionary hysteria at the very moment of its apotheosis in America.[61]

A contemporary observed that Otis was always in a *"reverie* when he speaks of Majesty," and so it has been suggested that Otis suffered from an "overidealization of paternal authority," manifested especially in his regard for George III as the "father of Mankind." And indeed, throughout the Stamp Act crisis, Otis dealt with the defiance of kingly authority implicit in his position by protestations of "unbounded affection to His Majesty's Royal person and family." When Otis did oppose the king on the Stamp Act he spoke "in tears." And even then he adopted the popular view that "a wicked and unfeeling Minister has caused a People, the most loyal and affectionate that ever King was blessed with, to groan under the most insupportable Oppression." Repeatedly, Otis proclaimed himself "his majesty's liege, true and faithful subject." And a year after the Stamp Act's repeal he still felt that "his Majesty like a tender kind benevolent Father" had wished to draw a veil over the Stamp Act troubles.[62]

However, this genuine if exaggerated submission to the king was accompanied by equally extreme attacks on his ministers, Hutchinson in particular. Otis's repeated mentions of the Jacobites, the Pretender, and the English Revolutions of 1649 and 1688, furthermore, amounted to veiled threats of regicide. He used the technique throughout his political career. Thus, arguing against the Writs of Assistance, he pointedly warned that a similar exercise of arbitrary power had "cost one king of England his head and another his throne." And later, in 1768, he attacked Governor Bernard by praising Oliver Cromwell and voicing approval for the execution of King Charles.[63] Thus, Otis's submission to the king shielded a powerful antagonism that took the form of attacks on his surrogates.

On one occasion Otis expressed his feelings toward the king in a manner that carried a clue to his underlying ambivalence. He wished that the British "Island was sunk in the Sea, so that the King and his Family were Saved." Here, as when he imagined the king fleeing to America, he indulged in the typical "rescue fantasy" of childhood. It has been said that the child who thus imagines saving his family from danger harbors an "attitude of defiance" that outweighs his apparently tender feeling. Otis's version was really no exception, for the rescue fantasy "is commonly enough displaced onto the Emperor, the King, or any other great man." (One of the verses on the paper pyramid designed by Paul Revere to celebrate repeal of the Stamp Act invited the king to America should he ever be in danger from insurrection.)[64]

Otis's continuing, unresolved anger toward his father, whose career he tried to rescue, was transferred both to a governor and a king. Otis alternately attacked and paid deference to Hutchinson at the same time as he alternately swore allegiance to and attacked the king in veiled allusions—first to regicide, then to the sinking of the ship of state. In the course of his career as a patriot, and especially through his attacks on Hutchinson, Otis very substantially upset that ship. Then, remorsefully, he ended his career by proclaiming his allegiance to Hutchinson, and attempting to rescue the State by upholding the king's prerogative as it was invested in the royal governor.

CHAPTER FIVE

John Adams

W HEN JAMES OTIS DIED IN 1783 John Adams wrote to Otis's sister, Mercy Warren, from Paris: "It was with very Affecting Sentiments that I learned, the Death of Mr. Otis, my worthy Master." Twenty-five years earlier, Adams had decided to become a lawyer partly out of admiration for Otis, his elder by ten years and a leading figure among the lawyers of Massachusetts. During Adams's two years of legal study in Worcester, Massachusetts, his teacher held up Otis as "by far the most able, manly and commanding Character of his Age at the Bar."[1] On several counts Otis offered an ideal figure for emulation. Like Adams he came from a farm village and a family that had risen from humble beginnings to financial security and local prominence. His father, Colonel Otis, practiced the same trade as Deacon Adams—that of cordwainer, or shoemaker—then went into business, on to local politics, and finally into province politics. The colonel married well, had three sons, and sent his oldest, James, to Harvard College. Deacon Adams also grew prominent in local though never in province politics, while remaining a cordwainer and farmer. He, too, married well, had three sons, and sent his oldest, John, to Harvard College.

The oldest sons from both families were plump, studious, high-minded, and self-righteous. Each bore his father's name and the family honor with self-conscious earnestness. Adams, who became friendly with Otis after being admitted to the bar, started slowly as a lawyer in the late 1750s, emerging to success only about the time that Otis delivered his argument in the Writs of Assistance case. By then he regarded himself as Otis's "pupil."[2]

The Adams who attended the Writs case was a somewhat dreamy

young lawyer still in search of himself. As he sat taking notes on the arguments, he hardly displayed the ambitiousness that he frequently confessed to in his diary. There he dreamed of a "leap into fame": a single grand stroke of brilliance by which he would simultaneously serve the cause of mankind and make himself prominent in Massachusetts. Now, as he listened, Otis made just such a gesture: his address to the court was learned, passionate, self-sacrificing yet self-advertising. "His exertions on this single occasion," Adams later remarked, "secured him a commanding popularity" that "never deserted him."[3]

Above all, Adams viewed Otis's speech as a defiance of authority, not simply of the crown and Parliament, but more dramatically of Otis's mentor. This was the lawyer for the Crown against whom Otis argued: Jeremiah Gridley, his former teacher and the leading figure at the Massachusetts bar. For Adams, recalling the Writs case nearly fifty years later, Otis's struggle with Gridley offered "a moral spectacle more affecting to me than any I have since seen upon any stage." It amounted to "a pupil treating his master with all the deference, respect, esteem, and affection of a son to a father, and that without the least affectation; while he baffled and confounded all his authorities, and confuted all his arguments and reduced them to silence." In his retrospective dramatization, Adams had forgotten that not Otis but Gridley had prevailed in the Writs case.[4]

By making the Writs case a struggle between responsibly daring youth and appreciative authority Adams translated it into a version of his personal myth. For Adams's own confrontations with authority imitated his relationship with his father as surely as Otis's did with his. Characteristically, Adams asserted his independence, as when he defied his father's wish that he become a minister rather than a lawyer, but he did so with a measure of respect. Afterward he expected approval of his principled acts. Thus, it was not surprising when he wrote that at the Writs case "Mr. Gridley himself seemed to me to exult inwardly at the glory and triumph of his pupil." Some years earlier when Adams came to Boston to be examined for the bar, then an informal procedure, he first presented himself at Gridley's house rather than at some lesser attorney's. Gridley tested Adams. Then, impressed with the young man's answers, he offered him advice on further studies and his future as a lawyer. This Gridley did, Adams wrote, "with the benignity of a parent in his Countenance."

Adams went next to Otis, who "received me more like a Brother

John Adams

than a father."[5] On this occasion Otis displayed his particular brand of defiance of authority. Wholly ignorant of accepted procedure, Adams had come to Bostton without a letter of introduction or any clear idea of how to gain admittance to the bar. Otis, contrary to accepted practice and what was considered good manners, told Adams that he need not bother with further calls on members of the bar. This was, of course, characteristically to advise against paying deference to authority—something that fell in with Adams's proclivity for independence.

At the same time as Adams, in later years, made the Writs case into a filial drama of defiance, he described a national drama that explained how Otis's argument gave birth to American independence. This, too, was filial. Shifting his focus to Thomas Hutchinson, the new chief justice, Adams "supposed" that he had arranged the physical setting of the trial so as to overawe defiance of authority. Hutchinson had introduced a new "scenery" of judicial "scarlet and sable robes, of broad bands, and enormous tie wigs" in order to lend a "theatrical," overbearing aspect to himself and the four judges who sat with him. In addition, "all the barristers at law of Boston, and of the neighboring county of Middlesex" were present and dressed "in gowns, bands, and tie wigs," while "two portraits, at more than full length, of King Charles the Second and of King James the Second [both of whom were famous for asserting the royal authority], in splendid golden frames, were hung up on the most conspicuous sides of the apartment." Adams emphasized that these were particularly imposing paintings of the highest excellence, and that they had been taken out of storage, "cleaned, superbly framed, and placed in council" by the new governor, Bernard, "no doubt with the advice and concurrence of Hutchinson."[6]

In this setting Otis spent several hours going through the Acts of Parliament that related to the colonies. His speech amounted to a diatribe on British attempts to hold down American growth. Otis listed a century of restrictive acts and "alternately laughed and raged against them all." England had imposed a "selfish, partial, arbitrary, and contracted system of parliamentary regulations in America," and Otis verged on asserting what Adams believed to be the incontrovertible case: that Parliament had no right whatever to legislate for America. Adams summed up Otis's recital of Parliament's restrictions on America with a familial comparison of his own: "Such were the bowels of compassion, such the tender mercies of our pious, virtuous, our moral and religious mother country towards her most dutiful and affectionate children!"

Adams's famous dictum that the Revolution took place in the minds and hearts of the people followed immediately after this account and referred especially to Otis's speech, to which Adams traced the entire Revolutionary process. Again using the familial analogy, he specified what he meant by "Minds" and by "Hearts." Whereas the people once had prayed for "the King and Queen and all the Royal Family, and all in Authority under them," they gradually changed their minds until, when they saw themselves abandoned by these "Powers," they found themselves praying for their own governments. Whereas they originally felt "an habitual Affection for England as their Mother-Country," their hearts' feelings altered upon discovering that she was "a cruel Beldam, willing, like Lady Macbeth, to 'dash their brains out.'" It was no wonder if their "fillial Affections" were changed into "Indignation and horror." Thus did Adams link together three filial dramas: Otis's defiance of Gridley, Otis's resentment at the king, and the subsequent change in people's attitudes to king and "mother country." Later, when independence was declared, Adams bade "Farewell! farewell, infatuated, besotted Stepdame."[7]

For Adams the Writs case involved yet one more drama, this one personal. All his life he somewhat questionably dated his own Revolutionary services from 1761, the year of the Writs. Yet he did not emerge as a patriot until the Stamp Act in 1765 nor gain real prominence until the First Continental Congress in 1774. However, 1761 marked a psychic turning point in Adams's life. It was the year of his father's death, and in his recollections he always regarded it as marking his own emergence into maturity—into independence, one might say. His claim that at the Writs case "the child Independence was born" may have been an exaggeration about history, but together with his pronouncement that "the seeds of patriots were then and there sown," it manifestly applied to himself.[8]

Along with his Revolutionary services Adams mistakenly placed other of his early achievements in 1761, including two that bore on the Writs case. These errors point to the roles played by Otis and Hutchinson in his birth as a revolutionary. First, Adams thought that he had attended the case as a barrister (a lawyer certified to argue before the Superior Court); second, he thought that Hutchinson had introduced the scarlet and sable robes for barristers on that occasion. In fact, both his own elevation to barrister and the introduction of robes in the court took place in the following year, 1762. By shifting these two memories to 1761 Adams, as it were, made himself into both a participant in Otis's drama and a charter anti-Hutchinsonian. It seems evident that here and elsewhere Adams chose the patriot Otis as a model for his adult identity. At the same time, in every possible way Adams viewed Hutchinson as the father-like, evil genius presiding over Massachusetts politics. Hutchinson was challenged by a symbolic son, Otis, whom he destroyed. But he would not succeed in the same way with another symbolic son then coming of age: John Adams would overthrow, not be cut down.[9]

Unlike Otis, Adams did not transfer resentment of his father to Hutchinson. As his ascription of kindly feelings to Jeremiah Gridley suggested, Adams had a loving father whom he revered and admired. In his imagination, however, Adams gave his father the role of moral judge. On the one occasion when Adams invented a fictional father in one of his writings, that figure warned his son against ambition and pledged him to high-minded public service. In contrast, when Adams depicted Hutchinson he repeatedly asserted that the key to his character was "unbounded ambition."[10] Thus, whereas Thomas Hutchinson represented for Otis the distasteful side of his father, for Adams he represented that which his father had warned against.

However, since Adams lacked Otis's clear motive for his dislike, it is difficult to pinpoint when he turned against Hutchinson. In recalling the Otis-Hutchinson feud over the chief justiceship, Adams wrote in 1818 that "a more deliberate, cool, studied, corrupt appointment never was made than that of Hutchinson to be Chief Justice. It was done for the direct purpose of enslaving this whole continent, and, consequently, Britain and man; and, if Otis did say he would set the province in a flame, it was one of the sublimest expressions that was ever uttered, and he ought to have a statue of adamant erected in honor of it."[11] But it was only in retrospect that Adams came to believe in Hutchinson's appointment as a means to insure a verdict favorable to the Crown in the Writs of Assistance case. The affair came to appear as part of "a black conspiracy against the liberties both of the new & the old world" only when the facts had faded from memory.[12]

Nevertheless, the appointment of Hutchinson as chief justice may

have represented a turning point for Adams as well as Otis. Previous
to it, according to Hutchinson's close friend, Peter Oliver, a paternal
Hutchinson had smiled on Adams just as he had on Otis. "Whilst he
was young at the Bar," Oliver wrote of Adams, "he behaved with
great Modesty; & as it is a general Misfortune incident to Gentlemen
of the Bar, to brow beat their Inferiors, so when any of his Seniors
took Advantage of him in this Way, the chief Justice Mr. Hutchinson
would, with his usual Humanity, support him, as well as show him
other Marks of Respect, out of Court." When the chief justiceship
came open, Adams partly drafted an essay calling for the appointment
of a legal expert—someone who, unlike Hutchinson or Colonel Otis,
had not spent his youth "in Husbandry Merchandize, Politicks."
Though Adams did not record his reaction when Hutchinson received
the appointment, Bernard Bailyn has speculated on the result.
"Adams," Bailyn writes,

> never forgot the outrage he felt at this elevation of a layman to the
> chief justiceship, so thwarting, insulting, and humiliating to his excru-
> ciatingly sensitive self esteem. For years the appointment would pro-
> vide him with an invaluable psychological device for handling impedi-
> ments to his passionate ambitions. An appointment so unmerited, so
> perverse, and so unjust to those like himself who were sacrificing their
> lives to the law could only be the result of dangerous, secret forces
> whose power would no doubt otherwise be felt and that would other-
> wise block the aspirations of powerless but honest and able new men.[13]

A few months after the Writs of Assistance case, however, Adams
admonished himself for "Swearing" and "Virulence" with regard to
the characters of several contemporaries, among them Hutchinson.
Unfortunately, he did not reveal what he had said about them. As late
as 1763, during the "1/4 of an Hour with Lt. Govr. Hutchinson" that
Adams spent one day, he betrayed no personal animus. Adams, Hutchinson, and lawyer Ezekiel Goldthwait discussed province history,
and Hutchinson alluded to patriot politics in a neutral manner. "This
to be sure was Familiarity and Affability!" wrote Adams in his diary,
with an uncertain but apparently ironical meaning in his exclamation
point. Yet, given Adams's usual explicitness when he suspected the
motives of others, he appears not to have meant anything sinister
here.[14]

At this period the Otis-Hutchinson feud was at its height, and
Adams appears to have been troubled by it. When his close friend

Jonathan Sewall ridiculed Otis as "Bluster," Adams responded with a series of newspaper articles calling for more civility of discourse. In the meantime, in an abusive—almost hysterical—unsent letter to Sewall, Adams attacked him for "satirizing and execrating one side," that of Otis, when really "both Parties deserve Curses." But within a few months Adams inexplicably switched his pseudonym, his newspaper, and his position away from the antigovernment and anti-Hutchinson side, and went so far as to defend Sewall. Adams's uncertainty about which party and which friends to join was to resurface more than once before the Revolution.[15]

Not until the Stamp Act did Adams clearly show animosity toward Hutchinson. With James Otis he was shocked by the Oliver riot on August 14, 1765. The "blind, undistinguishing Rage of the Rabble" had made "a very attrocious Violation of the Peace" which was "of dangerous Tendency and Consequence." Nevertheless, in the twelve-day interim before the attack on Hutchinson's house Adams blamed Hutchinson for the disturbances. Concurring in Otis's charges of plural office holding, Adams listed Hutchinson's appointive positions along with those he had secured for relatives. Was not the potential "Tyranny" of these arrangements, Adams asked rhetorically, "enough to excite Jealousies among the People?" In effect, Hutchinson, like Sewall, had contributed to the strained atmosphere of the times by his constant endeavors "to scatter Party Principles."[16]

Adams was particularly outraged and hurt by Hutchinson's maneuvering against attempts to reopen the courts—not the least because he was being deprived of his livelihood. Early in 1766 Adams complained in his diary, "Times are terrible and made so at present by Hutchinson Chief Justice." Soon afterward, however, at repeal of the Stamp Act, Adams relented. "I once thought," he reported saying of Hutchinson to Deacon Webb at tea, "that his Death in a natural Way would have been the most joyful News to me that I could have heard," but now he "hoped I was mistaken in my Judgment."[17]

Adams particularly welcomed the atmosphere of conciliation that seemed to issue forth from a "gracious" king, and it was his fervent wish to return to "the Kings Protection." As he reviewed the effects of the Stamp Act, Adams's mollified but cool feelings toward Hutchinson stood in sharp contrast to his enthusiasm for the king. It was true, he admitted, that Hutchinson's house had been "pull'd down." But the Hutchinson riot was not the first in New England, and it no

more deserved to be called "high Treason" than any of its antecedents. As for the king, Adams asked, "Has there been a disrespectful
Speech uttered of his Majesty or his Government, thro the whole
memorable Year 1765, even at Midnight? over the Bowl or the Bot-
tle—I believe not one."

At this point Adams, whose personal behavior frequently derived
its outlines from politics, stopped keeping his diary and to a great extent withdrew from politics. After repeal of the Stamp Act he endeavored to separate himself from the passions of party. In his autobiography he recalled, "I was solicited to go to the Town Meetings and
harrangue there. This I constantly refused."[18] Not until 1768, after
the Townshend duties had revived the old anti–Stamp Act sentiment,
did he emerge again in opposition.

During his period of silence, except for random diary jottings and
some perfunctory private letters, Adams wrote on one subject only:
Jonathan Sewall's published defenses of Governor Bernard and his administration. At the beginniing of Adams's legal career, Sewall, who
was his elder by seven years, had sought out, praised, and cultivated
friendship with his young colleague (something Adams incorrectly remembered as having taken place in the significant year 1761). In addition, he and Sewall had been treated by Otis as his "sons." Then
came Adams's discomfiture over Otis and Sewall in 1763, at which
time he had left a similar gap in his diary. Looking back on his relationship with Sewall, Adams recalled his friend's having possessed "a
lively Wit, a pleasing humour, a brilliant Imagination," adding, "I
know not that I have ever delighted more in the friendship of any
Man, or more deeply regretted an irreconcileable difference in Judgment in public Opinions."[19] Adams's replies to Sewall in 1767 and
1768—some of them published, others too intemperate to be sent to
the newspapers—reflect his anxiety over the permanent wedge being
driven between them at that time.

Most surprisingly for Adams, instead of employing his usual scholarly and exhaustive style of argumentation, he resorted for the most
part to denunciation. Writing in a country dialict as "Humphrey
Ploughjogger," Adams attacked the likewise pseudonymous Sewall as
"a most [almost] crazey." In another, unpublished, article Adams side-
stepped Sewall's rather persuasive arguments. After quoting these at
length, he compared their author to "King Lear in the cold Storm"
and asked his readers, "is this fellow Mad, or drunk?" In yet another

unpublished essay Adams composed a soliloquy for Sewall in which, like a character in a Mercy Otis Warren play, he confesses his insane ambition to be advanced by Bernard and Hutchinson.[20]

These writings appear to have reflected Adams's distressed state of mind at the time. He abhorred Sewall's side in the conflict but he feared the results if he should let himself become further involved. He therefore attacked Sewall, as he had Hutchinson, for supposedly exacerbating party divisions. Years later he recalled always answering his friend James Warren's plea that he speak at town meetings during this period with the expression, "That way madness lies." As Adams explained it, "The Symptoms of our great Friend Otis, at that time, suggested to Warren, a sufficient comment on these Words."[21] The episodes of anxiety and depression suffered by both patriots and loyalists in the next few years offered a further comment on Adams's words. From 1766 to 1768, it appears, Adams attempted to remove himself from party politics, and as a result suffered in his conscience. After his reemergence, this period of suffering colored his political behavior for the remainder of the Revolutionary period.

In 1768 Adams moved his family to Boston from his retreat in Braintree, and returned to political activity. He offered a hint of how he viewed his two-year silence when he referred in one of his pseudonymous articles to a "long Lethargy" from which he now was "roused."[22] Others were roused along with him by the impending Townshend duties, so that there was no apparent mystery to his withdrawal from affairs since the beginning of 1766. Yet Adams proceeded to make a mystery of his withdrawal period by insisting that it had never taken place. As early as 1770 he was representing himself as having been a staunch patriot throughout the 1760s, and in later life nothing so infuriated him as having his supposed involvement during this period overlooked. Thus, when in 1805 Mercy Otis Warren's *History of the Rise, Progress, and Termination of the American Revolution* omitted his services before the 1770s, Adams wrote her an outraged series of letters insisting on his continuous involvement from 1761 to the Revolution. Given the crisis rhythm of the 1760s, with the Stamp Act in 1765 and the Townshend duties in 1768 serving to arouse opposition such as his, there was hardly any disgrace in retiring from patriot agitation at other times. His unnecessary vehemence in claiming something different therefore calls attention to itself.

More than one loyalist claimed that Adams underwent an ordeal of choice between the patriots and loyalists approximately during the period in question. Once again, there need have been no embarrassment about this: uncertainty and wavering were typical experiences of conscience patriots. It seems clear, though, that Adams underwent a time of doubt during which he suffered a genuine *crise de conscience*. It has been shown that patriots and loyalists both frequently suffered from Puritan-like doubts about their "civic duty" in the troubled times before the Revolution.[23] When Adams firmly attached himself to the cause a few years later, he had good reason to try to forget his particular crisis of doubt, which at that point might have made him appear to be a backslider or potential dropout.

The patriots' challenge to the legitimacy of authority led quite understandably to personal conflicts over loyalty. Unable to choose sides yet tortured by the demand for a choice, the potential revolutionary often enters "a phase of withdrawal or passive alienation from politics." Frequently this takes the form, as it did with Adams, of disappointment in the way that others have responded to the political crisis. Adams, for example, complained that American "ardor" had quickly "cooled down" after the Stamp Act crisis. What was worse, his fellow townsmen, instead of rewarding his services against the act, had "neglected" him by failing to advance him from town office to the legislature at the next election.[24]

With the dying down of the revolutionary's first political crisis, those who, like Adams, still take a reformist approach often adopt what has been called the "innocent czar" theory to explain events. That is, they exonerate the king or czar, just as Adams and most of his fellow patriots did at the repeal of the Stamp Act, at the expense of his supposedly deceiving ministers. In Adams's case the "Arch Corrupter and Deceiver" remained Thomas Hutchinson, and it was chiefly against him that Adams proceeded to turn.[25] But he did so in a peculiar manner—as if he were transferring his rage at Sewall to a more prominent figure. This shift emerged from Adams's autobiographical accounts of a key incident that took place in 1769, just as he was ending his period of withdrawal.

As Adams told the story, Jonathan Sewall visited him on the orders of Governor Bernard in an attempt to lure him to the government side. When Sewall offered him the post of deputy advocate general of Massachusetts—Otis's old office—Adams's refusal was "very prompt." Despite Sewall's urgings, Adams insisted that "time would produce no change and he had better make his report to Bernard immediately." Sewall nevertheless returned "weeks afterwards" to renew the offer, only to be told that Adams's "Judgment and Inclination and determination were unalterably fixed."[26]

A few years later in London, the loyalists Richard Clarke and Samuel Quincy (the latter acquainted with Adams from childhood) gave a different account of the incident to Thomas Hutchinson. They had it that Adams told Sewall that he "was at a loss which side to take." After Sewall's first visit, which was not accompanied by a specific offer, Sewall supposedly asked Bernard to make Adams a justice of the peace in exchange for his allegiance to the government party. When Bernard delayed, this account went on, Adams took offense "and ever after joined in opposition."[27] It hardly accords with Adams's high-mindedness that he would consider deciding his allegiance in consideration of an office, and certainly not a lowly judgeship of the sort that interested Colonel Otis.

Nevertheless, in both stories a loyalist, whether mistaken or not, is shown to have been somehow convinced that allegiance remained an open question for Adams. Though actually his uncertainty lay not between patriotism and loyalism but between patriotism and neutrality, it comes as no surprise that the administration made several attempts to win Adams over in 1768 and 1769. For his part Adams in 1769 acted as advocate general in Sewall's stead by conducting a prosecution for the government while Sewall was away. The case itself was one perfectly calculated to shake Adams's patriot allegiance, for it concerned a "riot or Assault" on a customs officer, whose boat was "burned by a mob." From his disapproval of the Stamp Act "rabble" in 1765 throughout the Revolution, Adams steadily maintained his opposition to such lawlessness. Not only did he defend the British soldiers in the Boston Massacre—where fear of the mob had brought about the shooting—but in 1770 and 1771 he represented tarred and feathered victims of mobs. As late as 1774 Adams took the case of Richard King, a loyalist suing for damages from a mob that had broken into his house during the Stamp Act disturbances. In his summation Adams gave a vivid description of the terrors suffered by King and his family.[28]

In light of such expressions of conscience as these, one can see how Adams might resent any implications of backsliding. But Adams went further than a denial of ever having had any doubts about the patriot cause. He represented the administration's attempts to win him over as evidences of a conspiracy masterminded by Thomas Hutchinson. Thus, Adams went from early retrospects in which, as with the royal portraits in the Writs case, he *supposed* that Hutchinson lay behind the Sewall offer, to a later version in which he grew certain of Hutchinson's role, to a final version in which he recalled telling Sewall at their first interview that he could guess who was behind the offer. (When he named Hutchinson on the first occasion, Sewall is supposed to have "nodded assent.") Revealingly, Adams elsewhere made Hutchinson responsible for the key defections to the loyalist side of other moderates like himself. Hutchinson had "Seduced from my Bosom three of the most Amiable young Men from the cause of their Country to their own Ruin," Adams wrote, referring especially to Jonathan Sewall and Samuel Quincy (who bore the story of Adams's supposed wavering). Furthermore, in very old age Adams once asserted that Hutchinson had directly "practiced all his Arts upon me." Tantalizingly, Adams gave no details, except to say that, "my constant Answer was 'I cannot in conscience.' "[29]

Adams's supposed constancy here was reminiscent of his putative firmness with Sewall and his "constant" refusal to harangue at town meetings. In each case his attempt to depict himself as unwavering in the cause of patriotism had the opposite effect of suggesting a personal crisis of conscience. Hutchinson's part would appear to have amounted to little more than using his "familiarity and affability" to argue the loyalist side when, as a circuit-riding judge, he was thrown together with Adams and other lawyers like Sewall and Samuel Quincy. (In 1769, when Hutchinson was supposedly masterminding the Sewall offer, he actually *rejected* a proposal that Adams be offered the post of attorney general, which was the close equivalent of advocate general.)

The most likely cause of Adams's resentment against Hutchinson at this period was a trial in which Adams and Otis were to appear jointly before Hutchinson. Their client was a sailor who had killed a British officer while resisting impressment. "No trial," Adams later wrote, "had ever interested the community so much before."[30] It was expected that for his part Otis would argue constitutional principles, as he had at the Writs case. But it was at just this time that Otis's mental state began seriously to deteriorate, so that it fell to Adams to deliver the defense.

Adams labored until he had "ransacked every writer on the civil

law, that the town of Boston possessed." He appeared in the courtroom with a great pile of legal works, prepared to argue, in the manner of Otis, that Parliament had no right whatsoever to impress seamen. Once again Adams in old age recalled a scene of panoply:
presiding, in addition to Hutchinson as chief justice, were the governors of Massachusetts and New Hampshire, the judge of admiralty,
the local commander of the navy, "and councillors from several colonies, to the number of fifteen." After the preliminaries, just as Adams
began to speak, Hutchinson adjourned the case. He eventually ruled in
favor of Adams's client, but despite the legal victory Adams was
crushed by not being allowed to deliver his speech. "Never in my
whole life," he later wrote, "have I been so disappointed, so mortified,
so humiliated as in that trial." An acute historian has traced to this
disappointment Adams's transformation into a revolutionary.[31] Such
an analysis ignores the fact that though Adams often felt intense resentment, he rarely acted on it politically. Nevertheless, it does point
to the possibility that the incident represented a turning point for him.

In 1808 Adams explained Hutchinson's "secret motive" in calling
an adjournment: "to prevent me from reaping an harvest of glory."
(Hutchinson plausibly explained that his proceeding arose purely from
a matter of law.) By 1816 Adams's recollection had grown more vivid,
just as it had with regard to the Sewall offer, so that Hutchinson's look
as he rose to cut him off was "deeply graven on my retina." Still later,
Adams jokingly revealed his own intense state of anticipation as he had
prepared his brief. "I vainly felt as if I could shake the town & the
world," he recalled. But "Alas! for me, my glass bubble was burst! My
Boule de Savon was dissolved! All the inflammable Gas had escaped
from my Balloon and down I dropt like Gelater de Rosia." Finally in
1817 Adams revealed exactly what kind of fame he had looked for.
His plea, he wrote, "would have accellerated the Revolution more
than even the impeachment of the Judges, or Hutchinson's foolish
controversy about the Omniscience and Omnipotence & Infinite
goodness of Parliament did afterwards. It would have spread a wider
flame than Otis's ever did, or could have done."[32] Through the Corbet case, in other words, Adams might have leaped into fame in the
manner of Otis. More important, he might unequivocally have certified his patriot credentials—had it not been for Hutchinson.

Adams's great concern with public opinion was evident when, two
months after the Corbet case, he resumed his diary on a regular basis

for the first time since 1766. In recording a ride several miles out of his way to attend a Sons of Liberty dinner, he justified the detour in revealing terms. "I felt as if I ought not to lose this feast," he wrote, "as if it was my duty to be there." Why? "Jealousies arise from little Causes, and many might suspect, that I was not hearty in the Cause, if I had been absent whereas none of them are more sincere, and stead-fast than I am."[33] This has the appearance of mending fences. Once again Adams was assuring himself of his constancy while taking steps to erase any lingering impression of lukewarmness left over from his period of withdrawal from politics.

Adams was given the opportunity to certify his patriot credentials within the year when, soon after Hutchinson's designation as acting governor in place of Francis Bernard, the question of Adams's allegiance arose for the last time. On the morning after the Boston Massacre Adams and Josiah Quincy, Jr., were asked to serve as defense counsel for the British soldiers who had fired into the crowd. Although the patriot leadership presumably approved of their choice, in taking the case the two lawyers gave the appearance, at least at first, of being loyalist sympathizers. After thus risking their political reputations, both men quickly took steps to redeem themselves. Before the case came to trial the patriot leadership indicated its approval of Adams's course by designating him as a candidate for the legislature in replacement of Otis. Once elected, Adams took up where Otis had left off, quickly moving to the head of an opposition that challenged the new acting governor at every turn.

Adams succeeded in the legislature, if not in defeating Hutchinson's purposes, then at least in making his own loyalty clear. But by the end of the legislative session of 1770–1771 the strain of battle had left him in a state of anxious exhaustion. Following the adjournment Adams suffered from broken health and mental exhaustion. He resigned from the legislature (Otis, in a last, brief return to sanity, replaced him), and moved to his native Braintree. From here he went off to Connecticut for a mineral springs cure.

Friends ascribed Adams's intensity in the legislature to "some private pique" between himself and Hutchinson. This Adams denied. Nevertheless, he thought of his breakdown as having been caused by his opposition to Hutchinson. In the meantime, Hutchinson was elevated from acting governor to full royal governor of Massachusetts, and while Adams was away on his curative trip he read about Hutchinson's inauguration in June 1771. The newspapers carried the new chief executive's address at the opening of the legislative session and the legislature's "cordial answer" to it. Reading a description of the "elegant Entertainment" given that evening by Hutchinson, Adams let out his fury. "With great Anxiety and Hazard," he wrote in his diary, and "with loss of Health Reputation, Profit" he had "for 10 Years together invariably opposed" Hutchinson. With Hutchinson's elevation, it was as if all this opposition had been wasted. Adams's outburst revealed the intensity of his anti-Hutchinson emotion. But even more significant was the inaccuracy of the phrase "10 Years." For if he had been invariable in opposition for this length of time (that is, since the ubiquitous year 1761), it had been for the most part in his own mind.[34] As Adams's outburst and his decline into poor health revealed, his anti-Hutchinson campaign had grown at least in part out of a need to erase not only public doubt, but also a private, persistent uneasiness over his apostasy during 1766–1768.

After his recovery, much as when he blamed the loyalism of Sewall and Samuel Quincy on Hutchinson, Adams made the surprising claim that Hutchinson had "destroyed a Thatcher, a Mayhew, an Otis." There was an unintended sense in which Adams was right about Otis. But Benjamin Thacher, the teacher of the younger Josiah Quincy, had died of the after-effects of smallpox, while Jonathan Mayhew, the minister, suffered from chronic ill health and died after exerting himself in a church-related matter. Both had been deeply involved in opposition to Hutchinson, but by no stretch of the imagination had they been seriously injured by him. When Adams went on to mention his own "Constitution" as being "very infirm," he supplied the clue to his meaning: that Hutchinson destroyed patriots like himself.[35]

When Adams returned to politics in 1773, his "hatred of Hutchinson," as Bernard Bailyn put it, "had become obsessive." In contrast, in the course of attacking Hutchinson, Adams asserted that he and the American people "humbly look up to his present Majesty . . . as children to a father."[36] When later in the year Hutchinson's private letters were stolen and published, Adams and the other patriots were shocked by their contents, especially the proposal for an "abridgment" of English liberties as a means of controlling the unruly atmosphere in the streets of Boston.

Early in 1774 Adams wrote a diary meditation on the letters in which he declared, "Examples ought to be made of these great offenders Hutchinson and Peter Oliver, in Terrorem." The possibly deluded sincerity of the two men amounted to no defense, Adams argued, and he gave examples of other legally punishable acts done in good faith. The first example, oddly enough, consisted of those "who have pretended to be conscientiously persuaded, that the Pretender has a Right to the Throne." Other examples were Ravaillac and Felton, two mentally disturbed assassins of the previous century. One had murdered a French king, the other the duke of Buckingham, but only after coming to believe that the duke was involved in a regicidal plot. "The Liberty of private Conscience," wrote Adams of the assassins, with a chilling application to Hutchinson and Oliver, "did not exempt them from the most dreadful Punishment that civil Authority can inflict or human Nature endure." Here, shortly before Hutchinson's ouster, Adams participated in a final rehearsal of revolution. For he attached to Hutchinson, whom by now he regarded as "the vile Serpent," his own and his party's most extreme imagination of treason and its punishment.[37]

After Hutchinson had been driven out of Massachusetts Adams continued to regard him as the evil genius of the "junto" responsible for all of the province troubles (his supposed associates were Governor Bernard and Peter Oliver). Writing as "Novanglus" in 1775, Adams charged that "this desperate triumverate" had conspired in the revenue acts in order to divide part of the proceeds among themselves. Adams viewed Hutchinson, who was in England, much as the English did Bute after he was removed from influence. "If it was out of his power to do us any more injuries," Adams concluded, "I should wish to forget the past; but, as there is reason to fear he is still to continue his malevolent labors against this country, although he is out of sight, he should not be out of our minds. This country has everything to fear . . . from the deep intrigues of that artful man."

The emotionalism of "Novanglus," in which Adams mistakenly thought that his pseudonymous antagonist, "Massachusettensis," was Jonathan Sewall, recalled Adams's replies to earlier Sewall essays. (Adams persisted in his wrong identification of "Massachusettensis" well after he had evidence that the author was someone else.) With respect to Hutchinson, "Novanglus" went from denunciation to a perverse empathy. Commenting on Hutchinson's proposal to abridge English liberties he wrote, "My indignation at this letter has sometimes been softened by compassion . . . It carries on the face of it evident marks of *madness*. It was written in such a transport of passions, *ambition* and *revenge* chiefly, that his reason was manifestly over-powered . . . Indeed, he seems to have had a confused consciousness of this himself. 'Pardon me this excursion,' says he; 'it really proceeds from the state of mind into which our perplexed affairs often throw me.' "38

The Adams who felt his own infirm constitution to be threatened by politics, who had suffered a *crise de conscience* in 1766 (during which he characterized Jonathan Sewall as mad) and acute anxiety and illness in 1771, was closer in personality to Hutchinson than he realized. For his nemesis was also a man of conscience—one who had suffered nervous disorder in 1767 and subsequent fears for his health similar to those of Adams. It was not surprising, therefore, that after independence Adams began to show a remorse toward Hutchinson that recalled Otis's drunken apology of 1771. Adams thereby completed the pattern of revolutionary experience that first made itself evident in his period of withdrawal.

Insofar as the revolutionary act implies bringing down paternal authority, the emotions that follow it tend to resemble the remorse felt by a youth who has broken away from parental authority. Whereas in "My Kinsman, Major Molineux" Robin is soberly regretful about his kinsman, and whereas Otis was tearful, the remorse of Adams and certain other patriots found a political expression. They followed the pattern of the successful revolutionary, whose remorse often takes the form of incorporating in the new regime something of what the former paternal authority stood for. The notorious examples come from the periods of reaction in the French and Russian revolutions, during which there recurred the worst horrors of the old regime (at least as they had been depicted by the revolutionaries). American remorse, it appears, was of a gentler, subtler sort.

In the minds of the Massachusetts revolutionaries, Hutchinson stood for the old regime even more than the king or Parliament. Nothing points more certainly to him than the ways in which the patriots, especially Adams, unconsciously reinstated his principles after the Revolution. Before this process began, Adams revealed the special importance that it would involve in his case. During the first year of the new government, he learned while sitting in the Continental Congress that he had been appointed to Hutchinson's old office of chief justice of Massachusetts. Adams did not reveal his feelings on this occasion, but his acceptance of the appointment suggests much. In the 1760s, taking Otis's lead, he had objected to Hutchinson's plural office holding. Now, remarkably, in accepting the chief justiceship he laid himself open to the very same charge.

Furthermore, Adams held offices at this time that closely paralleled Hutchinson's at the beginning of Otis's campaign. In 1760 Hutchinson had been a justice of the peace, chief justice, a member of the Massachusetts Council, a judge in Suffolk County, and lieutenant governor. In 1776 John Adams was a justice of the peace, chief justice, a member of the Massachusetts Council, a judge in Suffolk County, and, though not lieutenant governor, a member of the Continental Congress and chairman of its Board of War. In response to congressional criticism Adams, though he was not the only patriot accused of Hutchinsonian plural office holding, resigned his seat on the Massachusetts Council. But, insisting that he had not accepted the chief justiceship from "any motives of Ambition"—as Hutchinson supposedly had—he remained in that office.[39] As it developed, he never had time to serve, and he resigned in 1777. The chief justiceship brought him only grief. Given the obvious difficulties it posed, Adams's acceptance of the office bears all the marks of unpolitical and unconscious motivation.

This example of what might be termed revolutionary self-punishment was followed by one of simple revolutionary remorse. In 1779 when Adams returned from a short diplomatic stay in Europe, he was appointed to the Massachusetts Constitutional Convention, where he soon became the drafter of the new constitution. Once again, he acted unpolitically and did so in a particularly suggestive way. A previous convention had foundered partly on the issue of whether or not to give the governor a significant power of veto over legislation. Surprisingly, Adams's draft, which for the most part sought moderation, failed to offer a compromise on this point. The question was hardly technical, for as one historian has put it, the governor remained "a symbol of the old kind of government."[40] Thus, in returning the veto power to him, Adams flew in the face of the strongest prejudices of his party—prejudices that he had shared when attacking Hutchinson as royal governor.

But Adams's act of restitution went further than a symbolic reinstatement of the powers of the old governorship. Bernard Bailyn has written of Hutchinson that "in his understanding of government he was of course conservative, but no more so than John Adams, who despised him and feared him and attacked him publicly and privately on every possible occasion but whose constitution for the Commonwealth of Massachusetts, which went into effect the month that Hutchinson died, exhibited to perfection the ideal of balance achieved through the independence and separation of powers which, in an older context, Hutchinson had struggled to retain."[41]

As time went on, Adams grew still closer to Hutchinson. Their theories of government had roots in a shared pessimism about human nature, and it was precisely with respect to this pessimism that Adams exceeded other revolutionaries in his return to elements of the old system.[42] Beginning with the Massachusetts Constitution it grew clear that Adams's Hutchinsonian philosophy implied basic disagreement with the growing democratic ethos of the American movement. Yet Adams suffered unpopularity for the rest of his life by stubbornly insisting on that philosophy.

He probably suffered worst for it in 1789 soon after the federal constitution went into effect. At that time he was elected vice-president, with the prospect of going on to the presidency just as Hutchinson had gone from lieutenant governor to governor. Almost immediately Adams became involved in the oddest controversy of his career. In the face of a rising tide of republicanism he advocated exalted titles and dress for the officers of the new government. His proposals, though he did not say so, recalled the panoply introduced into the Superior Court by Hutchinson when he became chief justice. Adams had ridiculed such splendor at the time and would do so again. But in 1789 he offered philosophical justifications for it. Citizens were not capable of living by abstraction alone, Adams argued; they required the display of symbols of authority. This was to endorse Hutchinson's purpose, as Adams had interpreted it, of using panoply to overawe the opposition to constitutional authority. The costumes in question in both cases were symbolic of paternal authority.[43]

As president of the United States, John Adams paid back Thomas Hutchinson one last time: in the coin of emulation. Like Governor Hutchinson, President Adams underwent an ordeal of personal attack both from without and within the government. Given his irascible temperament, it appears nothing short of miraculous that he responded as mildly as he did. His forbearance and forgiveness of enemies, in fact, recalled the equally extraordinary response of Thomas Hutchinson to his ordeal. (In the same way, President Adams's reputation of being susceptible to flattery recalled his own accusations against Hutchinson twenty-five years earlier.)[44]

Hutchinson in one instance—his call for an abridgement of English liberties—had not been entirely mild in response to the intense pressure brought against him, and he had lived to regret it. It was surprising, therefore, that when Adams's Congress passed a similar abridgement of English-American liberties in 1798—the Alien and Sedition Acts—Adams signed them into law. His administration, like Hutchinson's, had good reasons for the acts: a state of undeclared war with France, along with virulent, unmerited attacks in the press on the chief executive, and a similar atmosphere of disorder in the streets. Nevertheless, historians are agreed that Adams should have opposed the Congress. It is tempting to speculate that the example of Hutchinson influenced his failure to do so. Adams's loss of office matched Hutchinson's, in any case.[45]

In his Hutchinsonian forgiveness of enemies, Adams contrasted sharply with Samuel Adams, who called for draconian measures against all opponents of the new American governments. Thus, whereas Samuel Adams advocated the death penality for participants in the unsuccessful Shays's rebellion, Adams, over the objection of his party, pardoned the leader of the later Fries's rebellion from his death sentence.[46] The two old revolutionaries exhibited two kinds of relationship to the old regime. Samuel Adams unconsciously imitated what he had attacked it for; John Adams, closer to the typical American pattern, restored some of its old legitimacy.

As an old man Adams continued his presidential habit of forgiving enemies. He included even Alexander Hamilton, whose machinations actually were as dark as the sometimes wild speculations Adams had about others. Almost alone, though, Hutchinson continued to trouble him. "Many are the years," Adams confessed in 1816, "in which I have seriously endeavored to strip from my mind every prejudice, and from my heart every feeling, unfavorable to Mr. Hutchinson."[47] This he could not do. For Adams's demonizing of Hutchinson was integral to his understanding of the Revolution itself.

Adams ended his late speculations about Hutchinson on a perplexing note. "We need not fear that Mr. Hutchinsons Character will be injured with Posterity," he wrote of the most proscribed figure of the Revolution. "His every virtue, and his every Talent and his every Service will be recorded in polite Language, and blazoned in Splendid colours; when we, poor Beings who resisted him shall be thrown in Shades of darkness in the back ground."[48] Despite Hutchinson's defeat, it would appear, Adams forever regarded the exiled, unfortunate former governor as a figure surrounded with an aura of authority and success.

Adams's imagined heraldic device—with Hutchinson looming in the highlighted foreground, while the patriots are pictured as lowly subjects in the background—attests to the power of the Whig Sentimental vision. For in it the image of an overbearing father and his sons remained undimmed over forty years after Hutchinson's downfall. Despite the victory of his party over Hutchinson, and despite the universally proclaimed legitimacy of the nation whose president he had been, Adams continued to regard Hutchinson with a kind of awe. Adams ended by holding the former governor centrally responsible for what the revolutionaries did, and at the same time made a final restitution to him of his viceregal authority.

CHAPTER SIX

Joseph Hawley

Bᴇᴛᴡᴇᴇɴ 1766 ᴀɴᴅ 1776 Joseph Hawley emerged as a leading figure among the Massachusetts patriots. In the legislature, where he represented the western Massachusetts town of Northampton, he "really had much greater weight" than Samuel Adams.[1] Hawley was nearly selected for the first Continental Congress but one of his periodic illnesses caused him to decline. He did, however, serve in the Revolutionary provincial legislatures of Massachusetts soon afterward. Hawley was an older man who had failed to achieve prominence outside of western Massachusetts before the troubles with England (he had served in the Massachusetts legislature during the 1750s without particular distinction). His later fame was intimately bound up with his opposition to Hutchinson.

For the nearly twenty years before Hawley became a patriot his career was confined largely to Northampton, where he practiced law and served in many town offices, including selectman. As a country lawyer Hawley acquired a reputation similar to those of Adams and Otis. He was known for a scholarly knowledge of the law and for high ethics. Hutchinson wrote of him that "some instances have been mentioned of singular scrupulosity, and of his refusing and returning fees when they appeared to him greater than the cause deserved." Hawley's biographer writes, however, that outside of the law he had a reputation for being "rash and over-zealous at times."[2]

This was apparent at the very beginning of his career, when he took it upon himself to help his younger brother, Elisha, in a paternity suit. The Hawleys, a well-descended and well-connected family in the region, were greatly embarrassed when Elisha proved to be the father of illegitimate twins. The family of the young woman with whom he

131

had been involved, Martha Root, sued and won a large cash settlement. But Elisha, after escaping a forced marriage to Martha, came under the judgment of his church congregation, which ordered his temporary excommunication.[3] Such a proceeding required the approval and ordinarily the instigation of the minister, who in this case was the famous preacher of the Great Awakening, Jonathan Edwards.

Joseph Hawley appealed the excommunication to a church council of ministers, who heard both his testimony and that of Edwards. Though he advised his brother not to "labour to prove anything against her" but to let the burden of proof rest with the church fathers, Hawley himself testified to the council that he knew Martha Root as "a woman of the town"—that is, someone he had seen acting in a sexually provocative manner in public. The council recommended that Elisha be restored to church membership. Then, two years later, Hawley wrote Martha Root a letter of apology in which he admitted having "acted presumptuously" at the hearing and added, "I am heartily sorry, and freely and humbly ask your pardon and forgiveness."[4]

Hawley's confession initiated a pattern of behavior that repeated itself throughout his career. Typically, he involved himself in causes first with caution and then with precipitation, acting "presumptuously" in the heat of controversy. Later, he would regret his actions, and declare his wrongdoing either in private letters like the one to Martha Root, or in public confession. In 1828 Samuel Merrick of nearby Wilbraham, Massachusetts, reported that Hawley's life had been "full of sinning and repenting": "He came out so often in the broad aisle [of the church] to make his confession, that it became proverbial if he did anything supposed to be remiss, 'we shall have him in the broad aisle again.' "[5]

The pattern exhibited itself in Hawley's behavior toward Jonathan Edwards immediately after the Martha Root affair. Edwards was a cousin of Hawley, and had a history of familial connections with him going back to the period of the Great Awakening. In 1735, when Hawley was twelve, the first wave of a religious enthusiasm that would last through the 1740s was generated by the sermons of Jonathan Edwards. Many of his Northampton parishioners, gripped by concern for their souls, experienced religious conversion, though only after periods of agonized soul-searching. One among them, Hawley's father, was overcome by the general guilt proclaimed by Edwards. As Edwards recounted it, Satan was "let loose" in Northampton and "raged in a dreadful manner." Hawley's father, Edwards's uncle by marriage, was, Edwards wrote, "a gentleman of more than common understanding, of strict morals, religious in his behavior, and an useful, honorable person in the town; but was of a family that are exceeding prone to the disease of melancholy, and his mother was killed with it . . . He grew much discouraged and melancholy grew amain upon him." In the end, he "Laid violent Hands on himself, & Put an End to his Life, by Cutting his own throat."[6]

Hawley's father left a written confession of his spiritual corruption that anticipated the confessions later written by his son. (In the New York Public Library's collection of Hawley family papers it was until recently attributed to Joseph Hawley, Jr.) The elder Hawley imagined Christ's fiery vengeance on his soul after a heavenly tribunal; the tribunal would read him his sins and end by a "condemning of me to eternal fire."[7] The vision unmistakably derived from Edwards's famous hell-fire sermons—something that the young Hawley could hardly fail to appreciate.

Edwards was twenty years older than young Hawley—old enough to be his father. As Hawley put it, he was "much my Superior in age Station and accomplishments." Hawley later wrote that Edwards extended "many instances of his tenderness, goodness and generosity, to me as a young kinsman, whom he was disposed to treat in a most friendly manner." The relationship bore a parallel with those of the young lawyers Otis and Adams to Hutchinson, and it possibly influenced Hawley's own later relationship with Hutchinson. In 1739, four years after his father's death, Hawley followed in Edwards's footsteps by attending his alma mater, Yale, to become a minister. In 1742 Hawley returned to Northampton, apparently to complete his training with Edwards. For reasons unknown he left the same year to study at Harvard. At Yale he had received orthodox training of the sort that Edwards stood for. But Cambridge was a hotbed of Arminianism, the philosophy of free will that Edwards regarded as a heresy and took special pains to preach against.[8] To leave for Cambridge was overtly to defy Jonathan Edwards.

At Harvard Hawley was converted to Arminianism. This meant that he embraced the doctrine holding that man can aid in the work of his own salvation. Had Hawley's father been able to believe this, despite Edwards, his immediate motive for suicide would have been removed. That Hawley's conversion represented an act defying Edwards became evident when, twenty years later, he apologized for and repudiated his Arminianism in one of his letters of confession—this one to Edwards. Soon after his conversion in the early 1740s, Hawley served as an army chaplain with the New England expedition against Louisbourg, Canada. On his return he might again have been expected to follow in Edwards's footsteps to the extent of continuing as a minister. Instead he went to Suffield, Massachusetts, to study law with a former tutor of his at Yale now turned lawyer. This was in 1746. By 1748 Hawley had completed his studies, returned to Northampton, and engaged opposite Edwards on behalf of his brother. His decision to testify on that occasion, taken in the context of his relationship with Edwards, may have been influenced by a desire to best his former mentor.

If so, then Hawley's success in securing the church council's recommendation in favor of his brother did not satisfy this need. For a few months later he involved himself in the now famous struggle between Edwards and his parishioners in which Edwards was ousted from his pulpit. The issue here bore a certain relationship both to the death of Hawley's father and to his own Arminianism. This was because Edwards had aroused the ire of his congregation by taking a doctrinal position quite as extreme as the one on damnation with which he had provoked the Awakening. He now prounounced himself convinced that it was necessary to return to the strict old Puritan test and oath of sanctity as a preliminary to church membership. Edwards's and Hawley's common grandfather, Solomon Stoddard, had been responsible for doing away with such tests some sixty years earlier; thus, there was yet another family dimension to the issue at the outset.

In 1749 and 1750 there ensued a series of meetings in which the Northampton church congregation opposed Edwards's new stand and asked that he be removed as minister. The case was eventually taken to a church council similar to the one that took up the case of Elisha Hawley. Here, in a close vote, Edwards was ordered to step down as minister, largely on account of Hawley's taking sides against him. Before the proceeding ended, however, Hawley exhibited his characteristic changeableness in two surprising actions. After having served on the first few committees that developed the plans to oust Edwards, Hawley went one day to Edwards and told him that as a cousin he felt it incumbent on himself to withdraw from all involvement in the question. Apparently he had been slated to argue the congregation's case before the church council; his withdrawal, therefore, would take some of the pressure off Edwards.[9]

Soon after, "very inconsistently," as Edwards observed, Hawley returned to the attack, and with a vengeance. He did argue before the church council, where he successfully urged dismissal in what Edwards termed a "magisterial, vehement manner"—Hawley himself later described it as "a peremptory, devisive, vehement, and very immodest manner." It is not clear exactly when the following (probably embellished) story of Hawley's behavior, one told by a nineteenth-century historian, took place in this sequence of events, but it is worth recounting for its confirmation of stronger evidence that Hawley tended to act in bursts of emotion. He is supposed at some point to have been undecided which side to take in the Edwards controversy, and so stood outside a window listening to the congregation debate the matter. "At length, overcome with excitement, he leaped through the window and made a violent harangue against Edwards that lasted an hour and a half."[10]

Once converted, Hawley achieved the righteousness that came with religious "conviction" following the typical Puritan season of doubt. When he turned on Edwards he did so with an implacable will. At the church council he broke in on a minister who wished to sermonize on Edwards's services and long association with his congregation. Hawley succeeded in having him ruled out of order. Later, when after his dismissal Edwards continued to preach while the town searched for a replacement, Hawley saw to it that he not be permitted to continue in this temporary role. This he accomplished by presenting a long list of false charges against Edwards and his adherents.

Hawley's eventual remorse over Edwards followed the pattern of his apology to Martha Root. In 1755 he wrote two letters to Edwards in an apologetic tone but to some extent denying wrongdoing. Somewhat in the manner of Otis apologizing (or not apologizing) to Hutchinson, Hawley punctuated his letters with expressions of extreme "defference" and "respect." At about the same time he wrote a confession of sin reminiscent of his father's. He admitted to having imbibed the "Wicked Doctrines" of Arminianism "owing to the Natural Blindness and Pride of my heart." For a time he had found himself "tending to utter Deism and Infidelity," but he had returned to orthodoxy as of 1754, the year before his letters to Edwards.[11]

Two years after Edwards's death in 1758, an event generally perceived as a result of his exile from Northampton, Hawley wrote another confession. This he sent to the Reverend Hall, the man he had prevented from eulogizing Edwards at the church council. On this occasion Hawley confessed his guilt in the entire affair, and added that the charges he had brought against Edwards at the end "were really gross slanders" and "therefore highly criminal."[12] At Hawley's request, his letter was published—in the manner of the traditional Puritan *mea culpa* for religious or secular wrongdoing.

By now Hawley had become known for odd "Fits of Enthusiasm" in religious matters. The evidence for these comes entirely from the loyalist side, yet insofar as it confirms one's impression of Hawley's changeableness it is worth recalling. Peter Oliver told of Hawley's behavior while leading governmental investigatory commissions on tours of "publick Services" in the province. In one case Hawley insisted that his group hold morning and evening prayers "at every Inn where they lodged. But not long after, upon another like Tour, he was taken with a Fit of Deism, & then the Prayers were not only omitted but ridiculed." Hutchinson in his *History* reported an anecdote of similar religious extremism. It seems that on another trip Hawley was overtaken by the sabbath while still a few miles from home. Rather than violate the church's ban on travel, he is supposed to have remained on the spot over Saturday night and through Sunday. Also during the 1750s Hawley had a falling out with his cousin, Israel Williams, who had joined with him in the ouster of Edwards. It is not clear whether this was connected with regret over Edwards. But here, too, Hawley showed his characteristic extremism, for according to Williams his dislike took the form of public "sneers and jeers." These terms recall Otis's description of his "acrimonious" and "ludicrous" treatment of Hutchinson, and they correspond with Hawley's description of his having treated Edwards with "haughtiness" and "levity."[13]

Both Hawley's withdrawals and his pattern of "transgression and expiation" appear to follow the classic outline of manic-depressiveness, the malady that he most probably suffered from in later years. His letter to Reverend Hall in 1760 was said to have been written "in one of those fits of constitutional melancholy to which he was subject," and Peter Oliver indicated that the instances of Hawley's returning his clients' fees, which "were generally known to be moderate," also occurred "under the Influence of those Disorders"—that is, Hawley's fits of melancholia.[14]

A comparison of the symptoms exhibited in Hawley's father as described by Edwards, with those that Hawley described in himself, show decided similarities. Edwards mentioned a loss of capacity for business, and a loss of self-esteem in Hawley Senior. Hawley Junior described himself as having lost all "capacity for business." As for his self-esteem, though he did not mention it on this occasion, he made it clear during later illnesses that he was led to question all the deeds of his life. Furthermore, Hawley attributed his melancholia to the same kind of religious doubt suffered by his father. His depressed state, he believed, stemmed from his becoming "Embarrassed about Religion" and "Incapacitated to Judge in moral or religious matters."[15]

Hawley had good reason to feel himself the victim of a family taint. His father's mother was "killed with" depression, as Jonathan Edwards reported it, and his father driven to suicide by it. But depression, or melancholia, is neither an inherited trait nor a disease, though it can run in families. It is, among other things, a form of mourning for the loss of a loved one. The death of a parent at the age of twelve, as in Hawley's case, frequently leads to depression later in life. This depression expresses not only loss, but also anger at abandonment, which has come at the time in life when a youth begins to form his morality by emulating his parents. Hawley's violent campaigns against older men, then, may be viewed as attempts to revenge himself on his father, and his depressions may be viewed as periodic mournings for the same figure.[16] Whenever his revenge succeeded, he was seized with a remorse as unexpectedly extreme in its way as his original, unprovoked hostility.

The pattern was a classic one, down to the repetitions of the father's symptoms, and to Hawley's adopting a Puritan gravity of demeanor, apparently in direct imitation of his father's "strict morals" and "religious behavior." His contemporary, Timothy Dwight, said of Hawley that "his mind, like his eloquence, was grave, austere, and powerful," while Thomas Hutchinson described him as maintaining "great decency and propriety of behavior, and the appearance of gravity and seriousness."[17]

Hawley's illness in 1760 clearly had profound connections first with his father's death, and second with his unconscious avenging of that death through the ouster of Edwards. Writing to Hawley in 1754 Edwards had enforced the identification of himself as a father: "It had often been observed what a Curse Persons have lived under, & been pursued by, for their ill Treatment of their natural Parents: but especially may this be expected to follow such abuses offered by a People to one which in their own esteem is their spiritual Father." Six years later Hawley adopted a similar passage from Edwards's letter containing the accusation that Hawley had wronged an agent of the lord, and that, like his father, he deserved to die for it. "I have the greatest reason to tremble," Hawley wrote, "at those most solemn and awful words of our Saviour, Matt. xciii. 6, Whoso shall offend one of these little ones, which believe in me, it were better that a mill-stone were hanged about his neck, and that he were drowned in the depth of the sea."[18]

In the same letter that accused Hawley, Edwards reported himself ill from "Fits" that had left him with a trembling hand. If Hawley felt himself in some part responsible for these, then it would have appeared as if he had inflicted on Edwards the symptoms of the melancholic Hawley Senior. Edwards had in fact been "overwhelmed with melancholy" as a youth, and had written several times on the subject—once, of course, in connection with Hawley's father.[19] Thus, when in 1760 Hawley took upon himself the classic symptoms of melancholy, he recapitulated the suffering of both his father and Edwards. In doing so he commemorated the death of his father, while expiating the death of Edwards.

It is significant that in the same year Hawley entered patriot politics. He had served in the Massachusetts legislature on and off since the 1750s, during which time he was, like the Otises, "a most firm Friend to Government, & a great Friend to *Mr. Hutchinson* in his private as well as his publick Station." So, at least, later claimed Peter Oliver. In 1760, Oliver went on, Hawley, "from the Insinuations of *Mr. Otis* & his Adherents, turned inimical to Mr. *Hutchinson* & the Government." Unfortunately, Oliver did not specify how Hawley's change of allegiance is supposed to have manifested itself in 1760.[20]

In the array of family influences on Hawley, not only his father and Jonathan Edwards prove to have been significant, but also his mother. Rebekah Hawley had the reputation of being a powerfully eccentric person. Tradition has it that she was so devoted to making cheese and butter that when she was told her husband had cut his throat and was on the point of expiring, she calmly finished turning her cheeses before going to him. Hawley's relationship to Jonathan Edwards and to the Stoddard family, the most prominent in the town, was through her. She made much of the connection, arranging after her husband's death to remove herself from the traditional place of widows on the women's side of the aisle in church. Instead she sat with her mother and her brother, John Stoddard, in the family pew next to the Edwards family pew. Rebekah ostentatiously disapproved Hawley's choice of a fiancée in the early 1750s (as she later did that of his brother, Elisha); she succeeded in delaying his marriage, and then made life difficult for him and his wife. She moved in with them, arranged an apartment for herself separate from the rest of the house, and constructed a butter and cheese building where she spent much of her time. She was said to have inhibited and interfered with the couple's happiness until her death at the age of eighty.[21]

With her death she dealt her son a final blow, for she lived until June 2, 1766, the day following the twenty-first anniversary of his father's suicide. For a person of her iron will, the ability to remain alive just past a significant anniversary is by no means unprecedented. In fact, the most famous example in history of such a feat concerns Hawley's fellow patriot, John Adams. Both Adams and Thomas Jefferson, though ill, managed to keep themselves alive until July 4, 1826, the fiftieth anniversary of independence.

Depressives of Hawley's type—that is, those who are experiencing mourning for a dead parent—tend to suffer outbreaks on significant anniversaries having to do with their loss. Usually the anniversary of the death itself serves as the trigger, and this was presumably the case with Hawley in 1766. In addition, depression can set in when one reaches the age at which a lost parent died—something that also happened in Hawley's case some years later. At such anniversaries, it is common to suffer with the symptoms displayed by the lost parent. The depressive may or may not be aware of the connection, but awareness leads to the feeling that Hawley seems to have had of being gripped by a nemesis, and to the conviction that fate has decreed a repetition, in oneself, of the family catastrophe.[22]

The immediate occasion of Hawley's debut in the patriot cause and his struggle with Hutchinson was a Stamp Act–related legal case that came to be known as the Berkshire affair. On November 6, 1765, a few days after the Stamp Act went into effect, a Berkshire county deputy sheriff had arrested for debt a man in Lanesborough, Massachusetts, only to have him set free by some of his friends. On November 26, about three weeks after the thwarted arrest, the deputy went with reinforcements to Lanesborough to seize another debtor. This time he found himself in a melee. A gathering of people who had assembled at a tavern after a house-raising, with its traditional drinking and jollity, greeted the law with a fight. While the adults struggled, some boys set a bonfire upon which they burned "serveral persons in effigy." The adults dragged the deputy and some of his men out of the tavern and close enough to the fire for them to be singed, after which they were all sent packing.[23]

After the courts reopened, those who had humiliated the sheriff and his men were indicted for riot. Hawley then appealed on behalf of one of them before the Superior Court—Justice Thomas Hutchinson presiding. Hawley argued that the charge against his client was too severe, and that the Stamp Act and closing of the courts had created a state of general lawlessness that largely excused the Berkshire disturbance. Hutchinson in his charge to the jury gave it as the opinion of the court that riot was the correct charge. Thus, it appeared that when the jury returned from its deliberations the next morning it would uphold the conviction.

Hawley, however, "on revolving the case in the night," suddenly came to see it in an entirely new way. He decided that if the jury failed to reverse his client's conviction on the grounds he had set forth, then his client should be "charged anew, and with a crime of much higher nature, viz with High Treason." Apparently in a state of excitement reminiscent of the appeal proceeding on behalf of his brother, Hawley made this startling new proposal to Hutchinson when the court reconvened the next morning, only to have it dismissed. Hutchinson later explained that he had ruled "if the offense was treason, it was also a riot," and the Crown could still "prosecute for an inferior offense." From this moment may be traced Hawley's entrance into specifically anti-Hutchinsonian, patriot politics.[24]

It would seem that in turning on Hutchinson, Hawley underwent a conversion—hardly the first of his life. As with Edwards, whose place Hutchinson appears to have taken, the process took two steps. First there was the political estrangement of 1760 reported by Peter Oliver, and then the Berkshire case appeal, with its personal overtones (and its coincidence with the death of Rebekah Hawley). In 1768 Governor Bernard recalled Hawley's disappointment; he described Hawley as "a Man of ability but of violent & Changeable Passions, who about 15 Months ago left the Government party & joined Otis & became the most violent opposer of the Right of Parliament to legislate for

America as he called it." Hawley's sudden emergence as "the most violent opposer" resembled his having suddenly "become the most leading man in the town," as Edwards had put it, by joining the opposition to Edwards in 1750. This time, his conversion had the added force of coinciding with an emergence from melancholia. The phenomenon of melancholia followed by mania was a familiar one in Hawley's time, and had in fact been studied and written about by Edwards. As James Russell Trumbull, the historian of Northampton, put it in 1902: following Hawley's "seasons of depression came periods of great exaltation, during which he manifested extraordinary zeal for the cause of liberty."[25]

That all the patriots should have found their métier in opposition to Thomas Hutchinson was not surprising in itself, given Hutchinson's prominence. However, that Hawley's personal resentment over the Berkshire case should coincide with his political emergence makes a striking parallel not only with Otis and the Writs of Assistance case presided over by Hutchinson, but also with John Adams and the Corbet case, also presided over by Hutchinson. Out of resentment at Thomas Hutchinson as chief justice came important turns in the lives of these three lawyers, all of whom went on to careers as patriots.

Hawley never explained just what led him, on the night of the Berkshire case adjournment, to see the facts in the light of treason. But his writings in the following year indicate that he had suddenly perceived the revolutionary overtones of the entire Stamp Act situation. These writings contended that with the closing of the courts for lack of stamps, there had come a total suspension of justice in America. "Nothing is more plain," Hawley argued, "than that the people of such a country are in a worse state than a state of nature." This extreme view of the matter occurred to others at about the same time. In Boston in December 1765 John Adams was selected, along with James Otis and Jeremiah Gridley, to argue the case for reopening the courts despite the unavailability of stamps. On being notified of his appointment he mulled over the situation in his diary.

> What are the Consequences of the supposition that the Courts are shut up? The King is the Fountain of Justice by the Constitution—And it is a Maxim of the Law, that the King never dies.
>   Are not Protection and Allegiance reciprocal? And if We are out of the Kings Protection, are we not discharged from our Allegiance. Are not all the Ligaments of Government dissolved? Is it not an Abdication

of the Throne? In short where will such an horrid Doctrine terminate?
It would run us into Treason!

Hawley, in arguing that his client either be freed or charged with
treason, was moving in the same direction as Adams and others for
whom the Stamp Act represented a subjective turning point in allegiance. But Hawley, also like the others, was not yet prepared to con-
template directly the revolutionary implications of the situation. He
noted that "the king is presumed to sit in court" where justice is dis-
pensed in his name. "Who," he therefore asked with regard to closing
the courts,

> was the blameable cause and author of this shocking event? of this mis-
> chief & calamity, before unheard of, unless in a time of absolute civil
> war? A whole province outlawed for about the space of six months?
> This is a deep question with some, which I shall not presume to answer:
> But beg leave to say, I have not so much as the most distant thought
> that it was his sacred Majesty's our rightful King—I do not mean only
> to say he was not the author thereof as King, in which sense he cannot
> do wrong any more than he can die, but I mean, as a man he never
> commanded it, neither came it into his heart.[26]

For Hawley, as for most colonials, the idea that the king was
abandoning his American subjects remained only "the most distant
thought." Accordingly, for the time being the estrangement between
king and people found its best expression indirectly, in symbols of revolt. Hawley's client had been apprehended after a festive house-raising that recalled the Boston Stamp Act protests of August and the
more recent demonstrations on November 1 and November 5 (Pope
Day). The atmosphere in Lanesborough on the twenty-sixth had led
quite naturally to a symbolic immolation of authority in the form of
effigies in defiance of the sheriff's authority. It followed from the character of these events that Hawley, thinking the case over during the
night, arrived at the idea of the ultimate threat to authority—treason.

Nothing in the circumstances, however, suggested that Hawley
would thereafter grow obsessed with this case, and especially with
Hutchinson. Hawley argued before Hutchinson in September 1766.
In October he emerged from his obscurity in the legislature to take up
his client's cause there. This he was able to do in connection with a bill
providing compensation to Hutchinson and other victims of the Stamp
Act crowds. Hawley argued that His Majesty's "pious and benevolent
intention" was to pardon the offenders (among whom his client was

certain to be numbered) as well as to compensate the victims. Such an interference with the king's prerogative to pardon amounted to a radical challenge—and one that focused attention on Hawley. Under his influence the patriot party in 1766 took up the doctrine of no compensation without a general amnesty.[27]

Hawley's personal animus could not be mistaken. "The rioters," he was reported to have said, "had a claim to favor as well as the sufferers the chief of whom was a person of unconstitutional principles [that is, Thomas Hutchinson]." Hawley himself later reported that "divers persons" had charged, unfairly as he believed, that his speeches had "abused and done great injury to the judges of the superior court, and especially to the chief justice." At the same time Hawley's precipitation was equally notable. For, within a year of publicly joining the patriot side and toying with the idea of treason he is supposed to have proclaimed in the legislature that, "the Parliament of Great Britain has no right to legislate for us." Upon this, Otis, ever alert to potentially treasonous implications, rose and bowed to Hawley, saying, "He has gone farther than I myself have yet done in this House."[28]

Hutchinson's reaction to Hawley's attacks was characteristically balanced, generous, and psychologically acute. "I have never met with any misfortune more sudden and unexpected than Major Hawley's violent prejudice and opposition," he wrote to one correspondent, and to another he averred that he especially regretted being vilified "by a man of Mr. Hawley's character." To Hawley's cousin, Israel Williams, Hutchinson wrote that he did not intend to "lose the favorable opinion he once had of me and I doubt not that one time or other I shall convince him he is mistaken." Nevertheless, he observed that Hawley had "strangely appeared in opposition" to the compensation bill "to the surprise of everybody." Israel Williams, with the apparent aid of family insight (no doubt mixed with loyalist scorn), replied to Hutchinson's perplexity, "If he is not distracted the devil is in him." Williams knew Hawley's Arminian enthusiasm, his treatment of Martha Root, his role in the expulsion of Edwards, and his turning on Williams himself. Accordingly he predicted, "He will soon recant of what he has injuriously uttered elsewhere, if his mind be not Strangely blinded. His Prejudices and Zeal are apt to hurry him into great excess and mistakes sometimes."[29]

In the meantime, Hawley joined Otis and Samuel Adams in removing Hutchinson from his seat on the Massachusetts Council the following year. By then Hutchinson realized that he had inspired another obsessive, personal resentment. (This was the session during which Otis ran through the gallery shouting abuse at him.) Hawley, Hutchinson wrote, "thought he had not been properly treated by the Lieutenant-governor as chief-justice in the Court of Common Law, and to revenge himself, brought the publick abuse against him [Hutchinson] in the assembly." Hutchinson responded to Hawley's newspaper attacks with his usual forbearance: "What shall we do with Hawley? I can freely forgive him but how shall we save the honour of the court?" (Two years later Hutchinson asked Israel Williams in perplexity, "Is there no reconciling Major Hawley?")[30]

At this point Hutchinson, who by now regarded Hawley as "the principal demagogue in the province," arranged that Hawley should receive the rather mild rebuke of being suspended from appearing as a barrister before the Superior Court—something that did not affect the bulk of his legal practice. By the next court term Hutchinson had arranged for Hawley's reinstatement. In his turn Hawley delivered yet another letter of repentance, this one to the Superior Court. Here, as one native later recalled the "common report" of the day, he "came in and made a very humble confession and shed many tears."[31]

The semi-honorary position of barrister that was at issue came to hold important symbolic weight for the patriot lawyers, and to have a particular reference to Hutchinson after he became chief justice of the Superior Court. Josiah Quincy, Jr., became embroiled in a dispute over the necessity of wearing the barrister's "long robe" in this court. Hawley himself never forgave Hutchinson for his own temporary loss of barrister status the same year. Later, John Adams emphasized the symbolic importance of the new robes and formal panoply introduced by Hutchinson in 1762, confusing both the year of those innovations and his own elevation to barrister.

In January 1767 Jonathan Sewall defended both court and jury for upholding the guilty verdict. Writing as "Philanthrop," Sewall incidentally criticized Hawley's inflammatory speeches in the legislature on the matter, characterizing them as typical of unfair complaints against government and authority by the patriot party. Hawley chose to interpret Sewall as implying that the account of the Berkshire affair and trial which he had given to the legislature was inaccurate and that his plea for a charge of treason was misinformed. In a series of lengthy

essays, his first public writings, Hawley refuted these supposed con-
tentions.[32] Toward the end, Hawley mentioned having been in a "very
ill state of health" in February 1767, the month following Sewall's
first essay. Thus, both Hawley's newspaper dispute and his campaign
against Hutchinson in the legislature during 1767 appear to have been
related to the mental incapacity that first gripped him in 1766.

A description of Hawley's state of mind during 1767 suggests the
profound effect on him of the Berkshire affair and its sequelae. "He is
much altered from what he was," wrote Israel Williams, "is more
haughty, self-sufficient obstinate and less disposed to suspect himself
than formerly." Williams's description of Hawley's behavior is also
suggestive of a familiar Puritan phenomenon: the suffering of doubt
accompanied by anxiety, followed by a conversion and a new attitude
of certainty (often combined with intolerance of opponents). In 1766
Hawley's night of rethinking the Berkshire affair, during which he had
come to his conclusion about treason, had resembled the soul-searching of a Puritan. As Hutchinson put it, he thereafter threw off his religious enthusiasm to become an "Inthusiast in Politics," where he
made Hutchinson his "mark."[33]

In his newspaper articles Hawley insisted that he had been right to
ask that the court alter its charge to one of treason, and he hinted that
he was particularly incensed with Hutchinson for denying the motion.
As Hawley then proceeded to delve into the definition of treason, he
began to approach the idea of revolution. He offered as an example of
treason a group of men who for disobeying the law must be regarded
as levying "war against the office and authority of the king." What,
after all, was "war, rebellion, or insurrection," but treason? Suppose
that "two hundred men, with only clubs and staves [that is, armed like
the men in the Berkshire affair], should combine and undertake actually to murder the King." These men would be no more guilty of
treason than those in the Berkshire affair (if they *were* guilty), for both
groups have "absolutely broke and thrown off their allegiance to the
King and are become rebels."[34] Interference with service of the king's
writs was the equivalent of attempted regicide.

In his last newspaper letter Hawley explored his motives in writing, and revealed some of what he had begun to feel. Rhetorically he
asked whether he had written "in rebellion, or a spirit of sedition, and
to treat the King's Governors and Judges with contempt and disrespect [the grounds of his suspension by Hutchinson], and to destroy or

lessen that mutual trust and confidence in the community, upon which the public happiness in any degree depends."[35] He did not need to answer these questions, for of course he had written in no such spirit—at least consciously. Within a few years, though, Hawley became the confirmed rebel that he had called up in his imagination while turning over and over the concept of treason.

Hawley, Quincy, and the Adamses all took years to become patriots, and years after that to choose independence. But the aura of kingly presence with which government invested each of its officials made the *idea* of treason readily available to them once an example of disobedience had been raised. The Stamp Act crowds had provided such an example with their regicidal symbolism; the patriots who took up opposition in their writings raised the specter of regicide with an equivalent kind of indirection. At the Writs of Assistance case in 1761 James Otis alluded to the regicide of King Charles. So did John Adams in his "Dissertation on Canon and Feudal Law" in 1765. Hawley's overnight discovery of treason one may say, was the most dramatic example of a significant phenomenon: the imagining of revolution in symbolic terms years before any conscious decision to repudiate submission to the king. The newspaper essays in which Hawley first expressed such thoughts pointed unmistakably to revolution, but like the other patriots he did not immediately espouse active rebellion.

The result was the phenomenon of conscience patriotism: a constant, anguished reevaluation of one's own motives and opinions. Its results were sometimes bizarre, as in 1768 during an exchange in the legislature between Hawley and Otis. In one of his speeches on the question of Parliament's right to tax the colonies, Hawley returned to the frequently advanced proposal that the colonies establish representatives in Parliament. This possibility had been rejected by both sides as impractical. But as Hawley now recalled, it would remove the technical objection against taxation without representation. On this ground, apparently, Hawley indicated his support for the step. It amounted to yet another Hawley reversal—this one as startling as any of Otis's, for it conceded Parliament's absolute power over the colonies in exchange for token representation. One can only guess at Otis's reaction as he rose to dismiss the proposal. At some level of his consciousness he could not but identify Hawley's honest quixotism as similar to his own. Thus, at this moment the two most eccentric examples of Puritan conscience among the patriots faced one another.

"Otis," Bernard reported, "treated this [proposal by Hawley] as the revery of a Madman (H[awley] having a little wildness in his Constitution) being directly contradictory to his repeated assertions during all the last winter sessions." At this point, with a supreme sense of the ironies, the loyalist Timothy Ruggles rose to read from an earlier Otis tract that exactly expressed Hawley's present opinion. Otis obviously was not referring to Hawley's recent episode of melancholia. Nevertheless, the fact that the charge of madness had once again burst out in the heat of debate confirms the impression of widespread psychic strain in the period. What Hawley's cousin Israel Williams reported about him could have been applied to numerous less extreme cases among his fellow patriots: "It is said by many he is honest, but under the influence of strong, irregular passions." (Of specific interest for Hawley and his father is the modern observation that in "difficult social circumstances and in unstable times the number of depressions and depressive suicides increases.")[36]

The form that Hawley's passions now proceeded to take correspond closely to the behavior of melancholics during their "free intervals" between attacks of depression: "an obstinate and defiant attitude alternating with exaggerated docility and an excess of 'goodness.' " Thus, in 1769 when Hawley was elected from among the members of the lower house for the council, he declined to serve. Writing in 1823, William Tudor, the biographer of James Otis, asserted that early in the patriot struggle Hawley "resolved, and pledged himself, never to accept of any promotion, office, or emolument under any government. This pledge he severely redeemed. He refused even all promotion in the militia, was several times chosen a counsellor [that is, a member of the council], but declined; and would accept of no other public trust, than the nearly gratuitous one of representing his town."[37] Such refusal, or resolution to refuse, was common among the conscience patriots, and especially notable in James Otis and John Adams. But whereas his colleagues needed to convince themselves that they served the public strictly out of a sense of duty, Hawley's self-doubt could be assuaged only by self-denial. Thus, while serving as a town selectman early in his career, he had from time to time made the similar gesture of refusing to serve as moderator of the town meeting.

Frequently Hawley gave illness as his excuse for not serving, as when in 1756 he elected not to join in an inspection tour of forts because "the Weather is so Extremely hot that I would Instantly Bring the disorder to which I am Incident in hot weather." (Hawley appears to have suffered all his life from hypochondria. His letters to his wife invariably referred to his having a cold or "grievous cold." He would report to her that, at best, he was feeling as well as "is comon with me," or else "tollerably well for me."[38]

In 1770 Hawley emerged as a leading opponent of government. Contemporaries disagreed only as to whether he or Samuel Adams stood first in importance in the opposition during this period of Hutchinson's first session as acting governor. Until Hutchinson was driven from the province in 1774, Hawley concerned himself chiefly in bringing down his foe, whom, in yet another imputation of madness, he came to regard as "bereft." Hawley's biographer commented on this period: "If Hawley ever reviewed in his mind the terms he had served in the General Court, he must have realized that he had been associated with very little constructive work. Most of his energies had been expended in the struggle with the governor; for the rest he had mainly devoted himself to routine bills and special acts of a minor importance."[39] This is not necessarily to say that Hawley conducted a merely personal vendetta. Even among the conscience patriots he stood out as a man of principles. Nevertheless, like the rest he singled out Hutchinson with a peculiar emphasis on personality.

Once Hawley achieved certainty about Hutchinson and politics he entered what appears to have been his most effective phase. This extended from Hutchinson's elevation to acting governor in 1769 to Hutchinson's expulsion from Massachusetts in 1774, when Hawley again showed signs of illness. It was at this time that he refused to sign the Northampton Committee of Correspondence "covenants," and then declined appointment to the first Continental Congress. Both actions may have been further gestures of conscience, though the latter appears to have been chiefly connected with poor health. Whatever his condition at the time, Hawley was able to send a letter analyzing the political situation to his replacement, John Adams, in which he displayed notable insight and balance.[40]

After 1774 Hawley's melancholia no longer alternated with a manic phase. Though he never served in the Continental Congress he maintained contact with its members. Despite a return of symptoms starting in 1775, he served in the Revolutionary Massachusetts Provincial Congress and occasionally sat as a judge.[41] Then, in 1774 and 1775, three of Hawley's loyalist relatives were beset by patriot mobs.

One of the victims was his cousin, Israel Williams, and another was Williams's son; as a result of the attacks Williams's daughter-in-law suffered a miscarriage that brought her near death.

Like the other conscience patriots, Hawley disapproved of mobs: he "expressed a very strong disapprobation of such private disturbances and restraining People of their liberty."[42] But none of his contemporaries had to face up to a mobbing so close to home and so late in the struggle, and Hawley's shock evidently went deeper than his statement on public disturbances would indicate. For at this point his behavior departed from that of the other patriots: whereas they grew in conviction and unequivocal allegiance to the cause, he returned to doubt and self-examination.

In the month that his cousins were mobbed, Hawley suffered his third major illness. A few months later he reported on his "want of health, memory, weakness of body and Shocking impair of mind," and he added, "My state of mind has been for many weeks, much the same as it was about Ten years ago."

Both severe illnesses that he was referring to—1775 and 1766—coincided with public disturbances that affected him emotionally. Though he connected the current 1775 collapse of his health with politics, he did not specifically mention the riots, nor did he indicate that he might at this late date be experiencing remorse over his own treatment of Israel Williams some twenty years earlier. Instead, as Hawley understood it, he had been brought low by his attendance at the provincial legislature, which had just ended. There he had been disturbed by the "shocking backwardness" of towns to pay their excise taxes, by the "great deficiency of Gunpowder," and by "anxiety and Sollicitude" coming from his anticipation that "hostilities would very soon Commence."[43]

Yet these explanations were offered in a letter answering charges that his criticisms of rioters and his absence from the legislature indicated a turning against the cause. Defending himself just three months after he became ill, and writing in a still shaky hand, Hawley denied the charge of backsliding but with religious scrupulosity revealed his feelings as far as he could plumb them. His letter resembled his earlier religious confessions, especially in its refusal to shirk the truth.

The specific charges laid against Hawley were that he had expressed "disapprobation" of the cause, and that he had "forsaken or deserted it." He answered that his illness alone had sometimes kept him from the legislature, which far from forsaking he had wished to attend. As for his having expressed disapprobation of the cause, that presented a more complicated problem. His cousin Stoddard had sent him some loyalist pamphlets at about the time that Stoddard was beset by the mob, and Hawley had agreed to read them, though his illness had prevented him from more than looking at the tables of contents. On the other hand, Hawley's explanation went on to confess that when cousin Stoddard's brother had delivered the pamphlets, Hawley had told him that he was "entirely open to conviction."[44] This was old-fashioned religious terminology for having an open mind in a dispute. Nothing Hawley ever wrote more clearly demonstrated that for him the experience of revolution was modeled on the religious struggles of the Great Awakening.

The year 1776 marked both the Declaration of Independence and Hawley's reaching the age—fifty-three—at which his father had committed suicide. In the fall his melancholy came over him. He is supposed never to have truly recovered, so that one might say that, spurred by the memory of his father's suicide, Hawley sentenced himself to a living death. One of the several young boys who successively came to live with the childless Hawleys recalled that after this breakdown he "used to sit & muse & smoke . . . excessively." Friends visited and tried to distract him, usually without success. "In one of his gloomy turns" he feared that the British would win and that he would "lose his head." But, continuing his earliest pattern of swings in emotions, "in his bright turns he was full of zeal in the cause of liberty." Hawley continued to correspond occasionally with members of the Continental Congress, and in 1779 he outlined an essay on religion that suggested a return of interest in the disputes he had been attracted to as a young man writing his commonplace book.[45]

Then in 1780 Hawley displayed once and for all both the ambiguities of his patriot politics and their basis in religious scruples. He began by objecting to the formal establishment of religion in the new Massachusetts Constitution. In a long, philosophical letter he returned in spirit to the liberalism of his Arminian days (and perhaps justified Peter Oliver's description of him as being subject to "fits of Deism"). He did not turn on the Revolution itself, for he praised the idea of the new Constitution, but rather turned back to his own religious revolutionism. As Alan Heimert put it, Hawley's position on religion in 1780 "was a recapitulation of the first political premise of Revolutionary Calvinism."[46]

Despite his objections to the Constitution, Hawley was elected under it to the new state senate, the equivalent of the old council. However, because the Constitution called for a religious oath on taking office, Hawley refused yet another time to serve in public office. In a ringing statement of principle he denied the right of the state to compel religious oaths. The oaths in question recalled those demanded by Jonathan Edwards for church membership. More immediately, though, for Hawley they called to mind Thomas Hutchinson, whom he mentioned somewhat gratuitously toward the end of his statement. Hawley referred to the struggle, in which he had been instrumental, to keep Hutchinson off the Massachusetts council in 1767. "We have all heard of a Lieut. Govr. of the Massachusetts Bay," he wrote, "and some of us have known him very well who contended long and earnestly that he had a right to a seat in council without a voice [that is, without a vote]. I imagine that I can maintain a better argument than he did, that I have a right to a seat in the Senate of Massachusetts without a voice, but at present I shall not attempt to take it."[47] That Hawley should have imposed on the situation a strained parallel between himself and Hutchinson suggests that, like the other patriots, he felt both an affinity with and a degree of remorse toward him. Without too much stretch of the imagination it may be said that Hawley here delivered his last public apology.

Hawley's apostasy was followed between 1782 and 1787 by tax revolts in Northampton and neighboring towns that challenged the entire legitimacy of the new government. In February 1782 Samuel Ely and his followers began a series of disturbances calculated to close the courts. After Ely had been arrested, arraigned before Hawley, and jailed, a mob of his followers attempted to free him, just as in the Berkshire affair. Hawley viewed the Ely disturbances as a crucial test. Ely threatened to become a "ruling Tyrant," he wrote, and if "such Insurgents prevail, Britain prevails." Yet though Hawley remarked that "we are not Certain, who, besides the Devil, Sprang Ely into existence at first," he took a moderate and moderating role toward the rioters. He reviewed their grievances along with those of the former Continental soldiers who opposed them but were in 1782 "on the Point of turning to the Mobb." Like the loyalists who believed in sinister forces behind the patriot movement, Hawley now came to believe that British agents were responsible for the disturbances. In June 1782 he reported the shocking fact that "we have had it Huzza'd for George the third within 8 rods of our Court house."[48]

One can only wonder how Hawley felt this late in the Revolution at witnessing a popular revulsion against the movement with which he had allied himself. Of course his county and town made an exception in the new United Colonies, for nowhere else were there such counter-revolutionary outbreaks. Nevertheless, it appeared for a while that the violence of the Revolution, which he had disapproved, had begotten permanent violence. And as they expressed their resentment, the people used terms that went to the heart of Hawley's Revolutionary commitment. The people were "perpetually taught," supposedly by British agents, that "they were horribly deceived and deluded by those who first contended with Bernard and Hutchinson, and disputed against the Duties." The people had risen up, Hawley might well have added, against men like himself in particular. For, as he reported it, two thirds of them believed that *"they were miserably deceived by Hutchinson's oppressors."*[49]

Hawley seems to have receded more and more from the world after the Ely riots, so that there is no way of knowing how he was struck by the Shays riots in 1786, or even if he was aware of them. These continued through 1787 and ended in 1788; Hawley died shortly afterward.

At the time of his death Hawley's depressions appeared to his fellow patriots as an unfortunate affliction unrelated to his political career. Yet viewed in modern terms Hawley's pathology throws light on the national experience of revolution. It has been suggested that societies as a whole may suffer depression as a result of their loss of a familiar way of life or political arrangement. In such circumstances, "demands to restore a traditional morality" are common.[50] Hawley's loss of his father, when brought together with a national cause for mourning (in advance) the loss of England, resulted in an exaggeration in him of the national symptoms. Both his anger at representatives of the old regime and his love of its principles were stronger than those of others, yet recognizable to them. If he helped to make Thomas Hutchinson into a scapegoat, he made himself a sacrificial figure as well. For whereas Hutchinson had to bear the burdens of authority, Hawley underwent the sorrows of disobedience.

CHAPTER SEVEN

Josiah Quincy

W HEN THE FIERY YOUNG Boston patriot Josiah Quincy, Jr., died in 1775 he left behind him a mystery regarding his fluctuating opinions similar to the one connected with James Otis. Quincy became involved in politics in 1767, at about the age of twenty-three, in the aftermath of the Stamp Act. His political career lay closer to the Revolution than those of Otis, Adams, and Hawley, with the result that for him the great question was not so much that of Parliamentary supremacy as of independence itself. In a revealing study of Quincy's "vagaries," George H. Nash points out "a curious feature of his political behavior": "a discrepancy between a dominant radical posture and, at certain crucial moments, surprisingly cautious and restrained counsel and actions. It was a peculiarity that would become intensified in the final months of his life as he wavered, at times almost daily, between independence and reconciliation, between war and 'peaceful' coercion." Though Nash does not remark the parallel with the other patriots he comments that "the vagaries of the political career of Quincy reveal a pattern whose implications may extend far beyond the life of the man who made it."[1]

Quincy's politics began and ended with Thomas Hutchinson. On the day following the destruction of Hutchinson's house in 1765 Quincy, then twenty-one years old, wrote a compassionate memo on the shocking excesses of the "Rage-intoxicated Rabble."[2] Within a few years, however, he adopted the standard patriot view of Hutchinson, who became as central in his writings as in Otis's. Quincy ended his career in an obsession with Hutchinson that postdated those of the other patriots. In London in 1774 after Hutchinson's removal there, Quincy imagined himself in a struggle with the exiled governor, but

153

died before being able to convey his final impressions of Hutchinson's supposedly continuing role in American affairs.

Unlike Otis, the Adamses, and Hawley, Quincy was not an oldest but a youngest son. And yet, like the others, he bore his father's name and arrogated to himself the primary responsibility for honoring that name. His father, Colonel Josiah Quincy, was the leading citizen and justice of the peace in the village of Braintree, Massachusetts. The colonel was a man of means, the descendant of a long line of wealthy and distinguished Quincys. In 1749, when Josiah Junior was five and the family living in Boston, the colonel fell into a vast fortune—$300,-000—when a ship in which he held a one-third interest captured a Spanish galleon laden with silver. The next year he removed his family to Braintree. One tradition has it that he did so to retire, another that he retired six years later. The records show that he at least acted as overseer for the family glass business in Braintree, kept busy on town committees, and twice represented the town in the legislature.[3] It might be said, then, that he semiretired to a life of intermittent and unstrenuous public service. In 1775, the year before the second date given by tradition for the colonel's retirement, his wife died. Josiah was then eleven. Within six months the colonel remarried. His second wife died four years later, in 1759, and he remarried for the last time in 1762.

Despite these deaths, the colonel remained outgoing and funloving. Lacing his talk with confidential allusions to province affairs and well-placed friends (he had served on special commissions with Lieutenant Governor Hutchinson and with Governor Shirley), he evidenced a complacently high self-regard.

Next door to the colonel lived a young man whose very existence centered on the idea of self-sacrificing service to country on the old Puritan and Quincy family model. This was John Adams, who made "Coll Quincy" into a leading character in his diary.

Adams's "Coll Quincy" comes across as a genial, self-satisfied, and self-congratulatory figure. He likes to entertain the young people: his two sons and John Adams, all fledgling lawyers, and his spirited, flirtatious daughter Hannah, to whom John Adams almost proposed. (Josiah, then a teenager, is not mentioned by Adams.) The colonel goes sailing on the bay with the young people and entertains them in the evenings with philosophical and political talk, much of which advertises his own accomplishments. John Adams is irresistibly attracted by his worldliness—the colonel has been to Europe several times—and yet directs at him the resentment felt by high ambition in the face of self-satisfied indolence.[4]

Colonel Quincy's decision to retire may have been influenced by his father's death. Edmund Quincy, like *his* father before him, had been a prominent public figure in Massachusetts: a member of the council, and a judge of the Superior Court. In 1737 he had been sent to England on a boundary commission, and had taken his son Josiah with him. Soon after arriving in London he had died, at fifty-seven, of a faulty smallpox inoculation. It would not have been surprising if the son had henceforth avoided travel and strenuous government service. Certainly the colonel's death proved to be very different from either his father's or his sons'. According to tradition, "his passion for field sports remained in full force till the end, for his death was occasioned by exposure to the winter's cold, sitting upon a cake of ice, watching for wild ducks, when he was in his seventy-fifth year."[5]

Josiah Quincy, Jr., grew up with the specter of death constantly about him. In 1768 his brother Edmund died, making three deaths (those of mother, stepmother, and brother) in the immediate family in a little over ten years. In addition, in 1756, after the death of Quincy's mother, his cousin Abraham drowned. In 1765 Quincy's mentor and employer, Oxenbridge Thacher, died after having smallpox. Soon afterward and very near the beginning of his political career, Quincy, who had been a particularly frail child, learned that, like his brother, he had tuberculosis.[6]

Quincy's two older brothers, whose lack of ambition outraged John Adams, better reflected their father's character than did he himself, who came to be distinguished in a long line of Josiah Quincys as "the Patriot." The oldest brother, Samuel, put it well when he contrasted his own "love of ease" with the energy of young Josiah, who, "carried out by the zeal and fervour of imagination, strength of genius, and the love of glory, shall snatch at the wreaths of fame, through the turmoils of public action." On the other hand, Quincy shared his father's enthusiastic and impressionable nature, which expressed itself particularly in political matters. The colonel's ability suddenly to shift his political feelings has been criticized as an "emotional weakness." Similarly, his rather dramatic, tearful behavior toward relatives was judged by them as calculating and self-interested. It was not surprising, therefore, that the colonel eventually made his

Josiah Quincy

namesake and the youngest of his sons his favorite, for Josiah Junior shared both his emotionalism and his patriot politics.[7]

Quincy's political career redeemed the lives of two generations of Quincys: his own and that of his father. In his own generation one brother became a loyalist, while the other, who was mildly a patriot, died young. As for the colonel, his patriot sympathies and his "extreme view of the situation," similar to Quincy's, were not matched by any notable patriotic exertion. Quincy's attempt to make himself over in a sterner image is apparent in a letter to his father written in 1768. In it, after thanking the colonel for having made him financially independent, Quincy reported having taken a Puritanic vow of self-imposed adversity. "To apply for assistance, where my own foresight might have prevented the necessity, would be to me worse than death. Early in life I was fixed; experience has confirmed me, to suffer every stroke of adversity, let it be as severe as even imagination can paint, ere I would implore any earthly relief from distress, against which my own prudence might have armed me."[8] In other words, he made a conscious decision to reject a life of ease, and pointedly said so in a letter addressed to his easygoing father.

Like the other conscience patriots, Quincy displayed numerous Puritan traits of character. His diligent notes on cases, the *Quincy Reports,* remain a valuable source of New England legal history. When Oxenbridge Thacher died in 1765 and left Quincy his extensive law practice, in contrast to his father Quincy plunged into work to make himself worthy of his windfall. Late in 1767, for reasons that are not clear, Quincy spurned wearing the robe of a Superior Court barrister. Joseph Hawley's expulsion from this court at about the same time may have had something to do with his decision, or he may have been influenced by an abhorrence of the court's supposedly popish splendor as articulated by such men as John Adams. (In London in 1774 Quincy, in the Puritan fashion, called the theater a nursery of vice.)[9] Whatever the reason, Quincy's first public act after Thacher's death, a refusal of promotion, was both principled and self-sacrificing: he had assumed the mantle of conscience patriotism.

For all its idealism, Quincy's course in politics carried overtones of his father's relationship with Hutchinson. In 1747, when still being appointed to governor's commissions, the colonel had joined Hutchinson in investigating a Boston riot. The two men prepared a report condemning the rioters. Soon afterward, however, the colonel was ap-

pointed by the town to defend it against the governor's aspersions over
the riot. This put him on the opposite side from Hutchinson. Years
later, writing on the day following the Hutchinson mob, Quincy produced a disquisition on the dangers of crowds. There could not be
found "a more flagrant Instance, to what a Pitch of Infatuation an incensed Populace may arise, than the last Night afforded," he wrote.
He called on "ye Sons of *Avarice!*" and "ye Sons of *Popularity!*"—that
is, the instigators and defenders of mobs—to beware the anarchy
threatened by the *"Fury and Instability"* of "this Rage-intoxicated
Rabble."[10]

Yet Quincy's intense sympathy with Hutchinson on this occasion
soon shifted to violent hatred of him (though Quincy never abandoned
his opposition to crowd violence). His anti-Hutchinson feelings recapitulated the colonel's mild turn against Hutchinson, but Quincy's
fury appears to have been influenced by his mentor, Oxenbridge
Thacher.

Like James Otis, whom he joined in arguing the Writs of Assistance case, Thacher turned against Hutchinson in 1761. In the four
years of life remaining to him, Thacher established a reputation as
Otis's near equal in patriotic fervor, especially in regard to Hutchinson. He, too, attacked Hutchinson in the legislature and in newspaper
articles on the subject of plural office holding, and he, too, breached
the normal terms of deference in doing so. Up until and including the
Writs case, Adams observed, Thacher had had the reputation of an
especially mild-mannered, controlled personality. But thereafter
Thacher's "indignation" toward Hutchinson and the court party burst
out: "His Philippicks against the unprincipled Ambition and Avarice
of all of them, but especially of Hutchinson, were unbridled; not only
in private, confidential Conversations, but in all Companies and on all
Occasions. He gave Hutchinson the Sobriquet of 'Summa Potestas'
and rarely mentioned him but by the Name of 'Summa.' " Adams
claimed that as a result of the taxation issue Thacher grew "so anxious
and agitated that I have no doubt it occasioned his premature
death."[11] For Quincy, then, Thacher provided models of both opposition and martyrdom.

In 1767 Quincy joined Otis and Hawley in their efforts to deny
Hutchinson a seat on the governor's council on the grounds of plural
office holding. Over the pseudonym "Pro Lege" Quincy contributed
to the Boston *Gazette* a list of legal precedents for impeachment of

high officers like Hutchinson—an act reminiscent of his father's legal-
ism of 1747. In the preface to this list Quincy adopted the patriarchal
terms of Otis and Hawley. Hutchinson was a "rapacious Grasper of
Sovereignty, elected with a plenitude of power." But "strip yon gor-
geous Monarch of his Regalia," he wrote, "take from that despotic
Tyrant, the Powers with which a despised Rabble have invested him,"
and both would prove to be but mortal.[12]

. Despite its exaggerated resentment, when one compares this attack with later ones on Hutchinson by Quincy, it does not appear to
evince a special antipathy. For Quincy eventually outdid even Otis in
rhetorical extremity. Indeed, by all reports Quincy was easily agitated
on almost any question. His son later wrote that as a child Quincy had
been noted for "the extreme sensibility of his temperament," as well as
by "ardour and industry," and he added that "these qualities characterized him through life." John Adams caught Quincy in an apparently typical gesture in 1774, when the two were traveling the legal
circuit in Maine along with Quincy's brother Samuel. The lawyers
often traveled in a group with the judges; on arriving at a town where
the court was to sit they would be approached by prospective clients.
Adams observed in a letter to his wife that, when he and Samuel halted
because of a rain, "Josiah Quincy, allways impetuous and vehement,
would not stop, but drove forward, I suppose that he might get upon
the Fishing Ground before his Brother Sam, and me."[13] One assumes
that, as Adams indicated, Quincy spurred forward more out of excitement than to make money, for there is nothing in his record any more
than in those of the other conscience patriots to indicate cupidity.

When, beginning in 1767, Quincy began to write on politics for
the newspapers, the most remarkable feature of his essays was their
lack of argument. His attack on Hutchinson as "Pro Lege," like John
Adams's attack on Jonathan Sewall, amounted to little more than sustained denunciation. Philip Davidson has commented that "for all the
weight of his legal learning Quincy never burdened his effective essays
with heavy detail." Davidson theorizes that this was because he "knew
the central fact of crowd psychology—that emotion, not reason, determined action."[14] But as with the other patriots, and perhaps with
Quincy's father, presumptions of venality or calculation overlook a
genuine ardor of personality. Thus, Josiah Quincy, Jr., though easily
stirred himself, did not attempt to rouse the crowd. On the contrary,
he frequently risked his popularity by opposing it.

Rather than political calculation, Quincy's essays evidence a frenzied sensibility. This expressed itself in the current terms of Whig Sentimentalism. Whereas Otis gave expression to fantasies of destroying fathers, however, Quincy evoked a happy family life. He indulged in the imagination of ravishment in good Whig Sentimental manner. But his chief fear was of the murderer at the door: the nemesis that pursued his own family (and that, as he was writing his first political essays in 1767, was only months away from claiming his brother Edmund). To one who counseled "prudent means to obtain redress," Quincy, in an essay opposing English customs duties, replied, "Go, thou dastard! Get thee home!—A rank adulterer riots in thy incestuous bed, a brutal ravisher deflowers thy only daughter, a barbarous villain now lifts the murtherous hand and stabs thy tender infant to the heart—see the sapphire current trickling from the wound, & the dear Boy, now as he gasps his last, cries out the Ruffian's mercy." In the same essay Quincy readily admitted his emotionality. "My feeling heart," he wrote, "is alternately torn with doubt and hope, despondency and terror." And to anyone who might wish to criticize his approach, he declared, "If this, thou blasphemer! is enthusiasm, then will we live and die enthusiasts."[15]

Quincy was writing at the first crisis since the Stamp Act: the anticipated arrival in Boston of customs commissioners sent to collect the Townshend duties. Without specifying exactly what he meant, he called on his "countrymen" to take an oath: to "swear" that "we will die,—if we cannot live freemen!" Writing again as "Pro Lege" in 1768, Quincy imagined his own ravishment. "Should some dauntless Champion of the Cause of Freedom, providentially arise for their Defence," he wrote, the people "would fly, like a timid Herd, and leave the virtuous Hero to be sacrificed as a Victim."[16]

Later, Quincy began his attacks on Hutchinson by echoing the cry of "Pensioner!" with which Otis kept Hutchinson from his seat during the 1768 legislative session. Then, during the crisis over nonimportation that greeted Hutchinson on his appointment as acting governor, Quincy was caught up in the argument at a town meeting. William Molineux proposed to lead a crowd of demonstrators to Hutchinson's house in order to enforce adherence to what he regarded as the current terms of the nonintercourse agreement. Quincy rose to oppose the proceeding as involving high treason. But his warning, far from expressing sympathy with Hutchinson, contained an accusation against him that went further than anyone else's. The march being proposed was actually a plot laid by Hutchinson himself, Quincy declared. And he warned his fellow townsmen that "the Hutchinsons whose name they had long reason to dread had laid this trap in order to insnare them." He did not doubt, he added, that if they proceeded there would be many spies present "to take every advantage of them." This was the meeting at which Otis spoke distractedly—upon being appealed to by Quincy—and then ended by setting out with Molineux and Samuel Adams at the head of the crowd.[17] George H. Nash marks Quincy's opposition to the dominant patriot position on this occasion as the beginning of his curious changes of heart. If he is right, then it would appear that, as with the other conscience patriots, these had much to do both with Hutchinson and the crowd issue.

At the center of what Hutchinson, referring to Otis, termed the "mob-high eloquence" of the patriots lay a contradiction. Men like Quincy might identify emotionally with the crowd, but they were opposed to its lawlessness.[18] The reasons for this contradiction are apparent. Between 1765 and 1776 many patriots experienced a rising personal resentment at England—one that often found its surprising expression in crowd actions. When presented with the chance of cooperating with such actions, the conscience patriots demurred, as both Otis and Quincy did at the town meeting. Later, however, they often found ways to justify the illegality, while warning against any further disorder. This was the pattern for Joseph Hawley with the Northampton riot, for John Adams with the Boston Tea Party, and for Quincy with Molineux's march on Hutchinson's house.

Quincy voiced his approval a week later in an article supporting nonimportation, and a month later while representing a patriot client arrested for "Riot" and "tarring and feathering." Here he argued that the slightest disturbances were being blown up into cases of treason. Quincy also expressed his attachment to the cause by attacking Hutchinson. "Good GOD!" he wrote of him,

> What must be the distress, the sentiments, and feelings of a people, legislated, condemned and governed, by a creature so mercenary, so dependant, and so————but I forbear: my anguish is too exquisite——my heart is too full!

So full, in fact, that Quincy's newspaper opponent was able to point out that he had not "contended any of the points he had started."[19]

Viewed ethically, nonimportation was a subject on which Quincy could naturally take a fervent stand. In fact, nonimportation developed, with his help, into a righteous, almost religious issue that recalls the politics of the Puritans. The purpose of nonimportation became not only economic coercion of England but the renewal of "ancestral virtues," especially those of frugality and industry. With typical enthusiasm Quincy went further than others who extolled those virtues. In fact, he went so far as to wish that the abhorred revenue acts might be continued in force. That way America would be led to "break off— OFF FOREVER!—all social intercourse, with those, whose commerce contaminates, whose luxuries poison, whose avarice is insatiable, and whose unnatural oppressions are not to be borne."[20]

If nonintercourse was conceived as a self-purifying act, then coercive enforcement of it did not make sense. Thus Quincy could support nonimportation more fervently than Molineux, yet disapprove of its enforcement by crowds. Nevertheless, Quincy's political wavering here and elsewhere amounted to a crisis of conscience regarding the propriety of crowd behavior.[21] When the crowd appeared to be dormant his rhetoric intensified; when the crowd arose he retreated. This is the context in which he agreed on March 6, 1770, in a move celebrated in legend, to join John Adams in defending the soldiers arrested for firing in the Boston Massacre.

The following month Quincy accepted and tried another case related both to crowds and nonimportation. The two trials put him at the center of the crowd issue, and helped to produce a number of his seemingly contradictory writings and actions. The events resulting in the case of Ebenezer Richardson, which Quincy accepted and tried in April 1770, preceded the Massacre trials (which were put off until September). Richardson had interrupted a demonstration by a group of boys in front of the shop of Theophilus Lillie, the importer. Richardson had been chased into his house by a crowd, and then had fired the shot that killed the youth, Christopher Seider. For Bostonians, there were two massacres at the beginning of 1770, the one committed by Richardson and the other by the soldiers. Quincy defended the perpetrators in both cases.

When Richardson's case came to trial the crowd continued its presence, both within and without the courtroom, so that everyone present faced possible danger. Persisting in the conviction that he had expressed when taking on the Massacre case—that every defendant has a right to counsel—Quincy set out the legal precedents that showed Richardson guilty at most of manslaughter.[22] The crowd, however, intimidated the jurors into delivering a verdict of guilty. (Eventually Richardson received a king's pardon.)

A month after this trial Quincy presented the Boston town meeting with a set of instructions for its representative to the legislature. His document, which again returned him to the patriot fold (from the point of view of those who failed to understand the principles involved in his defense of Richardson), earned for him the reputation of a fiery agitator. The issue that the instructions argued was the same removal of the legislature to Cambridge by Hutchinson that drove John Adams to his nervous collapse. Since the legal precedents favored Hutchinson, Quincy was moved to an Otis-like attack on prerogative itself, which he denounced as an imposition supported by "mistical Jargon."

Quincy concluded with characteristic heat, "The further Nations recede and give way to the gigantick Strides of any powerful Despot, the more rapidly will the Fiend advance to spread wide desolation . . . 'The dogs of war let loose and hot for blood rush on to waste and havock!' " The Shakespearean language did not exceed other Quincy writings in extravagance, but perhaps because this one was officially adopted as town instructions, Hutchinson reacted with surprising anger: "Nothing can be more infamous than the Boston instructions. Is it possible they should pass without notice? Young Quincy, who goes by the name of Wilkes Quincy, penned them. He bids fair to be a successor to Otis, and it is much if he does not run mad also."[23]

That Quincy should be compared to John Wilkes and James Otis a month after defending Richardson and while still engaged to defend the Massacre soldiers is surprising, for both these cases put him if not directly on the government side, at least on the side of reason. It was true that he had just served on the committee that wrote an incendiary and slanted report of the "horred" massacre for distribution in England, but this hardly made him a Wilkes. However, like Otis and like Wilkes in the *North Briton,* Quincy had a way of attacking the king that breached acceptable critical bounds. In Quincy's case it was not a matter of forms of address, as with Otis, but of an overheated rhetoric in which "fiends" and king became synonymous. Otis might have been the one to earn the "Wilkes" title, it would seem, but for the coincidence that Quincy was cross-eyed like Wilkes. Quincy's eye, moreover, appears to have evoked a response not given even to Otis: a combination of awe and uneasiness arising from superstitions about the "evil eye."[24]

In his defense of the soldiers in September 1770, Quincy expounded upon the psychology of crowds. "The passions of man, nay his very imaginations are contagious," he argued. As an example of human suggestibility he offered "the pomp of funeral"—obviously referring to the recent funeral for Christopher Seider and its contribution to the passions of the Massacre. Quincy gave sympathetic accounts both of the crowd's passions and those of the soldiers. Then, in contrast to his fellow counsel John Adams, who argued legal points only, Quincy offered an emotional discourse, and may have had to be restrained. One tradition has him attacking the crowd, and therefore by implication the citizens of Boston, and then being persuaded by Adams to drop this line of argument. But such an attack by Quincy is not apparent in the exceptionally detailed shorthand notes of his argument. And Adams himself later wrote that he had cautioned Quincy to use restraint not in order to protect the reputation of Boston, but because their "Clients lives were hazarded by Quincy's too youthful ardour."[25] Once again, not political motives but personality seems to have dictated Quincy's political behavior.

Prior to 1770 this behavior was marked by an excess of feeling connected to the crowd. Thereafter, Quincy's emotions intensified and came to be directed largely at Thomas Hutchinson. Upon Hutchinson's elevation to governor in 1771, Quincy addressed him as "the MAN WHOM Conscience forbids to stile my Governor." In 1772 Quincy termed him "the serpent, subtlest beast of all the field" (a comparison used by John Adams and Samuel Adams, among others). One historian has called Quincy's hatred of Hutchinson at this point a "phobia," and another a species of "savagery." But Quincy rightly insisted that "having never received any *private* injury from him, I bear him no enmity."[26] Unlike Otis and Adams, who made the same claim, Quincy could have added that he had received no special kindnesses, either. By no means, then, can Quincy's antipathy be traced to unacknowledged personal resentment. Instead, it would appear that by the time he came to political consciousness the conviction of Hutchinson's evil had become a tenet of the patriot faith. In Quincy's case it is not his taking up anti-Hutchinsonianism that stands out, but the peculiar ferocity that he brought to this position.

As it develops, just as Quincy turned his politics toward Hutchinson he was put under emotional strain by illness. His son dated the beginning of Quincy's "pulmonary decline" from 1772, though the tuberculosis itself obviously had its onset well before then.[27] That Quincy's language should have grown more febrile as his consumption worsened in the early 1770s is not at all surprising. Indeed, it fits the pattern of behavior that doctors have observed as characteristic of the disease.

In effect, Quincy suffered two kinds of intensification of his political emotions: one having to do with the crowd atmosphere of Boston early in 1770, and the other with the effects of consumption. Alternating states of euphoria and depression have always been attributed to consumptives, who usually appear in literature as intermittently excitable types. But clinically speaking the one trait found universally among them is some kind of difficulty in expressing anger. Depending on the individual the anger may be obvious or hidden. When expressed it often takes the form of rebellious behavior; when kept hidden it can manifest itself in indirect rebellion, especially in the form of "strivings for independence." In either case, the anger is likely to be rerouted into "self-driving behavior."[28]

Quincy showed both characteristics: self-driving behavior as an ambitious young lawyer, especially after Thacher's death in 1765, and political rebellion thereafter. To be sure, hard work and rebellion were not exceptional. But they appear in Quincy's case to have combined in such a way as to make him prone to tuberculosis. According to Dr. E. D. Wittkower, "in individuals of a rebellious nature, resentment of imposed authority and imposed hardships often assumes a tuberculosis-precipitating function."[29] If, as it also appears, the onset of Quincy's disease coincided with or came soon after his entry into politics in 1767, then the form of that politics—vividly expressed resentment of the hardships imposed on Americans by British authority—had clinical significance.

Quincy's crossed eye offers one possible clue as to how he could have developed into a tuberculosis-prone type. Crossed eye or strabismus can aggravate a neurosis, especially when there is an internal conflict over expressing anger. In Quincy's case, then, a disability in addition to his physical frailty acted to exaggerate his emotional stress. Subsequently, upon exposure to his brother, Quincy apparently contracted his tuberculosis.[30] Thereafter, Quincy's waverings had reference not only to the perplexities of the movement toward independence, but also to the origins and the ebb and flow of the tuberculosis.

Early in 1772 the Richardson case remained unsettled, even though it had been argued months earlier. Quincy at this time published a newspaper essay on its current status. He chose the pseudonym "Callisthenes," after the follower of Aristotle whose bold expression of his opinions led to his imprisonment and death. (From the loyalist point of view the pseudonym had some reference to Richardson as a persecuted dissenter, but it was evidently meant to characterize Quincy himself.) Quincy argued that Richardson, still awaiting a decision on his appeal, should either be judged or freed. Yet as one analyst has described the essay, "On the one hand it seems to be urging Richardson's death, on the other it appears to be vigorously asserting his rights . . . Quincy's purpose in writing the letter defies explanation."[31] "Callisthenes," in fact, was an accurate mirror of Quincy's ambivalence over the crowd question: his legal training made him lean toward Richardson, while his patriot sympathies made him abhor his own client.

From this time forward the record of Quincy's patriot activities grows increasingly contradictory. A few months after the Richardson piece he launched a series of attacks on Hutchinson under the pseudonym "Marchmont Nedham." Once again the patriots were making an issue over Hutchinson's having moved the legislature's meeting place from Boston to Cambridge (where it had continued to meet since 1770). As usual, Quincy took up little space with argumentation, much with invective. But this time, although his meaning was clear enough in general, his argument could hardly be followed.

Quincy called Hutchinson's refusal to return the legislature to Boston a nefarious abandonment of the governor's role as *"father of this people,"* and asked, "Into what times are we fallen? NO BRITISH MONARCH EVER DARED THE LIKE EXPERIMENT.—INDEPENDANCE— *insult,—oppression—and madness* from the beginning were inseperable!" The obscure logic here might be paraphrased thus: "Insulting acts of oppression by the governor have from the beginning of his term had the same tendency: to goad the people into madness, and thence to independence." If this is what Quincy meant, then he was revealing his own agitated state of mind better than he was public opinion in the year 1772. Later the same year Quincy, again writing as Callisthenes, this time on the Massacre case, appeared to hint at a conspiracy in which false witnesses had been supplied at the trials.

This, he seemed to charge, had resulted in the acquittal of Captain Preston, the man charged with giving the order to fire. Again obscurely, Quincy concluded that "the blind may see—the callous must feel:—*the spirited will act.*"[32]

In this second Callisthenes article on cases that he had argued, Quincy, like John Adams, may have again wanted to dispel the impression that he harbored loyalist sympathies. But he succeeded chiefly in obscuring both his motives and intentions. Henceforward the veiled threat remained Quincy's characteristic mode of expression. If uncertain as to meaning, it effectively conveyed his partially suppressed resentment and consequent desire for "independance."

When, in reply to Quincy's "Marchmont Nedham" series, the government's newspaper writers clearly demonstrated the governor's legal right to convene the legislature in Cambridge, Quincy grew increasingly abusive of Hutchinson. Then one of these writers, "Lelius," accused Quincy of using the "language of a porter" (the very accusation that Jonathan Sewall had brought against Otis in 1763), and Quincy responded by expressing his "scorn and abhorrence" of Hutchinson, "the rapacious and lustful governor." Perhaps borrowing from Mercy Warren's denomination, "Rapatio," Quincy here assimilated Hutchinson to his own earlier Whig Sentimental treatment of England as a rapist. Lelius in response was moved to call Quincy a "madman," and Quincy, in turn, to add that Hutchinson was "a traitor to his species, with the genius and obstinacy of a devil." Quincy ended his Nedham series by promising that if his own life were "spared," he planned "in some future period, further to consider Mr. H. as a man, a citizen, legislator, judge and governor."[33]

This he never did. But he was not finished with Hutchinson. His next opportunity came a year later, after the Boston Tea Party. Earlier in 1773 Quincy, his disease advancing, traveled to the South for his health. Back in Boston he spoke at the town meeting that preceded the Tea Party. Just as in 1770 when Molineux stood waiting to lead the crowd, Quincy unsuccessfully counseled moderation.[34] Then, as after the march of the nonimportation crowd, Quincy defended the Tea Party. His argument, which appeared in a new series of "Nedham" essays, took the form of an attack on Hutchinson.

As usual, Quincy was hardly systematic. He stated once again that Hutchinson had failed to act properly as "a father of his people." Hutchinson, as supposedly revealed by the recent publication of his letters, was guilty of the very treason with which he charged the patriots. He was one who, while he "aims the fatal stroke against his country, sneaks like a coward behind the veil of darkness, and supplicates concealment from the face of day." Hutchinson, Quincy eventually charged, was "the great CAPITAL OFFENDER," the "origin of all our public calamities." The essays titled "Nedham's Remembrancer" ran to seven numbers in the Boston *Gazette,* growing increasingly hysterical about the never to be forgiven Hutchinson.[35]

Always literary, Quincy employed epigraphs from Milton and Shakespeare in this series, along with the allusions to raped virginity typical of Whig Sentimentalism. He asserted, in what might stand as a definition of this literary mode, that it was all the same "whether the scene of iniquity is in the lustful recesses of a brothel, or the *political* chambers of state": in either case Hutchinson was a tempter and debaucher. Hutchinson again appeared as the terrifying murderer who breaks in on the family to kill the children. *"He is,"* concluded Quincy, *"the man,* against whom the blood of my slaughtered brethren cries from the ground . . . I have, and shall, as strength is given me, pursue him." With chilling implication, the Nedham series ended by applying to Hutchinson the soliloquy in which the guilt-ridden Macbeth wishes his own death.[36]

Within a few months the repercussions of the Tea Party set in motion the Revolution itself. The Boston Port Act resulted in the blockade of Boston and Hutchinson's replacement by a military governor. Some still hoped for reconciliation, Quincy among them, but revolution and independence were now on all minds. In May 1774 Quincy published his last and longest essay, *Observations on the Boston Port-Bill.* With what Moses Coit Tyler termed "febrile intensity," Quincy, like the other patriots calling himself "one of infirm health," argued the unfairness of the punitive regulations imposed on Boston by Parliament. The latter part of the essay added lengthy observations "on Civil Society and Standing Armies." For these Quincy obviously had read widely, taking most of his American examples from Hutchinson's *History.*[37]

As always, more important than Quincy's argument was his rhetoric. This well expressed the general shock and resentment at the Port Bill, a measure that was all the more disturbing for having come suddenly, after a period of calm in American-British relations.[38] Tortuously but effectively Quincy traced a widespread phenomenon: the transfer of resentment, originally directed at American leaders, to George III and the leaders of Parliament. Quincy continued to attack Hutchinson, but now associated him with England and with the king. The word "parricide," which he—like Otis, Hawley, Mercy Otis Warren, and others—regularly applied to Hutchinson, continued paradoxically to suggest not the killing of a parent but a murder committed by the father. By accusing the father-king of harboring murderous impulses, Otis had inadvertently drawn attention to the parricidal implications in the patriots' own politics. However, whereas earlier Otis had been able to treat the king in terms of distant analogy, Quincy was dealing with reprisals against America that could hardly be treated abstractly. Thus, even though his argument against the Port Bill was officially directed toward Parliament, the king perforce came into the picture—for the first time as insistently as Hutchinson.

The Port Bill, Quincy ironically had it, came both from the members of Parliament, "those exalted characters," and from "that generous prince, styled the father of his people." Both parties were guilty of cruel and unnatural parental behavior against loyal children. In contrast, the children continued to act their natural parts. Quincy cited "the English colonist, replete with loyalty to his sovereign; the descendant from Britain, animated by love for a mother country." This loyal subject maintained "love for a parent country, love for a parent king." In violating the love of a people that wished only to maintain its freedom, the king was treating his loyal children as "worse than rebels." In the Port Bill pamphlet, "virtually alone of leading colonial writers, Quincy had reached the point of no longer believing the king to be an innocent bystander." Its popularity indicated that Quincy's deeply resentful but residually loyal feelings about the king now mirrored the popular mood.[39]

It was therefore significant that at the end of *Observations on the Port-Bill* Quincy indirectly gave expression to the very revolutionary impulse that he had begun by denying. His manner was so heavily symbolic as to make the modern reader imagine for a moment that he meant to anticipate Sigmund Freud's account of the band of brothers who slay the father in *Totem and Taboo*. In this work the brothers' act stands as the model of all revolutions that overthrow paternal authority. Quincy, as if in recognition of the bloody impulse implicit in revolution, ended his pamphlet by calling on his countrymen to dedicate themselves to the cause of freedom in a "Brutus-like" manner.

Brutus, Caesar's adopted son, joined in revolution with others who shared his resentment of Caesar's power over them. In Shakespeare's representation Brutus' fellow conspirator, Cassius, also has a filial relationship with Caesar. Because he had once saved Caesar's life, Cassius likens himself to Aeneas, who carried his father, Anchises, on his back out of the burning city of Troy. (The British cartoon attacking Lord Bute as a Caesar over his British children used lines from this same speech.) Steeped in Shakespeare as Quincy was, he could not but be familiar with the emphasis on filial ties uniting the band of conspirators in *Julius Caesar*. How striking, then, that he should quote Plutarch instead of his favorite Shakespeare in holding up Brutus and Cassius as heroic examples for Americans. The obvious explanation is that Plutarch's less ambiguous presentation of them as heroes better suited Quincy's purpose. And yet it was as though Quincy recalled Shakespeare's filial emphasis despite himself. For in the final sentence of his essay he wrote that "America hath in store her Bruti and Cassii—her Hampdens and Sydneys"; these coming figures, he declared, would prove "patriots and heroes, who will form a band of brothers." As with Shakespeare's sons of Caesar and Freud's primal horde, the business of this band of brothers would be killing. These American brothers, Quincy predicted, would be "men who will have memories and feelings—courage and swords:—courage that shall inflame their ardent bosoms, till their hands cleave to their swords—and their swords to their enemies' hearts."[40] The enemies are presumably any who may be opposed to American freedom. But the thrust of Quincy's "band of brothers" figure leads the swords ineluctably to the heart of King George III.

Late in 1774, a few months after writing the Port Bill pamphlet, Quincy again left Boston—partly for his health and partly to discredit Hutchinson. In exile, the former governor was being sought out for advice by influential members of Parliament. Quincy aimed to convince them that their past errors had arisen, as Bernard Bailyn put it, "from the misrepresentations fed the ministry by ruthless colonial officials, notably Thomas Hutchinson."[41] The five months that he spent in London at the end of 1774 and the beginning of 1775 provide the chief exhibit for George Nash in his study of Quincy's waverings.

Nash connects the vagaries of Quincy's politics with his emotionalism and advancing disease. Quincy's condition, in fact, now brought out more starkly than ever his conflict over independence. Impressionable as always, he shifted from a policy of accommodation to one of armed resistance as often as he conferred with the advocates of one or the other of these positions in London. He arrived with a strong prejudice against Benjamin Franklin, Massachusetts' official representative in England, who advised moderation on all sides. But by the end of his stay he wrote of a meeting with "Dr." Franklin, "I was charmed: I renounced my own opinion: I became a convert to his. I feel a kind of enthusiasm which leads me to believe that it was something almost supernatural which induced the discourse and prompted the Dr. to speak so fully and divinely." Franklin was understandably gratified, but he observed the danger of Quincy's condition: "I am much pleased with Mr. Quincy . . . [but] his zeal for the public, like that of David for God's house, will, I fear, eat him up."[42]

Franklin was particularly well qualified by his Boston upbringing to recognize the old Puritan zeal. Nowhere was its devil-hunting side more apparent than in Quincy's continuing "obsessive" concern with Thomas Hutchinson. Hutchinson had preceded him to London earlier in 1774, had met with the king, and had then settled into retirement. With a tenacity that recalled the continuing indictment of Lord Bute, Quincy insisted on regarding Hutchinson as the archvillain, the "one man" from whom "are all your miseries supposed to flow." Quincy regretted that Hutchinson had been allowed to "escape" from America. He searched out reports of his continuing influence, and so thoroughly convinced himself of it, that "Quincy's belief in Hutchinson's culpability may have impeded his progress to a truly revolutionary position." This was because if Hutchinson were to be regarded as alone responsible for the political situation, then not a revolution but exposure of Hutchinson was the answer to America's problems. Nash observes that conspiracy theories were commonly held among the patriots, but believes that Quincy's obsession with Hutchinson "seems to have been somewhat atypical."[43] It would be more accurate to say that Quincy differed from the Adamses, Otis, and Hawley not in the manner of his obsession but in remaining directly concerned with Hutchinson after his removal to England.

As Quincy's condition worsened, his politics grew increasingly eccentric. "From late December on, in fact, Quincy would frequently oscillate between advocacy of a settlement . . . and pursuit of complete independence—between peace, in other words, and war." In a single letter he reported beginning to spit blood, pointed to Hutchinson as the source of all miseries, and confessed his own emotionalism. He would rather lose all discretion, he confessed, than be "unpregnant of my cause, or lack gall to make oppression bitter." Very apt was it for him to quote Hamlet. For Quincy was another young man forced into a revolutionary situation not of his own making. And like Hamlet he wavered as the peculiar result of obsession with the villainy of one man. Hamlet's uncle Claudius has already committed the act of regicide that Hamlet contemplates; Quincy faced in Hutchinson a man whom he believed to have committed the "PARRICIDE" of destroying New England.[44]

Now desperately ill, Quincy's own blood flowed together with his earlier rhetoric and the last gasps of his revolutionary ardor. The patriots, he wrote, heavily inking the initial letter of the last word in his sentence, "must yet seal their faith & constancy to their liberties *with Blood.*"

If Quincy's condition thus influenced his politics, at the end his politics struck the final blow to his health. On January 23, 1775, the House of Commons voted down a pro-American petition in what amounted to an irreversible declaration of intransigence. That night in London Quincy came down with "a fever and spasms."[45] He had deceived himself about his health up to this point, but now admitted to being "very ill." Thenceforward he stopped writing to his wife and family, though he continued to make short entries in his diary.

Dwelling in London, Quincy had explicitly transferred his anger from Hutchinson to the king in advance of the other patriots. Less than two weeks before his collapse he wrote home that men like Lord Bute remained the "enemies" of America, and that "Hutchinson is still the same man." "But," he added, "ANOTHER CHARACTER, is in principle your adversary." This was, of course, the king. Quincy had just been admitted into the royal presence, "literally within the reach of his royal sceptre," and had found himself unawed. Or, more accurately, he found that though affected by the panoply he managed to recall himself to his radical sentiments "before the royal charm was over." He now called on Americans to show the king "a spirit going forth, which compels rulers to their duty."[46]

Thus, a year and a half before his fellow patriots delivered their first explicit attack on the king in the Declaration of Independence, the only one of Hutchinson's adversaries who came into the presence of the king prior to the Revolution experienced a dissolving of the royal bond. In recording this experience Quincy quoted Milton: "The trappings of a monarchy will set up a commonwealth."[47] The other patriots may not have been ready for revolution at this point, but they would have recognized the propriety of these words. For just as with Quincy, they associated revolution with Puritanism and with the English Puritan revolution that had culminated in the killing of a king.

Setting out for home early in 1775 with intelligence that he would not live to deliver, Quincy was either risking his life by leaving the comparatively mild London winter, or attempting a last service to his cause in the conviction that he had no chance of recovery in any case. He died at sea just before his ship reached America. Once again he had taken a course opposite to his father's in relationship to the family doom connected with travel. In 1738 Colonel Quincy had been deeply shocked by his father's death in London. He had written home to say that he was returning, only to add that he might after all take his planned vacation in Holland, which is exactly what he proceeded to do. Though the colonel had henceforward avoided all exertion or public service that might endanger his health, he seemed to be stalked by that very fate through the deaths of his sons. All three died at sea: Edmund in 1768 on his return from a voyage to the West Indies for his tuberculosis, Josiah in 1775 near the coast of Massachusetts, and Samuel in 1789 "within sight of the English coast" on *his* return from the West Indies.[48]

In his death as in his life Josiah Quincy, Jr., projected himself as a stern redeemer of the colonel's honor. The reversal in their roles was evident from a typically chatty letter sent by the colonel in 1773. Writing to Quincy in London, the colonel ended with apologies for the "Contents" of "this impertinent Scribles." Just before he set sail for America, Quincy mirrored this reversal of roles in one of his last pronouncements on the relationship between England and America. The English, he wrote, had come to a point where they looked "to the spirits of a distant people for salvation. Like an aged parent, Britain looks to her children for support & Defense."[49]

This image of redeeming children, together with Quincy's band of avenging brothers and John Adams's "poor beings" overshadowed by Hutchinson, perfectly expressed the ambivalence of America's conscience patriots. They felt themselves at once avengers and redeemers, defiers of authority and its salvation, usurpers and victims. Otis's imagination placed the king and royal family in a sinking ship, so that they could be rescued. Adams imagined Otis at the Writs case as besting authority in the person of his mentor, and then supposed Gridley to have smiled "with the benignity of a parent" at the insult. Though these men never banded together as a group in the manner of the crowds of the Revolution, they thought of themselves in collective terms, and always as the younger generation. In New England the sense of a generational dimension in political and religious issues had always been present, with controversialists tending to identify themselves either with the early generations of the Puritan "fathers" or with the later generations of their "sons." Thus, during the great Awakening, Old Light conservatives could assume a patriarchal stance and New Light innovators a filial one, even in cases where the difference in ages between the disputants should have reversed their imagery.[50] Patriots and loyalist authorities were now agreed in one thing at least: that the loyalists represented the parents and the patriots the children.

Thomas Hutchinson, quite independently of the transformations relative to him in the minds of his patriot opponents, thought of himself in such terms. As Carl Becker put it, "his profound irritation with America in general and with Boston in particular was the irritation of a proud and possessive father with a beloved but wayward child who fails to do him credit in high places."[51] All of this suggests a more than coincidental relationship between the personal rituals of the patriots and the public rituals of the crowd. Once again Hawthorne's "My Kinsman, Major Molineux" bears on the question, for there is reason to believe that the sudden political conversion of Robin in that story is evoked by the crowd's coming-of-age ritual. In the preceding biographical chapters such rituals have been viewed, in a manner of speaking, from the point of view of Robin. In the chapters that follow the rituals themselves are examined and their origins explored.

III

The Revolutionary Impulse

CHAPTER EIGHT

The Child, Revolution

THE BOSTON RIOTS OF August 1765 spread quickly to nearby
towns in Massachusetts, Rhode Island, and Connecticut, and
then south to New York, Pennsylvania, and the Carolinas.
Wherever distributors of stamps had been appointed from England, it
seemed, similar wild demonstrations forced them to resign. Crowds
marched to the appointee's homes in long processions carrying aloft an
effigy of the "Stampmaster," which they later burned. The prospective stamp distributor, sometimes only after his house had been sacked,
usually responded by announcing his resignation.[1]

The demonstrations were fed by news of what had taken place in
Boston, but each town supplied its local variations on the original
themes. For the most part these variations derived from English folk
punishments still prevalent in the colonies. In Newport, Martin
Howard, Otis's newspaper antagonist, was hung in effigy from a
twenty-foot gallows opposite the Town House. Alongside him were
the local stampman and Thomas Moffat, who had collaborated with
Howard on a series of proadministration newspaper letters earlier in
the year. The effigies were of course accompanied by a boot with a
devil peeping out of it, this device hanging over Moffat's shoulder.
And, in an unmistakable collocation of Whig rhetoric with crowd symbolism, Howard was labeled a "fawning, insidious, infamous Parricide"—the terms of Otis's attack on him as the Gentleman at Halifax.
In the same mode, Moffat was labeled a "leering Jacobite"—that is, a
traitor to the king.[2]

Howard and Moffat's newspaper letters had recommended the
cultivation of hemp in the colonies as a constructive response to the
Sugar Act, which awarded a bounty for every ton of this commodity

177

exported from America. Accordingly the effigies of the two authors were joined by a rope and a sign that had them say, "We have an hereditary, indefeasible right to an Haltar; besides we encouraged the growth of Hemp you know."[3] The joke here was by no means purely political, for the halter partly referred to a traditional folk punishment for sexual offenders and other trespassers against social norms. Whereas in Boston the symbolism had tended toward England and politics, in the rest of the country, beginning with Newport, more homely elements surfaced.

In Connecticut young people enacted a kind of modern mummers' play. This was a mock religious liturgy in which the names of political rebels were substituted for the usual objects of worship. "Instead of 'We beseech thee to hear us, good Lord!' was substituted, 'We beseech thee, O Cromwell, to hear . . . us.' 'O holy, blessed, and glorious Trinity!' was altered thus, 'O Chatham [that is, Pitt], Wilkes, and Franklin, have mercy upon us!' " In Lebanon, Connecticut, the stampmaster received a mock trial, while in Dumfries, Virginia, the stampmaster's effigy was placed backward on a horse, with a copy of the Stamp Act "tied round its neck with a halter." Then, in the partly mocking, partly religious language of one account, it "received the insults of the congregation, caning, whipping, (the Mosaick law) pillorying, cropping, hanging and burning, &c. &c."[4]

The sources of these ceremonies lay both in Pope Day and, as it was made particularly clear in Annapolis, Maryland, in traditional ceremonials of punishment. In Annapolis, "Malefactor like," the stampmaster's effigy was paraded in a cart to the accompaniment of church bells "Toling a solemn Knell." It was castigated at both the whipping post and the pillory. To indicate penitence, its head was evidently manipulated in the manner of Guy Fawkes–Pope day effigies. Finally it was hung on a gibbet and set alight by a flaming tar barrel beneath, into which it eventually fell. In Savannah, Georgia, a stampmaster's effigy replaced the usual one on Pope Day, 1766. It was beaten with cudgels and made to cry out in typical penitential tone, "No Stamps." Equally traditional, but more dramatic, was the effigy hanging of Stampmaster Ingersoll, alongside Lord Grenville, in Lebanon, Connecticut. Here the third figure, that of a devil, was equipped so that he "turned up his breech and discharged fire, brimstone, and tar in Ingersoll's face, setting him all in a blaze; which, however, Mr. Grenville generously extinguished with a hose . . . This was many times repeated." The usual attentions of the devil to the Guy were reversed so that Ingersol showed "fawning reverence" toward the devil, thus supposedly provoking the discharge.[5]

In Boston and most other places the first Stamp Act protests were followed by a period of waiting until November 1, the day the act went into effect. In New York, however, that day marked the first large-scale protests. On October 31 there were plans for a mock burial of a figure of Liberty to dramatize what was termed the country's last day of liberty. But this ceremonial, which eventually grew popular elsewhere, never took place. By this time, furthermore, the New York stampmaster had resigned. As a result, Cadwallader Colden, the aged lieutenant governor and temporary acting governor, became the focus of attention. It has been said that because of disputes with the legislature he was at this time "the most hated man in the province."[6] Even more so than in Boston, then, the agitation in the New York streets had to do with issues other than the Stamp Act.

At night on November 1 Colden was hanged in effigy by two separate groups. The first carried a portable gallows from which he and a devil were suspended alongside lighted lanterns. The "grand Deceiver of Mankind" hanging next to Colden held the by now mandatory boot in his hand to represent Bute. Colden had a drum fixed to his back, and in front a label with the words "The Rebel Drummer in the Year 1715," a taunting reference to his having marched as a drummer boy with the Pretender's forces against the king in the uprising of 1715. Just as those who supported the Stamp Act had to be "parricides," this king's representative had to be demeaned for his former endangering of the king.[7]

The second group carried a paper effigy of Colden mounted on an old chair and carried atop a seaman's head. This effigy received full ceremonial treatment: it was preceded by marchers carrying candles and torches; displayed in the center of town and at the fort, it was "shewn many Insults." Along the way, pistol shots were from time to time fired into the effigy.[8] At one point Colden's stable was broken into, his coach removed, and the effigy placed in it, in the manner of a pope's chair. When the two groups came together they burned their effigies and paraphernalia in a bonfire. Then, as in Boston, they sacked several private houses.

Outside New York the Stamp Act was greeted in November by demonstrations calculated to avoid the loss of control that had characterized the August crowds. In Boston effigies were again hung from the Liberty Tree, and then paraded as if at a funeral. This time colored portraits represented Grenville, whose administration was responsible for the Stamp Act, and "a former Boston citizen, John Huske, who had removed to England, become a member of Parliament, and was thought mistakenly to have proposed the American Stamp Act to Grenville." By including Huske, yet another incorrectly stigmatized scapegoat figure, the organizers of the demonstration were able to have one English and one American villain, just as on Guy Fawkes–Pope Day the foreign pope joined the English Guy Fawkes. The effigies were carried to the gallows, hung there for a time, and then taken down, to be torn to pieces in mock wrath by the crowd. A few days later on Pope Day the traditional north end–south end rivalry was formally ended by the peaceful marching of each group's effigies to the other's part of town, with a stop at the Liberty Tree, followed by a joint bonfire. Mackintosh and Swift, the south and north end leaders, appeared together in military dress and with attendants. In the meantime, the usual petty begging for money typical of Pope Day turned into the collecting of a large-scale public donation to the two groups.[9]

In Fredericktown, Maryland, at the end of the month an elaborate effigy procession was held featuring a funeral for Liberty. The stampmaster effigy was manipulated from beneath in the manner of a Guy, complete with the traditional nodding head "in Token of the utmost Sorrow and Confusion." (In another variation on the Guy, on Pope Day in Savannah, Georgia, the stampmaster's effigy "was obliged by several severe blows with a cudgel to call out in a pitiful tone, *No Stamps.*") The repentant Maryland effigy was buried together with Liberty, now "his beloved." At Wilmington, North Carolina, Liberty alone was paraded, its pulse tested, "and when finding some Remains of Life, they returned back to a Bonfire ready prepared, placed the Effigy [of Liberty] before it in a large Two-arm'd Chair, and concluded the Evening with great Rejoicings, on finding that LIBERTY had still an Existence in the COLONIES." But the ceremony in Newport, Rhode Island, was the most typical. At the moment of Liberty's interment a groan came from within the coffin, "Old FREEDOM was not dead." She became *"Liberty Revived,"* arising like the sun, as it was reported, "and the Stamp Act was thrown into the Grave and buried" in her place, followed by the tolling of bells.[10]

A View of the Year 1765

This altered copy of an English cartoon—one directed against Bute's 1763 excise tax—shows a supine America aided on the left by "B" (that is, Boston) leading the united colonies. Added to the original are Liberty on the left with her peleus and staff, and on the right American patriots who have "mounted aloft perfidious H[us]k[e]" on the newly designated Liberty Tree. (Huske was the New Hampshireman mistakenly supposed to have suggested the Stamp Act.) A real person rather than an effigy is represented in this case. In the English original, Wilkes, not Boston, attacked the dragon as Bute looked on at the right—in place of the Liberty Tree. (Bute is still suggested by the Scotch bonnet on the dragon.)

In the course of the eighteenth century the abstraction "liberty," along with its representation as a goddess, had become ubiquitous in both England and America. The English liberty movement on one occasion depicted Wilkes as "Liberty,"while on another a child dressed as "Liberty" was led through the streets of London. As the "master symbol of the protests" in America, Liberty appeared in a guise slightly different from that of the matron who had usually represented the idea in Roman and English iconology. She now became a young virgin—like the Indian maiden who had come to represent America. American patriots represented themselves as "sons" of Liberty in deference to the older, more mature version of Liberty, but in demonstrations they played the bereaved "swains" of a young Liberty. Recalling Whig Sentimentalism, this central symbolic figure of

American crowds was typically young and a virgin; lying defenseless and in décolleté, she is depicted as ineffectually attempting to protect herself from a rapacious figure representing England (or Lord Bute).[11]

In such protests the note of celebration was oddly pervasive. As a consequence, when repeal of the Stamp Act was observed in America six months after its November inception, the atmosphere in the streets continued that of the protests. Repeal day was combined with nearby St. Patrick's Day, as Otis later remembered. There were illuminations and bonfires, marching and drinking, and displays of allegorical representations. Along with cannon-fire and fireworks, these practices made up the usual form for celebrating English victories, royal births, birthdays, and weddings. Thus, the same forms that had been reversed in mockery for the protests were appropriated to commemorate victory. For the time being, the people's heroes, Pitt and Wilkes, were acclaimed, but their enemies not mentioned. A few months later, however, the "cowering Dastards, haughty Tyrants and merciless Parracides" who had supported the Stamp Act were recalled at the first annual commemoration of "the glorious 14th of August 1765." As with the protests, the celebrations and commemorations of 1766 and later years gathered at "the sacred Tree of Liberty" from which the first effigies had hung.[12]

Again following Boston's lead, virtually every town that conducted protests against the Stamp Act dedicated a Liberty tree. Over the years most pre-Revolutionary events gravitated to the tree: ritualized stampmaster resignations, repeal celebrations, commemorations of August 14, celebrations of Wilkes's election to Parliament, later protests against customs duties and the Tea Act, intimidation of loyalists, and the ushering in of independence. The trees were pruned, fitted out with commemorative plaques, and decorated with lanterns and flags. The pruning was to bring the number of branches to match such popularly celebrated totals as the ninety-two who voted against the governor (in support of the legislature's right to circulate a petition to other colonies). To signal meetings of the Sons of Liberty "they erected a flagstaff, which went through the tree, and a good deal above the top of the tree." In New York City and elsewhere Liberty Poles were erected for similar purposes and with similar ceremony. British soldiers and loyalists responded to the symbolism of the trees and poles by cutting them down. New York's largest riot, in 1770, erupted as the result of repeated attacks by British soldiers on the Liberty Pole.[13]

The Deplorable State of America, 1765

In this elaborate redrawing of an English cartoon, Britannia offers Pandora's box to her "daughter," America, the seated maiden (in the original, she is a bare-breasted Indian maiden). "Take it not. See poor Liberty," counsels Minerva, pointing to the supine, sexually indistinct figure that appears in place of the English version's clothed but clearly female Liberty. The tree has been made the Tree of Liberty, and given the date of the first Stamp Act riot in Boston. "W[illiam] P[it]t's dog" urinates on a Scottish (that is, Butean) thistle, from under which a snake emerges toward Liberty. In the left background is a gallows for hanging stampmasters, and added in front of it a grave from which one of them answers, "Yes, yes, I will!" to the question, "Will you resign?" In the right background stands a cart ready to carry a (tarred and feathered?) stampman.

More than one Liberty Tree was described as "sacred" by the patriots and as a sacrilegious "deity" or "idol" by their opponents. It has been suggested that the Liberty Tree functioned as a sacrament in the civil religion of the Revolution. Soon after the Revolution the poet Joel Barlow translated a French essay tracing the tree's origins to "ancient fertility ritual and myth." Other contemporaries recognized that the Maypole had "given place to the Liberty Pole," which one of them termed the "May-pole of sedition."[14]

The ceremonies that took place at Liberty Trees commonly had to do with execution by hanging. If not effigies of stampmasters and Bute or Grenville, a piece of paper, the Stamp Act itself, or any other offending document could be given a mock trial under a Liberty Tree, placed in the pillory, paraded effigy-like on a pole, hanged, and sometimes tarred and feathered prior to being burned. The offending writings of loyalists in New York were "burned at the stake; or, covering them with a coat of tar and feathers, they nailed them to a whipping post."[15] Hawthorne called the whipping post "the Puritan May Pole." Such proceedings did indeed resemble ancient fertility rituals, in particular those described in Frazer's *Golden Bough.*

According to Frazer the sacred tree used for fertility symbolized both the old king and his successor. A related symbolism appears in a journal entry made by the Boston printer and publisher, John Boyle, on November 1, 1765, describing "a vast Concourse of People [who] repaired in the Forenoon to the Royal Elm." The tree in question was of course the Liberty Tree, known informally as such since the previous August 14 and so named publicly in September.[16] Boyle's slip in calling it a "royal" instead of a popular elm was revealing. It indicated that the tree represented a transfer of sovereignty from king to people several years before one took place politically. Thus, when in the awakening of their nationalism the American people hanged in effigy representatives of the king, the sacred tree that they employed for their ceremony was in the deepest sense just what Boyle called it: a royal elm.

As the protests of the 1760s approached actual revolution, the same tree fittingly became the site for intimidating first customs informers and then loyalists. Here the ceremony employed was that of tarring and feathering. This humiliating and painful ordeal was described by patriots with the same punning mockery used for effigy burnings. The application of hot tar and sprinkling with feathers, for example, was referred to as dressing the victim in a "suit of the modern mode." In one town a "Committee for Tarring and Feathering" was jokingly announced as consisting of "Thomas Tarbucket, Peter Pitch, Abraham Wildfowl, David Plaister, Benjamin Brush, Oliver Scarecrow and Henry Hand-Cart." As at effigy burnings, the victim was often transported by cart, with the familiar itinerary of stops at the pillory and gallows being followed. (In one case, the hanging of a man's effigy preceded the tarring and feathering of his person.) There was usually a stop at the Liberty Tree or Liberty Pole as well, just as in England victims of tarring and feathering had once been tied to the Maypole. And finally, the sort of descriptive card that hung on the Stamp Act effigies (itself a reference to English hangings) was here placed around the victim's neck to specify his crime.[17]

These literalizations of the ways in which an effigy was treated derived from folk tradition. When the effigy or victim of tarring and feathering was supplied with a halter, and especially when the proceedings ended with the victim's physical expulsion from his community, the punishment derived from a tradition known as "rough music" in England and *charivari* in France. The victims of rough music were ridden "skimmington"—that is, backwards on a donkey—to the accompaniment of pelting, derisive laughter, and "drums beating, horns blowing, &c." In England in the seventeenth century the tradition was adapted to political protest when one John Williams, a "quasi-comic" popular leader of protests against enclosures took the name "Lady Skimmington." In the 1760s and 1770s in New England the skimmington was modified from an animal ride into a ride on a length of wood. A skimmington feature adopted for dealing with stampmasters, the mock trial, was occasionally used during the tarring and feathering of loyalists as well.[18]

On the continent and in England rough music was applied for the most part to henpecked husbands and in the case of a widow or widower's remarriage, especially to someone of very different age. Americans, however, appear to have employed rough music to punish the sexual transgressions of prostitution and adultery.[19] Boston's north end mechanics, who always made up one of the two Pope Day gangs, were long known for their rigid morality, and were prominent when crowds tore down local houses of prostitution. Not surprisingly, the rise in political disturbances during the 1760s was accompanied by a rise in skimmingtons and other folk punishments, often with political overtones. Thus, in North Carolina in 1765 the stampmaster's effigy was displayed along with that of a wife murderer. Then, once loyalist punishments began, American sexual offenders became as subject to tarring and feathering as to a skimmington ride. And, in a similar crossover of motifs, the two groups carrying effigies in New York City on the night of November 1, 1765, ended the night by "destroy[ing] several bawdy houses."[20]

Not only were people tarred and feathered, but property was as well. Tar and feathers was smeared on the shop doors, business signs, and windows of offending merchants during the nonimportation crisis; in one instance during Shays's rebellion in the 1780s it was applied to a political opponent's two horses. In place of tar other sticky substances were used, such as molasses, mud, "fish gurry," "Blubber Oil," and animal or human excrement. The latter, when mixed with urine, was termed "Hillsborough Paint" or "Hillsborough Treat" after Lord Hillsborough, the British secretary for colonial affairs. It was spread on the shop door belonging to Hutchinson's sons and on numerous human victims.[21] This practice, which had festival precedents, bore an obvious similarity to the pretended urinating by the Lebanon, Connecticut, effigy of Grenville. It also recalls two cartoons of the day: one of Lord Bute in which a mob shouts, "See his arse there! See his arse!" and another of an aged England attempting to hold his American sons by strings as two of them pull down their pants and present their backsides to him. These expressions of childlike, even infantile behavior effectively symbolized the regressive tendency in those patriot mobs that rioted against smallpox inoculation and destroyed playhouses.[22]

As with the practice of forcing householders to illuminate their windows, which could itself accompany the punishment of loyalists, the immediate reference of tar and feathers, presumably because it was known to all, was never mentioned by patriot writers. The lights, of course, derived from royal celebrations, and so amounted to a mockery of the Crown. But the case of tar and feathers had a more complicated reference. The loyalist historian, Peter Oliver, noted that while mounted on the traditional Pope Day cart both the pope and the devil could be covered with tar and feathers, though "it was generally the Devils Luck to be singular." Here, then, was the folk practice that united the two kinds of punishment, effigial and human. But Oliver did not mention that the boys on the pope cart whose role it was to torment the pope and devil, could themselves be covered with tar and feathers (over their clothes).[23]

In this they recalled the boys of the English May Day burry or "furry" dance, with their similar covering of burrs over some sticky substance to give a furry appearance. Clearly, tar and feathers did not represent punishment alone, but were connected to the mock celebratory side of the holiday as well. One of the earliest instances of the practice, from the fourteenth century, was part of a marriage celebration. The dissolute Charles VI of France, himself almost a mock king

*Poor Old England Endeavoring to Reclaim
His Wicked American Children*

The band of American brothers resists the leading strings of their "maimed"
British parent by employing regressively childlike mockery and scatology.
Two of the "children" have peashooters.

in his early excesses and later madness, appeared with five of his court-
iers at a masquerade ball. All were besmeared with tar or rosin and
covered with down. At about the time of the Revolution, the Sons of
Saint Tammany in Philadelphia celebrated their annual day of frolic
and pleasure, which fell on May Day, in similar fashion. On this occasion they smeared their bodies with "oil of the bear." The very goose
feathers used for tarring and feathering were linked with celebration
and especially with May Day, for the goose was a creature that might
be termed the totem animal of the English May Day. For example,
the geese of the English tradition were drawn on during a tarring and
feathering in Salem in 1768. Here, as the victim was carted through
the streets, "a live goose was repeatedly thrown at him."[24]
    Another poet of the period, John Trumbull, traced back even fur-

ther the source of tar and feathers in his poem, "M'Fingal," in which a loyalist is tied down to be tarred and feathered.

> Then lifting high the pond'rous jar
> Pour'd o'er his head the smoking tar:
> With less profusion erst was spread
> The Jewish oil on royal head.

Trumbull's suggestion here that the punishment was a mock coronation appears to be borne out by the earliest known example of tarring and feathering. In the twelfth century, King Richard the Lionhearted is reported to have announced that any of his fighting men caught stealing would be punished by having their heads shaved, tarred, and feathered. In a variation of the "crowning" motif, in colonial New York "on the feast of Bacchus at Shrove-tide . . . he who bore off the goose was declared to be king of the festival."[25] Whether in a frolicsome context or as a punishment, the symbolism of geese, their feathers, and oil or tar appears to have been connected with the coronation and its ceremony of anointment. As practiced by the American patriots, the tar and feather mockery or reversal of a king's crowning amounted to an act of symbolic overthrow. In yet another substitution, the patriots replaced George III with "the king's friends," the loyalists.

Wherever revolution expressed itself in ritual form, the motif of crowning, or at least the assumption of regal titles, was central. When, for example, on November 1, 1765, Mackintosh was given the mock-regal title "First Captain General of Liberty Tree," the ceremony amounted to a mock coronation. Mackintosh's New York counterpart, Isaac Sears, became known as "King Sears," and within a few years John Hancock, destined to become the first Revolutionary governor of Massachusetts, was being toasted as "King Hancock." (A month after his coronation as captain general, Mackintosh was also being called "Governor.")[26]

These mock elevations of American Revolutionary leaders evoked both "Great Wilkes Our King" and the American Pope Day. The Pope Day processional began as a mockery of the papal coronation. In the course of Pope Day's evolution, quasi-regal status was bestowed on men like Mackintosh and Swift, who came to be known as the champions, or "Captains," of their respective popes. In a perverse way, the pope effigies themselves grew popular as a result of the north

end–south end rivalry, so that when their captains were brought together on November 5, 1765, one diarist referred to the ceremony as
"a Union established between the South and North-End *Popes.*"[27]

The crowd leaders reminded contemporaries of the famous insur-
rectionaries of history. Jack Cade and the Neapolitan Thomas Aniello
("Massaniello") were mentioned by the loyalist opposition. The patriots themselves looked to Oliver Cromwell and the Corsican, Pascal
Paoli, both of whose initials they used to sign their handbills. Paoli's
birthday was celebrated in Boston, Mackintosh named one of his sons
after him, and at least one town changed its name to "Paoli" at about
the time that "Hutchinson" was being replaced by "Barre" as a place
name.[28] The succession of crowd leaders in Boston following Mackintosh continued the tradition of adopting Pope Day finery and its symbolic associations.

The first of these leaders was William Molineux, nicknamed
"Paoli Molineux," a merchant chosen by the patriot leaders to hold
crowd action within restraint. Molineux was rumored to have appeared in white wig and red cloak among the rioters just before the
Boston Massacre, and he also may have had a role in the Boston Tea
Party (though Mackintosh family tradition places Mackintosh there in
his place).[29] Historians have debated who the mysterious figures at
these two now almost mythical crowd events actually were. Yet it is
not their identities but their disguises that are important.

This was certainly the case with the most mysterious of them all,
Joyce Jr., who emerged in the 1770s. He was probably enacted by
John Winthrop, Jr., a young man from a family one step up in society
from Molineux. As "Chairman of the Committee for Tarring &
Feathering," Joyce Jr. presided over the enforcement of nonimportation, and the intimidation of loyalists.[30] He appeared on horseback
wearing a red cloak and white wig, a costume that recalls the figure
who appeared at the Massacre. Joyce Jr., too, derived from Pope Day,
where a participant with the same name accompanied the pope cart
mounted, masked, and in jackboots.

The original of both Joyce Juniors appears to have been George
Joyce, the officer in the English army who arrested Charles I and later
acted as one of his executioners. As the king's executioners had been
vizarded, Joyce Jr. wore a mask; as George Joyce was a soldier, Joyce
Jr. wore English army red; and as George Joyce was a Cornet of
Horse, Joyce Jr. appeared mounted—on an ass.[31] The reappearance of

this Pope day figure at ritual punishments of loyalists conveyed the festival's spirit of mockery into revolution. Joyce Jr. also brought with him the festival's ambivalence toward authority. For just as Mackintosh was both humilator and champion of the pope effigy, both in charge of its immolation and its defender against the north-enders, so did Joyce Jr. play a contradictory role. He was part of the pageant dedicated to ritual punishment of the pope conceived of as the king's enemy, and yet was himself the murderer of the king.

In "My Kinsman, Major Molineux," Hawthorne conveyed the same ambiguity about authority by emphasizing both the youthfulness of his revolutionary, and the circumstances of his personal revolt being directed at a substitute for his father. Toward his kinsman-substitute father, Robin feels the typically divided emotions of a son: dependence and revolt. In this state of mind, Robin makes of virtually every encounter during his search a drama of filial revolt and obedience. He speaks to a number of men while searching for his kinsman, and each time manipulates the encounter into a confrontation with authority. He elaborately defers to these successive authorities, but in each case he also reveals a certain arrogance which anticipates the moment when he will turn on his scapegoat-kinsman.[32]

The crowd in the story behaves in a parallel manner. It has substituted a local official, Major Molineux, and presumably a local issue (since this is not yet the time of the Revolution), for the Crown itself and for revolution itself. The crowd's resultant ambiguity appears in the form of ritually expressed awe as it dances in "mockery" around the tarred and feathered Major Molineux. Hawthorne's choice of the name "Molineux" conveys a final ambiguity—the result of a reversal of punisher and punished—which also bears on the function of Revolutionary crowd leaders. As it has been suggested, by giving William Molineux's name to the victim of a crowd, Hawthorne enacted a kind of expiation for the American Revolution's sins of excess. At the same time he may have been suggesting that this expiation was inherent in the facts. For, as Hawthorne possibly knew, William Molineux himself was eventually threatened by a Revolutionary crowd after Bostonians grew disgruntled at his loss of militancy and over charges of his business wrongdoing.[33] But this irony aside, the use of Molineux's name for a crowd *victim* seems to comment on the psychology of reversal implicit in the ritual of overthrow.

Hawthorne's crowd leader is not Molineux himself but a mounted figure unmistakably meant to suggest Joyce Jr. The appearance of this Pope Day and Revolutionary figure in the story, together with the parallel between Robin's ritual passage from youth with the country's coming of age, may be said to offer a ritual interpretation of the American Revolution. Among the implications of such an interpretation there stands out the importance of the child. Here, surely, Hawthorne was right in his choice of the youth, Robin. For in the rituals of the American Revolution, the importance of children, both physically and symbolically, was all pervasive. John Adams summed up the rhetoric of his fellow patriots when he spoke of the child, independence, and of the Revolution as a "vigorous youth," an *infans* brought to life by James Otis and nurtured by the gods.[34]

Adams's theme of the child was taken up in the collective symbolism of revolution. On Pope Day, Joyce Jr. rode among boys who accompanied the cart dressed in dunce caps. On the cart itself were more boys: those who played the devil's imps, and those who manipulated the pope effigy from beneath. In the politicization of Pope Day and the adoption of other festival motifs for protests, boys retained their centrality. Furthermore, boys appeared in important accompanying, and sometimes precipitating, roles at most of the protests from the Stamp Act through the Revolution. As previously they had attended the Pope, a group of boys attended the Oliver and Bute effigies in 1765. Here youth was also represented among the effigies by the "*young* Imp of the D——l" hanging beside Oliver. On the same occasion schoolboys were let out for the day to march in the procession, and were joined by drummer boys from the (English) regiment. Not surprisingly, when Governor Bernard, sitting in Council, received news of the protest, he dismissed it as a "boyish sport." The Hutchinson riot a week later was signaled by a group of "Boys and Children" lighting a fire in King Street, and later at Hutchinson's house "there was a number of boys from 14 to sixteen Years of age, som mere Children which did a great deal of damage." In Pennsylvania a broadside verse warned that if the stamp distributor executed his office, "May wanton Boys, to Town his Bones convey, / To make a Bonfire on a Rejoicing Day." In New York City the Stamp Act crowd in November "came up to the Fort Gate with a great number of boys carrying Torches & a scaffold." From then until repeal of the Stamp Act hundreds of little boys in New York "frequently tramped the streets at night shouting 'Liberty and No Stamps!' "[35]

Guy Fawkes.

Please to remember the fifth of November
    Gunpowder treason and plot ;
We know no reason, why gunpowder treason
    Should ever be forgot'
            Holla boys! holla boys' huzza—a—a'

A stick and a stake, for king George's sake,
A stick and a stump, for Guy Fawkes's rump'
            Holla boys! holla boys' huzza—a—a

Guy Fawkes

Seated in a chair and wearing the foolscap, the Guy, head characteristically tilted, is carried by boys, one of whom holds out his hat for coins.

The Life and Humble Confession of Richardson, the Informer

A crowd of boys and onlookers gathers in front of T. Lillie's importing shop
a short while before Richardson's shooting of the boy, Seider. The boys
have set up an effigial head on a pole.

At the beginning of the Townshend duties crisis in 1768, bands of
boys roamed through Boston. One group of about a hundred "lads"
paraded with drum and horns, and then surrounded a customs commissioner's house. At the end of 1769 boys were used to intimidate
merchants who refused to join the nonimportation movement. Hutchinson observed at the time that "Molineux and others have thought
it best that great numbers of Boys should collect upon such occasions
rather than men." On February 22, 1770, a school holiday like the
day of the demonstration against Stampman Andrew Oliver in 1765,
"many hundreds" of these boys "collected before the Shop of Mr.

Lillie . . . and a carved head upon a long Pole was fixed before his Shop Door." It was on this occasion that the youths were accosted by Ebenezer Richardson; they chased him to his house, where a crowd gathered and began to break in. When Richardson wildly fired his rifle out a window, so many youths were present that it was not surprising that one of them, Christopher Seider, was hit, rather than an adult. Seider's death became the occasion for a giant ceremonial funeral, starting from Liberty Tree, in which the coffin was preceded by "a vast Number" of boys let out of school for the occasion.[36]

From the loyalist point of view the boys at mob scenes were being "set on" by the patriot leadership to hide its own involvement. A patriot historian affirmed that the gangs of boys in many instances were hired. Yet, as with the patriot use of ritual, which the loyalists also interpreted as no more than a manipulation, the boys proved to carry symbolic weight of their own. The funeral for Christopher Seider was modeled on that conducted in London after the death of the boy, Allen, in one of the Wilkes riots. In both cases the spectacle of a child martyr proved to have political repercussions. But however manipulated the Seider funeral may have been, its organizers could not have intended it to inflame tensions in Boston to the degree that it did—or to result in Otis's raving breakdown on the same day. Mercy Warren's play, *The Adulateur,* again caught the mood. The boys at Lillie's shop become "sportive youths" who "play'd gamesome in the street." Seider is killed by an "inhuman ruffian," whose blood Brutus and Cassius vow to avenge on Rapatio-Hutchinson. Soon afterward at the Boston Massacre, it was a group of youths lighting a fire and tangling with soldiers early in the evening that led to the bloody confrontation at night. There, youths were among those killed. The funerals and public commemorations held for them during the next several years, modeled partly on the martyrdom of Christopher Seider and partly realizing the violations of youth in Whig Sentimental rhetoric, had a significant influence in raising an American Revolutionary consciousness.[37]

In America the revolutionary-ritual uses of youth tended to be obscured by loyalists and patriots alike. The loyalists, of course, saw the youths at demonstrations as mere pawns, while the patriot leaders, in order to dissociate themselves from a crowd action, typically would dismiss it as the work of "Young People, Servants and Negroes." This and other such formulaic evasions have been criticized as misrepresentations. They ignored the presence of adults, exaggerated the role of servants and slaves, and falsely described as children the many apprentices in their twenties who were present. On the other hand, apprentices were certainly youths if not children, and the evidence suggests that in Boston, Albany, and other towns, as with many crowd phenomena in history, young people predominated throughout the 1760s and 1770s.[38]

More significant than the actuality, however, was the attempt to exaggerate the presence of youth by reducing young men to boys in accounts of disturbances. Such accounts recall the American substitution of Sons of Liberty, Sons of Freedom, and Liberty Boys for the English Friends of Liberty, and the symbolic use in America not of Cornet Joyce but of Joyce *Junior*. Whenever Americans employed the family analogy, whether in their political writings or in the symbolism of crowds, they made themselves into children. This suggests that even if attributing their revolutionary disturbances to children was simply a way of avoiding prosecution, it nevertheless had meaning beyond this intention. Above all, the evasion demonstrated an essential continuity in the role played by boys on Pope Day and in the Revolution. For the traditional accounts of Pope Day and other disturbances were dismissive in the same manner as patriot accounts of demonstrations: all the trouble, it was usually said, was caused by "children," "young People Servants and Negros," or "negroes & other servants."[39]

Just as the Pope Day youths were used to symbolize the Protestant break from dependence on Rome, so in the Revolution were the same "boys & Negroes" used to symbolize a prospective break from Great Britain. In dismissing the actions of these youths as mere pranks, their elders implicated themselves in more ways than they were aware of. For such disclaimers put them in something like the position of the older generation in primitive coming-of-age rites. There, too, both generations have roles to play. The adults organize the ceremony in large part for their own purposes, manipulating the emotions of the neophytes. According to one analysis, the older generation's purpose is actually to protect itself.

The youths at coming of age represent a potential revolutionary threat to authority—which is to say, to their fathers. Over the millennia the fathers have developed ritual modes that effectively defuse this threat. In some cases the youths are encouraged to enact their unconscious aggressions in very direct ways; they behave "like dangerous criminals." They are, "licensed to waylay, steal, rape. This behavior is even enjoined on them. To behave antisocially is the proper expression of their . . . condition." In other cases the characteristically rebellious and aggressive feelings of boys arriving at maturity are deflected away from their natural targets, the fathers, by indirect means. The boys, under the tutelage of the fathers, who throughout make themselves appear as helpful and sympathetic, are systematically gulled. Often they are sent out into the wilds. There each of them must perform an act of courage—typically the killing of the tribe's totem animal. When a boy returns with the lion or other animal that he has killed he is ready to complete the coming-of-age ritual. What he does not realize, and what no one involved in the ritual any longer understands, is that his killing of a substitute has had the effect of deflecting the aggressive feelings that he harbored toward his father. (The animal that he has killed may be known officially as the totem "father" of the tribe.)[40]

Primitive peoples explain their coming-of-age rituals as occasions for transmitting the tribe's lore and values to the young. Yet the young are to a great extent misled, and they are put through numerous practices in no way related to instruction. In a similar way, New England legislatures proclaimed Pope Day, actually a time of riot and disorder, to be a serious memorial of the popish plot having as its purpose the instilling of "an Abhorrence of Popery & Forming a Spirit of Loyalty in the Youth of the Town."[41] Yet despite their formula of approval, New England elders were acutely aware of the disorderly content of Pope Day. As holidays approached they grew apprehensive of violence, which often involved apprentices.

The authorities were always aware of the holidays' youthful symbolism of subversion, as evidenced in the ordinance against children's holiday misbehavior denounced by James Otis. Earlier, the seventeenth-century English Puritans, once they came to power, forbade all childish "Floralia and Saturnalia"—their designations for the English popular recreations that were also associated with social disruption.[42]

Throughout Europe, from the Middle Ages through the eighteenth century, May and November marked the year's two great youth festivals. Boys and girls, along with young men and women, danced, performed mummery plays, exchanged love charms, went begging, and led processions like those of the sweeps on May Day. A boy and girl, crowned with wreaths of flowers, were made king and queen of the May. Boys were crowned "Fathers," lords of the May, mayors, judges, captains, admirals, barons, counts, princes, and kings, as well as priests, child abbots, archbishops, and pontiffs.[43]

The child crownings were performed in a spirit of mockery, with the crowned figure often being designated king of the revels. This king was ordinarily elected by his fellow members of a youth association, a kind of club made up of apprentices and young bachelors. The associations had as their special days the old May and November holidays. At these times they conducted pageants and crownings, begged for money, and sallied forth to administer rough music punishments. In the course of the sixteenth century the youth associations, regarded as too socially disruptive in their activities, were eliminated both on the continent and in England.[44] Their two annual days, their rough music, and their skimmingtons, however, continued.

The symbolic crownings of figures like Wilkes and Mackintosh recalled the mock child crownings, which shared an atmosphere of political threat to authority. Originally, as with the disorders of Pope Day, this atmosphere resulted partly from youthful high spirits and partly from the typical disobedience of youth. But at the same time the ceremonies that preceded the disorderliness of the youth festivals carried their own note of threat. On May Day, for example, the crowned child monarchs in France might hold mock, kangaroo courts before administering rough music punishments.[45] The threatening atmosphere of the youth days made its way, via the theme of regicide and the hooliganism of New England's Pope Day, into the rhetoric of the patriot party in America.

King Charles I, the monarch most frequently mentioned by the patriots after George III, although he did not himself appear on Pope Day, was a presence there by virtue of Joyce Jr., his executioner. When Joyce Jr. was later extracted from the Pope Day pageantry to serve as a punisher of loyalists, the holiday's regicidal-insurrectionary potential was drawn out. Patriot rhetoric had tapped this potential in a similar way when it represented the king's supporters as "regicides" and, in the end, the king himself as a "papistical tyrant."

Pope Day began as the commemoration of a historical event, the Gunpowder Plot, and a would-be regicide, Guy Fawkes. The holiday evolved by assimilating later attempts at overthrow and later regicidal figures, such as Cornet Joyce. When the American patriots chose their symbols and ritual from Pope Day, therefore, they brought into their political movement a holiday that had itself arisen out of and evolved in response to politics. In doing so they departed from the contemporary English practice with regard to ritualization, which in other respects they copied. For in England as on the continent, protesters tended to adopt the practices of the nearest convenient holiday in the calendar. In America, though, the initial Stamp Act protests took place in August, four months away from Pope Day, and yet still employed its practices. (The second round of protests, which actually bore less resemblance to Pope Day in many respects, did take place near Pope Day itself because the act happened to fall on November 1. But the use of the holiday's motifs had been established the previous August.)

Because of religious and cultural peculiarities that touched on the character of the American Revolution, Pope Day was the only adaptable New England holiday in existence at the time of the Stamp Act. English and American Puritans alike had disapproved of holidays, all of which to them smacked of Catholicism and paganism. In England the Puritans had been able to enforce a ban on such holidays and folk observances during the twenty years of their revolution from the 1640s to the 1660s. In France, over a longer period of time, the so-called forces of enlightenment acted to eliminate the many holidays that they regarded as contrary to reason. However, the French never went as far in their disapproval as the Puritans, nor ever matched the suppressions of those in America, who as of the time of the Stamp Act had maintained strict bans on holidays and folk observances for over a hundred and thirty years.[46] As a result of the Puritan hegemony, in eighteenth-century New England the only holiday that continued to include popular folk practices was Pope Day. Banned were Christmas, New Year's, Easter, May Day, and All Souls. As for Sunday, the English day for games and recreation, this was turned into a sober occasion for going to church—twice. New Englanders were granted a certain latitude for recreation on a number of holidays: Artillery Day, Election Day, and college Commencement Day, all of which took place in the spring. Election Day was timed to fall near Easter Sunday in contradiction of the Puritan ban on fixed days of observance, and it included "frolicking and mirth." Only in Philadelphia does May Day seem to have been an occasion for unrestrained fun. Here, accordingly, the anti–Stamp Act procession started from the place where fishermen traditionally erected their Maypole. Elsewhere the spring holidays were marked by sermons and were celebrated for the most part in the sober Puritan spirit. The American colonists, it may be said, suffered from festival deprivation.[47]

The only officially festive days in the year, when one could set off fireworks and drink toasts, were those connected with the monarchy: royal birthdays and accession days, and celebrations of English military victories. Therefore, given the colonial society's demand for decorum, and its prohibition of holidays in general, any expression of festival spirit meant either celebrating the tie with England or defying authority by misbehaving on a holiday. Thus it was that in America festival itself, and especially Pope Day, came to have subversive implications. Once these were made explicit and adopted for political ends, the holiday began to disappear.[48]

From 1765 onward, in fact, the life seemed to go out of Pope Day. Following the demonstrations in Boston on November 1, 1765, the outbreak expected by officials on the fifth never took place. Instead, the day proved to be a quiet one, with decorous anti–Stamp Act pageantry. Between 1765 and 1780 November 5 grew still quieter each year in what appears to have been a fairly steady trend. Newspaper writers began to condemn and town councils to prohibit its observance.[49] The Continental Congress, in order to establish good relations with Catholic Canada and Catholic France, denounced the wave of antipopery and effigy burning that burst forth in 1774 in response to the Quebec Act. The following year George Washington, citing the insult to Canada, prohibited his officers and soldies from practicing "that ridiculous and childish custom of burning the Effigy of the pope." But these official actions came well after a seemingly unaided decline of Pope Day. By 1780 the holiday had either disappeared or no longer seemed worth prohibiting or mentioning in newspapers or diaries. Then, apparently by smooth transition, it faded into Halloween, the similar children's holiday which takes place five days earlier. Like May Day, the ritual forms of Pope Day and Halloween persisted but acquired new associations: their bonfires, lanterns, devils, disguises, and begging all were assimilated to a mild, purely juvenile observance. The holiday's disguised insurrectionary content, it would appear, lost its suggestive power once it was made explicit by the Revolution.[50]

The one means by which this content lasted into modern history was via the fairgrounds, which had their own overtones of social disruption. For not only the license of festival days, but also the games played on Sundays took place at fairgrounds. Known as May games, and including some of the practices of May Day, these recreations were also outlawed by the English Puritans during their rule in the seventeenth century. They were permitted again after the Restoration, though they do not seem to have made their way to America. In the meantime, however, the Puritans, by virtue of their prohibitions, had made the fairgrounds implicitly a place of disorder and disobedience to law. Lastly, fairgrounds served, sometimes in conjunction with festivals, as a place for hiring. (One of the year's two traditional hiring days was November 5, which became Guy Fawkes day.)[51]

In the eighteenth century the hiring fairgrounds were logically chosen for the organizing of workers' protest demonstrations. The major London riots from the 1760s through the 1780s, in fact, either took place at or began at fairgrounds. Among these, the Massacre of St. George's Fields (during a demonstration for Wilkes) aroused the most intense reacton. Given the brutalities of ordinary London life, these deaths evoked an unusual outpouring of emotion—one that may in part have had to do with the festival associations of the name "St. George," a principal figure of the mummers' play, which was usually performed here. Years after the death of the boy Allen at the St. Geoge's Fields fairgrounds, the location served as the rallying point for the era's largest outbreak of crowd violence, the Gordon riots.[52]

A century later, in America, the hiring fair's relationship to both festival and revolution could be observed in the beginnings of the organized labor movement. During 1884, when a workers' demonstration for the eight-hour day was being organized, May 1 was the date chosen. At this time "there was no talk of 'spring festivals' or other ideas rooted in folklore"—or of the fact that this was the traditional German labor day. The May date was chosen "only" because it was "moving day, the annual date when leaves and other leases run out." On this day workers in both Europe and America could seek new employment or travel to new job locations. This meant that the modern May Day was related to the days set aside for the old hiring fairs.[53]

Though apparently unnoticed, this relationship had its effect when the planned demonstration finally took place in 1886 in Chicago, Illinois. For although the outcome was peaceful enough, the authorities reacted as if to a revolutionary outbreak. Three days later they fired into a group of strikers, killing six. The Haymarket Square bombing and melee in which seven were killed came on the following day.

Somehow the submerged revolutionary content of the old hiring days, last visible in the American Revolution, had played its role in this tragic series of events. For of all the medieval holidays of Europe, that of the hiring fair had lasted longest—into the nineteenth century in some places. As a result, those festival practices that also survived were the ones smuggled into these "most tenacious preservers of peasant customs." The customs in question included May games, morris dancing, and mummeries. Naturally they also included the general spirit of release and lawlessness on which the revolution had drawn: "farm servants, from several miles round [would] consider themselves as liberated from servitude on this day; and . . . [would] hie way, without leave, perhaps, to the statute."[54] As May Day grew into an international workers' day and then a Communist holiday, the events of 1886 were largely forgotten. Nevertheless, the day's festival origins, though still not acknowledged, once again made their way to the forefront.

At first the festival element presented itself as a convenience. One wing of the labor movement, wishing to ameliorate the Haymarket legacy as it was expressed in strikes and stridency, advocated a holiday with "pageants and games." This proposal was in effect defeated when the Communist International succeeded in taking over May Day as its official holiday. But later, in the 1920s, the American Federation of Labor made a similarly unsuccessful attempt to regain the day, in this case by starting up a rival, May 1 "Child Health Day." Here the federation inadvertently pointed back to May Day's original child associations. In the 1930s the Nazis in Germany apparently moved the day still futher away from its origins by purporting to make it once again a day of *labor*. What they meant, as it turned out, was a day of forced, unpaid "volunteer" work. Yet even here the latent spirit of festival reasserted itself, for the Nazis also made their May Day an occasion for youth pageants, flowers, and greenery.[55]

In the welter of festival traditions that lay behind the rituals of revolution, one member of the population in particular stands out: the young apprentice. As a member of a youth association he could participate in mock crownings, in rough music punishments, and in mummery plays, while as a worker he could join in the protest demonstrations that often derived from workers' pageants. His initiation into a guild represented Europe and America's closest approximation of the ancient primitive *rite de passage* of youth.

Late in his teens the apprentice underwent a ceremony that included most of the features of the primitive *rite de passage:* darkness, mystery, symbolic death and rebirth. The ceremony was unmistakably linked with those of Europe's secret societies, themselves supposed to have derived from primitive initiation cults. The most important secret society in America, the Masons, had many of the leading patriots and their followers as its members: the Sons of Liberty has been explained at various times as a secret society and as a branch of Masonry. The Masons were dedicated almost exclusively to conducting elaborate initiation rituals. In these, the new member was at the same time "made a man" and made a "mason"—that is, a symbolic worker. Just as with the youth associations, the special holidays of the Masons fell roughly at the summer and winter solstices. Since the same two periods were reserved for apprentice initiations, it is not surprising to find the motifs of the youth holidays in both. Thus, at the initiation of an English coachmaker, which took place "at the beginning of the winter season," the ubiquitous goose motif that found its way into tarring and feathering appeared when those participating in the ceremony "received a 'waygoose.' "[56]

The youth associations seem to have been devoted largely to coming of age. Instead of a single ceremony, they provided young men with a *rite de passage* that extended over several years—one that calls to mind the maturing of the American Revolution in the course of the 1760s. If such extended rituals can exist, then the castigating role of boys in their rough music phase may be understood in terms of an analogy with the displaced aggression of boys in primitive *rites de passage.* In the case of rough music an adult victim, usually an adult male, has been substituted for the totem animal. Just as with primitive initiations, and with the behavior of boys on Pope Day, the wild revelry of rough music was defended for supposedly having an educational function for youth. Actually, its cruelty appears to have derived from the period of license traditionally allowed the initiate in the *rite de passage.* The same tradition, when adopted by secret societies, came to resemble a "reign of terror." Here its characteristics became "license" for the members along with "great severity with regard to the morals of other people." This was precisely the attitude of the American patriots who conducted the intimidation of loyalists.[57]

In America, not only the period of license but the "brutal extortions" of money by members of the youth associations during rough music made their way into the Revolution. The extortions, too, came by way of Pope Day. (When Pope Day faded away, Halloween's begging for money in the form of "trick or treat" carried an echo of the previous extortionate atmosphere.) Along with begging came the "dreaded witticisms" of the punishers, as well as their generalized spirit of mockery—all found in America in the outrageous conduct of the boys on the pope cart toward the pope effigy and their practice of invading houses after the pageant. When this behavior took political form, Governor Colden in New York called it the "grossest ribaldry" of the "mob." Whatever degree of affinity the ribald spirit had with egalitarianism also had reference to the spirit of youth. In group coming-of-age rituals conducted over a long period of time among certain tribes, it has been observed that "among themselves, neophytes [sometimes known as "blood brothers"] tend to develop an intense comradeship and egalitarianism."[58]

Patriot rioters, however, were not youths, any more than were the initiates at Masonic ceremonies. They were adults who had adopted the spirit of youth initiation. In this respect, they offered an exception to the typical relationship between generations in *rites de passage.* For here they advanced from fearing and containing the youth generation to joining with it against a common foe perceived as a parent. This non-nurturant, threatening parent, Great Britain, served to merge the generations. From the impacted energy of their union arose a force of conviction, both private and collective, that drove the early stages of the American Revolution far beyond what even the participants themselves thought possible.

CHAPTER NINE

Festival, Ritual, and Revolution

O VER THE CENTURIES the festivals of mankind have undergone profound changes, adopting new dates, new names, and, where a performance is involved, new casts of characters. Yet no matter how far corrupted or co-opted, festivals have tended to retain their identity. Above all, their spirit of subversion never seems to remain suppressed for long. The very festivals that appear to have been successfully prohibited or taken over for official use may be those whose irrepressible elements will burst forth in the service of revolution.

Such a development can be seen in the long evolution of the holiday that became first New England's Pope Day, and then its ritual of revolution. The holiday's beginnings lay in a pre-Christian, Celtic anniversary of the dead celebrated by the Druids on November 1. In A.D. 837 Pope Gregory attempted to replace this still popular and still largely pagan observance of "All Souls" with a Christian observance dedicated to "All Saints." The Celtic practices of lighting bonfires and exorcising the dead proved impossible to abolish, however, and by the year 1000 the church had accepted All Souls as one of its approved holidays.[1] The celebrations of death found two millennia later in Guy Fawkes–Pope Day and Halloween testify to the persistence of the holiday's original impulse.

In the interim the remains of the old Celtic festival had continued to make themselves felt. In the sixteenth century, during the Catholic reign of Queen Mary in England, a number of medieval saints days prohibited by Protestant regimes were revived. One of these was St. Hugh's day, celebrated on November 17 by the ringing of bells. When Protestant Elizabeth happened to succeed Mary on a November 17, the Catholic practice of bell ringing on this day was taken over as the central feature of what was henceforward celebrated as Elizabeth's accession day. The official intention, to associate with Elizabeth "a holidaye wich passed all the popes holidayes," succeeded at first, and the Queen's accession day grew in importance through her long reign. But as the day became popular it accumulated practices and motifs—some of which would later appear in Pope Day—more appropriate to the old Celtic November 1, which was only three weeks distant in the calendar. The lighting of tar barrels was added, for example, along with the firing of guns, the setting off of fireworks, performances by children, and pageants.

For a considerable time these practices, along with the continued themes of anti-Catholicism, remained part of Accession Day. When the defeat of the armada from Catholic Spain on November 19, 1588, became an occasion for annual celebration, the pull of Accession Day soon proved so powerful that the two holidays blended and were celebrated on the seventeenth. After the death of Elizabeth the popular "Queen Elizabeth's Day" continued to be celebrated on November 17 even though James I had proclaimed March 24 as his own accession day. Eventually the subversive nature of the holiday began to reassert itself. In the prerevolutionary atmosphere of 1640, the fact that the Long Parliament began on November 17 was taken by many as an omen. Accession Day, without losing its identity, here went "from a day which had glorified the Tudor monarchy" to a "symbol of policies opposed to those of its successor." This was paradoxical but true to the original spirit of the holiday, which had always divided its enthusiasm between legitimacy and overthrow. Thus, on the day that Elizabeth succeeded Mary the bells had rung both subversively—to mourn the one—and loyally—to welcome the other. And thereafter the bells not only celebrated Elizabeth but also mocked the Catholics, to whom November 17 had belonged.[2]

This was not the end of the story, however. The next step in the recrudescence of the holiday's original spirit came later in the seventeenth century. Once again this took place under the guise of anti-Catholicism. And once again the borrowing of motifs had unexpected results. After 1679 Queen Elizabeth's Day was "converted into a satirical Saturnalia of the most turbulent kind" in which an effigy of the pope was paraded and then burned. The Test Act of the previous year had put the country into a state of great agitation by establishing an anti-Catholic oath as a requirement for holding government office. The act held, however, a special exclusion for James II, the Catholic brother of the childless King Charles II, permitting James to succeed to the throne. In reaction to this provision a special bill denying the throne to James was proposed, and in support of the idea a mock-Catholic procession was organized for Accession Day. It featured a pope in his chair of state, with a devil figure "frequently caressing, hugging, and whispering him, 'to destroy his majesty, to forge a prot-estant plot, and to fire the city again' [a reference to the Great Fire of 1666]; to which purpose he held an infernal torch in his hand."[3]

This panoply came directly from the papal coronation ceremony, then only about a century old. In ritual terms, the practices of yet an-other coronation were being added to the holiday. The new pope's cer-emonial chair, the *sedia gestatoria*, became the center of attention. The pope's two fan-carrying attendants were mocked by two boy atten-dants (whose ministrations would evolve into the exaggerated atten-tions of boys toward the pope effigy). A third attendant, who accompa-nied the pope as a constant reminder of life's brevity, was mocked on Accession Day by someone chanting a reminder of the pope's sup-posed involvement in the recent murder of Sir Edmund Berry God-frey, the event that had set off the anti-Catholic hysteria.

By Queen Elizabeth's Day 1681 the main features of Pope Day were evident. A mock papal procession was led by a figure of Godfrey "on Horseback all besprinkled with Bloud . . . and his head hanging on one side." This was followed by a pillory with effigies, another effigy "sitting upon a Chair, having a paper pinned upon his Breast," and lastly "his Holiness fixed upon a Sledge." Behind the pope, "all the way the Devil bobs him, and takes him by the Nose with a pair of Pincers." Torches, fireworks, and the burning of the effigies "at Temple-Bar, or in Smithfield" completed the show. When the Ameri-can patriots later organized a funeral for Christopher Seider, Thomas Hutchinson was reminded of the still notorious pageants featuring Godfrey.[4]

Queen Elizabeth's Day had now come nearly full circle. It had begun as an attempt to install a rival legitimacy to that of Catholic Mary, by means of imitation papal splendor and mockery of a Catholic holiday (St. Hugh's Day). Then Queen Elizabeth's Day had itself first become a holiday subversive of James I's official accession day, and then a mock holiday at the beginning of the Puritan revolution. Next it had served to express resistance to the succession of James II. Finally, its symbols were turned on the English monarchy itself by the American colonists.

The idea for a mock coronation pageant obviously derived from the feast of fools and child monarchs of the youth associations. Ironically, this tradition was largely Catholic. It had been prohibited in the sixteenth century, then revived in the seventeenth, along with St. Hugh's Day, May games, and mummeries. Banned again under Elizabeth, the pageant made its way back into favor by reappearing in the guise of an anti-Catholic exercise. More important, the addition of the pope brought to the holiday a permanent infusion of hysteria from England's most astonishing period of irrationality. The deranged informer, Titus Oates, whom James Otis recalled when he signed himself "James Oates," concocted an imaginary popish plot on the king's life. This led to a wave of executions of innocent Catholics, including members of Parliament, during 1679 and 1680, when the pope procession was inaugurated. The anti-Catholic hysteria, it has been said, "goaded the passions of men to a state of madness, and seemed for a while to extinguish the native good sense and humanity of the English character."[5]

In the meantime, in 1605, Guy Fawkes Day had entered the calendar to commemorate an attempted assassination. This holiday then took on added meanings when William of Orange ended the short reign of James II in the revolution of 1688. The annual commemoration of William's invasion of England on November 5, which fell coincidentally on Guy Fawkes Day and which resulted in his victory over James, appears to have led to the incorporation into Guy Fawkes Day of Queen Elizabeth's Day and its recent pope procession. In retrospect it appears that with every accession of saturnalian spirit and folk practices these holidays were being propelled toward their original, Celtic date at the beginning of November. Just when the amplified Guy Fawkes Day migrated to New England is not clear. It may well have been early in the 1730s, at the time of the Catholic Pretender's new, supposedly popish, plot and uprising against the king. But whatever the historical circumstances of the transit, it was characteristic of New Englanders that they should seize upon the antipapal elements of the holiday.

If one takes together the folk practices that were adopted in the American Revolution, it is apparent that they derived for the most part from English May and November festivals, with additional elements from midsummer as well as Christmas–New Year's. These periods had in common practices as diverse as mummeries, disguises, children's pageants, reversals of roles, and begging—all of which were adopted in political protests. This broad range of influence on the rituals of revolution presents a confusing picture until it is understood that the holidays in question derived from two basic sources: mankind's observances of the summer and winter solstices. Several forces have worked to disperse through the rest of the year the practices typical of the solstices. First, changes in the calendar shifted the dates of New Year's festivals like the Roman Saturnalia by as much as two months. Second, appropriations of holidays by religious and civil authorities brought about only slightly less extensive changes. Finally, two separate methods of determining the seasonal observances persisted in medieval and modern Europe and America, and resulted in two different sets of dates for essentially identical holidays.[6]

Yet, whatever the changes in a holiday's date or apparent subject, its roots in summer and winter always remained. And inasmuch as holidays at these times marked transitions from one season to the next, they were always "new" year's observances. At each, an effigy that was destroyed symbolized the death of the old, while the presence of children symbolized the birth of the new. (To this day, New Year's cards show these two figures in the forms of a diapered babe and an old man.) The course of the sun was imitated by illuminations: bonfires, torches, candle-lit windows, a flaming wheel rolled down a hill. Taken together, these practices amounted to *rite de passage* ceremonies conducted to observe the cycle of the year.[7]

The analogies with those other kinds of cycles, the successions of monarchs and governments, have always been evident, so that it was natural for the symbols of nature's passages to be adopted for inauguration ceremonies—and for that other method of succession, revolution. The revolution of the sun in its course, moreover, bore an equally good analogy with the peaceful and the violent successions of monarchs in human history. This meant that insofar as they served as *rites de passage,* holidays always carried potentially revolutionary undertones.

On Guy Fawkes–Pope Day these overtones were conveyed by a series of insurrectionary figures. Among these was Admiral Byng, who appeared in American pageants soon after the British admiral of that name was executed in England in 1757 for failing to do his utmost in a naval engagement. Because the court that condemned him to death absolved him of the charge of cowardice, however, he gained a measure of ambiguous popular sympathy. Thus, like Guy Fawkes he was a species of traitor, and therefore by definition threatening to the king; he was popularly reviled; and at the same time he elicited a jocular sympathy.

The mummers' play that accompanied May and November festivals conveyed a similar insurrectionary potential through the presence of villains dedicated to the symbolic overthrow of the king figures in the play. The mummers' play consisted of "a naive induction in which one of the performers craves the spectators' indulgence, asks for room, and promises a fine performance." Each one of its cast of champions then boastfully introduces himself. There are challenges, and a duel in which one of the champions falls wounded or dead. "A doctor is then summoned who vaunts his proficiency in medicine and proceeds to revive the fallen hero." After this ending the minor characters give a series of buffoonish entertainments, and money is collected.[8]

In the American, Pope Day version of the mummers' play, which has been identified as Cornish in origin, Father Christmas, a popular mummers' hero, might appear as the central character in the play. This Father Christmas traditionally enters saying, "I hope ould father Christmas will never be forgot."[9] Echoing his line was the popular colonial adage which had it that Pope Day was celebrated in order that the gunpowder plot would never be "forgot." Later, in the decline of Pope Day, New England almanacs commented, "Powder plot is not forgot. 'Twill be observed by many a sot"; and, by 1767 they reported, "Powder plot most forgot." (In each case there undoubtedly lurked a pun in the word "forgot," which referred to the collecting of money that was to follow the performance of the play.)[10]

Father Christmas, like other mummers' play heroes such as Saint George and King George, either killed or was killed by his antagonist. The winner then arranged for the doctor to bring his fallen antagonist back to life. This death and resurrection framework was based on "the idea of a conflict between the old year and the new, between the waxing and the waning life of the earth."[11] Thus, here was yet another analogy with political revolution. Not surprisingly, therefore, when the American revolutionaries seized on holiday motifs for their protests, they found the mummers' play as eligible as the Pope Day pageant itself. They imitated the play with their mock interments and resurrections of the figure of Liberty. Like the mummers' players, the political crowd expressed mock dismay at the death of Liberty, searched for signs of life, and then celebrated the discovery that she was "alive." Like mummery characters such as St. George and King George, the Liberty figure came to represent both a community—the ideal England conceived of as America—and the threat of its overthrow.

Both the characters and the symbols of festivals served to express the idea of revolution. Whether by the insertion of famous villains in the mummers' play or the effigy procession, or by the presentation of the act of overthrow, or by more subtle means such as the enactment of death and resurrection, the reversal of normal roles, or changes of costume, political crowds expressed their threat to order. In each instance, however, they conveyed a measure of loyalty along with their threat. Just as patriot rhetoric carried professions of love for the king along with its attacks on his state, and just as crowds tended to end demonstrations with shouts of "God Save the King," so their symbolism conveyed acceptance as well as defiance of the monarchy. The function of festival borrowings was not simply to express a threat, but to embody the divided feelings of those who ventured into dissent.

The ambiguities about revolution of patriots like Otis, Adams, Hawley, and Quincy, and of the crowds who praised their king even as they attacked his authority, found their readiest expression in the figure from whom Hawthorne derived his character, Robin. This was Robin Hood, the most popular choice to play the central, sacrificial role, and certainly the most symbolically dense figure in the English festival tradition.

Robin Hood appeared in both May and November. On May Day he, Maid Marian, and Friar Tuck were the three leading characters in the morris dance. After its performance Robin Hood and Maid Marian were crowned king and queen of the May. On Guy Fawkes–Pope Day, or at All Hallows, Robin Hood appeared together with Little John in the mummers' play. Here, with perfectly symmetrical ambiguity, the outlaw and thief of Sherwood Forest—a figure essentially of the usurping, king-slaying party—acts as a protector of the king's deer. He accuses a tanner of poaching, and they fight. At this point it becomes unclear just who falls and how. In one version Little

John seems to be substituted for the tanner and to fall. In another, Robin Hood fights indecisively until Little John takes his place and kills the tanner.[12]

This Robin Hood of the mummers' play differs from the outlaw of the well-known Robin Hood saga not only in having a dutiful relationship to the king, but also with respect to his prowess. For whereas in the play Robin Hood is as likely to win as lose, in the hand-to-hand combats depicted elsewhere he is invariably defeated. Indeed, the Robin Hood saga leads inexorably to Robin Hood's defeat, followed by his slow bleeding to death in Maid Marian's arms. This outcome, it has been pointed out, identifies him as yet another descendant of the fertility deities who die in order to nourish the earth. As such, he made an ideal addition to the mummers' play, itself an imitation of fertility ritual through its dying and resurrected characters.[13]

The year's succession, symbolized as a fatal struggle between youth and age, rebel and king, or son and father, found its most complete expression in Robin Hood. For he was both outlaw and ruler (the king of the May). In addition, he was both a would-be slayer of those he met in combat and a slain hero in the final scene of his saga. Finally, he was both man and boy, incorporating the idea of youth in two ways. In the first place he was often impersonated by a boy actor in the mummers' play and in the mock crowning of the May king and queen. In the second place, his name evoked the child or fairy figure "Robin of the Wood."[14]

Robin Hood served one function more. When, as was frequently the case, he was played by a chimney sweep—that figure of the child distilled to its symbolic essence—Robin Hood functioned not only as an individual symbol but a collective one as well. In England the sweeps traditionally united the rituals of labor with those of childhood. For the most part they were boys between eight and fifteen (those small enough to crawl into chimneys). Yet their calling entitled them to appear at workingmen's demonstrations. The appalling physical condition of these children, who in some cases were less than eight years old, was visible to all. Taken from their families and bound out to adult masters, they had to go through the streets shouting for work. Usually they were completely black from soot: a reform bill near the end of the eighteenth century called for masters to ensure that their charges be washed once a *week*.[15] When William Blake used the oppressed chimney sweeper to symbolize both innocence and experience, he was evoking the two traditional symbolic roles of sweeps in society.

As long as the Western imagination retained its memory of the feudal arrangement in which workers and peasants were conceived of as dependent children, the sweeps stood for all exploited workers. Furthermore, in a kind of ultimate exploitation, they were condemned never to become masters of their trade. Whereas every other guild had a ceremony elevating the apprentice to master or journeyman, at the equivalent age a sweep grew too large physically to continue his work. He was forced to go from being an actual master of his trade, though treated as an apprentice, to unemployment or some other employment. This unfortunate group of workers then, which gave the collective impression of remaining eternally young, was the only one to lack a coming-of-age ceremony symbolizing the passage to adult responsibility.

If they were denied a formal ritual, however, the sweeps were in some fashion compensated by being given a prominent role in the rituals of May Day. When the sweeps paraded on May Day their temporary change of roles was the most radical of all, for if revolution is conceived of as emanating from the bottom of society, the permanently arrested and exploited sweeps, the lowest of the low, lent themselves with peculiar aptness to its symbolization when they put on top hats and formal coats. Such reversal of status, which had always figured in the saturnalian aspect of the summer and winter holidays, perfectly suited a revolutionary situation. It expressed the political reversal implied in a change of government, and, in those cases where revolution led to social change, it symbolized the resultant reversals of personal status.[16]

Since their rituals impinged on society far more than privately held apprentice initiations, the sweeps presented themselves as logical candidates to conduct the rituals of revolution when those were adapted from the rituals of festival. Thus it was on their May Day that they first attacked Lord Bute.

A key feature of the *rite de passage* denied the sweeps is the period of social revolutionary license engaged in by the initiates. During this phase they demean themselves so as to appear to be among society's outcasts, the lowest of the low. Only after performing this role are they allowed to complete the passage to adult membership. The sweeps may be seen as a group perpetually in the *rite de passage* stage of outcast lawlessness. As such they threatened at any time to come into their rightful dominion as adults and to become, so to speak, the next masters of society. Thus they expressed in symbolic form the fustrations of society when its members began to desire that ultimate act of transition, the replacement of a monarch.

Modern society has perpetuated the symbolic pattern of the *rite de passage* to the extent of investing those who are lowest on the social scale with similar magical qualities. Workers and peasants have always represented a deep, autochthonous connection with the simple, profound truths of life. In the nineteenth century, Leslie Fiedler has suggested, dwarfs, or the "little people" as they were called, could "figure forth the revolutionary terror below the surface of Victorian optimism."[17] In the eighteenth century the sweeps bore the same revolutionary implications. In naming his boy revolutionary protagonist "Robin," Hawthorne also called attention to the ritual significance of the child in revolution.

But not only is the child connected with a ritual of coming of age in which he overthrows, but also a ritual defeat in which he is the one overthrown, or killed. This fate was magnified and ritualized after the killing of young Allen at St. George's Fields in London and again at the funeral of young Christopher Seider shortly before the Massacre in Boston. Over and over again in the works of Whig Sentimentalism "ruffians" are seen ritually cutting down innocent youths in the same way, sometimes with specific reference to martyrs such as Allen and Seider. It has been suggested that when the ritual of overthrow includes a defeated child or son figure, the responsibility for his death rests with the incumbent monarch. The subsequent commemorations of the child's death accordingly celebrate mankind's impulses toward social and political equality.[18]

In the mummers' play such a relationship obtained between monarch and child. It was possible for the May Day king, played in the afternoon by a chimney sweep, to step into the role of Robin Hood later in the day in the mummers' play. Here he might be assaulted by a king, fall dead, and then have his identity revealed as the king's son. The play differed from Whig Sentimentalism, however, in openly displaying a corresponding aggression on the part of sons. Just as Robin Hood embodied both man and boy, ruler and subject, in the play the winners and losers have interchangeable identities as sons or fathers. At the conclusion of the duel, the champion's antagonist is usually revealed to have been either his son or his father. If the father has won, he mourns until his son is revived; if the son has won, he mourns his father. Alternately one of the bystanders may suddenly reveal that he is the father of the defeated.[19]

In one of the plays in which King George falls, but without explicit identification of who is the father and who the son, a new character enters to conclude the play. Fidler Wit announces, "Father died the other night / And left me all his riches . . . Sing brothers sing." The hint here that the duel has to do with a struggle of brothers against the father at once looks forward to revolution and backward to the furthest sources of ritual. For the combats in the Robin Hood saga are of the same fraternal kind. These duels typically take place not between Robin Hood and, say, the sheriff of Nottingham or his men, but rather between Robin and one of his followers or prospective followers. His merry band is a band of brothers seeking to overthrow him. Fittingly, then, its members were often played by children, as were the characters of the mummers' play. When these actors were chosen from among members of the youth associations, or from among the sweeps, the duel or contest was restored to its original context of *rite de passage.*[20]

The members of the youth associations, furthermore, in real life carried forward one of Robin Hood's chief functions: the enforcement of traditional values. Robin Hood's stealing from the rich to give to the poor has precisely this moral purpose. In the American Revolution when youths dominated opposition to the Stamp Act, it was partly to protest a reversal of the same traditional values. The act, the argument went, threatened to rob the poor in order to enrich a few already wealthy stamp distributors. From the perspective of youths and their collective enactment of revolution, the beginnings of the American Revolution in Massachusetts display two sets of ritually tied brothers: the crowds organized by the "Sons" of Liberty, and the patriots joined together against Thomas Hutchinson. Josiah Quincy, Jr., well expressed the connection between the two when he called for a "band of brothers" with bloody swords to strike down monarchy.

Quincy's violent imagery accorded with the festivals that lay behind revolution. Their violence was conveyed in the blackened faces of both American Revolutionary crowds and their festival antecedents. Morris dancers in May and mummers in November traditionally performed with blackened faces, as did the participants in the American Pope Day. In France the entourage of the Abbey of Fools, "les Noircies," paraded naked, blackfaced, and covered with soot. All suggested something to do with burning—an impression strengthened by the accompanying bonfires and effigy burnings. In the morris dance the boy whose body was covered with burrs, and who performed the Robin Hood "furry dance," had his face blackened. He appears to have been associated with Jack in the Green. The latter, a somewhat later May Day figure, came to be played by a blackfaced chimney sweep. He walked "encased in a pyramidal framework of wickerwork" and he danced "on May Day at the head of a troop of chimney-sweeps, who collect pence." Alternately, he rode or was drawn on a sledge. In earlier observances Jack in the Green was slain and revived in a performance that evidently was the source for the mummers' play. He could also be burned.[21] Thus he was a sacrificial figure—like Robin Hood a vegetation-fertility deity such as those described by Frazer in the *Golden Bough.*

This ancient connection, although not understood in precisely these terms, was always apparent to observers of the festival. It was particularly evident to the fathers of the Christian church in their struggle against the stubborn remains and revivals of paganism—one extending from the seventh to the nineteenth century. During the American Revolution observers repeatedly noted the pagan sources of crowd ritual in much the same spirit of disapproval. Today, studies of crowds and revolutions tend to accept the notion that the dying god described in the *Golden Bough* lies behind the ubiquitous burning of effigies in revolutionary demonstrations. This symbolism, however, is taken as illustrative rather than operative.[22] If, in contrast, one regards the rituals of revolution as having a determining force of their own, and that derived from their ancient sources, then their origins take on more than passing interest.

When revolutionary crowds appeared in blackface they harked back to the ritual conflagrations of the earliest fertility ceremonies. From all indications these ceremonies gathered around a human sacrifice. As they evolved, the one who died, the king, was replaced by some other human victim, often a temporary, mock king, as in the Saturnalia. Later, animals and effigies were substituted for men. The Celtic sacrifice in Gaul and England was reported on by the Romans. It aimed at ensuring the fertility of the land by burning to death groups of condemned criminals and captured enemies, along with live animals, in a giant wicker frame.[23]

Festival and revolutionary practices alike frequently harked back to an actual victim. Boys in England dressed themselves as the villain, Guy Fawkes, just as in America they dressed as tar-covered devils. And just as effigies were designed to resemble persons, the published cartoon of an effigy could depict that person as actually hanging from a bough. Similarly, on one occasion instead of a Guy Fawkes effigy a real person was seized and carted through the usual proceedings. Andrew Oliver's effigy, when it was burned by the August 16 Stamp Act crowd, was termed a "Burnt-Offering." All of these hints were made explicit when the French revolutionaries of 1789 took the ultimate step back toward the original sacrifice: they decapitated their victims and impaled their heads on the traditional long poles used for carrying effigies. In the end, the charred victim was suggested only in the most indirect fashion by the candle inside the jack o'lantern of Halloween.[24]

Given the origins of festival evident in such proceedings, the scapegoatings of Lord Bute and Thomas Hutchinson appear as far more than political conveniences or anomalies. When held up to mockery in holiday-like demonstrations, these men were being joined to a tradition of politically inspired substitutions for the original victim. In Hutchinson's case especially, the "error" involved in choosing him, an opponent of the Stamp Act, as the chief victim of protest against it, proves to have been no error at all, but rather a necessity of the situation. In the attack on Hutchinson it was not the relatively minor issues of the Stamp Act and other revenue bills that mattered, but the coming to birth of a new nation. The scapegoat ceremony symbolized this national process, and at the same time was itself the reflection of political revolution in the distant past.

In the earliest times, after all, the victim himself was a substitute—most likely for a king or other leader. The original ceremony, therefore, had amounted to a transmission of political power by means of regicide, and so was itself an act of political revolution. Since a new king replaced the old, giving rebirth to the kingly powers, the ceremony celebrated both overthrow and legitimate succession. Here lay the ambiguity inherent in the mummers' play, Pope Day, and revolution, all of which simultaneously celebrated kingship and usurpation.

The ambiguity was well expressed in a striking pattern of doubling that may be observed throughout the revolutionary period as well as in its festival sources. Just as the ancient Roman Thargelia, a harvest festival, featured a parade of two *pharmakoi,* or scapegoats, and just as in the Bible two actual goats appear in the scapegoat sacrifice, so the original Guy Fawkes–Pope Day procession had focused on two figures, the pope and the devil, and in its political adaptations on one or another paired arrangement of figures.[25] The mummers' play had a cast of several characters, but when the proceedings resolved themselves into a marching pageant, two figures dominated, consisting either of two paraded effigies or two men carrying crosses. On Guy Fawkes Day the procession might feature two Guys and on Pope Day two popes or the pope and a devil. Oliver's effigy appeared alongside Bute as a boot in August 1765, Grenville's alongside Huske on November 1, Governor Colden's alongside a devil on November 5, and in 1774 Hutchinson appeared beside Wedderburne. (In the French Revolution the human heads on poles came in pairs.)

Boston and New York each had two groups of Pope Day celebrators, evidently derived from rival Guy Fawkes Day gangs in England. In both cities when these groups united to protest the Stamp Act they continued to construct their own effigies. These were paraded separately, then brought together to be burned in traditional fashion.[26] The same two groups had evidently risen in the revolt against Governor Andros in 1688. The members of one of them—the "North End Raggamuffins"—were recognized at the destruction of Hutchinson's house. A few months later the two groups marched separately to celebrate repeal of the Stamp Act, and a few years later met to join together before the Boston Massacre. In the spread of Stamp Act protests through the colonies, additional effigy doublings frequently appeared. As far away as the West Indies, when news of repeal reached Kingston in May 1766 islanders prepared an effigy of one John Howell which, after it was "paraded through the town, was brought aside a likeness of George Grenville, and the two set on fire."[27]

In the decline of Pope Day and the rise of direct action against loyalists, victims of tarring and feathering were frequently carted in pairs facing each other. Later, on the few occasions when effigies were revived, the old pattern persisted. The Quebec Catholic Relief Act of 1774 led to two popes being displayed in a temporary revival of Pope Day in Newport, Rhode Island. Still later, after the discovery of Benedict Arnold's conspiracy—an act of treason like Guy Fawkes's—the old processional was revived around the country. In New Milford, Connecticut, with the town's windows illuminated, Arnold was

French Revolutionary Procession

Actual heads (two again) are held aloft on poles in a spirit of revelry; the procession is led by a woman carrying a branch reminiscent of folk holidays and the sacrificial tree.

paraded with the devil to the rough music of firecrackers. His effigy was hanged, then cut down and buried. In Philadelphia his effigy, with a pitchfork-wielding devil behind it, had a moveable, constantly turning head—with two faces on it. Prints distributed as far north as Boston showed the two-headed effigy, the gibbet, and the pope cart with stage. Similarly, according to one observer, "Governor Hutchinson was often represented, with *two faces,* to denote his duplicity."[28] The symbolism, to be sure, indicated a traitor's divided loyalties. But were

Lords Bute and Grenville Hung in Effigy

The doubling motif of Pope Day is carried out in this depiction of Lords Grenville and Bute (in plaid kilt on the left) hanging in effigy. A chain links the two figures to "the Devil," who holds the Stamp Act or a stamped document.

not the patriots themselves traitors whose use of doubled effigies expressed their own divided loyalties?

If so, the harvest festival served them well once again, for doubled effigies were traditional. In *The Magic Art,* J. G. Frazer speculates that in harvest processionals one of the two figures represented a godlike spirit and the other its human representative.[29] In other words, two conceptions of the effigy appeared together: an older one of it as a god, and a newer one of it as (recently) human. Wherever two effigies continued to appear, this suggests, one of them was anterior in conception to the other. Here, then, was another symbolization of the old monarch who must die and the new one who takes his place. Politicized, it expressed in yet one more form the inevitabilities of overthrow and succession.

The rival Pope Day gangs of Boston and New York, which may be regarded as a collective instance of doubling, themselves reflected a traditional practice of festival: the athletic contest. Archery competitions in imitation of Robin Hood and his men offered one precedent, but of more obvious relevance were pitched battles like the tug of war. These imitated the change of the seasons conceived of as a struggle between winter and summer. In a comparable way, when a new king is to be invested among the Shilluk of the Sudan, "Nyikang," an effigy representing the mysteries of the kingship, is carried from the northern to the southern part of the kingdom. There, "Nyikang's army of the north meets in mock combat an army of the south, supporting the king-elect." The north- and south-end Pope Day gangs of Boston made ideal enacters of the similar struggle that is revolution. After the Revolution took place, their contest declined into another child's observance. Henry Adams recalled in his autobiography that "one of the commonest boy-games of winter, inherited directly from the eighteenth-century, was a game of war on Boston Common. In old days the two hostile forces were called North-Enders and South-Enders. In 1850 the North-Enders still survived as a legend, but in practice it was a battle of the Latin School against all comers."[30] The boys of the nineteenth century, although they had lost the ritual accompaniments of the battle, properly conducted it in the dead of the winter season, and furthermore brought out its potential class meaning by transforming a contest between two groups of workmen into one between children of different social classes.

The rituals of revolution have been accurately described as reversed ceremonies of legitimacy. But the ceremonies of legitimacy were themselves ambiguous. Inasmuch as they were attempts to eliminate the element of overthrow in the sources on which they, too, drew, they harbored the same contradiction as the rituals of revolution. The elaborate panoply by means of which kings maintained the awe that sustained their power amounted to a split of the original ceremonial. One part, the death of the old king, became a sacrifice of opponents;

*A Representation of the Figures Exhibited and Paraded through the Streets
of Philadelphia, on Saturday, the 30th of September 1780*

The Pope Day procession was revived for the last time to excoriate
Benedict Arnold. This depiction of the event shows the familiar, taunting
devil behind the seated villain. The doubling motif persists in Arnold's
two-facedness, and in the two ropes hanging from the gallows depicted on
the traditional lanthorn in front of him.

the other, the king's replacement by a conqueror, served to elevate the
kingly power itself. To punish criminals, who as Joseph Hawley
pointed out were all by definition traitors to the king, monarchy employed the sacrifice-like ceremonials of the public square. These extended from punishment in the stocks to hanging, and could include
such ceremonies as the public burning of Wilkes's *North Briton* Number 45. To celebrate monarchy there were feasts, illuminations, and
toasts to mark royal births, royal birthdays, accession days, and especially coronations.

The coronation ceremony derived both from the rites of passage
of the individual, and the related passage from the old year to the new.
Accordingly, its symbolism and timing, as with the *rite de passage,* emphasized new beginning. Egyptian coronations took place on "New
Year's Day or some other decisive new beginning in nature's cycle,"
and precisely at dawn—another natural beginning. (Conversely, those
Greek ceremonies that emphasized the passing of the older god rather
than the accession of the new, took place at sunset.) Charlemagne
chose Christmas, then still part of New Year's, for his coronation. And
as late as the seventeenth century Charles II was crowned on New
Year's Day to signify the restoration or rebirth of the monarchy.[31]

Charles's coronation was an exception, coming as it did after an interim, or death, not only of a king but of the succession itself. Yet however thoroughly the idea of death might ordinarily be expunged from the positive ceremonials of legitimacy, it lingered there as surely as in the negative ceremonials of punishment. The old king had fallen a sacrifice, and the new ruler had been implicated in his death. At the heart of the ritual that sustained legitimacy, therefore, lay revolution itself. The very process of succession implied "revolution" in both the political and technical meanings of the word. The sacrificial ceremony by which succession once took place, after all, was based on an analogy with the revolution of the earth and its seasons. As a result, the party of legitimacy in history and the party of revolution have had equal claim on and have drawn equally on the evolved practices of the sacrificial ritual.[32] It follows that as legitimacy is tainted with the crime of overthrow, so revolution is tainted by the worship of legitimacy.

That an equally powerful contradiction can reside in seasonal observances is evident from versions performed among tribal peoples. An African king may undergo both ritual and actual punishment in connection with sowing, or with first-fruits observances. He is presented as at once a child and, bedecked in green grasses, a fertility figure resembling Jack in the Green. During a saturnalian period of social disorder, featuring reversals of ordinary social roles, the king's subjects express their ambiguity toward him. In counterpoint to affirming their love and support for him, they chant to themselves with equal ritual sanction: "You hate the child king." They then turn directly to him chanting, "King, they hate thee."[33]

From this indication it is clear that the scapegoat king of the Saturnalia, when he was punished or put to death, absorbed profoundly hostile impulses on behalf of the true king. The king, any king, derives from a sacrificial figure. He therefore not only bears the guilt attaching to the sacrifice of his predecessor but also invites his own eventual sacrifice. The desire to overthrow the king thus logically reflects both his legitimacy and illegitimacy. He deserves punishment for the crime of usurpation, yet his service to the community derives from his own enactment of the same sacrifice. No wonder, then, that the practices of the Saturnalia—role reversals, disguise, mockery—have been able to imply revolution even when their symbolic meanings and derivations were but dimly understood.

It may be that the ancient symbolism remains most alive today in a country such as Ethiopia. After Haile Selassie was deposed in 1974, the new regime waited until New Year's Day (which there occurs in September under the Julian calendar) to remove him from his palace. On this day, "wearing a white embroidered shawl and white trousers—the traditional clothes for the Ethiopian new year," the fallen emperor was paraded from the palace to a "barren mud hut."[34] The need for a ceremonial of transition was seen elsewhere in 1974. Only a month earlier, on August 9, when it became known during the day that Richard Nixon planned to resign that night, there ensued a series of events that to one reporter "seemed almost stylized images of the last full day of a doomed regime." Across from the White House a crowd formed and soon "could be heard chanting in mockery of the ritual musical homage to the American Chief of State: 'Jail to the Chief. Jail to the Chief. Jail to the Chief.' " The crowd was "mostly young and 'crazy with joy.' " Its spirit reminded the reporter of the year's two great festival observances: "Far into the night, the streets were dense with traffic, the kind Washington never sees downtown even on a wild New Year's Eve. The cars drove around and around the White House, where kids cartwheeled and cavorted and whooped ... they looked like May Day protesters—young, bearded, blue-jeaned."[35]

In dramatic versions of overthrow like the mummers' play the sacrificial father is overthrown by his son, while in the collective ritual youth generation enacts the same overthrow. Given the explicit naming of the king as father of his people in royalist ideology, it should come as no surprise that Josiah Quincy thought of the American patriots as a band of brothers. "No great commitment to psychoanalytic theory is required," Michael Walzer has written, to describe revolution as "the successful struggle of the 'brethren' against the father."[36]

The Great Awakening of the 1740s in America had shown how even skeptical observers of a mass phenomenon could be caught up in its waves of emotion. Just as the Awakening had separated American intellectuals into "New Light" supporters and "Old Light" opponents of the revivals, in the 1760s the crowds helped separate them into patriots and loyalists. A crowd touches onlookers as well as participants. The patriots did not for the most part join the crowds, or even in every case witness their demonstrations. But along with everyone else they were vicariously involved in what amounted to a ritualization by the crowds of the colonies' feelings toward Great Britain.[37]

Like Hawthorne's Robin, whose *rite de passage* is projected onto a political uprising, the patriots' psychological crises were effectively expressed by the rituals of revolution. The patriots reacted in the first place with exceptional sharpness to being placed in a condition of dependency on England, yet insisted on their perfect submission. Josiah Quincy called himself England's "most dutiful son," while for John Adams the protesting colonists represented England's "most dutiful and affectionate children."[38] The same ambivalence toward authority was expressed collectively by the symbols of the crowds.

The patriots' conviction that they were building rather than pulling down was also well expressed by their rituals. For not only did peaceful political succession derive from a sacrificial ritual containing both loyalty and revolt, but as Greek tragedy, the Bible, Shakespeare, and the cultural theories of Freud (among others) agree, this ritual led to the establishment of civilization.[39] In Greek tragedy, as in the mummers' play, a bitter family conflict between parent and child typically results in the death of one and a ritual of atonement by the other. The Oresteia makes explicit the ritual's inauguration of law-abiding, civilized life. In the Abraham story in the Bible the planned ritual killing of a son by his father, in which a ram is substituted at the last minute, has a similar result: the establishment of a people. The conspirators in Shakespeare's *Julius Caesar,* like the American patriots who so often quoted their words, are quite unaware of the ritual aspect of their revolt and believe that they are engaged in the defense of Roman civilization. In *Totem and Taboo* Freud posits a precivilized murder of a father by his sons. Their act of atonement consists in establishing a ritual of sacrifice. They agree annually to mourn, memorialize, and honor their father, at the same time as they will reenact their deed in ritual. Most importantly, they include a vow to live at peace with one another—another example of the civilizing act.[40]

Freud, by extending the drama of overthrow from one child to a band of brothers, threw a new light on the parallel scenes in Greek tragedy and the Bible. Though in each instance one son stands out in the tragic contest, other children frequently come into the picture. So, too, with Shakespeare. In *King Henry V,* when Prince Hal, watching at his father's deathbed, places the crown on his own head, the old man awakens to rebuke him for wishing his death. Filled with remorse, Hal pledges reform, and then goes on to a kingship that is represented as establishing and defining English civilization. But the prince is not alone in his revolt against the old king. The rebel, Hotspur, is presented as a symbolic brother of Hal, while Hal's band of cronies are all violators of the king's laws. And, not only does Hal watch alone, but in a scene suggesting the band of brothers he stands among his actual brothers watching expectantly at his father's deathbed. In the Abraham story, too, Isaac is not the only young man to appear. It is written that Abraham took "two of his young men with him" when he set forth to make the sacrifice, and that after it was over he "returned unto his young men." These youthful witnesses from a distance may be thought of as learning the power over life held by their leader, Abraham. The ritual that Abraham performs, in other words, like the *rite de passage,* has been calculated to impose the control of the older generation over the younger.

The presence of more than one youth in diverse versions of the sacrifice may simply echo the ritual of overthrow, which would of course have been a collective observance. Or it may hark back still further to the original father-son struggle, indicating, as Freud thought, that it included a union of brothers (something that would have made tactical sense). If so, then the youths in the ritual who observed this original overthrow may well have undergone a *rite de passage* at the same time as they helped to celebrate succession.[41] In this combined rite the act of revolt would have been consecrated as an act of loyalty. For if instead of killing a lion or some other substitute the youths killed a man—symbolically or actually a father, and possibly the king or his scapegoat—then the act of adolescent transition was identified with political overthrow. So, too, with the youths' introductions to adult responsibility and to the values of their tribe: both would have been bound up with the ritual of overthrow. Thus, for the initiates to rebel meant to obey the imperatives of their people, to ensure the natural succession of generations, and to accomplish the transmission of values. Later, to revel (the word is etymologically identical with "rebel") meant to celebrate all these things in ritual.

Though originally united, the rituals of sacrifice and *rite de passage* at some point became separated from one another. They were partly reunited on those occasions when *rites de passage* were timed to coincide with changes of the season, and when youths enacted overthrow, as in the crowds of the American Revolution. This last coming together of the two rites, as Hawthorne's juxtaposition of them indicates, initiated a powerful interaction between individuals and the crowd. It was as if the revolutionary impulse had a kind of anthropological insight, and as if it gained strength from having made the correct ritual linkages.[42]

The ritual of revolution, then, was itself ambiguous in its deepest sources. Not only did the ritual of the seasons begin in a political act of overthrow, but it altered its aspect under the influence of political transitions and threats of transition later in history. It provided mankind with a language for the drama of succession, and was in turn influenced by the historical vicissitudes of that drama. The ritual also accommodated the drama of personal development by its capacity to attract groups of youths as its successive votaries. Their symbolic enactments of overthrow borrowed the language of ritual to mark the succession of generations, and adopted its motif of punishment to dramatize the struggle accompanying that succession. The American crowds and patriots, however clear and limited their conscious aims, spoke in this ritual language of punishment and overthrow. They banded together not only to protest acts of Parliament, but to rehearse a revolution.

CHAPTER TEN

The Rituals of the American Revolution

I N THE LIGHT OF RITUAL, both individual and collective, the anomalies of American response to the Stamp Act and to later British initiatives form a meaningful pattern. The psychological crises of patriots and the ambiguous rhetoric of their political writings may be regarded as ritualized expressions of a painful break with authority. The rhetoric of Whig Sentimentalism served to shift guilt over this break from the patriots themselves to the king's followers—loyalists and colonial government officials—by labeling these followers "parricides." The apparently unmotivated actions of American crowds, which also were accompanied by ambiguity and also concerned scapegoats, represented another kind of ritual. The crowds, expressing the ambiguities of revolution in forms such as death and rebirth, mock struggle, and mock worship, may be said to have enacted separation from England as the coming of age of America.

The questions of exactly how and to what extent ritual affects history remain open. It has been asserted that because ritual is "cyclical and repetitive," and is dedicated to sameness rather than change, it occurs outside history. On the other hand, ritual has been described as possessing a "subversive dynamic."[1] The American case appears to come closest to the anthropologist Victor Turner's definition of a class of rituals that "anticipates deviations and conflicts." Included in this class are "periodic rituals and life-crisis rituals." Of course, conflict is not the same as revolution. Furthermore, even in the case of rituals that specifically mime overthrow, it has been shown that the effect may be to channel emotions *away* from violence and revolution. On the other hand, if rituals cannot be said to initiate revolution, they can significantly influence its timing and style.[2]

This was true during the revolution of 1848 in France, which in rural areas coincided with Mardi Gras and which adopted that holiday's symbols. Similarly, in its early stages the recent revolution in Iran, which developed without the apparent benefit of ritual (though not without that of religion), peaked in forty-day cycles that coincided with the Moslem periods of mourning. In America the timing and design of the first Stamp Act protests manifestly derived from festival and its rituals.[3]

The element of ritual in American demonstrations appears to have contributed both to the nurturing and containment of the revolutionary impulse. Thus, the ritual symbols that helped spark the violence at the end of the Oliver riot were thereafter employed as means of control. When ritual was largely absent, as in the Hutchinson riot, there was less control. The difference between the Stamp Act protest of August 14 and the Hutchinson riot of August 26 may be expressed as that between a ritualized and a merely collective action—with far more violence resulting in the latter case. In ten years of turmoil, it has often been remarked, no lives were taken in American pre-Revolutionary demonstrations. In retrospect the restraint of American crowds, given the powerful emotions aroused by the English revenue acts and the thousands of protesters who took to the streets, appears far more remarkable than their violence.

It used to be said that Americans were by nature less violent than Englishmen or Europeans, but recent scholarship has dismissed this explanation. Once again, the element of ritual is worth considering. Just as in England there was less violence among ritualized Wilkes crowds than among groups on strike, so in America there was less violence by ritualized protest crowds than by crowds arising from other disputes of the period.[4]

Despite their reduced violence, however, the ritualized American protests were the ones that led on to revolution. Thus, it would appear that the ritualization of protest can act to contain violence in the short run, but has the potential of fostering revolution in the long run. Over the years from 1765 to 1776 in America, ritual was bound up with the growth of a revolutionary mentality and the binding together of a revolutionary class. When at last the implications of the prerevolutionary enactments of overthrow were realized by Revolution itself in 1776, the country was swept by a final wave of effigy burnings and destructions of the king's symbols of legitimacy. Thereafter, such demonstrations disappeared into the realities of the Revolutionary war. In contrast, in England, where the Wilkes protests were not followed by revolution, the ensuing decades were marked by an increase in street violence.

Along with other unconscious forces at play, then, the rituals of the American Revolution had their influence on events. Just how much is a matter for historians to decide. But taking ritual together with the other causes, of which contemporaries were largely unaware, the development of Revolutionary sentiment in America can be tentatively described in the following terms.

From the period of the Great Awakening in the 1740s until the early 1760s, the American colonists were caught up in England's war with France. At the termination of hostilities the colonists had gained two kinds of independence. They were no longer in danger from the French, and partly as a consequence of this and partly because they had proven their own fighting ability, they were no longer entirely dependent on British arms. As long as the war had lasted, American rhetoric was marked by anti-Catholic religious fanaticism and by the warmest loyalty toward the mother country. It was for this reason that Francis Bernard, arriving to take over the Massachusetts governorship in 1760, looked forward to an uneventful administration. Then, between 1760 and 1765 the passions directed at France shifted to England. Looking back in 1770 a Boston writer recalled the change that had taken place since the official end of the war in 1763.

> In the year 1763, and before that unhappy period, so great was the veneration the Colonists had for the old countries, that it was by much, more easy to incense a Marylander against a Virginian, or any one Colonist against another, to such a degree, that they would decide their difference by fighting, than to stimulate any one of them to fight with an Englishman; but the stamp-act, and subsequent revenue laws, have already raised a flame in the colonies, which will not now be speedily allayed.[5]

At the same time as the colonists were expressing their hatred of France and their love of England, their rhetoric displayed what has been termed a "growth in symbols of American community." That is, Americans began to reveal an increasing if not entirely conscious sense of American independence. This sense was buttressed by a century-long rise in the spirit of individual autonomy equally observable in France, England, and America. At this point two developments in particular brought into play the nascent nationalism of Americans. First was the economic depression of the early 1760s that recalled so many local, Hutchinson-related issues in Boston. Second was the enforcement and extension of British revenue measures intended partly to recoup the expenses of the war. Coming as they did in a time of depression, these measures appeared particularly harsh. Yet not their harshness but their moderation may actually have been the crucial factor in the colonists' reaction. For there was something patronizing in the imposition from above of these well thought out, reasonable directives, especially in view of the colonists' growing spirit of autonomy. In the context of the victory over France it was as if a fatherly authority had suddenly attempted to renew control just when independence had been won. It followed that the rhetoric of American opposition began to depict England as a non-nurturant parent attempting to fetter and inhibit a growing people.[6]

The tensions generated by the opposition to British revenue measures were further exacerbated by riots and uprisings in both England and the colonies during the course of the 1760s and 1770s. In England, festival-related disturbances operated in a manner that is said to typify episodes of collective behavior: "The world is portrayed in terms of omnipotent forces, conspiracies, and extravagant promises, all of which are imminent."[7] Such beliefs were fostered by the techniques of publicity developed by English radicals, and these techniques provided American patriots with a ready-made iconography of opposition. Particularly applicable were the motif of youth and the personification of good and evil in figures like Pitt, Wilkes, and Bute. Wherever religion came into English opposition politics, moreover, Americans magnified it in their adaptations. Thus Bute's disproportionate importance in America points to a fascination with the issue of Catholicism. The anti-Catholic strain in the English campaign against Bute provided a bridge that eased the migration of American feelings from Catholic France to Protestant England.

The class most affected by the new spirit of autonomy included the newly powerful merchants, lawyers, and newspaper publishers who were also those most affected by the Stamp Act. Bred in the habits of Puritan conscience, the patriots who came from this class found the rituals of overthrow as enacted at mass protests both expressive of their own ambiguous feelings toward authority and frighteningly anarchic. The inconsistencies of their attitude toward crowds mirrored their consequent uncertainties about resistance to authority, as did their writings, which were marked by swings of opinion and a puzzling rhetoric.

The ambiguities of these writings found their subjective correlative in protests derived from the Pope Day celebrations. In its variations from the English Guy Fawkes Day the New England Pope Day had established, well before the 1760s, the special emphasis on autonomy and independence that would eventually mark the Revolution. Most significantly, in replacing Guy Fawkes with the pope and in choosing a name for their major holiday, Americans had put the father—pope or "papa"—at the center, and depicted themselves as his revilers. From this dynamic of opposed generations it was but a short step to a ritual of revolution. In this ritual, scapegoats such as Hutchinson replaced the pope. But like Guy Fawkes and the pope himself, these scapegoats referred ultimately to the king, as 1776 eventually made clear.

If the rituals of independence rode on a wave of growing eighteenth-century personal autonomy, it did not follow that individual patriots necessarily represented psychological types more highly evolved in personal traits of independence than their contemporaries. On the contrary, what evidence exists seems to show a great deal of uneasiness among patriots over the implications of freedom.[8] Just as in a rite of passage, before they could advance to a more autonomous stage of existence, the patriots had to undergo a process that released regressive tendencies. Like Hawthorne's Robin, they experienced these tendencies first in crowd spectacle, and then as personal crises of conscience.

The rituals of the American Revolution, then, were of two kinds: public and private. They were enacted both by crowds and in the minds and hearts of the patriots. The rituals were what might be termed prospective or prophetic rites of transition. That is, they predicted, anticipated, and even encouraged revolution—were "rehearsals" of revolution—without being the thing itself. Carrying with them all the ambiguities attendant on the process of dawning revolutionary consciousness, the rituals celebrated a passage from one state of being to another: from the reign of a king to that of the American people.

Notes

Introduction

1. John Adams to Hezekiah Niles, February 13, 1818, in L. H. Butterfield, "John Adams: What Do We Mean by the American Revolution?" in Daniel J. Boorstin, *An American Primer* (Chicago, 1966), 248, 250. Adams referred specifically to 1760 and 1761, then to the period at large.

2. Jack P. Greene, "Revolution, Confederation, and Constitution, 1763–1787," in *The Reinterpretation of American History and Culture*, ed. William H. Cartwright and Richard L. Watson, Jr. (Washington, D.C., 1973), 272, 271. Compare Bernard Bailyn's remark that the Stamp tax "was generally considered to be an innocuous and judicious form of taxation," *The Origins of American Politics* (New York, 1970), 159. See also the chapter "Fact and Fiction" in Carl Ubbelohde, *The Vice-Admiralty Courts and the American Revolution* (Chapel Hill, N.C., 1960).

3. Daniel W. Bjork, "The American Revolution as a 'Screen Memory,'" *South Atlantic Quarterly* 75 (1976): 275–289. James H. Hutson, "The American Revolution: The Triumph of a Delusion?" in *New Wine in Old Skins: A Comparative View of Socio-Political Structures and Values Affecting the American Revolution*, ed. Erich Angermann et al. (Stuttgart, 1976).

The historian of Anglo-American imperial relations, Lawrence H. Gipson, perhaps the least psychologically oriented scholar of the Revolution in this century, summarized the underlying causes of the Revolution as psychological in the preface to *The Coming of the Revolution, 1763–1775* (New York, 1962), xi.

For a suggestive essay on subjective factors, containing references to recent psychologically oriented studies of the Revolution, see Bruce Mazlish, "Leadership in the American Revolution: The Psychological Dimension," in *Leadership in the American Revolution* (Washington, D.C., 1974). Gordon Wood forcefully makes the case for consideration of unconscious and irrational factors in "Rhetoric and Reality in the American Revolution," in *Essays on the American Revolution*, ed. David L. Jacobson (New York, 1970), 54. See also the epilogue to Philip Greven, *The Protestant Temperament: Patterns of Child-Rearing, Religious Experience, and the Self in Early America* (New York, 1977).

1. The Rehearsal of Revolution

1. On previous riots in America see Alan Rogers, *Empire and Liberty: American Resistance to British Authority, 1755–1763* (Berkeley and London, 1974).

2. The revenue acts, taken together, did not propose to raise more than a portion of the cost of the British military in America. Edmund S. Morgan and Helen M. Morgan, *The Stamp Act Crisis: Prologue to Revolution* (Chapel Hill, N.C., 1953), 22–23.

3. For a possible source of the marriage license rumor, for seamen and soldiers' exclusions, and for provisions that offered a way to escape from servitude by identifying evaders, see "An Act for Granting and Applying Certain Stamp Duties, and Other Duties in the British Colonies and Plantations in America . . . ," *Great Britain Laws, Statutes, etc., 1765. At the Parliament, Jan. 10, 1765* (Philadelphia, 1765).

4. Andrew Preston Peabody, "Boston Mobs before the Revolution," *Atlantic Monthly* (September, 1888), 324. For a loyalist opinion on smuggling, see *Peter Oliver's Origin and Progress of the American Rebellion: A Tory View*, ed. Douglass Adair and John A. Schutz (San Marino, Calif., 1961), 46–48.

5. John Kern, "The Politics of Violence: Colonial American Rebellions, Protests, and Riots, 1676–1747" (Ph.D. diss., University of Wisconsin at Madison, 1976), 209. "Mother Gin" was also known as "Madam Geneva." See George Rudé, *The Crowd in History: A Study of Popular Disturbances in France and England, 1730–1848* (New York, 1964), 51. On drink and riot see Chapter 2 below, "Their Kinsman, Thomas Hutchinson." Also Thomas Hutchinson, *The History of the Colony and Province of Massachusetts-Bay*, ed. Lawrence Shaw Mayo (Cambridge, Mass., 1936), 3:90.

6. See Edmund S. Morgan, "The Puritan Ethic and the American Revolution," in Morgan, *The Challenge of the American Revolution* (New York, 1976).

7. Catherine L. Albanese, *Sons of the Fathers: The Civil Religion of the American Revolution* (Philadelphia, 1976), 6. Here and below the definition of ritual is borrowed in part from Victor Turner, *The Forest of Symbols: Aspects of Ndembu Ritual* (Ithaca, N.Y., 1967), 19, 22, 95. I am also indebted to Turner's *The Ritual Process: Structure and Anti-Structure* (Chicago, 1969) and *Dramas, Fields, and Metaphors* (Ithaca, N.Y., 1974).

8. The events of August 14, 1765, have been reconstructed from a variety of sources: *The Boston-Gazette and Country Journal*, August 19, 1765; Malcolm Freiberg, ed., "An Unknown Stamp Act Letter," *Proceedings of the Massachusetts Historical Society* 78 (1966): 142n (hereafter cited as *PMHS*); Samuel G. Drake, *The History and Antiquities of Boston* (Boston, 1856), 693 (hereafter cited as Drake's *Antiquities*).

9. Boston *Gazette*, August 19, 1765. Franklin B. Dexter, ed., *Extracts from the Itineraries and Other Miscellanies of Ezra Stiles D.D. LL.D., 1755–1794 . . .* (New Haven, Conn., 1916). The boys were evidently those let out of school for the occasion. On "dying speeches" see Dirk Hoerder, *Crowd Action in Revolutionary Massachusetts, 1765–1780* (New York, 1977), 46. *Boston Post-Boy and Advertiser*, August 26, 1765. Hutchinson, *History of Massachusetts-Bay,* 3:87. Freiberg, "An Unknown Stamp Act Letter," 141.

10. James K. Hosmer, *The Life of Thomas Hutchinson: Royal Governor of the Province of Massachusetts Bay* (Boston and New York, 1896), 1:89. Morgan and Morgan, *The Stamp Act Crisis*, 124. J. Almon, *A Collection of Interesting, Authentic Papers . . .* [Prior Documents] (London, 1777), 10. Jonathan Mayhew to Thomas Hollis, Auugust 19, 1765, *PMHS* 69 (1947–1950): 175. See also Clifford K. Shipton, *Sibley's Harvard Graduates . . .* (Boston, 1933–), 7:394, quoting from Samuel Mather's letter.

11. Lawrence H. Gipson, *The British Empire before the American Revolution* (Caldwell, Idaho, and New York, 1936–67), 10:293n: Francis Bernard to Board of Trade ("ye" Province changed to "the"). Compare Hutchinson's account: "forty or

fifty tradesmen, decently dressed," cited above, and Morgan and Morgan, *The Stamp Act Crisis,* 181.

12. *New York Times,* June 9, 1976. *New York News,* September 29, 1974.

13. Robert Middlekauff, "The Ritualization of the American Revolution," in *The Development of an American Culture,* ed. Stanley Coben and Lorman Ratner (Englewood Cliffs, N.J., 1970), 35.

14. For another account of the Stamp Act disturbances, stressing their connection with Pope Day, see Alfred Young, "The Rapid Rise and Decline of Ebenezer Mackintosh," an unpublished paper presented at the Shelby Cullom Davis Center, Princeton University, January 23, 1976, 8. This paper will appear as a chapter in Young's forthcoming *The Crowd and the Coming of the American Revolution: From Ritual to Rebellion in Boston, 1745–1776.* I was unable to see the paper by Young, which was presented at the Anglo American Labor Historians Conference, 1973, as "Pope's Day, Tar and Feathers, and Cornet Joyce, Jun." Professor Young informs me that he focuses on the mechanics of one city, Boston, and his interpretation differs from my own. See also Jonathan Mayhew to Thomas Hollis, *PMHS* 69:174–175: "The Boot was old, and had a new green sole, or as I understand it is to be mentioned in the Prints of this day, a *Green-vile* sole. A punning device, which I suppose the Chancllr of the Exr [that is, the Chancellor of the Exchequer, George Grenville], will easily understand." On the planning of the Oliver demonstration see George P. Anderson, "Ebenezer Mackintosh: Stamp Act Rioter and Patriot," *Publications of the Colonial Society of Massachusetts* 26 (1924–1926): 30.

15. "Self-discipline": Young, "Ebenezer Mackintosh," 28. Gustave LeBon, *The Crowd: A Study of the Popular Mind* (1895; reprint Dunwoody, Ga., 1968), 42. LeBon is rejected by many scholars, notably by George Rudé and others of the "rational crowd" school, such as Dirk Hoerder, *Crowd Action in Revolutionary Massachusetts.* See, for example, E. Dupréel, "Y a-t-il une foule diffuse?: L'Opinion publique," in Georges Bohn et al., *La Foule* (Paris, Centre International de Synthèse, 1934). Also Ernst Kris, "New Contributions to the Study of Freud's *The Interpretation of Dreams:* A Critical Essay" (1954), in *Selected Papers of Ernst Kris* (New Haven, Conn., and London, 1975). For a balanced view see the essays in *Readings in Collective Behavior,* ed. Robert R. Evans (Chicago, 1969), especially Carl J. Couch, "Collective Behavior: An Examination of Some Stereotypes."

16. E. J. Hobsbawm, *Primitive Rebels: Studies in Archaic Forms of Social Movement in the 19th and 20th Centuries* (Manchester, 1959). E. P. Thompson, "The Moral Economy of the English Crowd in the Eighteenth Century," *Past and Present* 50 (1971): 76–136. "There was no direct causal relationship between deprivation and protest" (Dale Edward Williams, "Were 'Hunger Rioters' Really Hungry? Some Demographic Evidence," *Past and Present* 71 [1976]: 74).

17. Pauline Maier, *From Resistance to Revolution: Colonial Radicals and the Development of American Opposition to Britain, 1765–1776* (New York, 1974), 210. Other studies attribute dogged loyalty to the king to special local conditions or the political exigencies of a particular stage of the Revolution. See Stephen E. Lucas, *Portents of Rebellion: Rhetoric and Revolution in Philadelphia, 1765–1776* (Philadelphia, 1976), 179. Jerrilyn Greene Marston, "The Abdication of George III," *New England Historical and Genealogical Register* 129 (1975): 133. Stella F. Duff, "The Case against the King: The *Virginia Gazettes* Indict George III," *William and Mary Quarterly* 6 (1949): 391.

18. William David Liddle, "A Patriot King, or None: American Public Attitudes towards George III and the British Monarchy, 1754–1776" (Ph.D. diss., Claremont

College, 1970), 195–196, 203–207. See also supplement to the Boston *Gazette,* November 11, 1765, for "Huzzah for George the Third" in Newport.

19. Liddle, "A Patriot King," 3–4, 309, 321–322. See also Marston, "The Abdication of George III," 133; and Darrett B. Rutman, "George III: The Myth of a Tyrannical King," in *Myth and the American Experience,* ed. Nicholas Cords and Patrick Gerster (New York and Beverly Hills, 1973). On European parallels see Charles Tilly, "Collective Violence in European Perspective," in *The History of Violence in America: Historical and Comparative Perspectives,* ed. Hugh Davis Graham and Ted Robert Gurr (Washington, D.C., 1969), 21.

20. Winthrop D. Jordan, "Familial Politics: Thomas Paine and the Killing of the King, 1776," *Journal of American History* 60 (1973): 295–296. Lucas, *Portents of Rebellion,* 167–168. Joseph Hawley to Elbridge Gerry, February 18, 1776, in James T. Austin, *The Life of Elbridge Gerry* . . . (Boston, 1828), 1:161. Burnings: Liddle, "A Patriot King," 423–425. For attempts to explain the sudden shift in attitude toward the king, see 445–446; and Jordan, "The Killing of the King," 297. Also, Albanese, *Sons of the Fathers,* 186; and Philip Davidson, *Propaganda and the American Revolution, 1763–1783* (Chapel Hill, N.C., 1941), 184.

21. Jordan, "The Killing of the King," 307–308. For toasts see, for example, *Supplement to the Boston-Gazette,* September 16, 1765.

22. Isaiah Thomas, *The History of Printing in America* . . . (Albany, N.Y., 1874; reprint New York, 1964), xxix. The connections between Pope Day and the American Revolution were pointed out by Esther Forbes in *Paul Revere and the World He Lived In* (Boston, 1942), especially 93–96. The Pope Day sources of American Revolutionary crowd iconography have most recently been explored by Alfred Young in both published and unpublished articles. See the Afterword by Alfred Young, ed., *The American Revolution: Explorations in the History of American Radicalism* (De Kalb, Ill., 1976), and n. 14 above.

23. Justin Winsor, ed., *The Memorial History of Boston* . . . (Boston, 1881), 5:172.

24. R. S. Longley, "Mob Activities in Revolutionary Massachusetts," *New England Quarterly* 6 (1933): 102. Anderson, "Ebenezer Mackintosh," 26.

25. See Michael Kammen, *A Season of Youth: The American Revolution and the Historical Imagination* (New York, 1978), especially ch. 6. For youths in demonstrations, see Chapter 8 below, "The Child, Revolution."

26. Q. D. Leavis, "Hawthorne as Poet," *Sewanee Review* 59 (1951): 179–205. For a discussion of various interpretations of the tale, see Peter Shaw, "Fathers, Sons, and the Ambiguities of Revolution . . . ," *New England Quarterly* 49 (1976): 559–576.

27. Edwin G. Burrows and Michael Wallace, in "The American Revolution: The Ideology and Psychology of National Liberation," *Perspectives in American History* 6 (1972): 292 (using Weinstein and Platt's *The Wish to Be Free*), remark: "The habit of obedience is permanently broken and the old prohibitions against the recognition of latent hostility crumble."

28. Lawrence H. Leder has written that Americans in the 1760s "easily fell into their traditional mass paranoia." *America—1603–1789: Prelude to a Nation,* 2d ed. (Minneapolis, 1978), 167.

29. Davidson, *Propaganda,* 193. For the New York Sons of Liberty: Kenneth Silverman, *A Cultural History of the American Revolution: Painting, Music, Literature, and the Theatre in the Colonies and the United States from the Treaty of Paris to the Inauguration of George Washington, 1763–1789* (New York, 1976), 97. It should be noted that Edward Countryman and others have expressed skepticism on this point. "The Problem of the Early American Crowd," *Journal of American Studies* 7 (1973):

86; and Jesse Lemisch, "Radical Plot in Boston (1770): A Study in the Use of Evidence," an essay review of Hiller B. Zobel, *The Boston Massacre* (1970), in *Harvard Law Review* 84 (1970): 480, 485–504.

30. Patrick Henderson, "Smallpox and Patriotism: The Norfolk Riots, 1768–1769," *The Virginia Magazine of History and Biography* 73 (1965): 415.

31. Gerard H. Clarfield, "Salem's Great Inoculation Controversy, 1773–1774," *Essex Institute Historical Collections* 106 (1970): 285. The Marblehead controversy is known, too, by the name of nearby Salem, which was also involved. George A. Billias, "Pox and Politics in Marblehead, 1773–1774," ibid., 92 (1956): 54. C. H. Webber and W. S. Nevine, *Old Naumkeag . . .* (Salem and Boston, 1877), 269. Actually, dogs of a certain size were killed. Whether this or the killing of all dogs was the seventeenth-century practice is not clear.

32. Michael Kammen, "The American Revolution as a *Crise de Conscience:* The Case of New York," in *Society, Freedom and Conscience,* ed. Richard M. Jellison (New York, 1976). See also George Rosen, "Emotion and Sensibility in Ages of Anxiety: A Comparative Historical Review," *American Journal of Psychiatry* 124 (1967): 79–284.

33. "Patriots never seek office" became a formula. See Bernard Bailyn, *The Origins of American Politics* (New York, 1970), 143.

34. These are Neil J. Smelser's preconditions for revolution in *Theory of Collective Behavior* (New York, 1963), as examined critically by E. L. Quarantelli and James R. Hundley, Jr., "A Test of Some Propositions about Crowd Formation and Behavior," in *Readings in Collective Behavior,* ed. Robert R. Evans (Chicago, 1969), 542. The authors find support for this first of Smelser's preconditions, 545.

2. *Their Kinsman, Thomas Hutchinson*

1. Robert M. Zemsky, "Power, Influence, and Status: Leadership Patterns in the Massachusetts Assembly, 1740–1755," *William and Mary Quarterly* 26 (1969): 502–520. Bernard Bailyn, *The Ordeal of Thomas Hutchinson* (Cambridge, Mass., 1974), 376. Malcolm Freiberg, "Thomas Hutchinson: The First Fifty Years (1711–1761)," *William and Mary Quarterly* 15 (1958): 42.

2. Freiberg, "Thomas Hutchinson: The First Fifty Years," 51. For Franklin see below, n. 46. Both Franklins held these opinions some years later.

3. Ibid.

4. Malcolm Freiberg, "Prelude to Purgatory: Thomas Hutchinson in Provincial Massachusetts Politics, 1760–1770" (Ph.D. diss., Brown University, 1950), 38. Hutchinson's fate has most often been attributed by modern scholars to excessive "prudence." See Malcolm Freiberg, "How to Become a Colonial Governor: Thomas Hutchinson of Massachusetts," *The Review of Politics* 21 (1959): 651. Also, Edmund S. Morgan, "Thomas Hutchinson and the Stamp Act," *New England Quarterly* 21 (1948): 480; and Bailyn, *Ordeal,* 68, 378.

5. G. B. Warden, *Boston, 1689–1776* (Boston and Toronto, 1970), 133. Hutchinson was eventually voted out of legislative office in 1749. Malcolm Freiberg, "Thomas Hutchinson and the Province Currency," *New England Quarterly* 30 (1957): 199. See also Hutchinson's comment on himself: "Nothing made him more obnoxious to [a] great part of the people than his quarrel with paper money." *The Diary and Letters of His Excellency Thomas Hutchinson, Esq. . . . ,* ed. Peter Orlando Hutchinson (Boston, 1884), 1:53.

6. Warden, *Boston,* 140. On the Hutchinson house-burning see Hutchinson,

Diary and Letters, 1:54. Herbert L. Osgood, *The American Colonies in the Eighteenth Century* (Gloucester, Mass., 1924), 3:350. John Adams, *The Works of John Adams, Second President of the United States* . . . , ed. Charles Francis Adams (Boston, 1856), 10:232. John Adams always praised Hutchinson as a monetary genius. On the 1741 ouster of Belcher, see John A. Schutz, "Succession Politics in Massachusetts, 1730–1741," *William and Mary Quarterly* 15 (1958): 520.

7. John C. Miller, *Samuel Adams: Pioneer in Propaganda* (Boston, 1936), 26. Deacon Adams's losses have been called exaggerated. See George Allen Billias, *The Massachusetts Land Bankers of 1740,* University of Maine Studies, 2d ser., no. 74 (Orono, Me., 1959), 19. On the "uprising," 35. See also Osgood, *The American Colonies,* 3:357. William V. Wells, *The Life and Public Services of Samuel Adams* . . . (Boston, 1865), 1:6–15. Miller, *Samuel Adams,* 19.

8. Miller, *Samuel Adams,* 26. On the role of Otis's father in the currency dispute, see Chapter 4 below, "James Otis." Thomas Hutchinson, *The History of the Colony and Province of Massachusetts-Bay,* ed. Lawrence Shaw Mayo (Cambridge, Mass., 1936), 3:212. See James K. Hosmer, *The Life of Thomas Hutchinson* . . . (Boston and New York, 1896), 1:82–83, on Samuel Adams's emergence at the time of the Sugar and Stamp Acts.

But John Adams also traced Samuel Adams's career to the 1740s and 1750s. See John Adams to William Tudor, February 9, 1819, *Works of John Adams,* 10:364. On Hutchinson's "Design": Samuel Adams to Arthur Lee, April 19, 1771, in *The Writings of Samuel Adams,* ed. Harry Alonso Cushing (New York and London, 1906), 2:165. See also Billias, *Massachusetts Land Bankers,* 42: "The residue of bitterness it [the land bank] left in colonial minds must be given its place among the contributing causes of the war for independence."

9. Osgood, *The American Colonies,* 3:357.

10. In the long term, Hutchinson's bill seems to have had beneficial results. Lawrence Henry Gipson discusses money bills in *The Coming of the Revolution* (New York, 1962), 121–157. See also Freiberg, "Thomas Hutchinson: The First Fifty Years," 47.

11. Thomas Hutchinson to the Earl of Hillsborough, January 22, 1771, in "Governor Hutchinson's Letters," *Proceedings of the Massachusetts Historical Society* 19 (1881–1882): 129 (hereafter cited as *PMHS*). On Loyalist theories of patriot motives, see Mary Beth Norton, *The British Americans: The Loyalist Exiles in England, 1774–1789* (Boston, 1972), 147: "The refugees absolutely refused to accept as valid the Americans' continual protestations of loyalty to Great Britain before 1776." Bailyn, *Ordeal,* 375.

12. Hosmer, *Thomas Hutchinson,* 1:48n.

13. Warden, *Boston,* 149, 150, 152.

14. There is some dispute over the question of what kept Hutchinson from England. See Freiberg, "How to Become a Colonial Governor," 651; and Freiberg, "Prelude to Purgatory," 62; also *Dictionary of American Biography,* s.v. "Hutchinson, Thomas" (by Carl Becker). Both Becker and Freiberg note that Hutchinson himself requested a delay in going. See also Hosmer, *Thomas Hutchinson,* 73. This is not incompatible, however, with a campaign against his going, and may indeed have been a typically compromising response. Clifford K. Shipton, *Sibley's Harvard Graduates* . . . (Boston, 1933–), 8:436.

On anti–Stamp Act agitation: Ralph Volney Harlow, *Samuel Adams: A Study in Psychology and Politics* (New York, 1923), 31, 32–33, 38, 77–78; and Miller, *Samuel Adams,* 75. "Cloven foot": *Boston-Gazette and Country Journal,* February 21, 1763. "Cotton Mather": Arthur M. Schlesinger, *Prelude to Independence: The Newspaper*

War on Britain, 1764–1776 (New York, 1957), 130–131. "Fiend": Shipton, *Harvard Graduates,* 8:209.

15. Morgan, "Thomas Hutchinson and the Stamp Act," 466–467.
16. Ibid., 468, 486–487, 489.
17. Ibid., 463.
18. *Works of John Adams,* 10:343. At about the same time, and later, too, Hutchinson's *History of Massachusetts-Bay* and its accompanying documents provided the evidence and arguments for numerous patriot tracts. Catherine L. Albanese, *Sons of the Fathers: The Civil Religion of the American Revolution* (Philadelphia, 1976), 20.
19. Dirk Hoerder, *Crowd Action in Revolutionary Massachusetts, 1765–1780* (New York, 1977), 101. George Richards Minot, *Continuation of the History of . . . Massachusetts Bay* (Boston, 1803), 2:213. Also compare Alfred Young, "The Rapid Rise and Decline of Ebenezer Mackintosh," an unpublished paper presented at the Shelby Cullom Davis Center, Princeton University, January 23, 1976, 8–9. Thomas Hutchinson, *History of Massachusetts-Bay,* 3:88. See also Boston *Gazette,* August 19, 1765, and Samuel G. Drake, *The History and Antiquities of Boston* (Boston, 1856), 697 (hereafter cited as Drake's *Antiquities*). Also Dirk Hoerder, "Boston Leaders and Boston Crowds, 1765–1776," in *The American Revolution,* ed. Alfred F. Young (De Kalb, Ill., 1976), 243.
20. Caleb H. Snow, *A History of Boston . . .* (Boston, 1825), 260. On the two groups: Drake's *Antiquities,* 699, and "Interleaved Almanacs of Nathan Bowen," *Essex Institute Historical Collections* 91 (1955): 189. Francis Bernard to the Earl of Halifax, August 31, 1765, in Merrill Jensen, ed., *American Colonial Documents to 1776* (New York, 1955), 677 (vol. 9 of *English Historical Documents*).
21. Hutchinson, *Diary and Letters,* 67. Shipton, *Harvard Graduates,* 8:175. Thomas Hutchinson to Thomas Pownall, "Letterbooks of Thomas Hutchinson," Archives of the Commonwealth, Boston, Massachusetts, 26:149. Diary of Josiah Quincy, Jr.," August 27, 1765, in *PMHS* 4 (1858): 48. Bowen, "Interleaved Almanacs," 190. Thomas Hutchinson to Thomas Pownall, August 31, 1765, quoted by Malcolm Freiberg, "Footnote to a Riot: Or, How Not to Preserve a House," *Old Time New England* 48 (1958): 106.
22. Lawrence H. Gipson, *The British Empire before the American Revolution* (Caldwell, Idaho, and New York, 1936–67), 10:296. Freiberg, "Thomas Hutchinson: The First Fifty Years," 50–51. For Bernard's opinion see Josiah Quincy, Jr., *Reports of Cases . . . ,* ed. Samuel M. Quincy (New York, 1865; reprint, 1969), 416n. Drake's *Antiquities,* 698. For the possible influence on the rioters of a sermon by Jonathan Mayhew, see Charles W. Akers, *Called unto Liberty: A Life of Jonathan Mayhew, 1720–1766* (Cambridge, Mass., 1964), 205–207. Morgan, "Thomas Hutchinson and the Stamp Act," 468.
23. Gordon E. Kershaw, *The Kennebeck Proprietors, 1749–1775* (Maine Historical Society, 1975), 261–262. See 272 for Kennebeck involvement in the procurement of Hutchinson's letters in 1773, an incident described further on in this chapter. For additional causes see Dirk Hoerder, "People and Mobs: Crowd Action in Massachusetts during the American Revolution, 1765–1780" (Ph.D. diss., Free University of Berlin, 1971), 165 [held by State University Library, Stony Brook, N.Y.]; and Freiberg, "Prelude to Purgatory," 113–121.
24. Hoerder, "People and Mobs," 158, 164. Francis Bernard to General Thomas Gage, August 27, 1765, in *The Barrington-Bernard Correspondence . . .* (Cambridge, Mass., and London, 1912), 228.
25. Shipton, *Harvard Graduates,* 8:178. Freiberg, "Prelude to Purgatory," 149, 166.

26. On the effects of a letter by the inflammatory essayist "Junius," reprinted in America, on the February 15, 1770, nonimportation crowds, see "Extracts of Two Letters from Boston," March 13, 1770, Sparks MSS, 10, vol. 3, by permission of the Houghton Library, Harvard University. For other newspaper reports from England see, for example, *The Pennsylvania Journal,* May 17, 1770, and May 24, 1770, as well as *The Virginia Gazette* (Purdie and Dixon), March 22, 1770. All three carry news of shocking behavior directed at the king.

27. On Puritan governors see Michael Walzer, "Puritanism as a Revolutionary Ideology," *History and Theory* 3 (1961): 85. For Hutchinson at the Massacre see Hiller B. Zobel, *The Boston Massacre* (New York, 1970), 202–205; Thomas Hutchinson to the Earl of Hillsborough, March 1770, in *PMHS* 6 (1862–1863): 484; "Extracts of Two Letters from Boston," Sparks MSS 10, 3:6. On Seider: Thomas Hutchinson to General Thomas Gage, February 25, 1770, in Massachusetts Archives 26:448. Adams's Crispus Attucks: *Diary and Autobiography of John Adams,* ed., L. H. Butterfield et al. (New York, 1964), 2:84.

28. See Hutchinson's own discussion of the incident in *Diary and Letters,* 1:27–28. Also Bailyn, *Ordeal,* 157.

29. Schlesinger, *Prelude to Independence,* 137, 138, 140. And see Davidson, *Propaganda,* 147–148. See William David Liddle, "A Patriot King, or None: American Public Attitudes towards George III and the British Monarchy, 1754–1776" (Ph.D. diss., Claremont College, 1970), 269–277. Also Bailyn, *Ordeal,* 172–173. Donald C. Lord and Robert M. Calhoon write that Hutchinson "probably" did not have his hands "completely tied" ("The Removal of the Massachusetts General Court from Boston, 1769–1772," *Journal of American History* 55 (1969): 737).

30. Gipson, *The Coming of the Revolution,* 213. "Answer of the House of Representatives to the Speech of the Governor of Sixth January" (January 26, 1773), in *Speeches of the Governors of Massachusetts, 1765–1775* (Boston, 1818), 349. For the whole issue see Richard D. Brown, *Revolutionary Politics in Massachusetts: The Boston Committee of Correspondence and the Towns, 1772–1774* (Cambridge, Mass., 1970), 86–91.

31. Bailyn, *The Ordeal of Thomas Hutchinson,* 227, 223n, and on the meaning of "abridgment," 250–251. See also Hutchinson, *The History of Massachusetts-Bay,* 3:293–294n; and Malcolm Freiberg, "Missing: One Hutchinson Autograph Letter," *Manuscripts* 8 (1956): 179–184.

32. Gipson, *The Coming of the Revolution,* 217. Steven J. Rosswurm, " 'That They Were Grown Unruly': The Crowd and Lower Classes in Philadelphia, 1765–1780" (Master's thesis, Northern Illinois University, 1974), 89–90. *The Virginia Gazette,* July 7, 1774. Cf. Boston *Gazette,* June 27, 1774; both about N.Y. effigies. Publication of Charles I's letters preceded *his* overthrow.

33. Newspaper campaign: Merrill Jensen, *The Founding of a Nation* (New York, 1968), 447. "Parricide": Bailyn, *Ordeal,* 243. One study remarks that at this period "opposition writers in Massachusetts often used more space (and venom) attacking Hutchinson than they did criticizing Parliament and the ministry." Liddle, "A Patriot King," 347n. Mercy Otis Warren, *The Adulateur, A Tragedy, As It Is Now Acted in Upper Servia* (Boston, 1773), reprinted in *The Magazine of History,* extra number 63 (Tarrytown, N.Y., 1918): 10, 8 (1773 pagination). "The Defeat," Boston *Gazette,* May 24, 1773.

James H. Stark, *The Loyalists of Massachusetts and the Other Side of the American Revolution* (Boston, 1910), 172. The name of the town was changed in 1774. See Malcolm Freiberg, "Prelude to Purgatory," 80.

34. Bailyn, *Ordeal,* 28. Thomas Hutchinson to John Pownall, July 3, 1773, in

K. G. Davies, ed., *Documents of the American Revolution, 1770–1783* (Dublin, 1974), 180–181. William Franklin to Benjamin Franklin, July 29, 1773, in *The Papers of Benjamin Franklin,* ed. Leonard W. Labaree (New Haven and London, 1959–), 20:332. Benjamin Franklin to William Franklin, ibid., 439.

35. Davidson, *Propaganda,* 183. Shipton, *Harvard Graduates,* 8:208. Benjamin Woods Labaree has Hutchinson desirous of a showdown. *The Boston Tea Party* (New York, 1964), 132.

36. Bailyn, *Ordeal,* 238.

37. On what may be termed the semi-royal nature of Hutchinson's instructions to move the legislature, see Leonard W. Labaree, *Royal Government in America: A Study of the British Colonial System before 1783* (New York, 1958), 28; and Bailyn, *Ordeal,* 172–173. South Carolina provides the only other instance of a removal of a legislature. See Sydney George Fisher, "The Twenty-Eight Charges against the King in the Declaration of Independence," *Pennsylvania Magazine of History and Biography* 31 (1907): 302.

For the opinion that Hutchinson was intended, see Donald C. Lord and Robert M. Calhoon, "The Removal of the Massachusetts General Court from Boston, 1769–1772," *Journal of American History* 55 (1969): 752; and Bailyn, *Ordeal,* 173. Two other clauses in the Declaration may refer to Hutchinson, based on the popular belief that he had brought on the Massacre and then manipulated the trials so as to free the soldiers: "FOR quartering large bodies among us: FOR protecting them, by a mock Trial, from Punishment for any Murders which they should commit on the Inhabitants of these States."

38. Bailyn, *Ordeal,* 278, 337–338.

39. John Adams to William Tudor, June 1, 1817, in *Works of John Adams,* 10:262, 261.

40. There is no distinct report of Hutchinson's being given this detail, but he had good intelligence of what transpired at his house. See Hutchinson, *Diary and Letters,* 1:395.

41. Ibid., 2:341–361. For contemporary maps of London showing the locations in question, see Norton, *The British Americans,* 74 and endpapers. Thomas Hutchinson, Jr., to his brother, May 26, 1780, in Egerton MSS, British Museum, no. 2659.

42. John Adams to Abigail Adams, June 17, 1780, and June 23, 1780; John Thaxter to Abigail Adams, June 18, 1780, in *Adams Family Correspondence,* ed. L. H. Butterfield and Marc Friedlaender (Cambridge, Mass., 1973–), 3:367, 368, 370. Thaxter's letter shows sufficient signs of echoing his chief to support the speculation that he was doing so with regard to Hutchinson. Lord Mansfield's house was actually destroyed *after* Hutchinson's death. Benjamin Franklin to Michael Carmichael, June 17, 1780, in Hutchinson, *Diary and Letters,* 2:359.

43. Thomas Hutchinson, Jr., to Elisha Hutchinson, June 8, 1780, Egerton MSS, British Museum, no 2659. See Chapter 3 below, "John Wilkes and the Earl of Bute," for the link between "No Popery," and John Wilkes. Thomas Hutchinson to unidentified correspondent, September 24, 1774, Egerton MSS, no. 2661.

44. Thomas Hutchinson to William Parker, August 26, 1770, in Massachusetts Archives 26:540.

45. Thomas Hutchinson to Israel Williams, July 20, 1773, Massachusetts Archives 27:516. Hutchinson, *Diary and Letters,* title page, identified as coming from the flyleaf of his diary. "Hyperion," Boston *Gazette,* September 19, 1768. Josiah Quincy, Jr., used this pseudonym. See Chapter 7 below, "Josiah Quincy."

46. Warren, *The Adulateur,* 7, 11.

3. *John Wilkes and the Earl of Bute*

1. John Brewer, "The Misfortunes of Lord Bute: A Case-Study in Eighteenth-Century Political Argument and Public Opinion," *The Historical Journal* 16 (1973): 29. Merrill Jensen, *The Founding of a Nation: A History of the American Revolution, 1763–1776* (New York, 1968), 164. Lawrence Henry Gipson, *The Coming of the Revolution, 1763–1775* (New York, 1962), 33.

2. Lawrence Henry Gipson, *The British Empire before the American Revolution* (Caldwell, Idaho, and New York, 1936–67), 8:51. See Mrs. E. Stuart Wortley, ed., *A Prime Minister and His Son* (New York, 1925), 10, for masquerades. J. A. Lovat-Fraser, *John Stuart, Earl of Bute* (Cambridge, 1912), 89, 96. John Brewer, "The Faces of Lord Bute: A Visual Contribution to Anglo-American Political Ideology," *Perspectives in American History* 6 (1972): 111. For typical perplexity by a historian over why Bute should have been libeled as he was, see Gipson, *The British Empire*, 9:23.

3. Brewer, "Faces of Bute," 103, 111. Bruce Ingham Granger, *Political Satire in the American Revolution, 1763–1783* (Ithaca, N.Y., 1960), 76; and Philip Davidson, *Propaganda and the American Revolution, 1763–1783* (Chapel Hill, N.C., 1941), 149. Cartoons: E. P. Richardson, "Stamp Act Cartoons in the Colonies," *The Pennsylvania Magazine of History and Biography* 96 (1972): 275–297. See also Kenneth Silverman, *A Cultural History of the American Revolution: Painting, Music, Literature, and the Theatre in the Colonies and the United States from the Treaty of Paris to the Inauguration of George Washington, 1763–1789* (New York, 1976), 265. On chimney sweeps see M. Dorothy George, *London Life in the Eighteenth Century* (New York, 1965), 246; A. R. Wright, *British Calendar Customs* (London, 1938), 2:239. See also M. D. George, "America in English Satirical Prints," *William and Mary Quarterly* 10 (1953): 512.

4. Ian R. Christie, *Myth and Reality in Late-Eighteenth Century British Politics and Other Papers* (London, 1970), 34. Richard Pares, *King George III and the Politicians* (London, 1953), 107. Brewer, "Misfortunes of Bute," 35. The subtitle of a 1780 pamphlet, used as an epigraph by Brewer for his "Faces of Bute," conveys the persistence and intensity of the Bute myth: "Proving that all the evils and Misfortunes that have befallen this Kingdom, from the close of the last glorious War to the present ruinous and disgraceful Period, originated in one sole individual and Identical Person." See also Christie, *Myth and Reality*, 39.

5. On Bute's illness: Horace Walpole to Horace Mann, November 6, 1769, in *Horace Walpole's Correspondence with Sir Horace Mann*, ed. W. S. Lewis et al. (New Haven, Conn., 1967–), 17:52. Effigy accounts: *The Middlesex Journal; Or, Chronicle of Liberty*, March 30–April 2, 1771; and *The London Chronicle*, March 30–April 2, 1771. *Gentleman's Magazine*, April 1, 1771. Davidson, *Propaganda*, 391–392.

6. Lewis Namier, *England in the Age of the American Revolution*, 2d. ed., rev. (1961; reprint New York, 1963), 168 and passim on Bute's character. Bute's letter is dated March 24, 1761—that is, on the eve of his accession to the position of secretary of state.

7. Bernard Bailyn, *The Ordeal of Thomas Hutchinson* (Cambridge, Mass., 1974); see "The 'Scape-Goat' " chapter. Brewer, "Faces of Bute," 114, 110. Bernard Bailyn, *The Ideological Origins of the American Revolution* (Cambridge, Mass., 1967), 122–123, 147–149.

8. Charles C. Trench, *Portrait of a Patriot: A Biography of John Wilkes* (Edinburgh and London, 1962), 89.

9. John Brewer, *Party Ideology and Popular Politics at the Accession of George III* (Cambridge, 1976), 97–99.

10. Thomas Nutall to Lady Chatham, November 12, 1761, in *Correspondences of William Pitt, Earl of Chatham*, ed. William Stanhope Taylor and J. H. Pringle (London, 1838), 2:167.

11. The princess appeared on April Fools according to "another account" reported in *The London Chronicle*, March 30–April 2, 1771, cited above. *The Fall of Mortimer, An Historical Play* [Dedicated to the Right Honourable John Earl of Bute &c &c &c] (London, 1763), viii. 2d title page: "Revived From Mountfort, with Alterations" (italicized in the original). Frederic George Stephens, *Catalogue of Prints and Drawings in the British Museum*, div. I, IV, no 4329. See M. D. George, "America in English Satirical Prints," 515.

12. Gipson, *The British Empire*, 8:51. Trench, *Portrait of a Patriot*, 91, 93. The Mortimer parallel was repeated in *North Briton*, no. 5.

13. Pares, *King George III*, 101n. Stephens, Catalogue of Prints and Drawings, nos. 4245, 4442.

14. William Jay Fliegelman, "The American Revolution against Patriarchy, 1770–1800" (Ph.D. diss., Stanford University, 1977), 39–40. Brewer, "Faces of Bute," 105, from *Political Register*, (1767).

15. John Adams, "Governor Winthrop to Governor Bradford," in *Papers of John Adams*, ed. Robert J. Taylor et al. (Cambridge, 1977), 1:194 (Adams has "shall" for "will" in the quotation); and 2:100. New York Sons of Liberty: *Supplement to the Boston-Gazette*, February 19, 1770. "Casca": *Boston-Gazette and Country Day Journal*, November 22, 1773. "Tarquin": Edmund S. Morgan and Helen M. Morgan, *The Stamp Act Crisis: Prologue to Revolution* (Chapel Hill, N.C., 1953), 90. Lloyd J. Matthews, "Patrick Henry's 'Liberty or Death' Speech and Cassius' Speech in Shakespeare's *Julius Caesar*," *Virginia Magazine of History and Biography* 86 (1978): 299–305. See also Bernard Bailyn, *The Origins of American Politics* (New York, 1970), 148–149.

16. *Diary and Autobiography of John Adams*, ed. L. H. Butterfield et al. (New York, 1964), 1:200–201.

17. "God of Liberty": Brewer, *Party Ideology*, 153. George Rudé, *Wilkes and Liberty: A Social Study of 1763 to 1774* (Oxford, 1962), 184.

18. Ibid., 186–187. For a discussion of Pitt and others who anticipated Wilkes's appeal to public opinion and even to the "mob," see Lucy Sutherland, "The City of London and Eighteenth Century Politics," in *Essays Presented to Sir Lewis Namier*, ed. Richard Pares and A. J. P. Taylor (London, 1956), 64.

19. Brewer, *Party Ideology*, 190–191. For Brewer's use of the anthropological categories of Victor Turner, see 118 and 116n. The other historians who have explored extra-rational motivations are E. P. Thompson, E. J. Hobsbawm, and Natalie Zemon Davis. The *Briton* newspaper referred with its title to the phrase in the king's accession speech, "I glory in the name of Britain," believed by some to have been interpolated by Bute. On the interpolation see Namier, *England in the Age of the American Revolution*, 128. "North Briton," then, constituted a gibe at the king under cover of an attack on Bute. As Raymond Postgate observed, "There is nothing whatever in the *North Briton* about social conditions or economics in the modern sense at all" (*That Devil Wilkes*, rev. ed. [London, 1956], 33).

20. Rudé, *Wilkes and Liberty*, 22. William Purdie Treloar, *Wilkes and the City* (London, 1917), 28, citing October 22, 1764, letter of Wilkes.

21. The *North Briton*, no. 38, February 19, 1763; and no. 45, April 23, 1763, in *The Works of the Celebrated John Wilkes, Esq.; Formerly Published under the Title of*

The North Briton . . . (London, 1763), 2:151, 228. Horace Bleackley, *Life of John Wilkes* (London and Toronto, 1917), 60.

22. King insulted: "Mr. Rigby" to the Duke of Bedford, November 26, 1762, *Correspondence of the 4th Duke of Bedford* . . . , ed. Lord John Russell (London, 1846), 3:160. Bute on the campaign against him: Robert R. Rea, *The English Press in Politics, 1760–1774* (Lincoln, Neb., 1963), 35. George III's warning: Brewer, "Misfortunes of Bute," 38. Wilkes's refusal of an invitation: Bleackley, *John Wilkes,* 69. No. 45: *Works of . . . Wilkes,* 3:228. Further on (239–240), no. 45 contains some phrases with strong political implications: *"The King of England* is only the first magistrate of this country," and "The people too have their *prerogative."*

23. Bleackley, *John Wilkes,* 105, 107.

24. *Parliamentary History of England 1753–1765,* 15:1380–1381. *The Life and Correspondence of Philip Yorke,* ed. Philip C. Yorke (Cambridge and Chicago, 1913), 3:461.

25. Gipson, *The British Empire,* 9:39. Rea, *The English Press,* 103–104.

26. London *Public Advertiser,* November 3, 1769. See also *Middlesex Journal: Or Chronicle of Liberty,* April 13–15, 1769; April 20–22, 1769; and April 22–25, 1769.

27. Jack P. Greene, ed., *The Nature of Colony Constitutions: Two Pamphlets on the Wilkes Fund Controversy in South Carolina by Sir Egerton Leigh and Arthur Lee* (Columbia, S.C., 1970), 5, 14. Arthur M. Schlesinger, *Prelude to Independence: The Newspaper War on Britain, 1764–1776* (New York, 1957), 36.

28. "Symbolic": Robert Middlekauff, "The Ritualization of the American Revolution," in *The Development of an American Culture,* ed. Stanley Coben and Lorman Ratner (Englewood Cliffs, N.J., 1970), 34. "Talismanic": Silverman, *Cultural History of the American Revolution,* 112–113. "Cabalistic": Trench, *John Wilkes,* 121. See also Catherine L. Albanese, *Sons of the Fathers: The Civil Religion of the American Revolution* (Philadelphia, 1976), 65.

29. Windows: Bleackley, *Life of Wilkes,* 191. Ambassador: Horace Walpole, *Memoirs of the Reign of King George the Third* (New York and London, 1894), 2:130.

30. Bleackley, *Life of Wilkes,* 233, 247, and 215 for all the other charges outstanding against Wilkes.

31. Directly after the St. George's Fields Massacre (see below) striking sailors attacked and drove off the Wilkite crowds. Horace Walpole to Sir Horace Mann, May 12, 1768, *The Letters of Horace Walpole* . . . , ed. Mrs. Paget Toynbee (Oxford, 1903–1905), 7:188. However, the "watermen," whose dispute was partly with the sailors, took up the Wilkes banner. When prevented from writing "No King!" at the bottom of a petition, they settled for "Liberty and Wilkes for ever!" E. P. Thompson, "Eighteenth Century English Society: Structure, Field of Force, Dialectic," an unpublished paper presented to the Shelby Cullom Davis Center Seminar, Princeton University, February 6, 1976, 44–45.

32. *Gentleman's Magazine,* May 1768. For detail about Cornhill, see Rudé, *Wilkes and Liberty,* 53.

33. See, for example, *Annual Register* (1769), 84, for a coach with depiction on its side of "soldiers firing at young Allen."

34. Bleackley, *Life of Wilkes,* 218, 249. Brewer, *Party Ideology,* 179. See also Gary T. Marx, "Issueless Riots," in James F. Short and Marvin E. Wolfgang, eds., *Collective Violence* (Chicago and New York, 1972), 57–58.

35. Brewer, *Party Ideology,* 190. *Public Advertiser,* November 7, 1769. Postgate, *That Devil Wilkes,* 61.

36. Rudé, *Wilkes and Liberty,* 43 (from *Annual Register,* March, 1768). For a list

of occasions calling for illuminations, see Dirk Hoerder, *Crowd Action in Revolutionary Massachusetts, 1765–1780* (New York, 1977), 46.

37. Brewer, *Party Ideology*, 163, 185–186. Bleackley, *Life of Wilkes*, 194. Presumably the crowd *sang* "Great Wilkes Our King." For the cries: Rea, *The English Press*, 150; Bleackley, *Life of Wilkes*, 220; Charles Brietzcke to Edward Weston, March 23, 1769, in *Historical Manuscripts Commission Reports on the Manuscripts of the Earl of Eglinton* . . . , vol. 10, app. 1 (London, 1885), 414. Brewer, *Party Ideology*, 190.

38. Bleackley, *Life of Wilkes*, 249–250; see 277 for more angry crowds when Wilkes failed in his bid for the lord mayoralty of London.

39. The Quebec Act may have influenced the Gordon riots of 1780, along with the Catholic Relief Act. See George Rudé, "The Gordon Riots: A Study of the Rioters and Their Victims," *Transactions of the Royal Historical Society*, 5th ser., 1 (1956): 101.

40. Carl Bridenbaugh, *Cities in Revolt: Urban Life in America, 1743–1776* (New York, 1955), 114. Rudé, "The Gordon Riots," 112. Protestant hysteria was also apparent in "sporadic riots against Wesleyans and Quakers in 1751 and 1759." See R. B. Rose, "The Priestly Riots of 1791," *Past and Present* 18 (1960): 70.

41. "The charges [regarding the peace treaty] appearing in the North Briton do not merit the slightest attention" (Gipson, *The British Empire*, 9:32).

42. Geoffrey Holmes, "The Sacheverell Riots: The Crowd and the Church in Early Eighteenth-Century London," *Past and Present* 72 (1976): 84n.

43. Nicholas Rogers, "Popular Protest in Early Hanoverian London," *Past and Present* 79 (1978), 71–79. Reginald R. Sharpe, *London and the Kingdom* . . . (London and New York, 1895), 3:5.

44. *The Political Register*, no. 17, August 1768 (London, 1768): 137 (signed "B.F.").

45. On Wilkes and sexual license see Brewer, *Popular Ideology*, 190.

46. Jonathan Sewall on James Otis: *Boston Evening Post*, February 14, 1763, signed "J." Pauline Maier, "John Wilkes and American Disillusionment with Britain," *William and Mary Quarterly* 20 (1963): 384, 385–387.

47. Stella F. Duff, "The Case against the King: The *Virginia Gazettes* Indict George III," *William and Mary Quarterly* 6 (1949): 390. Douglass Adair, "The Stamp Act in Contemporary English Cartoons," *William and Mary Quarterly* 10 (1953): 538. E. P. Richardson, "Stamp Act Cartoons in the Colonies," *Pennsylvania Magazine of History and Biography* 96 (1972): 288.

48. Fred Weinstein and Gerald M. Platt, *Psychoanalytic Sociology: An Essay on the Interpretation of Historical Data and the Phenomena of Collective Behavior* (Baltimore and London, 1973), 108. John Kern, "The Politics of Violence: Colonial American Rebellions, Protests, and Riots, 1676–1747" (Ph.D. diss., University of Wisconsin at Madison, 1976), 207, 214, 221, 245, 260–264.

49. Robert McCluer Calhoon, *The Loyalists in Revolutionary America, 1760–1781* (New York, 1973), 160. Thomas Hutchinson, *The History of the Colony and Province of Massachusetts-Bay*, ed. Lawrence Shaw Mayo (Cambridge, Mass., 1936), 3:74.

50. Caleb H. Snow, *A History of Boston* . . . (Boston, 1825), 259n (the words appear in capitals). Weavers' riot: *Virginia Gazette* (Purdie and Dixon), May 24, 1770. Glovemakers' riot: Pauline Maier, *From Resistance to Revolution: Colonial Radicals and the Development of American Opposition to Britain, 1765–1776* (New York, 1972), 75. Boston *Gazette*, August 19, 1765. Duff, "The Case against the King," 385–386, 388, 390. "Hancock and Liberty": William Ander Smith, "Anglo-Colonial Society and the Mob" (Ph.D. diss., Claremont College, 1965), 125.

For other American reports of British disturbances in 1763, 1765, 1768, and 1771, see Boston *Gazette,* March 21, 1763; *New York Gazette,* July 22, 1765; Dirk Hoerder, "People and Mobs: Crowd Action in Massachusetts during the American Revolution, 1765-1780" (Ph.D. diss., Free University of Berlin, 1971), 257n (held by the State University Library, Stony Brook, N.Y.); and *Pennsylvania Gazette,* May 23, 1771.

51. Chester Noyes Greenough, "New England Almanacs, 1766-1775, and the American Revolution," *Proceedings of the American Antiquarian Society* 45 (1935): 300. *Virginia Gazette* (Purdie and Dixon), June 21, 1770. *Pennsylvania Journal,* May 23, 1771, where Wilkes was still reported as the opposite of Bute. Wilkes's birthday in Boston and South Carolina: Rudé, *Wilkes and Liberty,* 149.

"Wilkes Quincy": Bailyn, *Ideological Origins,* 121. Alexander McDougall of New York as the "Wilkes of America": Maier, "John Wilkes and American Disillusionment," 386. Hutchinson told King George that Samuel Adams was "a sort of Wilkes in New England": see "Extracts from the Journal of Thomas Hutchinson," *Proceedings of the Massachusetts Historical Society* 15 (1877): 330. Samuel Adams was also called "the American Wilkes"; see John Cary, *Joseph Warren: Physician, Politician, Patriot* (Urbana, Ill., 1961), 83. John Lamb of New York was also called "The Wilkes of America," see Herbert M. Morais, "The Sons of Liberty in New York," in *The Era of the American Revolution: Studies Inscribed to Evarts Boutell Greene* (New York, 1939), 283.

4. *James Otis*

1. Clifford K. Shipton, *Sibley's Harvard Graduates . . .* (Boston, 1933-), 11:270. On Otis being blamed see 264; also, *Peter Oliver's Origin and Progress of the American Rebellion: A Tory View,* ed. Douglass Adair and John A. Schutz (San Marino, Calif., 1961), 48-49, 52-53. For Otis's disapproval of violence, see John J. Waters, Jr., *The Otis Family: In Provincial and Revolutionary Massachusetts* (New York, 1975), 156-157. Bernard later wrote that Colonel Otis initially had hoped for a place on the panel of judges when a promotion to the Superior Court should make one free, and that Otis turned on Hutchinson when Hutchinson kept his old posts as well as the new, thus leaving no such vacancy. Francis Bernard to the earl of Shelburne, December 22, 1776, Public Record Office (London), C.O. 5/756, folios 5-8 (hereafter cited as PRO). Transcripts of Crown-copyright records in the Public Record Office appear by permission of the Controller of Her Majesty's Stationery Office.

2. Ellen E. Brennan, *Plural Office Holding in Massachusetts,1760-1780: Its Relation to the "Separation" of Departments of Government* (Chapel Hill, N.C., 1945), 30. John J. Waters and John A. Schutz, "Patterns of Massachusetts Colonial Politics: The Writs of Assistance and the Rivalry between the Otis and Hutchinson Families," *William and Mary Quarterly* 24 (1967): 560-561.

3. *Diary and Autobiography of John Adams,* ed. L. H. Butterfield et al. (New York, 1964), 1:226 for the currency of the story. Otis's denial that he made precisely the threat reported by Bernard (*The Boston-Gazette and Country Journal,* April 4, 1763) makes it clear that Bernard took his meaning, if not his characteristically elaborate circumlocutionary delivery. See below on Otis's style. John C. Miller, *Samuel Adams: Pioneer in Propaganda* (Boston, 1936), 220.

4. Hugh F. Bell, " 'A Personal Challenge': The Otis-Hutchinson Currency Controversy, 1761-1762," *Essex Institute Historical Collections* 6 (1970): 297-298. Merrill Jensen, *The Founding of a Nation: A History of the American Revolution, 1763-1776* (New York, 1968), 74.

5. John Adams to Mercy Otis Warren, September 10, 1783, *Warren-Adams Letters: Being Chiefly a Correspondence among John Adams, Samuel Adams, and James Warren, 1743–1814,* in *Collections of the Massachusetts Historical Society* 72–73 (1917, 1925), 2:224 (hereafter cited as *CMHS*). Clifford K. Shipton, "James Otis and the Writs of Assistance," *Proceedings of the Bostonian Society,* January 1961: 22; and see Shipton, *Harvard Graduates,* 11:278–279. On Otis's injuries: Hiller B. Zobel, *The Boston Massacre* (New York, 1970), 147–149. At the time, Otis was reported beaten by Robinson and just barely saved from death. See the *London Public Advertiser,* November 3, 1769; also, Thomas Young to John Wilkes, September 6, 1769, "John Wilkes and Boston," *Proceedings of the Massachusetts Historical Society* 47 (1913–1914): 209 (hereafter cited as *PMHS*).

6. Thomas Hutchinson, *The History of the Colony and Province of Massachusetts-Bay,* ed. Lawrence Shaw Mayo (Cambridge, Mass., 1936), 3:64. William Tudor, *The Life of James Otis of Massachusetts* (Boston, 1823; reprint New York, 1970), 24. Though Hutchinson is referred to in the anecdote as "Chief Justice," the case probably preceded his tenure in that office. The nature of the proceeding, an apparently trivial one, and the biographer's intention of illustrating Otis's early practice suggest Hutchinson's period as a lower-court judge. Thus, it would not seem to be a case of Hutchinson attempting to mollify Otis after taking the chief justiceship.

7. See James Otis, Jr., to James Otis, Sr., February 7, 1742, and April 4, 1743, in Otis Family Manuscripts, Butler Library, Columbia University, New York, New York. See, for example, James Otis, Sr., to James Otis, Jr., February 13, 1756, in Otis Papers, New York Public Library, New York, New York.

8. Waters, *The Otis Family,* 65, 131. The term "factotum" in the preceding paragraph is borrowed from the index. Shipton, *Harvard Graduates,* 8:165.

9. Waters, *The Otis Family,* 107, 105.

10. "Idolized": *Peter Oliver's Origin and Progress,* ed. Adair and Schutz, 28. Joseph Otis to James Otis, Sr., January 8, 1749/50, in Otis Family MSS. Use of Otis's library: *Diary and Autobiography of John Adams,* 1:57, 158, 169.

11. According to Peter Oliver, *Diary and Autobiography of John Adams,* 1:225. *Dictionary of American Biography,* s.v. "Otis, James" (by S. E. Morison), regarding the period 1766–1768 (hereafter cited as *DAB*). Waters, *The Otis Family,* 143–144. Brennan, *Plural Office Holding,* 67.

12. For such an estimate of Hutchinson, see Malcolm Freiberg, "Thomas Hutchinson: The First Fifty Years (1711–1761)," *William and Mary Quarterly* 15 (1958): 54.

13. Bell, "A Personal Challenge," 310. James Otis, Boston *Gazette,* April 11, 1763. Bell, "A Personal Challenge," 314.

14. John Adams to William Tudor, March 29, 1817, in *The Works of John Adams, Second President of the United States . . . ,* ed. Charles Francis Adams (Boston, 1856), 10:248. On the weakness of Otis's case see Maurice A. Smith, *The Writs of Assistance Case* (Berkeley, Calif., 1978), 327–330 and passim on Otis's resignation, and 130 on the possibility that the king's death was not the precipitant of the writs crisis (all discussed below). *Works of John Adams,* 2:523.

15. *Works of John Adams,* 2:523. Shipton, *Harvard Graduates,* 11:252.

16. *Works of John Adams,* 2:524.

17. Brennan, *Plural Office Holding,* 26. See Waters, *The Otis Family,* 120–125 on the beginning of Otis's anti-Hutchinson campaign and on prerogative.

18. Boston *Gazette,* December 28, 1761, postscript to article by Otis. Shipton, *Harvard Graduates,* 8:159. Boston *Gazette,* December 21, 1761. Bell, "A Personal Challenge," 314.

19. Waters and Schutz, "Patterns of Massachusetts Colonial Politics," 564. Ship-

ton, *Harvard Graduates,* 11:255, quoting fom Bernard manuscript. On Otis's rationalism see Waters, *The Otis Family,* 136–137.

20. Hutchinson, *The History of Massachusetts-Bay,* 3:69. See also James Otis to Jasper Mauduit, October 28, 1762, *CMHS* 74 (1918): 78. Shipton takes this letter as the "first sign" of an accommodation with Bernard, which is to ignore Otis's vote in favor of the grant of land to Bernard earlier in the year (*Harvard Graduates,* 11:256–257). The letter may not be connected with any of Otis's actions in 1762, on the other hand, but may point to his second reconciliation with Bernard. This took place the following year and is discussed below.

21. A good example of a charge of madness is that leveled against Josiah Quincy, Jr., in 1772. See his response in his "Marchmont Nedham" article, Boston *Gazette,* June 29, 1772. On the links between public and private disturbances see Otto Fenichel, "Depession and Mania," in *The Meaning of Despair: Psychoanalytic Contributions to the Understanding of Depression,* ed. Willard Gaylin (New York, 1968), 140. See also n. 28 below.

22. *Diary and Autobiography of John Adams,* 1:225, entry of June 5, 1762, referring to the May elections. "Letter Concerning James Otis," *PMHS* 4 (1858–1860): 53. Tudor, *James Otis,* 8–9. See below for indirect collaboration of this incident. Bernard Bailyn finds "signs of mental instability" in Otis's writings between 1761 and 1764; see Bernard Bailyn, ed., *Pamphlets of the American Revolution 1750–1776* (Cambridge, Mass., 1965), 414.

23. *Diary and Autobiography of John Adams,* 1:226.

24. James Otis to Jasper Mauduit, *CMHS,* 77.

25. For a political explanation see Waters and Schutz, "Patterns of Massachusetts Colonial Politics," 566. "Some Political Writings of James Otis," ed. Charles F. Mullett, *The University of Missouri Studies* 4 (1929): 261 (Preface). See also Shipton's praise, *Harvard Graduates,* 11:257–258. Tudor, *James Otis,* 120 (italics deleted).

26. William Edward Hartpole Lecky, *A History of England in the Eighteenth Century* (New York, 1892–1893; reprint New York, 1968), 3:73, 71.

27. Tudor, *James Otis,* 125, 126. Moses Coit Tyler, *The Literary History of the American Revolution, 1763–1783,* 2d ed. (New York and London, 1898), 1:43. James Otis, *A Vindication of the Conduct of the House of Representatives of the Province of the Massachusetts-Bay . . . ,* in "Some Political Writings of James Otis," ed. Charles F. Mullett, *The University of Missouri Studies* 4 (1929): 25.

28. 1763 truce: Brennan, *Plural Office Holding,* 68. The colonel's investiture took place in February 1764. For a Hutchinson letter on the truce, now calling Otis a "clever fellow," but possibly ironic, see Shipton, *Harvard Graduates,* 11:258. On the king: Boston *Gazette,* February 28, 1763, anonymous article attributed to Otis by Brennan, *Plural Office Holding,* 57n. In the same article Otis complained that government writers habitually used the term "madman" to describe opponents. Advertisement: Boston *Gazette,* March 28, 1763. "Retirement": Brennan, *Plural Office Holding,* 67–68. Brennan sets the reconciliation a bit later in 1763. It is difficult to chart Otis's changing attitudes toward the administration, especially as most of the information for these comes from Bernard and Hutchinson themselves, whose reactions were understandably uncertain and confused. The confusions over Otis's position at any given time serve to illustrate the wavering character of his politics.

29. Boston *Evening-Post,* February 14, 1763, signed "J.," (that is, Sewall) with servant's remark in italics. Otis's anonymous denial in Boston *Gazette,* February 28, 1763. Boston *Evening-Post,* July 11, 1763.

30. Lawrence Henry Gipson, "Aspects of the Beginning of the American Revolu-

tion in Massachusetts Bay, 1760–1762," *Proceedings of the American Antiquarian Society* 67 (1957): 21n. Boston *Gazette*, April 4, 1763, Otis's italics.

31. Boston *Gazette*, April 11, 1763.

32. Thomas Hutchinson to Israel Williams, April 15, 1763, quoted in Bernard Bailyn, *The Ordeal of Thomas Hutchinson* (Cambridge, Mass., 1974), 61.

33. In addition to the reversals supposed to be evident among these, there may have been reversals with regard to Otis's speeches, which were not recorded. Also, in 1765 Otis published *Considerations on Behalf of the Colonists. In a Letter to a Noble Lord.* This was a reply to the Englishman Soame Jenyn's *Objections to the Taxation of Our American Colonies, Briefly Considered,* in which Otis returned to the tone if not the content of his 1764 attack on Parliament. On this work see James R. Ferguson, "Reason in Madness: The Political Thought of James Otis," *William and Mary Quarterly* 36 (1979): 211. Ellen Elizabeth Brennan, "James Otis: Recreant and Patriot," *New England Quarterly* 12 (1939): 695.

34. Jensen, *The Founding of a Nation,* 85. Bailyn, *Pamphlets,* 410, 415. Hutchinson referred to Otis's "loose, unconnected peformance[s]" that "abound[ed] with digressions and apparent irrelevancies" (Ferguson, "Reason in Madness," 195). Ferguson calls Otis "confused, uncertain, and ultimately inconsistent," and argues his "retreat" on the issue of Parliamentary authority ("Reason in Madness," 198, 203). Otis, "The Rights of the British Colonies Asserted and Proved," in "Some Political Writings," 74.

35. See Brennan, "Recreant and Patriot," 722–723. For modern denials see Bailyn, *Odeal,* 116. *DAB,* s.v. "Otis, James" (by S. E. Morison).

36. Tyler, *Literary History,* 1:47. Martin Howard, *A Letter from a Gentleman at Halifax to His Friend in Rhode Island Containing Remarks upon a Pamphlet Entitled The Rights of the Colonies Examined* (Newport, R.I., 1765), referring presumably to Otis's 1764 *Rights* on King Charles and ship money. (See Otis, "The Rights of the British Colonies Asserted and Proved," in "Some Political Writings," 87.) On Otis's style, see Howard, *A Letter from a Gentleman at Halifax,* 4, 6–7, 21. Howard offered his ironic praise of Otis in a comparison with a similar essay by Governor Stephen Hopkins of Rhode Island.

37. Martin Howard, *A Defence of the Letter from a Gentleman at Halifax, to His Friend in Rhode Island* (Newport, R.I., 1765), especially 29.

38. Howard, *A Letter from a Gentleman at Halifax,* 11. Otis, "A Vindication of the British Colonies," in "Some Political Writings," 140. That it had deposed a king was the claim of the song's author: see *Encyclopedia Britannica,* 11th ed., s.v. "Lillibullero." See also Lewis Winstock, *Songs and Music of the Redcoats* (Harrisburg, Pa., 1970), 24–25. The title is also spelled Lilliburlero.

39. Otis, "A Vindication of the British Colonies," in "Some Political Writings," 137. On the use of Filmer's *Patriarcha* by Otis and others, see Edwin G. Burrows and Michael Wallace, "The American Revolution: The Ideology and Psychology of National Liberation," *Perspectives in American History* 6 (1972): 172–173, 175. See also 287 for a writer signing himself "Hampden," Otis's pseudonym, picking up this point in 1776. Otis in Boston *Gazette,* February 28, 1763 (with "cutting out" a conjectural reading). On the imagery of violation see Kenneth Silverman, *A Cultural History of the American Revolution: Painting, Music, Literature, and the Theatre in the Colonies and the United States from the Treaty of Paris to the Inauguration of George Washington, 1763–1789* (New York, 1976), 82–107 and especially 106 on the play *The Prince of Parthia.*

40. Howard, *Defence of the Letter from a Gentleman at Halifax,* 25. *Works of John*

Adams, 10:295, with Adams's dating of the period as 1764 adjusted by S. E. Morison in *DAB* to 1765, as pointed out by Brennan, "Recreant and Patriot," 692.

41. Shipton, *Harvard Graduates,* 11:262. Alluding to Otis's tone, Martin Howard wrote that "the madness of others shall be a lesson to him," *Defence of the Letter from a Gentleman at Halifax,* 29.

42. Francis Bernard to John Pownall, May 6, 1765, in Bernard Papers; quoted by Brennan, "Recreant and Patriot," 711. Otis, "Brief Remarks on the Defence of the Halifax Libel, on the British-American-Colonies," in "Some Political Writings," 170.

43. Otis, "Brief Remarks on the Defence of the Halifax Libel," in "Some Political Writings," 158, 159, 160–161. See also 163 where Otis again takes up both the Pretender theme and "Lillibullero."

44. Ibid., 170.

45. Silverman, *Cultural History,* 139, 643. Howard referred to derisive use of the epithet by newspaper writers in *Defence of the Letter from a Gentleman at Halifax,* 24. The end of the refrain, "Tumtititi, tititumti, tumti-prosodee," had a footnote attached that assigned its source as "Jacobus de Prosodia," another reference to Otis as prosodist. The Orpheus-violin story has been regarded as apocryphal, but Waterhouse's reference suggests its authenticity, lending further credence to Peter Oliver's claim mentioned above that Otis's mental disturbance dated to the 1740s.

46. "The aptness of thy nose to bleed": Boston *Evening-Post,* March 28, 1763. James Otis, Sr., to Joseph Otis, February 4, 1766. Otis Family MSS. "It has been amply demonstrated that alterations in nasal function accompanying conflict situations are often sufficient to produce pathologic tissue changes" (Flanders Dunbar, "Anxiety, Stress and Respiratory Diseases Especially Tuberculosis," in Phineas J. Sparer, ed., *Personality, Stress, and Tuberculosis* [New York, 1956], 217).

47. John Adams to William Tudor, March 11, 1818, in *Works of John Adams,* 10:295. Otis as "Freeborn Armstrong," Boston *Gazette,* February 3, 1766. Bailyn, *Ordeal,* 66. Francis Bernard to the Earl of Shelburne, December 22, 1766, PRO (London) C. O. 5/756, folios 6–7. On Otis's connection with the Kennebec land claims discussed in the chapter on Hutchinson above—claims that gave him, along with Samuel Adams, an interest in the destruction of Hutchinson's papers—see G. B. Warden, *Boston, 1689–1776* (Boston and Toronto, 1970), 356–357n. Shipton, *Harvard Graduates,* 11:265–266, quoting Governor Bernard.

48. On denunciation of mobs: Shipton, *Harvard Graduates,* 11:266. Otis on taxation: *Diary and Autobiography of John Adams,* 1:295. Hallowell, who reported Otis's words, was the customs official whose house was mobbed earlier on the same evening as Hutchinson's. His report about Otis may possibly have been of an earlier conversation. Otis defended Parliament in January, writing as "Hampden." Shipton, *Harvard Graduates,* 11:267–268.

Otis voted for a proadministration colonial representative to join the new House agent in protest against the Stamp Act. Jensen finds this a shocking reversal, *Founding of a Nation,* 105. Otis voted to support Bernard's March proroguing of the legislature from early April to late April 1766. Jensen explains this as merely a matter of politics (*Founding of a Nation,* 145).

49. Tudor, *James Otis,* 250–251. See Waters and Schutz, "Patterns of Colonial Politics," 566, where this contrast is given a political explanation.

50. Shipton, *Harvard Graduates,* 11:273. Brennan, *Plural Office Holding,* 92. See Josiah Quincy, Jr., *Reports of Cases . . . ,* ed. Samuel M. Quincy (New York, 1865; reprint New York, 1969), 442 (hereafter cited as *Quincy Reports*) for a list of contemporary references to Otis as mad. Shipton, *Harvard Graduates,* 11:275.

51. *Diary and Autobiography of John Adams,* 1:271 (re: 1765). For examples of

Otis's recreancy in 1768 see Dirk Hoerder, *Crowd Action in Revolutionary Massachusetts, 1765–1780* (New York, 1977), 184; and Jensen, *Founding of a Nation,* 246. Odes: Boston *Evening-Post,* November 30, 1767, January 11, 1768, and see Samuel Waterhouse, *Proposals for Printing by Subscription the History of Adjutant Trowel & Bluster* (Boston, 1766). Hutchinson wrote in 1766 that Otis was "without dispute a madman" (Bailyn, *Ordeal,* 72).

52. Tudor, *James Otis,* 356. *Diary and Autobiography of John Adams,* 1:343, states that one of the pieces being written by the patriots with Otis that day led directly to the fight with Robinson. "Five Weeks after the fight, John Adams remarked that Otis was much better mentally than he had been for a long time." Shipton, "James Otis and the Writs of Assistance," 24. On Otis's gloom: "Additions to Thomas Hutchinson's *History of Massachusetts-Bay,*" ed. Catherine Shaw Mayo, *Proceedings of the American Antiquarian Society* 59 (1949): 24; also, Andrew Oliver to Francis Bernard, December 3, 1769, in *Quincy Reports,* 464. Hutchinson makes Otis's gloom appear to have been habitual; he may simply have had the report from Oliver, or had it from the same source as Oliver.

53. Canes: "Additions to Thomas Hutchinson's *History,*" 15. *Diary and Autobiography of John Adams,* 1:348, 349. While excoriating Hutchinson Otis quoted, "In my father's House are many Mansions . . ."

54. Boston *Evening-Post,* November 30, 1767. On Hawthorne's choice of the name "Molineux" see Peter Shaw, "Their Kinsman, Thomas Hutchinson; Hawthorne, the Boston Patriots, and His Majesty's Royal Governor," *Early American Literature* 11 (1976): 183–190; and Peter Shaw, "Fathers, Sons, and the Ambiguities of Revolution in 'My Kinsman, Major Molineux,'" *New England Quarterly* 49 (1976): 559–576. "Extracts of Two Letters from Boston Dated March 13, 1770," Sparks MSS, Houghton Library, Harvard University, Cambridge, Mass., 3:56–57. *Pennsylvania Chronicle,* February 26–March 5, 1770.

55. *Diary and Autobiography of John Adams,* 1:350. Benson J. Lossing, *The Pictorial Field Book of the Revolution* (New York, 1859), 1:493n. See also *Peter Oliver's Origin and Progress,* ed. Adair and Schutz, 36; and see Thomas Hutchinson to John Pownall, October 17, 1771, in Massachusetts Archives 27:246 on Otis's drunkenness.

56. *Letters and Diary of John Rowe . . .,* ed. Anne Rowe Cunningham (Boston, 1903), 201. See also Joseph Otis to James Otis, Sr., March 19, 1770, Otis Family MSS.

57. Boston *Gazette,* April 11, 1763.

58. Tudor, *James Otis,* 25. This unsubstantiated tale may be a conflation with the newspaper defense of the king's birthday youths. If so, it would indicate that these seemingly different holidays were associated together in the contemporary mind.

59. Shipton, *Harvard Graduates,* 11:281–282, quoting from Hutchinson's London diary.

60. Otis in 1771: *Diary and Autobiography of John Adams,* 2:20 (June 1771); Adams's opinion: 55 (February 1772). "Bound hand and foot": Thomas Hutchinson to Francis Bernard, December 3, 1771, in William V. Wells, *The Life and Public Services of Samuel Adams . . . ,* (Boston, 1865), 1:439; see also 458. "Banter": Hutchinson, *History of Massachusetts-Bay,* 3:244. Support of article: Shipton, *Harvard Graduates,* 11:283. In October 1772, Otis worried about his offering a petition being considered a "Contempt" in law. "Is mere Impertinence a Contempt?" he asked John Adams. *Diary and Autobiography of John Adams,* 2:65–66. See also Arthur M. Schlesinger, *Prelude to Independence: The Newspaper War on Britain, 1764–1776* (New York, 1957), 147.

61. Hutchinson, *History of Massachusetts-Bay,* 3:244. James Warren to Mercy

Otis Warren, June 18, 1775, in *Warren-Adams Letters,* 1:59–60. Otis as "Hamp-den," Boston *Gazette,* January 26, 1766. Oates may have come to mind for Otis on account of another parallel: Oates's outline of the popish plot was written in Greek, and Otis was one of the few men in America who knew Greek. At about this time Otis destroyed his manuscript of a book on Greek prosody along with his other papers.

62. "Reverie" and "overidealization": John J. Waters, "James Otis, Jr.: An Ambivalent Revolutionary," *History of Childhood Quarterly* (Summer 1973), 143. "Unbounded affection": Shipton, *Harvard Graduates,* 11:270, quoting from a private letter. On Otis's tears at courts-reopening speech, December 1765: *Quincy Reports,* 02. "Faithful subject": Boston *Gazette,* January 13, 1770. "Kind and benevolent father": Otis as "Freeborn American," February 9, 1767, *Supplement to the Boston-Gazette.* Identified by Malcom Freiberg, "Prelude to Purgatory," 164 and n. 16. In 1765 Otis called the king "the father of all his people"; see "Considerations on Behalf of the Colonists . . . ," in "Some Political Writings," 112.

63. Waters, *The Otis Family,* 123. Shipton, *Harvard Graduates,* 11:274.

64. Waters, "Ambivalent Revolutionary," 154. Harold Bloom, *The Anxiety of Influence: A Theory of Poetry* (New York, 1973), 64, quoting Freud. Revere verses: Boston *Gazette,* May 16, 1766.

5. John Adams

1. John Adams to Mercy Otis Warren, September 10, 1783, in *Warren-Adams Letters; Being Chiefly a Correspondence among John Adams, Samuel Adams, and James Warren, 1743–1814,* in *Collections of the Massachusetts Historical Society* 72–73 (1917, 1925), 2:224. *Diary and Autobiography of John Adams,* ed. L. H. Butterfield et al. (New York, 1964), 3:275.

2. *The Works of John Adams, Second President of the United States . . . ,* ed. Charles Francis Adams (Boston, 1856), 4:6.

3. John Adams to Hezekiah Niles, January 14, 1818, ibid., 10:276.

4. John Adams to William Tudor, July 9, 1818, ibid., 10:327. Adams remembered the case as never being settled, whereas actually the writs were upheld after being confirmed in England as acceptable practice. See Maurice H. Smith, *The Writs of Assistance Case* (Berkeley, Calif., 1978), 507.

5. John Adams to William Tudor, August 6, 1818, in *Works of John Adams,* 10:343. *Diary and Autobiography of John Adams,* 3:272, 273. See Robert M. Zemsky, *Merchants, Farmers, and River Gods: An Essay on Eighteenth Century American Politics* (Boston, 1971), 81–82, on Adams's entry into the legal profession. On going to see Otis, compare *Diary and Autobiography of John Adams,* 1:56.

6. John Adams to William Tudor, December 18, 1816, in *Works of John Adams,* 10:233. *Diary and Autobiography of John Adams,* 3:276. John Adams to William Tudor, March 29, 1817, in *Works of John Adams,* 10:245.

7. John Adams to William Tudor, August 21, 1818, in *Works of John Adams,* 10:350. John Adams to Hezekiah Niles, February 13, 1818, in L. H. Butterfield, "John Adams: What Do We Mean by the American Revolution?" in Daniel J. Boorstin, *An American Primer* (Chicago, 1966), 229–230. John Adams to Abigail Adams, July 15, 1776, *Adams Family Correspondence,* ed. L. H. Butterfield et al. (New York, 1965–), 2:49.

8. John Adams to William Tudor, March 29, 1817, in *Works of John Adams,* 10:247–248.

9. Peter Shaw, *The Character of John Adams* (Chapel Hill, N.C., 1976), 45–46, 46n.

10. Ibid., 51. *Diary and Autobiography of John Adams*, 2:55.

11. John Adams to William Tudor, March 11, 1818, in *Works of John Adams*, 10:298.

12. John Adams to William Tudor, December 17, 1816, Adams Papers Microfilm, *Massachusetts Historical Society*, reel 123. See also Josiah Quincy, Jr., *Reports of Cases . . .*, ed. Samuel M. Quincy (New York, 1865; reprint New York, 1969), 411n. Smith, *Writs of Assistance Case*, 147, has recently speculated that Adams may have been right about the reason for Hutchinson's appointment. But compare Emily Hickman, "Colonial Writs of Assistance," *New England Quarterly* 5 (1932): 84–85.

13. *Peter Oliver's Origin and Progress of the American Rebellion: A Tory View*, ed. Douglass Adair and John A. Schutz (San Marino, Calif., 1961), 83. *Diary and Autobiography of John Adams*, 1:167–168. Bernard Bailyn, *The Ordeal of Thomas Hutchinson* (Cambridge, Mass., 1974), 51.

14. *Diary and Autobiography of John Adams*, 1:218, 232–233.

15. *Papers of John Adams*, ed. Robert J. Taylor et al. (Cambridge, Mass., 1977), 1:63. For an analysis of Adams's ambivalence in 1763 see Robert A. East, "The Strange Pause in John Adams's Diary," in *Toward a New View of America: Essays in Honor of Arthur C. Cole*, ed. Hans L. Tefousse (New York, 1977).

16. *Diary and Autobiography of John Adams*, 1:260, 281.

17. Ibid., 1:305, 308, 311, 324. Brackets supplied by editors of the Adams papers have been omitted, and an abbreviation has been expanded (311).

18. Ibid., 1:323, 292, 291; and 3:290–291.

19. *Works of John Adams*, 4:6. *Diary and Autobiography of John Adams*, 3:278. On the break in Adams's diary and his forgetfulness see East, "The Strange Pause," 30n.

20. *Papers of John Adams*, 1:181, 185, 189. See Carol Berkin, *Jonathan Sewall: Odyssey of an American Loyalist* (New York and London, 1974), 31–34, for Sewall's arguments.

21. *Diary and Autobiography of John Adams*, 3:291.

22. Shaw, *Character of John Adams*, 57.

23. Michael Kammen, "The American Revolution as a *Crise de Conscience:* The Case of New York," in *Society, Freedom, and Conscience: The American Revolution in Virginia, Massachusetts, and New York*, ed. Richard M. Jellison (New York, 1976), 133.

24. David C. Schwartz, "A Theory of Revolutionary Behavior," in *When Men Revolt and Why: A Reader in Political Violence and Revolution*, ed. James C. Davies (New York, 1971), 114. *Diary and Autobiography of John Adams*, 1:312–313n, with "neglected" conjectured by the editors.

25. Schwartz, "Revolutionary Behavior," 116. John Adams to Abigail Adams, June 30, 1774, in *Adams Family Correspondence*, 1:116.

26. *Diary and Autobiography of John Adams*, 3:288–289.

27. *The Diary and Letters of His Excellency Thomas Hutchinson, Esq.*, ed. Peter Orlando Hutchinson (Boston, 1884), 2:220.

28. See *Legal Papers of John Adams*, ed., Kinvin Wroth and Hiller B. Zobel (Cambridge, Mass., 1965), 2:103, 219, 254, 264. It is perhaps significant that Josiah Quincy, Jr., who defended the Massacre soldiers with Adams, was also engaged with him in the case of the assault on the customs officer, and that Otis was one of the attorneys opposing him.

29. John Adams to William Tudor, November 25, 1816, and John Adams to William Tudor, November 16, 1816, in Adams Papers, reel 123.

30. Bailyn, *Ordeal,* 151. John Adams to Jedidiah Morse, January 20, 1816, in *Works of John Adams,* 10:209–210.

31. *Works of John Adams,* 207, 205. John Adams to William Tudor, December 30, 1816, Adams Papers, reel 123. The historian is Clifford K. Shipton.

32. John Adams to John Quincy Adams, January 8, 1808, Adams Papers, reel 118. John Adams to Jedidiah Morse, January 20, 1816, *Works of John Adams,* 10:206. John Adams to William Tudor, December 30, 1816, Adams Papers, reel 123. "Gelater de Rosia" is my conjectural reading. John Adams to William Tudor, January 11, 1817, Adams papers, reel 123. For Hutchinson's explanation see his *History of the Colony and Province of Massachusetts-Bay,* ed. Lawrence Shaw Mayo (Cambrdige, Mass., 1936), 3:167n.

33. *Diary and Autobiography of John Adams,* 1:341–342. See *Papers of John Adams,* 2:171, for a 1766 contact with the Sons of Liberty.

34. Only a year later Adams mistakenly dated his dispute with Hutchinson "in the Spring of the Year 1771" instead of in Fall 1770. In moving it he revealed the association that his illness had in his mind with Hutchinson. *Diary and Autobiography of John Adams,* 2:53, 54, 56n; "10 years": 2:35 (June 1771).

35. Ibid., 2:55 (this was another unpublished essay). See also 2:75, for a different version of their demises. For Mayhew's health and death see Charles W. Akers, *Called unto Liberty: A Life of Jonathan Mayhew, 1720–1766* (Cambridge, Mass., 1964), 105, 219–220.

36. Bailyn, *Ordeal,* 2. "Answer of the House of Representatives" (January 26, 1773), in Alden Bradford, *Speeches of the Governors of Massachusetts, 1765–1775* (Boston, 1818), 357, 363.

37. *Diary and Autobiography of John Adams,* 2:192–193. "Vile Serpent": 2:81.

38. John Adams as "Novanglus": *Papers of John Adams,* 2:277; and *Works of John Adams,* 4:71. *Papers of John Adams,* 2:221–222n. *Works of John Adams,* 4:120. For two discussions of Adams's inexplicable failure either to accept or recall the fact that Daniel Leonard and not Sewall was the author of "Massachusettensis," see Mellen Chamberlin, *PMHS* 6 (1890–1891), 253–254 and 399–400.

39. Adams was also a justice of the quorum and a colony-wide justice. Ellen E. Brennan, *Plural Office Holding in Massachusetts, 1760–1780: Its Relation to the "Separation" of Departments of Government* (Chapel Hill, N.C., 1945), 114–115. *Diary and Autobiography of John Adams,* 3:361n, 362. Ironically, Adams's resignation came in a letter to James Otis, Sr., April 29, 1776; see *Works of John Adams,* 9:374.

40. Stephen Patterson, *Political Parties in Revolutionary Massachusetts* (Madison, Wis., 1973), 227; and Jackson T. Main, *The Upper House in Revolutionary America, 1763–1788* (Madison, Wis., 1967), 163.

41. Bailyn, *Ordeal,* 377.

42. Merle Curti, *Human Nature in American Historical Thought* (Columbia, Mo., 1968), 17–22.

43. See Shaw, *Character of John Adams,* 227–229.

44. Ibid., 252–253.

45. For the importance of Hutchinson to Adams in later life: ibid., 293, 305, 306–307.

46. William V. Wells, *The Life and Public Services of Samuel Adams* . . . (Boston, 1865), 1:246.

47. John Adams to William Tudor, November 16, 1816, in *Works of John Adams,* 10:230. See also Shaw, *Character of John Adams,* 305n, 309.

48. John Adams to William Tudor, November 25, 1816, in Adams Papers, reel 123.

6. Joseph Hawley

1. "Additions to Thomas Hutchinson's *History of Massachusetts-Bay*," ed. Catherine Shaw Mayo, *Proceedings of the American Antiquarian Society* 59 (1949): 38.
2. E. Francis Brown, *Joseph Hawley, Colonial Radical* (New York, 1931), 49–50, 96.
3. Kathryn Kish Sklar, "Joseph Hawley: A Case of Conscience in Northampton in the 1740s," an unpublished paper presented to the American Studies Association convention, 1976, 14.
4. Brown, *Joseph Hawley,* 72, 73. Joseph Hawley to Martha Root, August 8, 1750, Hawley Papers, Manuscripts and Archives Division, New York Public Library, Astor, Lenox, and Tilden Foundations. The quotation is taken from Hawley's draft version. "Yr." expanded to "your."
5. Samuel F. Merrick to George Bliss, April 28, 1828, *Papers and Proceedings of the Connecticut Valley Historical Society* 9 (Springfield, Mass., 1912), 33.
6. Jonathan Edwards, "A Faithful Narrative," in *The Great Awakening,* ed. C. C. Goen (New Haven and London, 1972), 206. "Narrative of Surprising Conversions," in *Jonathan Edwards, Representative Selections,* rev. ed., ed. Clarence H. Faust and Thomas H. Johnson (New York, 1962).
7. Joseph Hawley, Sr., Hawley Papers.
8. Brown, *Joseph Hawley,* 37. Sereno Dwight, *The Works of President Edwards* . . . (New York, 1829), 1:425. Brown, *Joseph Hawley,* 26.
9. Ibid., 31–32.
10. Ibid., 37. *Edwards, Representative Selections,* 397. Dwight, *Works of Edwards,* 1:423. Charles Lyman Shaw, "Joseph Hawley, The Northampton Statesman," *Magazine of American History* . . . 22 (1889): 489–490.
11. Joseph Hawley to Jonathan Edwards, January 21, 1755, Hawley Papers; also, January 11, 1755. Brown, *Joseph Hawley,* 37. Fragment, no date, Hawley Papers, 13. It would appear to have been written near the date at which Hawley abandoned his Arminianism, which it gives as 1754. The Word "Natural" is a conjecture.
12. Brown, *Joseph Hawley,* 39.
13. Oliver and Hutchinson anecdotes: *Peter Oliver's Origin and Progress of the American Rebellion: A Tory View,* ed. Douglass Adair and John A. Schutz (San Marino, Calif., 1961), 37–38; Thomas Hutchinson, *The History of the Colony and Province of Massachusetts-Bay,* ed. Lawrence Shaw Mayo (Cambridge, Mass., 1936), 3:213. In other anecdotes Hawley is reported upbraiding a neighbor for sawing wood on the sabbath, and interrupting a raw young replacement minister's sermon, then taking his place in the pulpit to finish it. "Northampton Reminiscences" (by "S.E.B."), *Hampshire Gazette,* July 25, 1876.
"Sneers": Robert J. Taylor, *Western Massachusetts in the Revolution* (Providence, R.I., 1964), letter of Williams, 23; and see 25 for another example of Hawley's changeableness (in 1759). "Haughtiness": Brown, *Joseph Hawley,* 37.
14. "Transgression and expiation": Otto Fenichel, "Depression and Mania," in *The Meaning of Despair: Psychoanalytic Contributions to the Understanding of Depression,* ed. Willard Gaylin (New York, 1968), 150. "Constitutional melancholy": "The Revival under Whitefield," *Christian Examiner* 4 (1827): 491. *Peter Oliver's Origin and Progress,* ed. Adair and Schutz, 39. Oliver also reported that Hawley's letter to Hall was written "in the Depths" of a "religious Melancholy," 38.
15. Brown, *Joseph Hawley,* 15, 94, re: 1764. Febichel, "Depression and Mania," 137.

16. Sandor Rado, "Psychodynamics of Depression from the Etiological Point of View," in *The Meaning of Despair*, ed. Willard Gaylin, 101.

17. Timothy Dwight, *Travels in New England and New York*, ed. Barbara Miller Solomon (Cambridge, Mass., 1969), 1:244. Hutchinson, *History of Massachusetts-Bay*, 3:213.

18. Jonathan Edwards to Joseph Hawley, November 18, 1754, in *Edwards, Representative Selections*, 400–401. Joseph Hawley to "the Reverend, Mr. Hall," May 9, 1760, in Dwight, *Works of Edwards*, 1:425. Edwards, apparently quoting the Biblical lines from memory, had shifted their voice so as to make Christ, with whom he explicitly associated himself as a martyr, directly warn such as Joseph Hawley to "take heed" lest they offend him.

19. *Edwards, Representative Selections*, 392. Gail Thain Parker, "Jonathan Edwards and Melancholy," *New England Quarterly* 41 (1968): 194.

20. *Peter Oliver's Origin and Progress*, ed. Adair and Schutz, 37, Oliver's italics.

21. Judd MSS, 1:493, Forbes Library, Northampton, Mass. Sylvester Judd, *Hampshire Gazette*, June 15, 1852.

22. Brown, *Joseph Hawley*, 20, 21. George H. Pollock, "Anniversary Reactions, Trauma, and Mourning," *Psychoanalytic Quarterly* 39 (1970): 347–371.

23. Joseph Hawley, Boston *Evening-Post*, July 6, 1767.

24. Hawley, Boston *Evening-Post*, July 13, 1767. *The Diary and Letters of His Excellency Thomas Hutchinson, Esq. . . .*, ed. Peter Orlando Hutchinson (Boston, 1884), 1:73.

25. Bernard: Malcolm Freiberg, "Prelude to Purgatory: Thomas Hutchinson in Provincial Massachusetts Politics, 1760–1770" (Ph.D. diss., Brown University, 1950), 319. Leading man: Dwight, *Works of Edwards*, 1:411; and see Brown, *Joseph Hawley*, 98, on Hawley's election to the legislature in 1751 apparently as the result of his prominence gained in ousting Edwards. See Parker, "Edwards and Melancholy." James Russell Trumbull, *History of Northampton, Massachusetts . . .* (Northampton, Mass., 1902), 2:81n.

26. The "state of nature" and "shocking event" passages are both from Hawley, Boston *Evening-Post*, July 13, 1767. The MS of Hawley's newspaper article offers some evidence of how important his overnight decision appeared to him, for it is heavily revised where it describes the experience. It mentions "revolving [& ?] sounding [? x'd out] ye Case in ye Night." MS in Hawley Papers. Adams on treason: *Diary and Autobiography of John Adams*, ed. L. H. Butterfield et al. (New York, 1964), 1:270, diary entry dated December 21, 1764. A crossed-out phrase has been removed.

27. Hawley was the chairman of the committee report quoted: Brown, *Joseph Hawley*, 107. For Otis's attribution of Hawley's leadership in this affair see Freiberg, "Prelude to Purgatory," 307n.

28. Brown, *Joseph Hawley*, 109. (The report of Hawley's remarks was conveyed to Thomas Hutchinson.) Hawley, Boston *Evening-Post*, January 18, 1768. William V. Wells, *The Life and Public Services of Samuel Adams . . .* (Boston, 1865), 1:127.

29. Thomas Hutchinson to John Rivington, March 27, 1767, Massachusetts Archives 26:271. Thomas Hutchinson to Israel Williams and to William Bollan, December 2, 1766, and November 22, 1766; Israel Williams to Thomas Hutchinson, n.d., all in Brown, *Joseph Hawley*, 109–110, 110n. Israel Williams to Thomas Hutchinson, January 5, 1767, Massachusetts Archives 25:140.

30. On the Hawley-Samuel Adams alliance and for Hutchinson on Hawley's "revenge," Brown, *Joseph Hawley*, 112. "What shall we do?": Brown, 67. Thomas Hutchinson to Israel Williams, September 6, 1769, Williams Papers, Massachusetts

Historical Society. Hawley hinted at his breakdown in the Boston *Evening-Post,* July 13, 1767.

31. Thomas Hutchinson to William Bollan, October 31, 1767, Massachusetts Archives 25:210. Thomas Hutchinson to Israel Williams, May 9, 1772, Williams Papers. See also Arthur M. Schlesinger, *Prelude to Independence: The Newspaper War on Britain, 1764–1776* (New York, 1957), 95. Samuel F. Merrick to George Bliss, April 28, 1828, *Papers and Proceedings of the Connecticut Valley Historical Society,* 9:33. Merrick's letter reveals that Hawley's disbarment was actually moved by Edmund Trowbridge, though with Hutchinson's agreement.

32. Hawley, Boston *Evening-Post,* January 5, 1768. Sewall's attack, which also brought a newspaper retort from John Adams, did not concentrate on Hawley. Sewall was answering another newspaper writer, "X," who had asserted the unfairness of compensation for victims of Stamp Act mobs without amnesty for the rioters. See Carol Berkin, *Jonathan Sewall: Odyssey of an American Loyalist* (New York and London, 1974), 40.

33. Brown, *Joseph Hawley,* 112. Freiberg, "Prelude to Purgatory," 164.

34. Hawley, Boston *Evening-Post,* January 25, 1768.

35. Ibid., February 1, 1768.

36. Freiberg, "Prelude to Purgatory," 319n. Fenichel, "Depression and Mania," 140. Brown, *Joseph Hawley,* 112.

37. Karl Abraham, "A Short Study of the Development of the Libido" (1924), reprinted in *On Character and Libido Development: Six Essays* (New York, 1966), 72. Ellen E. Brennan, *Plural Office Holding in Massachusetts, 1760–1780: Its Relation to the "Separation" of Departments of Government* (Chapel Hill, N.C., 1945), 95–96. William Tudor, *The Life of James Otis of Massachusetts* (Boston, 1823; reprint New York, 1970), 255.

38. Anne Baxter Webb, "On the Eve of Revolution: Northampton, Massachusetts, 1750–1775," (Ph.D. diss., University of Minnesota, 1976), 189, 190. Joseph Hawley to Mercy Hawley, 1754, 1774, 1770; similar remarks appear in a letter of 1768, and in one to Joseph Clarke, the couple's adopted son: "I am ordinary well" (April 4, 1776). All in Hawley Papers. Also, a letter to Mercy Hawley, January 10, 1772—"I am in ordinary health"—Williams Papers. Joseph Lyman of Hatfield, Mass., Hawley's friend, said in his funeral oration that Hawley "at three different periods of life, for several years, [fell] under the full dominion of his hereditary indisposition." The periods were presumably 1760, 1766, and 1775–1776. The Reverend Timothy Alden, *A Collection of American Epitaphs . . .* (New York, 1814), 3:81.

39. "Mr. Hawley," wrote Hutchinson, "was equally, and perhaps more, attended to" (Brown, *Joseph Hawley,* 119). According to Samuel Cooper, Hawley was "behind no man in influence" (ibid., 127–128). John Adams wrote to William Tudor, January 24, 1817, "The Patriots could carry nothing in the house, without the support of Major Hawley" (*The Works of John Adams, Second President of the United States . . . ,* ed. Charles Francis Adams [Boston, 1856], 10:240). On Hutchinson's being "bereft": Joseph Hawley to Mercy Hawley, June 8, 1772, Hawley Papers. Brown, *Joseph Hawley,* 128.

40. George Henry Merriam, "Israel Williams, Monarch of Hampshire, 1709–1788" (Ph.D. diss., Clark University, 1944), 112. The letter to John Adams was the famous "broken hints" letter. See *Works of John Adams,* 9:641–643.

41. For Hawley's late letters see Hawley Papers; and [Elias Sill Hawley], *Historical Sketch of Major Joseph Hawley . . .* (Buffalo, N.Y., 1890).

42. Joseph Hawley to Theodore Sedgwick, May 10, 1775, Hawley Papers. The contractions have been expanded.

43. Ibid.
44. Ibid.
45. MS transcription of statement by William Botter, a ten-year-old who came in 1776 to live with the Hawleys. Judd MSS, 1:477. The essay is in the Hawley Papers.
46. Alan Heimert, *Religion and the American Mind: From the Great Awakening to the Revolution* (Cambridge, Mass., 1966), 523. See Brown, *Joseph Hawley*, 130–132 on the notable consistency of Hawley's religious toleration and separation.
47. "Joseph Hawley's Criticism of the Constitution of Massachusetts," ed. Mary Catherine Clune, *Smith College Studies in History* 3 (1917): 55.
48. Robert E. Moody, "Samuel Ely: Forerunner of Shays," *New England Quarterly* 5 (1932): 108. Joseph Hawley to Caleb Strong, June 23, 1782, Hawley Papers. "Turning to the Mobb": Joseph Hawley to Ephraim Wright, April 16, 1782, *American Historical Review* 36 (1931), 777. Joseph Hawley to Caleb Strong, June 24, 1782, Hawley Papers. Brown quoted this letter as having "Hurra'd" for what I read as "Huzza'd." We both have an apostrophe for the superscript "d."
49. Ibid., italics in original.
50. Fred Weinstein and Gerald M. Platt, *Psychoanalytic Sociology: An Essay on the Interpretation of Historical Data and the Phenomena of Collective Behavior* (Baltimore and London, 1973), 106n.

7. Josiah Quincy

1. George H. Nash, "From Radicalism to Revolution: The Political Career of Josiah Quincy, Jr.," *Proceedings of the American Antiquarian Society* 79 (1969): 254.
2. Josiah Quincy, Jr., *Reports of Cases . . .* , ed. Samuel M. Quincy (New York, 1865; reprint New York, 1969), 168–170. Hereafter cited as *Quincy Reports.*
3. Clifford K. Shipton, *Sibley's Harvard Graduates . . .* (Boston, 1933–), 8:467, 466. *Memoir of the Life of Josiah Quincy, Jr. of Massachusetts: By His Son, Josiah Quincy* (Boston, 1825), 4–5 (the 2d. ed., 1874, with additions, has been consulted). Quincy Senior was also justice of the peace.
4. See *Diary and Autobiography of John Adams,* ed. L. H. Butterfield et al. (New York, 1964), 1:140–141.
5. On his death: James H. Stark, *The Loyalists of Massachusetts . . .* (Boston, 1910), 367. Inoculation: [L. H. Butterfield], *A Pride of Quincys: A Massachusetts Historical Society Picture Book* (Boston, 1969), unpaged pamphlet.
6. *Diary and Autobiography of John Adams,* 1:122n. *Memoir of Quincy,* 7.
7. Samuel Quincy to Josiah Quincy, Jr., June 1, 1774, in *Memoir of Quincy,* 151. Shipton, *Harvard Graduates,* 8:470, 469, 471.
8. Ibid., 472. *Memoir of Quincy,* 26 (written December 1768).
9. On the theater: *Memoir of Quincy,* 233. On the adoption by young revolutionaries of the principles rather than the practice of parents, see Kenneth Keniston, *Young Radicals; Notes on Committed Youth* (New York, 1968), 55–60; and Philip Abrams, "Rites de Passage: The Conflict of Generations in Industrial Society," *Journal of Contemporary History* 5 (1970), 175–190. Also see n. 27 below.
10. Shipton, *Harvard Graduates,* 8:469. *Quincy Reports,* 168, 173.
11. Shipton, *Harvard Graduates,* 10:324–325. On Thacher's preventing Hutchinson from going to England see Ellen E. Brennan, *Plural Office Holding in Massachusetts, 1760–1780: Its Relation to the "Separation" of Departments of Government* (Chapel Hill, N.C., 1945), 69. John Adams to Hezekiah Niles, February 13, 1818, in L. H. Butterfield, "What Do We Mean by the American Revolution?" in Daniel

Boorstin, *An American Primer* (Chicago, 1966), 233. In his edition of Adams's *Works*, Charles Francis Adams evidently corrected the Latin to *"potestatis."* See also *Diary and Autobiography of John Adams*, 1:110.

12. *Quincy Reports*, 581 (from *The Boston-Gazette and Country Journal*, January 1767).

13. *Memoir of Quincy*, 7. John Adams to Abigail Adams, July 4, 1774, in *Adams Family Correspondence*, ed. L. H. Butterfield et al. (New York, 1965), 1:122.

14. Philip Davidson, *Propaganda and the American Revolution, 1763–1783* (Chapel Hill, N.C., 1941), 7.

15. Boston *Gazette*, October 5, 1767. See also Quincy as "Hyperion," Boston *Gazette*, September 28, 1767. The former essay was reprinted in the *New York Journal*, October 22, 1767: Bernard Friedman, "The Shaping of the Radical Consciousness in Provincial New York," *Journal of American History* 56 (1970): 801n.

16. Quincy as "Hyperion," Boston *Gazette*, October 3, 1767, in *Memoir of Quincy*, 24. Quincy as "Pro Lege," Boston *Gazette*, January 4, 1768. For similar imagery of rapine see Merrill Jensen, *The Founding of a Nation: A History of the American Revolution, 1763–1776* (New York, 1968), 295.

17. George Mason to unknown recipient, January 24, 1770, in Narrative of Proceedings at Boston from February 7th to March 14th 1770, Sparks MSS 10, 3:55–70, Houghton Library, Harvard University, Cambridge, Mass.

18. Quoted from an unsent letter by Carl Becker, *The Eve of the Revolution: A Chronicle of the Breach with England* (New Haven, Conn., 1921), 174.

19. Notes on Josiah Quincy's "Plea for the prisoner," Joseph Hawley's Commonplace Book, Hawley Papers, New York Public Library, New York, New York. Quincy as "An Independent," Boston *Gazette*, February 26, 1770. See below on the shooting of Christopher Seider, which Quincy's piece may reflect.

20. Edmund S. Morgan, "The Puritan Ethic and the American Revolution," *William and Mary Quarterly* 24 (1967): 9. Quincy as "An Independant," Boston *Gazette*, February 12, 1770 (with "unnatural" as a conjectural reading).

21. For the importance of the crowd in Quincy's case see Nash, "Radicalism to Revolution," 286; and see Quincy as "Nedham's Remembrancer," Boston *Gazette*, January 10, 1774.

22. Quincy defended taking the case in a letter to Josiah Quincy, Sr., who, in keeping with his limited conscience, disapproved when he first heard of it. *Memoir of Quincy*, 34–38.

23. *A Report of the Record Commissioners of the City of Boston Containing the Boston Town Records, 1770 through 1777* (Boston, 1887), 18:29, 31, 32 (May 15, 1770). Closing single quotation mark supplied. Richard Frothingham, *Life and Times of Joseph Warren* (Boston, 1865; reprint New York, 1972), 156–157 (letter of Thomas Hutchinson, May 22, 1770). See Hiller B. Zobel, *The Boston Massacre* (New York, 1970), 228–229 and n. 47, for further Hutchinson reactions.

24. See *Legal Papers of John Adams*, ed. L. Kinvin Wroth and Hiller B. Zobel (Cambridge, Mass., 1965), 3:11n. The Gilbert Stuart portrait of Quincy, which shows his crossed eye, was painted well after Quincy's death.

25. Ibid., 166. Marginalia in John Adams's copy of Gordon's *History*, quoted by Hiller B. Zobel, "Newer Light on the Boston Massacre," *Proceedings of the American Antiquarian Society* 78 (1968): 120n. See also John Phillip Reid, "A Lawyer Acquitted: John Adams and the Boston Massacre Trials," *American Journal of Legal History* 18 (1974): 189–207.

26. Quincy as "Hyperion," Boston *Gazette*, November 25, 1771, in Arthur M. Schlesinger, *Prelude to Independence: The Newspaper War on Britain, 1764–1776*

(New York, 1957), 141 (italics removed). Quincy as "Marchmont Nedham," Boston *Gazette,* June 6, 1772 (Epigraph) and June 29, 1772. "Phobia": Shipton, *Harvard Graduates,* 15:483, 480. "Savagery": Bernard Bailyn, *The Ordeal of Thomas Hutchinson* (Cambridge, Mass., 1974), 249.

27. *Memoir of Quincy,* 70.

28. E. D. Wittkower, "Psychological Aspects of Pulmonary Tuberculosis: A General Survey," in *Personality, Stress and Tuberculosis,* ed. Phineas J. Sparer (New York, 1956), 157. Wittkower found "conflicts over aggression" in all 300 patients used for his study.

29. Ibid., 158.

30. Ernest A. Rappaport, "Anger, Apathy and Strabismus," *The Eye, Ear, Nose and Throat Monthly* 38 (1959): 478. Among ophthalmologists, "a fairly large number of writers . . . have noted a high correlation of strabismus with neurotic traits" (Edgar L. Lipton, "A Study of the Psychological Effects of Strabismus," *The Psychoanalytic Study of the Child* 25 [1970]: 148, 156). Intensity such as Quincy's can bring on strabismus, or exacerbate it. Conversely, strabismus can bring about the psychological reaction.

31. Editorial note in *Legal Papers of John Adams,* 2:410. "Callisthenes" appeared in the Boston *Gazette,* February 10, 1772.

32. Quincy as "Marchmont Nedham," Boston *Gazette,* June 8, 1772. Boston *Gazette,* September 28, 1772.

33. Quincy as "Marchmont Nedham," Boston *Gazette,* June 15, 1772. On Otis's "porterly reviling" see Jonathan Sewall as "J," in Boston *Evening-Post,* February 14, 1763. Boston *Gazette,* July 6, 1772.

34. Francis Drake, *Tea Leaves* (Boston, 1884), p. LX [so numbered]. Historian George Bancroft obliged posterity by inventing the words of Quincy's speech on this occasion.

35. Quincy as "Nedham's Remembrancer, No. I," Boston *Gazette,* December 20, 1774. "Nedham's Remembrancer, No. II," December 27, 1773. "Nedham's Remembrancer, No. III," January 3, 1774. The charge was repeated in no. VII, February 7, 1774. See no. IV, January 10, 1774.

36. "Nedham's Remembrancer, No. VI," January 31, 1774. "Nedham's Remembrancer, No. VII," February 7, 1774.

37. This work was published under Quincy's own name. Its full title: *Observations on the Act of Parliament Commonly Called the Boston Port-Bill; With Thoughts on Civil Society and Standing Armies.* Found in *Memoir of Quincy,* appendix. Moses Coit Tyler, *The Literary History of the American Revolution, 1763–1783,* 2d ed. (New York and London, 1898), 1:273. The year before, John Adams had similarly taken Hutchinson for his text in the draft of a reply to the governor.

38. This was the so-called "quiet period" of the Revolution, from 1771 to 1774.

39. *Observations on the Port-Bill* in *Memoir of Quincy,* 372, 375, 376, 386. William David Liddle, "A Patriot King, or None: American Public Attitudes towards George III and the British Monarchy, 1754–1776" (Ph.D. diss., Claremont College, 1970), ca. 320.

40. *Memoir of Quincy,* 469. Quincy may have borrowed from John Dickinson's *Farmer's Letters,* which told Americans in 1767, "You will be a 'band of brothers.' " In *Empire and Nation,* ed. Forrest McDonald (Englewood Cliffs, N.J., 1962), 83.

41. Bailyn, *Ordeal,* 319.

42. "Journal of Josiah Quincy, Jr. . . . in England," ed. Mark A. DeWolfe Howe, *Proceedings of the Massachusetts Historical Society* 50 (1916–1917): 468. *The Writings*

of Benjamin Franklin, ed. Albert H. Smyth (New York, 1905–1907), 6:310 and cf. 9:94.

43. Bailyn, *Ordeal,* 320. *Memoir of Quincy,* 257, 256. "Journal of Quincy in England," 446, 450. Nash, "Radicalism to Revolution," 268. Bernard Bailyn shows that Quincy met with reports that, in describing machinations, blamed Bernard and Hutchinson equally; yet Quincy singled out Hutchinson (Bailyn, *Ordeal,* 320). Nash, "Radicalism to Revolution," 269n.

44. Ibid., 275. Josiah Quincy, Jr., to Abigail Phillips Quincy, December 7, 1774, *Memoir of Quincy,* 259. Quincy as "Nedham's Remembrancer," Boston *Gazette,* January 31, 1774.

45. Josiah Quincy, Jr., to Joseph Reed, December 17, 1774, Reed Papers, New-York Historical Society. *Memoir of Quincy,* 337. On the House of Commons vote see Nash, "Radicalism to Revolution," 280.

46. *Memoir of Quincy,* 303, 314, 303.

47. Ibid., 314.

48. Josiah Quincy, Sr., to Edmund Quincy, IV, February 23 and March 2, 1737/38, Quincy Papers, Massachusetts Historical Society. Stark, *Loyalists of Massachusetts,* 375, 366.

49. Josiah Quincy, Sr., to Josiah Quincy, Jr., April 9, 1773, Quincy Papers. Josiah Quincy, Jr., to Joseph Reed, December 17, 1774, Reed Papers.

50. See Donald Weber, "The Image of Jonathan Edwards in American Culture" (Ph.D. diss., Columbia University, 1978), 21–42.

51. *Dictionary of American Biography,* s.v. "Hutchinson, Thomas," (by Carl Becker).

8. *The Child, Revolution*

1. Pauline Maier, *From Resistance to Revolution: Colonial Radicals and the Development of American Opposition to Britain, 1765–1776* (New York, 1974), 54–55.

2. Edmund S. Morgan and Helen M. Morgan, *The Stamp Act Crisis: Prologue to Revolution* (Chapel Hill, N.C., 1953), 145. William Almy to Elisha Story, August 29, 1765, *Proceedings of the Massachusetts Historical Society* 55 (1922): 236, 235 (hereafter cited as *PMHS*). Boston *Evening-Post,* September 2, 1765.

3. Morgan and Morgan, *The Stamp Act Crisis,* 49; and Boston *Evening-Post,* September 2, 1765.

4. The Reverend Samuel Peters, *General History of Connecticut* ... (New York, 1877), 232. The piece was taken to have been written by Franklin. *Georgia Gazette,* October 24, 1765. For a similar ritual in New Haven, Conn., see Philip G. Davidson, "Sons of Liberty and Stamp Men," *North Carolina Review* 9 (1932): 41.

5. *Supplement to the Boston-Gazette,* September 16, 1765 (dateline Annapolis, August 29). The figure was of Zacharia Hood: see Paul H. Giddens, "Maryland and the Stamp Act Controversy," *Maryland Historical Magazine* 27 (1932): 84–85. For more on effigies of Hood see Governor Horatio Sharpe to Lord Baltimore, September 10, 1765, and Sharpe to Lord Calvert, same date, in *Archives of Maryland,* 14 [Correspondence of Governor Sharpe, vol. 3] (1895), 223, 225. Savannah: Report in Boston *Gazette,* supplement, January 27, 1766. Peters, *General History,* 234n. After the effigies were burned it was decided to give them formal Christian burial, and the mob tried to enlist a clergyman for the purpose. They ended by conducting a funeral themselves, complete with a coffin, through which they drove a stake, 234–235.

6. N.Y. plans: Robert R. Livingston to General Robert Monckton, November 8,

1765, *Collections of the Massachusetts Historical Society* 10 (1871): 560 (hereafter cited as *CMHS*). For a burial of "Liberty" on October 18, 1765 in Charleston, South Carolina, see Edward McCrady, *The History of South Carolina under the Royal Government, 1719–1776* (New York, 1899), 556. Colden "hated": Roger J. Champagne, "Liberty Boys and Mechanics of New York City, 1764–1774," *Labor History* 8 (1967): 117. For the opinion that the New York riot was directed more at Colden and Major James, an English artillery officer who had insulted the mob, than at the Stamp Act, see Roger J. Champagne, "The Sons of Liberty and the Aristocracy in New York Politics, 1765–1790" (Ph.D. diss., University of Wisconsin, 1960), 66–67.

7. Henry B. Dawson, *The Sons of Liberty in New York* (New York, 1859), 93–94 (New-York Historical Society pamphlet). John Austin Stevens, "The Stamp Act in New York," *Magazine of American History* 1 (1877), 361. Stevens explained that "it was a bitter satire upon the zeal with which Colden, then on a visit from New York to his home in Scotland, voluntarily took up arms against the Pretender and his own countrymen, in support of the King." F. L. Engelman says that the reference was simply to Colden's having been on the Pretender's side ("Cadwallader Colden and the New York Stamp Act Riots," *William and Mary Quarterly* 10 [1953]: 571). Also, see letter cited in note 13 below for the rumor in New York of Colden's having served with the Pretender. The above account of the effigy is based also on the *Boston Post-Boy and Advertiser,* November 11, 1765. The term "parricides" had been used not long before, to refer to supporters of the Stamp Act in New York who would supposedly murder their fathers. See Champagne, "The Sons of Liberty and the Aristocracy," 53.

8. Letter from New York written by E. Carther (signature uncertain), November 2, 1765, in *New York City during the American Revolution* (New York, 1861), 45. *Maryland Gazette,* December 10, 1765.

9. Boston *Evening-Post,* November 4, 1765. Lawrence Henry Gipson, *The Coming of the Revolution* (New York, 1962), 103. "Boyle's Journal of Occurences in Boston, 1759–1778," *New England Historical and Genealogical Record* 84 (1930): 170–171. Dirk Hoerder, *Crowd Action in Revolutionary Massachusetts, 1765–1780* (New York, 1977), 122. Samuel G. Drake, *The History and Antiquities of Boston* (Boston, 1856), 709–710 (hereafter cited as Drake's *Antiquities*). Boston *Gazette,* November 11, 1765. Merrill Jensen, *The Founding of a Nation: A History of the American Revolution, 1763–1776* (New York, 1968), 147.

10. Boston *Gazette,* supplement, January 27, 1766 (re: November 5, 1765). *Maryland Gazette,* December 10, 1765 (re: November 30, 1765). *Continuation of the North-Carolina Gazette,* November 20, 1765. Boston *Gazette,* November 11, 1765. Bernhard Knollenberg, *Origin of the American Revolution, 1759–1766* (New York, 1960), 231. For other burials of Liberty see *Extracts from the Itineraries . . . of Ezra Stiles . . . ,* ed. Franklin B. Dexter (New Haven, Conn., 1916), 513. Also I. N. Phelps Stokes, *The Iconography of Manhattan Island . . .* (New York, 1915), 4:753.

11. On the great popularity of Liberty in colonial American newspapers see Elizabeth Cook, *Literary Influences in Colonial Newspapers, 1704–1750* (New York, 1912), 89–90. Wilkes as Liberty: John Brewer, *Party Ideology and Popular Politics at the Accession of George III* (Cambridge, 1976), 169. Child as Liberty: *Leeds Mercury,* April 4, 1769. On rape: Kenneth Silverman, *A Cultural History of the American Revolution: Painting, Music, Literature, and the Theatre in the Colonies and the United States from the Treaty of Paris to the Inauguration of George Washington, 1763–1789* (New York, 1976), 85–86, 252–253. See also, Douglass Adair, "The Stamp Act in Contemporary English Cartoons," *William and Mary Quarterly* 10 (1953): 538–542.

E. P. Richardson, "Stamp Act Cartoons in the Colonies," *Pennsylvania Magazine of History and Biography* 96 (1972): 275–297. On the development of the Liberty figure see especially Frank H. Sommer, "The Metamorphoses of Britannia," in *American Art, 1750–1800: Toward Independence* (New Haven, Conn., 1976).

12. Boston *Gazette*, Supplement, May 26, 1766. Boston *Gazette*, Supplement, June 2, 1766. Boston *Evening-Post*, May 26, 1766. St. Patrick's Day: Dirk Hoerder, "People and Mobs: Crowd Action in Massachusetts during the American Revolution, 1765–1780" (Ph.D. diss., Free University of Berlin, 1971), 258–259 [held at State University Library, Stony Brook, N.Y.]. Boston *Gazette*, August 18, 1766.

13. Pruning: George P. Anderson, "Ebenezer Mackintosh: Stamp Act Rioter and Patriot," *Publications of the Colonial Society of Massachusetts* 26 (1924–1926): 49 (hereafter cited as *PCSM*). Also, Philip Davidson, *Propaganda and the American Revolution, 1763–1783* (Chapel Hill, N.C., 1941), 185, which describes pruning to the number 92. Flagstaff: Governor Francis Bernard to Lord Hillsborough, together with facsimile of Liberty Tree broadside in *Bulletin of the Boston Public Library*, 4th ser., 1 (1919): 328. See also Davidson, *Propaganda*, 184–186; and Arthur M. Schlesinger, "Liberty Tree: A Genealogy," *New England Quarterly* 25 (1952): 435–458. Lee R. Boyer, "Lobster Backs, Liberty Boys, and Laborers in the Streets: New York's Golden Hill and Nassau Street Riots," *New-York Historical Society Quarterly* 67 (1973): 231–308. See also, for Boston, Boston *Evening-Post*, September 19, 1768, and for New York, Boston *Gazette*, Supplement, February 19, 1770; and *New York Gazette*, January 2, 1770, March 22, 1770.

14. Catherine L. Albanese, *Sons of the Fathers: The Civil Religion of the American Revolution* (Philadelphia, 1976), 65, 63, 67 (for "sacrament"), and see 64. Schlesinger, "Liberty Tree," 448, 445. On Barlow: Robert D. Richardson, Jr., "The Enlightenment View of Myth and Joel Barlow's Vision of Columbus," *Early American Literature* 13 (1978): 37. Also, Schlesinger, "Liberty Tree," 426n, and 451 on Trumbull. "May-pole of sedition": William Gordon, *History of the Rise, Progress, and Establishment of the Independence of the United States of America* (London, 1788), 300.

15. Hoerder, *Crowd Action*, 130. Parading on a pole: Benjamin W. Labaree, *Patriots and Partisans: The Merchants of Newburyport, 1764–1815* (Cambridge, Mass., 1962), 19. For "hanging" of stamped papers removed from a ship see Anderson, "Ebenezer Mackintosh," 49–50. New York loyalist writings: Moses Coit Tyler, *The Literary History of the American Revolution* (New York and London, 1898), 1:351.

16. "Boyle's Journal," 170. For the naming of the tree see Boston *Gazette*, Supplement, September 16, 1765. Boyle used the term "Liberty Tree" at the outset, on August 14, 1765. For the suggestion that Liberty Tree can be compared with Frazer's sacred tree as a representative of monarchy, see Winthrop Jordan, "Familial Politics: Thomas Paine and the Killing of the King, 1776," *Journal of American History* 60 (1973): 305–306.

17. For the committee: Arthur M. Schlesinger, "Political Mobs and the American Revolution," *Proceedings of the American Philosophical Society* 99 (1955): 247n. Carting: Walter Kendall Watkins, "Tarring and Feathering in Boston 1770," *Old-Time New England* 20 (1929): 34. Maypole: R. S. Longley, "Mob Activities in Revolutionary Massachusetts," *New England Quarterly* 6 (1933): 113. Descriptive card: Stephen J. Rosswurm, " 'That They Were Grown Unruly': The Crowd and Lower-Classes in Philadelphia, 1765–1780" (Master's thesis, Northern Illinois University, 1974), 50, 62.

18. In England, the term for use of a piece of wood was "riding the stang." In France the term for a donkey ride was *chevauchée de l'ane*. For a "ride Scimiter" see Boston *Post-Boy and Advertiser*, October 29, 1774. "Lady Skimmington": A. W.

Smith, "Some Folklore Elements in Movements of Social Protest," *Folklore* 77 (1967): 243. For the use of a halter in tarring and feathering see Boston *Evening-Post,* September 19, 1768. Drums and horns (in Norwich, Conn.): see Boston *Post-Boy and Advertiser,* July 4, 1774. For a mock trial see Violet Alford, "Rough Music or Charivari," *Folklore* 70 (1959): 508. For a folk precedent for these literalizations, "smugging" or drafting a man to play the role of the Guy effigy, see William Hone, *The Every Day Book . . .* (London, 1866), 1:718, and chapter 9 below, n. 26.

19. Alford, "Rough Music," 506. For a skimmington to punish an adulterer see Boston *Post-Boy and Advertiser,* November 5, 1764.

20. On the north-end mechanics see Carl Bridenbaugh, *Cities in the Wilderness: The First Century of Urban Life in America, 1625–1742* (New York, 1938), 388–389. Bridenbaugh's reference is actually to north-end *Church* mechanics, an equivalent term. For the rise in riots of all types: Hoerder, *Crowd Action,* 51. Wife murderer: *North Carolina Gazette,* January 20, 1765 (McCarter). Tarring and feathering for a sexual offense: Boston *Evening-Post,* November 6, 1769; Hoerder, *Crowd Action,* 194; Esther Forbes, *Paul Revere and the World He Lived In* (Cambridge, Mass., 1942), 212 (for an incident in the 1790s). For the punishment of a whore by means of a mock burial service similar to those employed against the Stamp Act, see the MS diary of Noyes Belcher, 1774, American Antiquarian Society. Robert R. Livingston to General Robert Monckton, November 8, 1765, *CMHS* 40 (1871): 562.

21. For the festival precedents, see Louis and Selma Fraiberg, "Halloween: Ritual and Myth in a Children's Holiday," *American Imago* 7 (1950): 318. Among the shops smeared with tar and feathers was that of Theophilus Lillie the night before the boys' demonstration that ended in the shooting of Christopher Seider. "Extract of a Letter from Boston dated 14th March 1770," in "Documents concerning the non-importation controversy," Sparks MSS 10, 3, no page no., Houghton Library, Harvard University, Cambridge, Mass.

For the various uses of tar and feathers see David S. Lovejoy, *Rhode Island Politics and the American Revolution, 1760–1776* (Providence, R.I., 1958), 176. Windows: Maier, *From Resistance to Revolution,* 128; excrement: 127n. Horses: Forbes, *Paul Revere,* 212. Hoerder, *Crowd Action,* 220; Lord Hillsborough: 340. Hoerder, "People and Mobs," 371, 570. Houses smeared: *Letters and Diary of John Rowe . . .,* ed. Anne Rowe Cunningham (Boston, 1903), 146; with "Blubber Oil" as well as excrement and feathers: Wallace Brown, *The King's Friends: The Composition and Motives of the American Loyalist Claimants* (Providence, 1965), 34–35.

22. Cartoons: Herbert M. Atherton, "The 'Mob' in Eighteenth-Century Caricature," *Eighteenth-Century Studies* 12 (1978): 49. On excrement, regression, and "pregenital activity" among crowds see Phyllis Greenacre, "Crowds and Crisis: Psychoanalytic Considerations," *The Psychoanalytic Study of the Child* 27 (1972): 144–145. Also Andrew Peto, "On Crowd Violence: The Role of Archaic Superego and Body Image," *International Review of Psycho-Analysis* 2 (1975): 450.

23. *Peter Oliver's Origin and Progress of the American Rebellion: A Tory View,* ed. Douglass Adair and John A. Schutz (San Marino, Calif., 1961), 94. For tarring and feathering combined with the use of lights see Forbes, *Paul Revere,* 209, and for the tarred boys, 95.

24. On the boys and on the burry dance, see the chapter 9, below. Also Lewis Spence, *Myth and Ritual in Dance, Game, and Rhyme* (London, 1947), 150. Alford, "Rough Music," 512. Also Longley, "Mob Activities," 113, where the wrong king is named. Francis Von A. Cabeen, "The Society of the Sons of Saint Tammany of Philadelphia," *The Pennsylvania Magazine of History and Biography* 26 (1902): 336 (regarding a 1785 performance of the ceremony). Watkins, "Tarring and Feath-

ering," 30. On English May Day and geese: A. R. Wright, *British Calendar Customs* (London, 1938), 2:242.

25. Longley, "Mob Activities," 112–113. Stokes, *Iconography of Manhattan Island,* 4:146. Compare the "way goose" received at the initiation of London coachmakers "at the beginning of the winter season." E. J. Hobsbawm, *Primitive Rebels: Studies in Archaic Forms of Social Movement in the 19th and 20th Centuries* (Manchester, 1959), 154.

26. Philip G. Davidson, "Sons of Liberty and Stamp Men," *North Carolina Historical Review* 9 (1932): 39. Hoerder, *Crowd Action,* 240. "Gov. Mackentosh": Clifford K. Shipton, *Sibley's Harvard Graduates . . .* (Boston, 1933–), 7:398.

27. "Boyle's Journal," 171, italics added.

28. Jack Cade and Masaniello: Hoerder, *Crowd Action,* 141; William Tudor, *The Life of James Otis of Massachusetts* (Boston, 1823; reprint New York, 1970), 221n. Paoli: Hoerder, *Crowd Action,* 94; Albanese, *Sons of the Fathers,* 23; Davidson, *Propaganda,* 79n, 182; "Recollections of a Bostonian," *Colombian Centinel,* November 10, 1821. George P. Anderson, "Pascal Paoli, an Inspiration to the Sons of Liberty," *PCSM* 36 (1924–1926): 180–210; Anderson, "Ebenezer Mackintosh," 45. For a report from Corsica on "Clement Paoli, brother to Pascal," see *Virginia Gazette* (Purdie and Dixon), May 11, 1769. Ironically, the town of Paoli, Pa., became the last stop on Philadelphia's exclusive Main Line commuter railroad. A Paoli hospital still exists in Philadelphia.

29. "Paoli Molineux": John C. Miller, *Samuel Adams: Pioneer in Propaganda* (Boston, 1936), 87. Hoerder, Crowd Action, 228n, 262. Anderson, "Ebenezer Mackintosh," 51. See also Maier, *From Resistance to Revolution,* 129f; *Legal Papers of John Adams,* ed. L. Kinvin Wroth and Hiller B. Zobel (Cambridge, Mass., 1965), 3:172, 173, 176, 177. And Abigail Adams to John Adams, April 20, 1777. *Adams Family Correspondence,* ed. L. H. Butterfield et al. (New York, 1965), 2:218.

30. Albert Matthews, "Joyce Jr.," *PCSM: Transactions* 8 (1902–1904): 93.

31. Forbes, *Paul Revere,* 95. Matthews, "Joyce Jr. Once More," *PCSM: Transactions* 9 (1906–1907): 282.

32. See Peter Shaw, "Fathers, Sons, and the Ambiguities of Revolution in 'My Kinsman, Major Molineux,' " *New England Quarterly* 49 (1976): 559–576.

33. See Roy Harvey Pearce, "Hawthorne and the Sense of the Past, or, the Immortality of Major Molineux," (1954), reprinted in Pearce, *Historicism Once More: Problems and Occasions for the American Scholar* (Princeton, 1969). Hoerder, *Crowd Action,* 252–253.

34. John Adams to William Tudor, March 29, 1817, in *The Works of John Adams, Second President of the United States . . .* ed. Charles Francis Adams (Boston, 1856), 10:247–248.

35. "Boyish sport": Edmund S. Morgan, *Prologue to Revolution: Sources and Documents on the Stamp Act Crisis, 1764–1766* (Chapel Hill, N.C., 1959), 107. "Boys and Children": Hoerder, *Crowd Action,* 104, and on drummers, 154. How drummer boys, presumably from the English regiment, became involved is not explained. Boys at Hutchinson's: *Deacon Tudor's Diary . . . ,* ed. William Tudor (Boston, 1896), 19. For boys starting a riot in a similar way in New York see Stokes, *Iconography of Manhattan Island,* 753. Also Davidson, "Sons of Liberty and Stamp Men," 56. Pennsylvania broadside: Bruce Ingham Granger, "The Stamp Act in Satire," *American Quarterly* 8 (1956): 378.

November boys in New York: Governor Cadwallader Colden to H. S. Conway, November 5, 1765, *Collections of the New-York Historical Society for the Year 1877* (New York, 1878), 457. For "boys and sailors" in New York on October 31, 1765,

just before the November demonstrations ("there was a design to execute some foolish ceremony of burying Liberty"), see Robert R. Livingston to General Robert
Monckton, November 8, 1765, in *CMHS*, 560. For boys in English "no popery"
disturbances see George Rudé, *The Crowd in History: A Study of Popular Disturbances
in France and England, 1730–1848* (New York, 1964), 208–209.

36. Boys in 1768: Hoerder, *Crowd Action*, 157; and Hoerder, "People and
Mobs," 257. On February 22, 1770: Thomas Hutchinson to Commodore Thomas
Hood, February 23, 1770, Massachusetts Archives 26:444. School holiday: *Legal
Papers of John Adams*, 2:397. Funeral: Bernard Bailyn, *The Ordeal of Thomas Hut-
chinson* (Cambridge, Mass., 1974), 136n. On the "vast Number" of boys: *Diary and
Autobiography of John Adams*, ed. L. H. Butterfield et al. (New York, 1964), 1:349.
"Five hundred": Hoerder, *Crowd Action*, 222.

37. Thomas Hutchinson to General Thomas Gage, February 25, 1770, cited by
the editors, *Legal Papers of John Adams*, 2:398. William Gordon, *The History of . . .
the United States*, 1:277. Mercy Otis Warren, *The Adulateur, A Tragedy, As It Is Now
Acted in Upper Servia* (Boston, 1772), reprinted in *The Magazine of History*, extra
number 63 (Tarrytown, N.Y., 1918): 10–11, 15. On boys in the composition of the
Massacre crowd and among those killed see Pauline Maier, "Revolutionary Violence
and the Relevance of History," *Journal of Interdisciplinary History* 2 (1971): 131, and
126 for further use of boys in June 1770.

38. Hoerder, *Crowd Action*, 48; Hoerder, "People and Mobs," 360. "Boys and
negroes": John E. Alden, "John Mein: Scourge of Patriots," *PCSM* 34 (1937–
1942): 588. Eighteenth-century references to boys, lads, youths, and negroes sometimes meant adults. This is especially evident with "negroes," who are usually cou-
pled with "boys," and evidently regarded as a species of child. The terms of the evasion are more significant than the reality, as the following paragraph makes clear. See,
as well, Boston *Gazette*, September 5, 1774: "Mostly boys and negroes."

Beverly McAnear, "The Albany Stamp Act Riots," *William and Mary Quarterly*
4 (1947): 490. On the importance of youths in European riots see Natatlie Z. Davis,
"The Rites of Violence: Religious Riots in Sixteenth-Century France," *Past and Present* 59 (1973): 87. For a summary and analysis of recent studies of crowd makeup see
Carl J. Couch, "Collective Behavior: An Examination of Some Stereotypes" (1968),
reprinted in Robert R. Evans, ed., *Readings in Collective Behavior* (Chicago, 1969),
especially 111–112. Also, on the ages of demonstrators, George Wada and James C.
Davies, "Riots and Rioters," *Western Political Quarterly* 10 (1957): 870.

39. On American versus English usages see Albanese, *Sons of the Fathers*, 75; and
Jordan, "Familial Politics," 305. Referring to 1738 and 1754: Hoerder, "People and
Mobs," 101, 180. James Freeman Notebook, November 5, 1764, Massachusetts
Historical Society. The term "sons of liberty" had appeared in England, in George
Lillo's play, *The Christian Hero*, and earlier in America in the 1750s, but both were
obscure precedents. See Silverman, *A Cultural History of the American Revolution*, 82;
and Maier, *From Resistance to Revolution*, 82n.

40. *Peter Oliver's Origin and Progress*, ed. Adair and Schutz, 89. Mary Douglas,
Purity and Danger; An Analysis of Concepts of Pollution and Taboo (New York and
Washington, 1966), 96–97. The author refers to the youths' "marginal" condition,
the technical term for their period of mania. Theodore Reik, *Ritual: Psychoanalytic
Studies*, 2d ed. (New York, 1958), 112, 149. See also Géza Róheim, *The Eternal Ones
of the Dream: A Psychoanalytic Interpretation of Australian Myth and Ritual* (New
York, 1945), 75.

41. Council Records of Massachusetts, quoted by Hoerder, "People and Mobs,"

80–81. On how Pope Day became a party issue, with the popular party in its favor and the government, or court party, wishing to curb its excesses, see John Kern, "The Politics of Violence: Colonial American Rebellions, Protests, and Riots, 1676–1747" (Ph.d. diss., University of Wisconsin at Madison, 1976), 284–285.

42. Max Beloff, *Public Order and Popular Disturbances, 1660–1714* (London, 1938), 22. A riot of London apprentices on May 1, 1517, led to this day's coming to be known as the "evil" May Day. "Floralia": Robert W. Malcomson, *Popular Recreations in English Society, 1700–1850* (Cambridge, 1973), 7.

43. Philippe Ariès, *Centuries of Childhood* (New York, 1962), 77–78. Spence, *Myth and Ritual,* 32. James G. Frazer, *The Magic Art and the Evolution of Kings,* 2 vols. (London and New York, 1911), 2:62. Yves-Marie Bercé, *Fête et Révolte: Des mentalités populaires du XVIe au XVIIIe siècle* (Paris, 1976), 26. Natalie Z. Davis, *Society and Culture in Early Modern France* (Stanford, 1975), 110, 98, 99.

44. Bercé, *Fête et révolte,* 11, 21–22. Natalie Zemon Davis, "The Reasons of Misrule: Youth Groups and Charivaris in Sixteenth-Century France," *Past and Present* 50 (1971): 41–75. Re: Scotland: Joseph Strutt, *The Sports and Pastimes of the People of England* . . . , enlarged ed. (1801; reprint London, 1903), 340.

45. Bercé, *Fête et révolte,* 37.

46. Ibid., 69–70.

47. Edmund F. Slafter, "The Character and History of *The Book of Sports,*" *PMHS* 19 (1906): 87–95. Also Davis, *Society and Culture,* 120. On the Long Parliament's substitution of a fast day for Christmas, see E. K. Chambers, *The Medieval Stage* (London, 1903), 1:391. Samuel Eliot Morison, "A Poem on Election Day in Massachusetts about 1760," *PCSM* 18 (1915–1916): 57, 60. Philadelphia Maypole: Rosswurm, "That They Were Grown Unruly," 41. On the Puritans' denial of ritual see Michael Zuckerman, "Pilgrims in the Wilderness: Community, Modernity, and the Maypole at Merry Mount," *New England Quarterly* 50 (1977): 255–277.

48. Militia training days and election days were partly celebratory. For a full list of New England holidays see Hoerder, *Crowd Action,* 46. On the destruction of holidays by politicalization see Bercé, *Fête et révolte,* 88; and on the modification of holidays by politicalization see Paul Friedrich, "Revolutionary Politics and Communal Ritual," in *Political Anthropology,* ed. Marc J. Swartz et al. (Chicago, 1966).

49. See Letters and Diary of John Rowe, passim, especially 1769 and 1774. Also, Hoerder, "People and Mobs," 232, 233; and Maier, *From Resistance to Revolution,* 67–68, 140. For the "decorum" on Pope Day 1768, supposedly agreed to in 1765, see Oliver M. Dickerson, comp., *Boston under Military Rule, as Revealed in a Journal of the Times* (Boston, 1936), 19. See the letter attacking Pope Day "Madness" and "Infatuation," *Massachusetts Gazette,* November 5, 1767. For Newbury, R. I., vote against effigies in 1774 see Hoerder, "People and Mobs," 81. For the prohibition of Pope Day in Portsmouth, N.H., 1768, see Charles M. Andrews, *Colonial Folkways* . . . (New Haven, Conn., 1920), 128.

50. F. J. Zwierlein, "End of No-Popery in the Continental Congress," *Thought* 11 (1936): 357–377. *Writings of Washington,* ed. John C. Fitzpatrick (Washington, D.C., 1931), 4:65 (General Orders, November 5, 1775). Drake's *Antiquities,* 663, notes that Boston's last Pope Day took place in 1774. For further examples of holiday suppression and disappearance see Bercé, *Fête et révolte,* 117–120, 152.

51. See Spence, *Myth and Ritual,* 34. The other hiring day was St. John's Day in December: see Wright, *Calendar Customs,* 3:156, 279–280.

52. On child actors: Spence, *Myth and Ritual,* 72. On St. George's Fields: Lloyd C. Rudolph, "The Eighteenth-Century Mob," *American Quarterly* 2 (1959): 455.

53. Josef Pieper, *In Tune with the World: A Theory of Festivity* (New York, 1965), 55. Maurice Dommanget, *Histoire du premier mai* (Paris, 1953), 37.

54. Bercé, *Fête et révolte*, 185–186, my translation. Malcomson, *Popular Recreations*, 23–24.

55. Alexander Trachtenberg, *History of May Day* (New York, 1934), 12, 26 (pamphlet). Pieper, *In Tune with the World*, 55–58.

56. Davis, *Society and Culture*, 113. Reik, *Ritual*, 151. See also Albanese, *Sons of the Fathers*, 135; and Hobsbawm, *Primitive Rebels*, 151–152, where Masonic ritual is shown to have derived from artisans' rituals. J. S. M. Ward, *Freemasonry and the Ancient Gods* (London, 1926), 119, agrees on the derivation of Masonic ritual from "primitive initiatory rites." Albanese, *Sons of the Fathers*, 58, 130, 132, 135. Sydney Morse, "Freemasonry in the American Revolution," in *Little Masonic Library, Book III* (Kingsport, Tenn., 1924, 1926), 233–234. "Waygoose": Hobsbawm, *Primitive Rebels*, 154.

57. Davis, *Society and Culture*, 107, 303n. Géza Róheim, *Animism, Magic, and the Divine King* (1930; reprint New York, 1972), 281.

58. "Brutal": Bercé, *Fête et révolte*, 21–23. Neophytes: Victor W. Turner, *The Ritual Process: Structure and Anti-Structure* (Chicago, 1969), 95. Blood brothers: Jacob A. Arlow, "A Psychoanalytic Study of a Religious Initiation Rite: Bar Mitzvah," *The Psychoanalytic Study of the Child* 6 (1951): 355.

9. Festival, Ritual, and Revolution

1. Richard Sterba, "On Hallowe'en," *American Imago* 5 (1948): 213. See *Encyclopedia Britannica*, 11th ed., s.v. "Hallowe'en" for Roman additions.

2. Roy C. Strong, "The Popular Celebration of the Accession Day of Queen Elizabeth I," *Journal of the Warburg and Courtauld Institutes* 21 (1958): 103, 88.

3. R. Chambers, ed., *The Book of Days* . . . (Edinburgh, 1864), 2:588. William Hone, *The Every Day Book* . . . (London, 1866), 745.

4. Hone, *The Every Day Book*, 744. Pope John Paul I in 1978 refused to employ the Sedia Gestatoria, or papal chair, for his installation or, for a time, for his public appearances. *The Procession, or, the Burning of the Pope* (printed for William Goble, 1681), pamphlet held by New-York Historical Society. For Hutchinson's recollection of Godfrey, see Thomas Hutchinson, *The History of the Colony and Province of Massachusetts-Bay*, ed. Lawrence Shaw Mayo (Cambridge, Mass., 1936), 3:194.

5. E. K. Chambers, *The Medieval Stage* (London, 1903), 1:326, 347, 352, 366. John Lingard, *The History of England* . . . (Edinburgh, 1902), 346.

6. James G. Frazer, *The Golden Bough: A Study in Magic and Religion*, abr. ed. (1922; reprint New York, 1944), 133, 633, 651, 654–655. See also Jane Ellen Harrison, *Epilegomena to the Study of Greek Religion and Themis: A Study of the Social Origins of Greek Religion* (1921, 1927; reprint New York, 1962, 1966), 184. Also see Chambers, *Medieval Stage*, 1:110–112. Chambers writes, "All the folk-customs of the winter half of the year, from Michaelmas to Plough Monday, must be regarded as the flotsam and jetsam of a single original feast," 249.

7. See Arnold Van Gennep, *The Rites of Passage* (1909; reprint Chicago, 1964), 178–179.

8. Admiral Byng himself appeared as one of these in the Pope Day mummers' play. Here he was identified by the mouthing of "bing bing," a mnemonic that recalls the puns on Bute's name. R. J. E. Tiddy, *The Mummers' Play* (1923; reprint 1969), 153, 73.

9. Justin Winsor, ed., *The Memorial History of Boston* . . . (Boston, 1881), 3:172. Tiddy, *The Mummers' Play,* 148.

10. Esther Forbes, *Paul Revere and the World He Lived In* (Boston, 1942), 93. For Ames's Almanac, 1767, see "Diary of the Rev. Samuel Checkley, 1735," ed. Henry W. Cunningham, *Transactions of the Colonial Society of Massachusetts* 12 (1908–1909): 289.

11. Tiddy, *The Mummers' Play,* 71. Tiddy adds that the old figure may be regarded as a scapegoat. See also Harrison, *Epilegomena and Themis,* xxxiii, xxxix.

12. Lewis Spence, *Myth and Ritual in Dance, Game, and Rhyme* (London, 1947), 32n.

13. Tiddy, *The Mummers' Play,* 209, 250. Also Spence, *Myth and Ritual,* 143, 32; and Chambers, *The Medieval Stage,* 1:218.

14. Spence, *Myth and Ritual,* 32, 24.

15. M. Dorothy George, *London Life in the Eighteenth Century* (1925; reprint New York, 1965), 244–245. There were cases of these boys not washing for years.

16. A. R. Wright, *British Calendar Customs* (London, 1938), 2:239.

17. Leslie Fiedler, *Freaks: Myths and Images of the Secret Self* (New York, 1978), 267. On the "liminal" potential of dwarfs see Victor W. Turner, *The Ritual Process: Structure and Anti-Structure* (Chicago, 1969), 110.

18. Ludwig Jekels, "The Psychology of the Festival of Christmas," *International Journal of Psycho-analysis* 17 (1936): 71.

19. See the Lutterworth *St. George Play,* also called *The Christmas Mummers' Play,* in Chambers, *Medieval Stage,* 2:296–297.

20. Tiddy, *The Mummers' Play,* 231. The same connection is evident in the initiation ceremony of English woolcombers, where the lines recited "echo the cadences of the mummers' play." A. W. Smith, "Some Folklore Elements in Movements of Social Protest," *Folklore* 77 (1967): 251.

21. For morris dancers: Spence, *Myth and Ritual,* 142. For *"les noircies"* see Yves-Marie Bercé, *Fête et révolte: Des mentalités populaires du XVIe au XVIIIe siècle* (Paris, 1976), 27. For black face: Ernest Crawley, *The Mystic Rose: A Study of Primitive Marriage and of Primitive Thought in Its Bearing on Marriage,* enl. ed. (New York, 1927), 1:332. Chambers, *Medieval Stage,* 1:199. Spence, *Myth and Ritual,* 150. Frazer, *Golden Bough,* 129. For the sledge: E. O. James, *Seasonal Feasts and Festivals* (New York, 1961), 311. For death and rebirth and burning of the Jack see *Encyclopedia Britannica,* 11th ed., s.v. "Drama."

22. Chambers, *Medieval Stage,* 1:95. *Peter Oliver's Origin and Progress of the American Rebellion,* ed. Douglass Adair and John A. Schutz (San Marino, Calif., 1961), 54. See Natalie Z. Davis, *Society and Culture in Early Modern France* (Stanford, 1975), 101–102. For contemporaries on pagan sources see Catherine Albanese, *Sons of the Fathers: The Civil Religion of the American Revolution* (Philadelphia, 1976), 64. Also, some twenty years later, Joel Barlow's translation of a "Genealogy of the Tree of Liberty," from an unknown French source, in MS at Houghton Library, Harvard University, Cambridge, Mass.

23. See Lord Raglan, "Myth and Ritual," in *Myth, A Symposium,* ed. Thomas A. Seboek (Bloomington, Ind., 1958). Raglan gives this order: men-animals-effigies. Just what the order may have been remains in dispute. See also Chambers, *Medieval Stage,* 1:133–134. Frazer, *Golden Bough,* 653–654. Frazer discusses other late, symbolic versions. It should be noted that the Roman report, by Julius Caesar, has been called in question.

24. Hone, *The Every Day Book,* 718. Boy Guys: John Brand, *Observations on Popular Antiquities . . . ,* rev. ed. with the additions of Sir Henry Ellis (London, 1877),

216. "Burnt-Offering": Dirk Hoerder, "People and Mobs: Crowd Action in Massachusetts during the American Revolution, 1765–1780" (Ph.D. diss., Free University of Berlin, 1971), 154 [held at the State University Library, Stony Brook, N.Y.], from Boston *Evening-Post,* August 19, 1765. On the source of the jack o'lantern: Louis and Selma Fraiberg, "Hallowe'en: Ritual and Myth in a Children's Holiday," *American Imago* 7 (1950): 299.

25. On the Thargelia see E. O. James, *Seasonal Feasts and Festivals* (New York, 1961), 139. Leviticus 16:1–24, is cited by Géza Róheim in *Animism, Magic, and the Divine King* (London, 1930), 335; see also 363. Also James G. Frazer, *The Magic Art and the Evolution of Kings* (London and New York, 1911), 2:76–77.

26. In addition, Mackintosh and Swift made a pair on November 1, 1765, in Boston. For the two New York groups and their two effigies: *Maryland Gazette,* December 10, 1765. For English Guy gangs: Hone, *The Every Day Book,* 716. For effigies of Huske and Grenville in Boston: Boston *Evening-Post,* November 4, 1765.

27. Walter Muir Whitehill, *Boston, A Topographic History* (Cambridge, Mass., 1968), 29. "Extracts from the Interleaved Almanacs of Nathan Bowen, Marblehead, 1742–1799," ed. W. H. Bowden, *Essex Institute Historical Collections* 91 (1955): 190. Hiller B. Zobel, *The Boston Massacre* (New York, 1970), 71. On the Boston Massacre: "Extract of Two Letters from Boston, Dated March 13, 1770," in "Documents concerning the non-importation controversy," Sparks MSS 10, 3, no page no., Houghton Library, Harvard University, Cambridge, Mass. In some cases, Newport's for example, three or more effigies appeared, as once dozens of Guys had been hung and then burned. Donna J. Spindel, "The Stamp Act Crisis in the British West Indies," *Journal of American Studies* 11 (1977): 210, quoted from the *South Carolina Gazette,* July 21, 1766.

28. Arthur M. Schlesinger, "Political Mobs and the American Revolution," *Proceedings of the American Philosophical Society* 99 (1955): 247. Charles Royster, " 'The Nature of Treason': Revolutionary Virtue and American Reactions to Benedict Arnold," *William and Mary Quarterly* 36 (1979): 188–189. "Recollections of a Bostonian," *Columbian Centinel,* November 10, 1821.

Among numerous other examples of doubling: announcement of plans to exhibit effigies of the stamp distributor and his deputy in St. Christopher, October 31, 1765: *Maryland Gazette,* December 10, 1765. A crude cartoon of Lords Grenville and Bute hanging from a gibbet: *Boston-Gazette and Country Journal,* February 24, 1766. "Two Informers" reported to have been tarred and feathered together in Newburyport, R.I., Boston *Evening-Post,* September 19, 1768. Also, see the descriptions at the beginning of Chapter 8, above.

29. Frazer, *The Magic Art,* 2:76–77. Frazer refers to the wood spirit, specifically.

30. See F. M. Cornford, "The Origin of the Olympic Games," chapter in Harrison's *Epilegomena and Themis.* E. E. Evans-Pritchard, *The Divine Kingship of the Shilluk of the Nilotic Sudan* (Cambridge, 1948), 27–28. *The Education of Henry Adams, An Autobiography* (Boston and New York, 1918), 55.

31. Henri Frankfort, *Kingship and the Gods: A Study of Ancient Near Eastern Religion and the Integrations of Society and Nature* (Chicago, 1948), 103–104, 102 on Egypt. On Charlemagne: Chambers, *Medieval Stage,* 1:390. On sunset ceremonies: Harrison, *Epilegomena and Themis,* 375. On Charles II's coronation: Chambers, *The Book of Days,* 2:26. On New Year's and solstitial enthronements see Ivan Engnell, *Studies in Divine Kingship in the Near East* (Oxford, 1943; 2d ed., 1967), 10, 33.

32. For a somewhat different view, emphasizing the "charisma" of kings, yet deriving from this power that of the rebel, see Clifford Geertz, "Centers, Kings, and Charisma: Reflections on the Symbolics of Power," *Culture and Its Creators: Essays in*

Honor of Edward Shils, ed. Joseph Ben David and Terry N. Clark (Chicago and London, 1977), 168.

33. Max Gluckman, *Rituals of Rebellion in South-East Africa* (Manchester, 1953), 12–14. See also the reversals with the king himself in the Ndembu installation ritual (Turner, *The Ritual Process,* 102–103).

34. *New York Times,* September 15, 1974.

35. *New York Post,* August 8, 1974, story by Helen Dudar.

36. Michael Walzer, *Regicide and Revolution: Speeches at the Trial of Louis XVI* (London and New York, 1974), 26.

37. See George H. Pollock, "Mourning and Adaptation," in *Culture and Personality,* ed. Robert A. Le Vine (Chicago, 1974), 71.

38. Edwin G. Burrows and Michael Wallace, "The American Revolution: The Ideology and Psychology of National Liberation," *Perspectives in American History* 6 (1972): 193. Adams's phrase, cited in chapter 5 above, is from *The Works of John Adams, Second President of the United States . . . ,* ed. Charles Francis Adams (Boston, 1856), 10:350.

39. See most recently, René Girard, *Violence and the Sacred* (1972; Baltimore and London, 1977).

40. As the Abraham story—like the mummers' play—indicates, the son makes as likely a victim as the father, so that in many religions, Christianity among them, the death of the young god rather than that of the father is celebrated. See Róheim, following note.

41. Géza Róheim, "Dying Gods and Puberty Ceremonies," *Journal of the Royal Anthropological Institute* 59 (1929): especially 194. On the identity of initiation and New Year's ceremonies see Harrison, *Epilegomena and Themis,* 184.

42. Harrison connects All Souls, one of the sources of Pope Day, with the fertility ritual. *Epilegomena and Themis,* 275, 294.

10. *The Rituals of the American Revolution*

1. Daniel Fabre, "La Fête éclatée," *L'Arc* 65 (1974): 68. And see Mona Ozouf, "La Fête sous la Révolution française," in *Faire de l'histoire: Nouveaux objects,* ed. Jacques LeGoff and Pierre Nora (Paris, 1974). Yves-Marie Bercé, *Fête et révolte: Des mentalités populaires du XVIe au XVIIIe siècle* (Paris, 1976), 36, 60; "subversive dynamic," 16. René Girard, *Violence and the Sacred* (1972; Baltimore and London, 1977), 125, 132.

2. Victor Turner, *The Forest of Symbols: Aspects of Ndembu Ritual (Ithaca, N.Y., 1967),* 45. Robert J. Bezucha, "Masks of Revolution: A Study of Popular Culture during the Second French Republic," in *Revolution and Reaction: 1848 and the Second French Republic,* ed. Roger Price (London and New York, 1975), 236–253. See also Natalie Zemon Davis, *Society and Culture in Early Modern France* (Stanford, 1975), 110, 98, 99.

3. Bezucha, "Masks of Revolution," 238. And see Davis, *Society and Culture,* 69. For Iran: *Washington Post,* September 9, 1978.

4. Gordon S. Wood, "A Note on Mobs in the American Revolution," *William and Mary Quarterly* 33 (1966): 635–642. John Kern, "The Politics of Violence: Colonial American Rebellions, Protests, and Riots, 1676–1747" (Ph.D. diss., University of Wisconsin at Madison, 1976). Also on the violence of the 1760s and its underlying causes, see James A. Henretta, *The Evolution of American Society: An Interdisciplinary Analysis* (Lexington, Mass., 1973), 125–128.

5. Chester Noyes Greenough, "New England Almanacs, 1766–1775, and the American Revolution," *Proceedings of the American Antiquarian Society* 45 (1935): 288.

6. See Richard J. Merritt, *Symbols of American Community 1735–1775* (New Haven, Conn., and London, 1966). On the possible effects of the depression see James C. Davies, "Toward a Theory of Revolution," *American Sociological Review* 27 (1962): 5–19. Also, Raymond Tanter and Manus Midlarsky, "A Theory of Revolution," *Journal of Conflict Resolution* 11 (1967): 264–280. Kenneth S. Lynn has related the growth of autonomy to the psychologies of individual patriots in *A Divided People* (Westport, Conn., 1977).

7. Neil J. Smelser, "Theoretical Issues of Scope and Problems," (1964), reprinted in *Readings in Collective Behavior,* ed. Robert R. Evans (Chicago, 1969), 90.

8. N. E. H. Hull, Peter C. Hoffer, and Steven L. Allen, "Choosing Sides: A Quantitative Study of the Personality Determinants of Loyalist and Revolutionary Political Affiliation in New York," *Journal of American History* 65 (1978): 344–366.

Acknowledgments

All or part of the manuscript was read and improved by Carol Berkin; John Catanzariti; my editor, Aida Donald; Malcom Freiberg; my copy editor, Maria Kawecki; John Lovejoy; John Thompson; my knowledgeable assistant, Geraldine Murphy; and, as always, my wife, Penelope. Messrs. Catanzariti and Lovejoy shared with me their special knowledge of primary sources. Dr. George Weinberg helped devise the part titles. To all an additional, formal thank you.

My thanks are due also to the staffs of the libraries where I worked: the American Antiquarian Society; the British Museum; Columbia University; the Massachusetts Historical Society; the New-York Historical Society; the New York Public Library; the Forbes Library, Northampton, Massachusetts; the Public Record Office, Boston; and the State University, Stony Brook, New York.

Sources for written and visual materials appear in the notes and the list of illustrations. Funds for photocopying and purchase of microfilm were provided by the Stony Brook Graduate School, and a grant-in-aid for the summer of 1976 was awarded by the American Council of Learned Societies.

In somewhat different form, Chapter 5 appeared as "John Adams' Crisis of Conscience," *Journal of the Rutgers University Libraries* 42 (June 1980): 1–25.

Index

Abraham and Isaac, 224–225
Accession days, 104, 199, 205–206, 221
Adams, Deacon Samuel, 28, 109–110
Adams, Henry, 220
Adams, John, 1, 22–24, 109–130, 210; and Thomas Hutchinson, 27–28, 30, 32–33, 37, 43, 46, 133, 144, 163, 171; and Parliamentary authority, 39; and Gordon riots, 45; and *Julius Caesar,* 57; and George III, 57–58; and James Otis, 80, 84, 88, 100, 102–103, 106; and Boston Massacre, 120, 123, 162, 164, 167; and Joseph Hawley, 131, 148; death of, 139; and Stamp Act, 141–142; and treason, 146; and conscience patriotism, 147, 173–174; and Josiah Quincy, 153–154, 157, 159, 164; and Colonel Quincy, 154–155; and Oxenbridge Thacher, 158; and Boston Tea Party, 161; and child symbolism, 191, 224
Adams, Samuel, 24, 78, 129; and Thomas Hutchinson, 27–28, 31–32, 148, 161, 164, 171; and Parliamentary authority, 39; and James Otis, 106; and Joseph Hawley, 131, 143; and treason, 146
Alien and Sedition Acts, 129
Allen, William, 66, 194, 200, 213
Andros, Governor, 217
Aniello, Thomas, 189
Apprentices, 201–203
Arminianism, 133–135, 143, 150
Arnold, Benedict, 217–218, 221
Attucks, Crispus, 37

Bailyn, Bernard, 39, 94, 115, 124, 127–128
Barlow, Joel, 183
Barré, Colonel Isaac, 32, 40
Becker, Carl, 174
Belcher, Governor, 28
Bell, Hugh F., 78
Berkshire affair, 139–145, 151
Bernard, Governor Francis, 10–11, 31, 39–40, 46, 84, 99–100, 229; and Thomas Hutchinson, 34–37, 52, 77–78, 123; and George III, 85; and James Otis, 86–88, 90–91, 97, 101, 107, 147; and Jonathan Sewall, 117, 118; and John Adams, 119–120, 125; and Joseph Hawley, 140–141, 152; and Stamp Act riots, 191
Bolingbroke: *Patriot King,* 52, 57
Bollan, William, 81, 87
Boston-Gazette, 9, 11, 57, 72, 103; and Josiah Quincy, 158–159, 168
Boston Instructions, 31, 163
Boston Massacre, 24, 66, 71, 189, 213, 217; and Thomas Hutchinson, 37–38, 41, 44; celebration of, 104–105; and John Adams, 120, 123, 162, 164; and Josiah Quincy, 162–164; 166–167; role of youths in, 194
Boston News-Letter, 10
Boston Port Bill, 41, 43; and Josiah Quincy, 168–170
Boston Post-Boy, 10
Boston Tea Party, 25, 41, 168, 189; and John Adams, 161; and Josiah Quincy, 167

275

Boyle, John, 184
Boylston family, 22
Brewer, John, 60, 71
Briton, 60
Bunker Hill, 106
Burke, Edmund, 58
Bute, Lord, *see* Stuart, John
Byng, Admiral, 208–209

Cade, Jack, 189
Catholic Relief Act, 68, 217
Charles I, 45, 62, 95, 107, 146; and George Joyce, 189, 197
Charles II, 70, 112, 206, 221–222
Charles VI (France), 186–187
Child symbolism, 191, 193–197, 199, 201, 208, 213; and chimney sweeps, 211–212
Clarke, Richard, 120
Colden, Governor Cadwallader, 179, 203, 217
Coming-of-age rituals, 18–21, 126, 174, 195–197, 214, 224; and apprentices, 201–203; and seasonal cycles, 208, 221; and chimney sweeps, 212–213; and sacrifice, 225–226
Committees of Correspondence, 22, 148
Conscience patriotism, 23–24, 146–147, 149, 173–174, 231; and crowd demonstrations, 161–162
Continental Association, 21
Continental Congress, 113, 126–127; and Joseph Hawley, 131, 148, 150; and anti-Catholicism, 199
Corbet case, 121–122, 141
Cornhill (London), 62, 63, 65
Coronation ceremony, 221–222. *See also* Mock coronation
Cromwell, Oliver, 57, 70, 107; and Stamp Act riots, 178, 189
Currency issue, 27–30, 35, 86
Customs commission, 5, 8; and John Hancock, 73; and Writs of Assistance, 84; and Josiah Quincy, 160

Davidson, Philip, 159
Declaration of Independence, 150; and George III, 15, 20, 41, 43, 172; and Parliamentary authority, 39; and political demonstrations, 68
Dress: as a sign of protest, 11–12, 16
Droit Le Roy, 63
Dwight, Timothy, 137

Edward III, 53
Edwards, Jonathan, 132–138, 140–141, 143, 151

Effigies, 216–221; and Stamp Act riots, 9–11, 48, 177–186; and Pope Day, 11, 16–18, 69, 188–190, 199, 203, 210; and the devil, 12, 16; and George III, 15; and anti-inoculation riots, 21; of Thomas Hutchinson, 40, 41; of Lord Bute, 50, 52, 53, 68, 72, 191; and John Wilkes, 58, 62, 67, 72; and anti-Catholicism, 68, 205, 206; and Berkshire affair, 140; of Andrew Oliver, 191; and change of season, 208; burning of, 215, 228
Ely, Samuel, 151–152
Essay on Woman (John Wilkes), 64–66

Fawkes, Guy, 15, 18, 69, 180, 192, 197, 209, 216–217, 231. *See also* Guy Fawkes Day
Fertility rituals, 184, 211, 215, 222
Festivals, 199–201, 204–217, 220, 228, 230
Filmer, Sir Robert, 96
Fort Hill (Boston), 11, 16
Franklin, Benjamin, 26–27, 40–41, 45, 171, 178
Franklin, William, 27, 41
Frazer, Sir James George: *The Golden Bough,* 184, 215; *The Magic Art,* 219–220
French and Indian War (Great War), 5, 229, 230
French Revolution, 20, 126, 216, 217, 218
Freud, Sigmund, 13, 169, 170, 224–225
Fries's rebellion, 129

Gage, General, 41
George I, 70
George II, 49
George III, 14–15, 41, 54, 151, 188, 197; and Lord Bute, 49–50, 52, 55; and political corruption, 57–58; and John Wilkes, 61, 67; and James Otis, 85, 90–91, 106–107; and Josiah Quincy, 169, 170, 172
Gin Act riots (London), 7–8, 69
Gipson, Lawrence H., 40, 55
Glorious Revolution, 63, 69, 99, 107
Godfrey, Sir Edmund Berry, 206
Goldthwait, Ezekiel, 115
Gordon riots (London), 44–45, 69, 200
Great Awakening, 21–22, 46, 174, 223, 229; and George Whitefield, 31; and Jonathan Edwards, 132, 134; and Joseph Hawley, 150
Grenville, Lord George, 12, 180; effigies of, 18, 178, 184, 186, 217, 219

Gridley, Jeremiah, 82, 110, 113–114, 141, 174
Guy Fawkes Day, 69, 104, 200, 217; origins of, 15, 204, 207; and Stamp Act riots, 178–180; and Pope Day, 197; and insurrectionary figures, 208; and mummers' play, 210; and independence, 231

Hall, Reverend, 136
Halloween, 199, 203, 204, 210, 216
Hamilton, Alexander, 129
Hancock, John, 73, 188
Hawley, Elisha, 131–132, 134, 139–140
Hawley, Joseph, Jr., 15, 22–24, 131–152, 210, 221; and Thomas Hutchinson, 32, 169, 171; and Parliamentary authority, 39; and Josiah Quincy, 153–154, 157–161
Hawley, Joseph, Sr., 132–135, 137–138, 147, 152
Hawley, Rebekah, 138–139, 140
Hawthorne, Nathaniel, 225; "My Kinsman, Major Molineux," 18–20, 33, 43, 71, 73, 126, 174, 190–191, 210, 213, 224, 231; "Edward Randolph's Portrait," 37–38, 44, 45
Haymarket Square bombing (London), 200, 201
Heimert, Alan, 150
Henry, Patrick, 57
Hillsborough, Lord, 186
Hofstadter, Richard, 30
Howard, Martin, 95–100; and Stamp Act riots, 177–178
Howell, John, 217
Huske, John, 180–181, 217
Hutchinson, Anne, 46
Hutchinson, Thomas, 2, 8, 16, 49, 51, 191, 193, 206, 230; as scapegoat, 18, 20, 24–47, 50, 52, 57, 73, 194, 214, 216–218, 228, 231; and events in England, 48, 72; and James Otis, 77–93, 100–103, 105–108, 133, 135; and John Adams, 112–116, 118–130, 133; and Joseph Hawley, 131, 136–145, 148, 151–152; and Josiah Quincy, 153, 157–161, 163–164, 166–174

Impressment of seamen, 121–122
Impressment riots, 72
Independent Advertiser, 28
Ingersoll, Stampmaster, 178–179
Intolerable Acts, 14

Jacobites, 63, 70; and William Pitt, 53; and Lord Bute, 61; and John Wilkes,

62; and James Otis, 97, 104, 107; and Thomas Moffat, 177
James I, 205, 206
James II, 45, 96, 99, 112, 206–207
James III, 16
James IV, 16
Jefferson, Thomas, 139
Jensen, Merrill, 78
Jewish Naturalization Act, 69
Joyce, George, 189, 197
Joyce Jr., 189–190, 191, 195, 197

King, Richard, 120
King's Bench Prison, 65, 66

Land Bank, 27–30, 40, 46, 72
Le Bon, Gustave, 13
Liberty Tree, 12, 14, 34, 180–184; and John Wilkes, 64; and mock coronation, 188; and Christopher Seider's funeral, 194
Lillibullero, 95–98
Lillie, Theophilus, 162, 193–194

Mackintosh, Ebenezer, 180, 188–190, 197
Market riot, 72
Masons, 202, 203
Massachusetts Constitution, 150–151
Massachusetts Constitutional Convention, 127–128
Massachusetts Historical Society, 88
May Day, 186–187, 196–201, 207, 210, 223; and chimney sweeps, 212, 215; and role reversals, 213
Mayhew, Jonathan, 124
Maypole, 183–185, 195
Mein, John, 17
Merrick, Samuel, 132
Miller, John C., 31
Mock coronation, 188, 201, 207
Moffat, Thomas, 177–178
Molineux, William, 37, 102, 160–161, 167; and nonimportation, 162; and Stamp Act riots, 189, 190, 193
Mortimer, Roger, 53, 55
Mummers' play, 209–211, 213–214, 216–217, 224

Nash, George H., 153, 161, 170
Nonimportation movement, 36–37, 161–162, 186
North Briton, 59, 60–62, 163; Number 45, 59–66, 70, 91, 221

Oates, Titus, 106, 207
Oliver, Andrew, 6, 9–13, 16; as scapegoat, 18, 48, 72, 116, 191, 193,

216–217, 228; and Thomas Hutchinson, 33–34, 35
Oliver, Peter, 81, 82, 88–89, 186; and John Adams, 115, 125; and Joseph Hawley, 136, 138, 140, 150
Osgood, Herbert L., 30
Otis, Colonel James, 24, 80–93, 98, 107, 109, 120; and Thomas Huchinson, 27, 30, 77
Otis, James, Jr., 22–24, 58, 71, 77–108, 194, 207, 210; and Thomas Hutchinson, 27, 31, 33, 36–37, 46, 133, 135–136, 144, 169, 171; and John Adams, 109–127; and Joseph Hawley, 131, 138, 143; and Stamp Act, 141, 182; and treason, 146; and conscience patriotism, 147, 173–174; and Josiah Quincy, 153–154, 158–161, 163–164; and Jonathan Sewall, 167; and Martin Howard, 177; and child symbolism, 191, 196
Otis, Joseph, 87
Otis, Samuel, 88

Paine, Thomas: *Common Sense,* 14–15
Paoli, Pascal, 189
Pares, Richard, 55
Peabody, Andrew Preston, 7
Pitt, William, 8, 10, 57, 58, 230; and Stamp Act, 48; and patriotism, 53, 62; and liberty, 73; and Stamp Act riots, 178, 182, 183
Political Register, 70
Pope, Alexander, 64
Pope Day, 11, 15–18, 69, 104–105, 142, 216–217, 220–221; and Stamp Act riots, 178–180, 185, 198–199; and tar and feathers, 186; and mock coronation, 188–189; and Joyce Jr., 189–190, 191; role of youths in, 195–197, 202–203; origins of, 204–208; and insurrectionary figures, 208; and mummers play, 209–210, 214; and independence, 231
Pownall, Governor, 81
Preston, Captain, 167
Pretender's Rebellion, 53, 69
Priestley riots, 69, 70
Princess Dowager, 53–56, 68
Public Advertiser (London), 63
Puritanism: and religious revivals, 1, 21; and religious symbolism, 12; and preparation for salvation, 23, 135, 145; and currency issue, 30; and hysteria, 45–46, 171; and civic duty, 119, 154; and church membership, 134; and repentance, 136; and public demeanor, 137; and conscience patriotism, 146; and self-

denial, 157; and nonimportation, 162; and revolution, 173; and coming-of-age rituals, 174; and holidays, 198–199, 200

Quakers, 46
Quebec Act, 68, 199
Queen Anne, 70
Queen Elizabeth's Day, 70, 205–207
Queen Mary, 204–205, 206
Quincy, Colonel Josiah, 154–159, 173
Quincy, Edmund, II, 155, 160, 165, 173
Quincy, Hannah, 154
Quincy, Josiah, Jr., 22–24, 72, 153–174, 210, 214, 223–224; and Thomas Hutchinson, 34–35, 103, 144; and Boston Massacre, 123; and treason, 146
Quincy, Samuel, 120, 121, 124, 155, 159; death of, 173
Quincy family, 154–157

Randolph, Edward, 38
Religious revivals, 1, 21. *See also* Great Awakening
Revere, Paul, 49, 51, 107
Richardson, Ebenezer, 162–163, 166, 193–194
Rites of passage, *see* Coming-of-age rituals
Ritual: defined, 9, 13. *See also* Coming-of-age rituals; Fertility rituals
Robin Hood, 210–211, 213–215, 220
Robinson, John, 102
Root, Martha, 132, 135, 143
Rudé, George, 58–60
Ruggles, Timothy, 88, 147
Russian Revolution, 126

Sacheverell, Dr. Henry, 69–70
Sacheverell riots, 69
St. George's Fields (London), 65, 68; Massacre of, 66, 71, 200, 213
St. Hugh's Day, 204, 206, 207
St. Patrick's Day, 104, 182
Saturnalia, 64, 71, 73, 196, 208; and status reversal, 12, 212; and Queen Elizabeth's Day, 205, 207; and human sacrifice, 215, 222
Scapegoating, 216–217, 222, 225, 231; and "My Kinsman, Major Molineux," 18–20, 190; and Thomas Hutchinson, 31, 35, 38, 41, 46, 52; and Lord Bute, 50, 52, 60–61; and Saturnalia, 71; and Stamp Act riots, 180
Sears, Isaac, 188
Seider, Christopher, 37, 71, 103, 162, 164; as martyr, 193–194, 206, 213
Seilern, Count de, 65
Seven Years War, 81

Sewall, Jonathan, 92, 116–121, 124–126; and Joseph Hawley, 144–145; and John Adams, 159; and James Otis, 167
Sewall, Stephen, 77
Shakespeare, William, 163, 168, 170, 172; *Hamlet*, 53–55, 172; *Julius Caesar*, 55–57, 170, 224; *King Lear*, 117; *King Henry V*, 224–225
Shays's rebellion, 129, 152, 186
Shipton, Clifford K., 86, 96
Shirley, Governor William, 28, 84, 87; and Colonel Otis, 81, 82; and James Otis, 89; and Colonel Quincy, 154
Smallpox inoculation, 21–22, 155, 186
Smuggling, 5, 7, 8, 35, 84
Sons of Liberty, 21, 32, 40, 57, 214; and John Adams, 123; and Liberty Tree, 182; and child symbolism, 195; and Masonry, 202
Sons of Saint Tammany, 187
Stamp Act, 1, 5–9, 180, 227, 229, 230; and George III, 14–15; and patriot leaders, 22, 31–32; and Samuel Adams, 28, 31; and Thomas Hutchinson, 40, 216; and William Pitt, 49; and John Wilkes, 71; and James Otis, 93–97, 100, 107; repeal of, 101, 104, 117, 119, 182, 191, 217; and John Adams, 113, 116, 118; and Berkshire affair, 139–145; and Josiah Quincy, 153, 160
Stamp Act Congress, 98, 100
Stamp Act protests, 5–13, 15, 177–203, 219; and George III, 14; and ritual violence, 20–21, 142, 146, 214, 216–217, 228; and Thomas Hutchinson, 33–36; and events in England, 48, 72; and James Otis, 101, 103; and John Adams, 120
Stoddard, John, 139, 150
Stoddard, Solomon, 134, 138
Stuart, Charles Edward (the Pretender), 61, 107, 125, 179
Stuart, John (Lord Bute), 8, 9, 17, 170, 212; as scapegoat, 18, 24, 48–73, 125, 171, 172, 191, 216–217, 219; and American patriots, 46; and Stamp Act riots, 179, 181–184, 186; and anti-Catholicism, 230
Sugar Act, 1, 6, 7, 31; and hemp production, 177–178

Tea Act, 182
Test Act, 205–206
Thacher, Benjamin, 24, 124
Thacher, Oxenbridge, 155, 157, 158, 165
Totem animal, 187–188, 196, 202
Tower Hill (London), 50
Townshend Acts, 1, 14, 40, 117, 118, 160
Townshend, Charles, 32, 44
Trowbridge, Edmund, 24, 31
Trumbull, John, 187–188
Tudor, William, 147
Turnbull, James Russell, 141
Turner, Victor, 227
Tyler, Moses Coit, 168

Walzer, Michael, 62, 223
Warren, James, 118
Warren, Joseph, 39
Warren, Mercy Otis, 46, 109, 167, 169; *Adulateur*, 37, 40, 194; *Defeat*, 40; *History of the Rise, Progress, and Termination of the American Revolution*, 118
Washington, George, 199
Waterhouse, Samuel, 98, 100
Webb, Deacon, 116
Wedderburne, Alexander, 40, 217
Whitefield, George, 31
Wilde, Oscar: *Importance of Being Earnest*, 86
Wilkes, John, 8, 17, 36, 45, 59, 103, 194, 200, 228–229; and freedom of the press, 50; and Lord Bute, 53–55; as hero, 58–73, 181, 188, 230; and George III, 91; and Josiah Quincy, 163; and Stamp Act riots, 178, 182
William III, 70
William of Orange, 70, 207
Williams, Israel, 136, 143–145, 147, 149
Williams, John, 185
Winthrop, John, Jr., 189
Wittkower, Dr. E. O., 165
Writs of Assistance, 33, 35, 58, 71; and James Otis, 83–85, 107, 109–110, 112, 121, 141, 174; and John Adams, 113, 114, 115; and treason, 146; and Oxenbridge Thacher, 158